COUNSELING AND PSYCHOTHERAPY
A Multicultural Perspective

THIRD EDITION

Allen E. Ivey
University of Massachusetts, Amherst

Mary Bradford Ivey
Amherst, Massachusetts, Regional Schools
University of Massachusetts, Amherst

Lynn Simek-Morgan
Florida International University

With contributions from
Harold E. Cheatham and Sandra Rigazio-DeGilio

ALLYN AND BACON
Boston • London • Toronto • Sydney • Tokyo • Singapore

Copyright © 1993, 1987, 1980 by Allyn and Bacon
A Division of Simon & Schuster, Inc.
160 Gould Street
Needham Heights, MA 02194

Series Editor: *Raymond Short*
Series Editorial Assistant: *Christine Shaw*
Production Administrator: *Elaine Ober*
Editorial-Production Service: *Trinity Publishers Services*
Text Designer: *Nancy McJennett*
Cover Administrator: *Linda Dickinson*
Cover Designer: *Lauran Book Design*
Manufacturing Buyer: *Megan Cochran*

Library of Congress Cataloging-in-Publication Data

Ivey, Allen E.
    Counseling and psychotherapy: a multicultural perspective / Allen
E. Ivey, Mary Bradford Ivey, Lynn Simek-Morgan; with contributions
from Harold E. Cheatham and Sandra Rigazio-DiGilio. — 3rd ed.
        p.   cm.
    Includes bibliographical references and indexes.
    ISBN 0–205–14226–5
    1. Cross-cultural counseling.   2. Psychotherapy—Cross-cultural
studies.   I. Ivey, Mary Bradford.   II. Simek-Morgan, Lynn.
III. Title.
BF637.C6I93   1993
158′.3 — dc20   92–20262
                                                                CIP

Printed in the United States of America

10 9 8 7 6 5 4 3 2 1   96 95 94 93

Contents

4   Decisional Counseling: The Basis of All Counseling and Therapy   71

5   Multicultural Counseling and Therapy: Changing the Foundations of the Field   93

Harold E. Cheatham, Allen E. Ivey, Mary Bradford Ivey,
Lynn Simek-Morgan

6   Developmental Counseling and Therapy: Integrating Alternative Perspectives   124

**PART II   Historical Theories of Counseling and Psychotherapy:
The First, Second, and Third Forces   159**

**7   Psychodynamic Counseling and Therapy:
Conception and Theory   161**

**8   Psychodynamic Counseling and Therapy: Applications
for Practice   184**

**9   Cognitive-Behavioral Counseling and Therapy:
Behavioral Foundations   215**

To Carolyn Attneave and Gilbert Wrenn,
whose contributions to multicultural counseling and therapy
will live forever

Preface

Change is in the air. Listening to students and professionals from throughout the world has brought us to a profound awareness of the need for an integrated multicultural approach to counseling. Many are asking for a new view of counseling and therapy that respects and builds on the past but focuses on building new frameworks for a multicultural, multinational approach to the helping process.

Counseling and Psychotherapy: A Multicultural Perspective, Third Edition, is an all-new textbook designed to help start this process of coping with an ever-changing world. This book is for use in undergraduate and graduate courses in counselor education, psychology, human services and mental health, and social work. It discusses in detail the three traditional forces of counseling and therapy: psychodynamic, cognitive-behavioral, and existential-humanistic. In addition, major attention is given to the recently arrived fourth force in the field—multicultural counseling and therapy.

We need to equip students so that they can take complex theory into action. They need to be able to grasp major theoretical ideas, use research findings, and then construct interventions in a culturally and gender-sensitive fashion. We have found that students particularly enjoy the way this book shows how to apply abstract theory to concrete practice.

Those who have used the two earlier editions will find this a very different book. It has been totally rewritten and reorganized and includes many new concepts. We have integrated the research into each chapter rather than providing a separate presentation. There are two chapters on each of the major theoretical orientations and new chapters on multicultural counseling and therapy, developmental counseling and therapy, and family systems.

Multicultural counseling and therapy, the fourth force, appears early in this book, as it gives a new perspective to the field. Historical theories of counseling and therapy have roots in European and North American culture. We have found that if we start learning about counseling and therapy from a basis of awareness of cultural issues, our students become more critically and actively involved in their learning. And, as students become more involved, all of us enjoy the learning experience more fully.

We have continued our emphasis on worldview and multiple perspectives and the need for each counselor or clinician to generate his or her own construction of the helping process. At the same time, you will note that we advocate for each theory presented. Our life experience has moved us from "Which theory is best?" to a belief that each theory has some value for most clients. We also have found that integrating two or more theories simultaneously in the session can be helpful to clients. Thus, we believe it is important for students to understand and master the basics of sometimes competing ideologies.

The first major section of this book focuses on three foundational theories of helping. Empathy, microskills, and decisional counseling are presented in the early chapters both as sets of skills and as theories within themselves. Students who master these concepts and theories early are better prepared to understand and work with multicultural issues and can use the ideas of the first three chapters to understand historical theories in more depth.

Throughout this book, you will find a multicultural emphasis. Our clinical, counseling, and teaching experience has taught us that counseling and therapy can be more interesting, enjoyable, and effective if we allow ourselves to become aware of ourselves and our clients as cultural beings. Exhibit 2.3 in chapter 2 asks us to look at our own ethnic heritage and how it might affect our worldview and counseling style. This type of experience (and other practical exercises in this book) seems to bring the theoretical concepts "alive" and simultaneously may empower the reader to take ownership of the book. We hope you will use this book as a tool for further understanding, rather than as an end in itself.

We like to think of this book as a new reading of traditional material. Each time we work through the writings of such giants as Freud, Rogers, Frankl, and Skinner, we come away more deeply impressed by their wisdom and the value of their contributions. At the same time, more modern theorists such as Beck, Meichenbaum, Ellis, and the authoritative writings of the family therapists have enriched the basic legacy.

Even more recent are the multicultural theorists, who are just beginning to be recognized. Some, such as Carolyn Attneave, Donald Cheek, and Paulo Freire, have been writing for a considerable period of time, yet only now are their messages beginning to be heard. Their voices are rising with new authority, supported by work completed in more recent years (for example, Jean Baker Miller, Mary Fukuyama, Thomas Parham, Bruce Taub-Bynum, and Derald Sue). Clearly, the fourth force of multicultural counseling and therapy (MCT) is arriving on the therapeutic scene prepared to make an impact on the therapeutic field.

The multicultural approach enriches and complements historical ideas. Throughout this book, we have attempted to show how the integrity of traditional theory can be enhanced through increased cultural awareness.

Family theory (chapter 13) and developmental counseling and therapy (chapter 6) are new to this edition. Family methods are especially appropriate supplements to traditional one-on-one interviewing. We would argue that individual therapy and counseling without awareness of family issues is incomplete. This is an important theme in the psychodynamic and developmental counseling and therapy (DCT) chapters. Our experience is that DCT offers an integrative paradigm for other theories while also providing specific assessment and treatment skills.

"No research without action. No action without research." We believe strongly in Kurt Lewin's famous statement. Chapters now include research exhibits, and the concluding chapter focuses on the importance of including some form of research and evaluation in every counseling and therapeutic encounter.

This book is supplemented by a student workbook/casebook and a teacher manual available from the publisher, Allyn and Bacon. The teacher manual is available on Macintosh™ in Microsoft Word 5.0™. (To obtain a copy, write Allen Ivey, Box 641, North Amherst, MA 01059, and please enclose a formatted disk and return envelope.)

We'd like to acknowledge and thank the many people who have helped this third edition become a reality. First, we'd like to acknowledge chapter coauthor Harold Cheatham of The Pennsylvania State University and chapter author Sandra Rigazio-DiGilio of the University of Connecticut. In addition, they commented on several chapters of the book as well. Maurice Howe, Education Australia, has been an active presence in this book from beginning to end. His sage comments in the early phases of this project were followed by extensive editing and commentary on the final portions of the manuscript. These three people have been vital to the process.

Chapter comments by the following authors were especially helpful:

4. Decisional Counseling—Sunny Hansen, Leon Mann, William Matthews, and Robert Marx

5. Multicultural Counseling and Therapy—Mary Fukuyama, Donald Locke, Migdalia Rivera, and Derald Sue

6. Developmental Counseling and Therapy—Evelyn Brooks, Machiko Fukuhara, Fran Howe, Oscar Gonçalves, and Koji Tamase

7./8. Psychodynamic Counseling and Therapy—Fran Howe, and Bruce Taub-Bynum

9. Cognitive-Behavioral Counseling and Therapy: Behavioral Foundations—Donald Cheek, Donald Meichenbaum, and Beth Sulzer-Azaroff

10. Cognitive-Behavioral Counseling and Therapy: Cognitive Approaches—Aaron Beck, Albert Ellis, and Institute for Reality Therapy

12. Existential-Humanistic Tradition: Logotherapy and Gestalt Therapy—Viktor Frankl, Elisabeth Lucas, Alfred Längle, and Joseph Fabry

Special appreciation is expressed to Stephen Weinrach, Villanova University, for his incisive criticism of the first draft of this manuscript. He, perhaps more than anyone else, sensed that this book moves beyond the old way of viewing theories and perhaps represents an entirely new approach. He caught the multicultural spirit of this book and encouraged us to make these ideas even clearer. As a result of his comments and the efforts required to meet his suggestions, we now think of this book as the fourth edition! The third edition, the one Dr. Weinrach first reviewed, never truly saw the light of day. He was also there for guidance and support in the critical final stages of the manuscript.

Thomas Parham and Derald Sue have been both challenging and supportive as we sought to develop a book that takes multicultural issues more fully into account. They have raised many difficult issues and brought our understanding to new levels. We look forward to learning more from and with them in the future.

Other reviewers of the manuscript provided key insights and suggestions. They were Harold Cheatham, Al Petipas, John Romano, and Don Smith. Elizabeth Koss and Bruce Oldershaw were critical in maintaining stability and organization in the midst of the chaos of writing. Truly, without them, it wouldn't have happened. happened.

Finally, we'd like to thank Ray Short, editor at Allyn and Bacon. His patience and support were endless and are truly appreciated. Evelyn Mercer Ward, the manuscript editor, is now working with us for the third time. It is a joy to have a literate and scholarly colleague such as she. We look forward to more collaboration with future books. She and John Ward of Trinity Publishers Services have combined to make collegial the final stages of a difficult process. Cynthia Cornell served as consultant for color choice on this book, and we appreciate her skillful advice.

Writing a book is a leap of faith involving many others beyond the authors. You are seeing the result of a process that began five years ago as we attempted to see how students and professionals conceptualized the field. We listened and learned and read much wonderful new theoretical and research literature. Yet, most informative have been the challenges provided by multicultural authorities. As authors, we no longer think about the field as we did five years ago. Change is indeed in the air. We look forward to your comments and reactions to this book. And, again, we will listen and do our best to engage in a mutual process of reconstructing our views of counseling and psychotherapy.

The Culturally Intentional Counselor and Therapist: Introduction and Overview

CHAPTER GOALS

Counseling and psychotherapy theory, practice, and research have become increasingly sophisticated and effective during the past decade. Along with expanded competence, however, the field is coming to a realization that present theories are limited by lack of awareness of multicultural and gender issues. The task of the next decade is to reexamine the field thoroughly from a multicultural perspective. There are said to be up to 400 theories of counseling and therapy. This book seeks to summarize some of the most useful and also to present some of the most important thinking in the multicultural arena.

As a counselor or therapist, you are participating in building a future—yours and the field's—that will depend on how effectively you relate to clients of varied ethnic and cultural backgrounds. This chapter presents an overview of four key concepts important in helping you generate your own construction of counseling and psychotherapy.

1. *Worldview.* The way you and your clients make sense of things depends on your way of *making meaning in the world.* Each individual makes unique meanings, but these meanings also have universal human qualities.

2. *Cultural intentionality.* Although we are all unique humans, we are also influenced by multicultural factors. It is critical that as a counselor/therapist you develop awareness in yourself and others of how issues such as race/ethnicity, culture, and gender affect the way you and your clients construct meaning in the world.

3. *The scientist-practitioner.* Counseling and psychotherapy are based in scien-

tific study. It is our task as responsible clinicians and counselors to draw on research as we plan our interventions.

4. *Ethics*. All our helping interventions rest on a moral base. As a counselor or therapist, you will be constantly called on to make ethical decisions. Effective practice is ethical practice.

Relativity: Perspective and Reality

We are all in the same world, but each of us makes different sense of what we see. Consider and reflect on the print entitled "Relativity" (figure 1.1). Where is your attention drawn? As you rotate the print, each new perspective proffers a new meaning. As you focus on the figures, you may find yourself wondering: Where are they going? What relation does each figure have to the others?

In discussing his drawing, Escher (1960) indicates the two figures at the top set of stairs: "Two people are moving side by side and in the same direction, and yet one of them is going downstairs and the other upstairs. Contact between them is out of the question, because they live in different worlds and therefore have no knowledge of each other's existence" (p. 15).

Counseling and therapy operate on the assumption that significant contact between client and counselor is possible. You, as a counselor or psychotherapist, are called on to show creativity and artistry in the way you observe and interact with your clients as they walk down life's path. If you can enter your clients' worlds for a time and join them on their journey, you may find a new understanding and respect for how their worlds are different from your own. Sometimes, simply validating your clients' alternative perceptions of reality may be all that is needed. Other clients may want to change direction, to find new perspectives and new ways of acting. In these cases, your task is more difficult because you will need to see their ways of thinking and being, to share yourself and your knowledge, and to work with them to seek new directions for the future.

This book is about joining the client's world and learning to respect ways of thinking and behaving that are different than your own. Psychotherapeutic and counseling theory are systematic ways of thinking that may help you expand both your own ways of being and those of the clients you serve.

Worldview: Examining How You Think About the Client's World

Consider again the Escher print and Escher's comments about the two individuals walking on the same stairs, but in different directions. Imagine that a client, walking in a different direction, comes to you for help and says, "My eight-year-old isn't doing

Figure 1.1   "Relativity," by M. C. Escher
SOURCE: Cordon Art (Baarn, Holland) © 1953 M. C. Escher. Reprinted by permission.

well in school. It worries me. I never succeeded either. I hated school. My parents sometimes had to beat me to get me out of the door. But the same approach doesn't seem to work with him. Now I'm told by the school counselor that I'm being abusive and that they are going to file a complaint with youth services. They said that my child might be taken away unless I change. I don't want to be here. What are you going to do to help me?"

How would you respond to this client? What feelings and thoughts are going through your mind as you think about this person? Take a moment to think about yourself, your "gut" feelings about a case of this type, and then on a sheet of paper write down your possible response. After you have written your response, compare and contrast your ideas with those presented in the following section.

Effect of Theoretical Orientation on Therapeutic Response

Child abuse is an issue that the professional helping field has avoided until recently, but now most therapists and counselors would agree that direct action is necessary to protect the child from abuse. At the same time, the general "wisdom of the field" is that the child should stay in the home if possible. Although most therapists, regardless of theoretical orientation, would agree that abusive behavior has to stop, the way therapists respond to the parent's question varies with their worldview, as the following subsections indicate.

The Existential-Humanistic Worldview

The existential-humanistic worldview seeks to understand how the client makes sense of the world. Believing firmly in self-actualization, these therapists often listen to clients carefully in the belief that clients will ultimately find their own positive direction in life. Thus, the response of the existential-humanistic therapist might be:

> It sounds as if you are deeply troubled and angry about being here. At the same time, I hear that you desperately want to straighten things out. Am I hearing you accurately?

The Psychodynamic Worldview

The psychodynamic worldview stresses that the past is often a prelude for the future. Research clearly indicates that those who abuse often suffer from abusive childhoods themselves. A psychodynamic counselor believes that change will not be lasting unless clients have some sense of how their present actions relate to their past experience. A possible response from such a professional might be:

> You say you were beaten by your own parents and now you find you are doing the same thing with your own child. It will take some time, but our goal is to find out how your past experiences are being reflected in your present behavior with your child. Let's start by you sharing some of your own thoughts and feelings during childhood.

The Cognitive-Behavioral Worldview

The cognitive-behavioral worldview is more oriented to action and short-term treatment. Relaxation training, parent education, and stress management are some of many techniques and strategies that might be used. The cognitive-behavioral counselor will focus on short-term observable change but will keep an eye to the future and work with the client for long-term maintenance of behavioral change. The counselor's response might be:

> There's a lot happening in your life. We'll be doing a lot of things in our time together. What I find most helpful as a beginning step is dealing with your personal frustration

and issues of loss of self-control. We'll be working on some very practical issues of how you think and behave to help you work with your child more effectively and to feel better about yourself. We'll start with some stress management.

The Family Systems Worldview

Family counselors and therapists remind us that so-called individual problems are often developed in a family context. Rather than working with individuals, family therapists argue that it is more effective to work with family systems. For example, the abusive parent in the interview may be currently experiencing abuse from the partner and transferring it to the child. A response from this therapist might be:

> The next time we get together, I'd like you to bring in your child and your partner. Our behavior and our thoughts are generated in a system of relationships. We'll explore how your family interactions reflect your present problems. But, for the moment, let us start with developing a family chart or genogram. Knowing about your family of origin can help us look more completely at the context.

The Multicultural Worldview

The multicultural counselor tends to see *individuals in a family and cultural context*. Such counselors would consider three levels of client experiencing and might conceptualize the case as follows and then use appropriate language in translating these issues for the client:

> We'll need to look at your issues from three levels. First, we want to stop the abusive behavior, and we'll work on that by using some cognitive-behavioral techniques. Second, people tend to become more assaultive under oppressive conditions. For example, those who suffer economic oppression and the loss of a job are more likely to lose control. Third, we need to work together to focus on issues of injustice in our community and take direct action for a more humane system.

The multicultural worldview takes into account that individual and family problems are often the result of external environmental factors, including a poor economy, racism or sexism, and so on. Sometimes a client with economic or self-image problems may only be seeking treatment because of an oppressive environment. The multicultural worldview stresses that individual and family counseling can only be fully effective if supplemented by direct action in the community.

Multiple Realities and Worldviews in Counseling and Therapy

The five frames of reference presented above are only a small portion of ways in which clients' problems can be conceptualized. Needless to say, the techniques and methods of each of the theoretical frameworks lead to very different treatment methodologies.

Which is the "correct" worldview and treatment? Once upon a time—and not so long ago—counseling and therapy theory operated on the assumption that there existed a "best" therapy. Students and professionals were encouraged to select one theory and then defend that position. Not too surprisingly, we have learned that each of the systems has something to contribute. The importance of listening to the unique human being before you, as stressed by the existential-humanists, has become foundational to all helping approaches. The psychodynamic framework's emphasis that past history affects the present is becoming more widely accepted, although it is still somewhat controversial. And cognitive-behaviorist techniques have been shown to be especially effective in producing change. These three systems are examples of the *individualistic* worldview and share a common belief that working with one person is enough to produce long-term change. The *systemic* worldview, exemplified by family therapy, and the *multicultural* orientation are a direct challenge to these traditions of professional helping.

We take the position in this book that effective counselors and therapists need to become familiar with the skills, competencies, and knowledge base of multiple theories. Some clients respond best to individualistic methods, some to family orientations, and some to a multicultural orientation. Many clients profit from a combination of approaches. It is important that you develop expertise in several approaches so that you can meet the needs of your culturally diverse clientele more effectively.

Examining Your Own Worldview

In the simplest terms, the concept of worldview can be described as the way you think the world "works." Metaphorically, each of us tends to view the world through a different pair of glasses. In a religious sense, there are Buddhist, Christian, Jewish, and Moslem "glasses" that give meaning to our world. In an ethnic/racial sense, there are African-American, European-American, and Native American "glasses." Each of us has multiple lenses—racial, cultural, contextual—through which we view the world.

The Language of Multicultural Identity

There is no fully satisfactory set of terms that describes the vast array of multicultural experience comprising our world. According to Bumpus (1991), very few in the United States are satisfied with census categories such as White, Black, or Hispanic. He asks: "What is a 'White' student? Is there a 'White' culture? . . . People of European descent are of many cultures . . . (for example, Irish-American, Polish-American). . . . Multiculturalism should reflect more than skin color. . . . We have cultural groups who can't even be defined by traditional anthropological terms . . . [including] lesbians, gays, single parents, and bicultural families" (p. 4).

Recognizing these difficulties of terminology and language, we will attempt to respect the many possible perspectives on multicultural identity. At times the terms *White* and *Black* will be used (due to common usage or the context of the discussion), and both will be capitalized according to recognized American Psychological Association standards of usage. However, more specific terminology will often be used, such as Asian-American (Japanese-American, Cambodian-American, and so on), African-American, European-American[1] (German-American, Italian-American, and so on), Latina/o (Puerto Rican, Chicana/o, Mexican-American), and Native American. (It should be noted that many believe the term *American* to be inappropriate because it fails to include South American peoples.)

It is important to recall that the only real Americans are Native Americans. As such, the term *Native American* will not be hyphenated, out of respect for the hospitality and patience of Native Americans with their many "uninvited guests." They, like African-Americans, who were forced to come to this country through slavery, had little say in the colonization and governing of North America. The authors also recognize that the Hopi, Sioux, and Yakima Nations each vary among themselves as much as or more than French-Canadians and Irish-Canadians.

Moreover, this book will also attempt to give some attention to groups that can be considered as distinct cultures—for example, the culturally deaf, those with physical issues, lesbians and gay males, Vietnam and Persian Gulf veterans, and others.

Although this book attempts to use respectful ethnic and cultural terms, it is important that you not label or stereotype your clients. Instead, you may assist clients in finding their own definition of being in a multicultural world. Many clients are bicultural or multicultural. If their issues are culturally related, you will find you work more effectively if you use their descriptions rather than labeling them from your frame of reference.

The Building Blocks of a Worldview

As we have seen, counseling and psychotherapy have a vast array of "glasses" through which the world is seen. The multicultural pair of glasses reminds us that each of us views the world through the lens of culture. In examining your own worldview, four foundations may be considered: individual, family, multicultural, and universal (see figure 1.2).

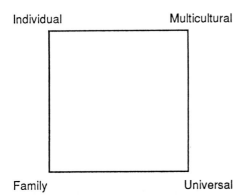

Figure 1.2   The Four Building Blocks of Worldview

Each individual has a unique life experience, even within the same family, and this recognition has long been central to individually oriented counseling and therapy. As we grow and develop in a family context, our experience in the family is basic to the ways we view the world. Your family experience has been important in the way you construct and think about reality. It is of great benefit in your development as a helper to think about your own family influences on your worldview.

The culture is transmitted to us through extended family, friends, the neighborhood, community, government, and the media. Our attitudes and behaviors toward issues of ethnicity/race, affectional orientation, and the effects of aging and disability, among others, are affected by these cultural transmission agents. Although it is not easy to define culture, its impact on our worldview is profound. As Sue (1991) comments:

> The danger . . . is that counselors who hold a world view different from their clients and are unaware of the basis for this difference are most likely to impute negative traits to clients. Theories of human development and their translations into counseling and psychotherapy are influenced by the social-cultural framework from which they arise. It would be erroneous for us to believe that there is only *one way* toward the path of normality and health. (p. 300)

However, we are all human, and in this sense, we share a universal humanity with others—*we are in the world*. We encourage you to think about your own ideas about the universal meaning of being human. Often, such ideas involve the religious or spiritual realms. Regardless of individual, family, and multicultural experience, we all share in being-in-the-world. Throughout this book, we hope you will examine your worldview as an individual, as a family member, as a multicultural being, and as a traveler through human experience.

Cultural Intentionality

A common theme underlying most approaches to interviewing, counseling, and psychotherapy, regardless of culture, is expansion of alternatives for living—the development of intentionality or purpose. The intentional individual, or the fully functioning person, can be described as follows: The person who acts with intentionality has a sense of capability. She or he can generate alternative behaviors in a given situation and "approach" a problem from different vantage points. The intentional, fully functioning individual is not bound to one course of action but can respond in the moment to changing life situations and look forward to longer-term goals.

The broad construct of intentionality underlies the several descriptions of theoretical goals for counseling we have discussed. Your task is to generate ever-increasing ways to respond to the complex situations and clients you may work with. In turn, you will seek to help individuals and families generate intentionality—new ways of responding to ever-changing life conditions.

Intentional living occurs in a cultural context. Cultural expertise and intentionality imply the following three major abilities:

1. *The ability to generate a maximum number of thoughts, words, and behaviors to communicate with self and others within a given culture.*

Common to people who come for assistance on personal issues is immobility, the inability to act intentionally and resolve problems—the experience of feeling fixed in one place. Immobility is described differently in the several helping theories.[2] For example, Gestalt therapists talk about splits and impasses, Rogerian therapists talk about discrepancies between ideal and real self, and psychodynamic theorists discuss polarities and unconscious conflicts.

A multiculturally oriented therapist might examine the person's historical, cultural, and social context, giving special attention to the different modes of being that exist among different cultural groups. A family therapist might work with the entire family in the belief that the "identified patient" somehow is enacting family wishes. These are only a few of a myriad of therapeutic approaches, any one of which can be used effectively to free clients so they can generate new behaviors and be more fully functioning.

This points to an underlying purpose or overall goal of all counseling and therapy, which is to increase response capacity and the ability to generate or create new behaviors and thoughts.

2. *The ability to generate the thoughts, words, and behaviors necessary to communicate with a variety of diverse groups and individuals. Both clients and counselors need to communicate within their own culture and learn the ability to understand other cultures as well.*

It has been demonstrated in several research studies that 50 percent of Third World or minority individuals do not return for a second counseling interview (see Sue & Sue, 1990). In addition, a large number of majority culture individuals also fail to complete the helping process.

Most counseling theories operating in North America are rooted in European-American, middle-class culture. However, what is appropriate behavior for the European-American may be unsuitable for an African-American or Latina/o. For example, the expression of emotions necessary in client-centered and psychodynamic therapy may be totally inappropriate and alien for some Asian-Americans and Native Americans (as well as many European-Americans). Thus, not only the goal but also the very process, style, and techniques of traditional helping may be inappropriate for those of minority cultures.

Fortunately, most theories and approaches stress the importance of evaluating whether or not the therapeutic methods are appropriate for the particular client. The counselor must reflect, analyze, and choose appropriate responses and techniques. A therapist who is skilled and knowledgeable in many theories thus has a strong basis for cultural intentionality. It is rapidly becoming evident that culture, religious background, socioeconomic status, age, and gender can be as important as the unique personality of the client and the problem itself.

3. *The ability to formulate plans, act on many possibilities existing in a culture, and reflect on these actions.*

"Unfreezing" an individual so that he or she is able to generate new behaviors is vital, but the simple generation of new ways of responding and acting creatively is not enough. At some point, the person must become committed to action and decide on an alternative. Not all counseling theories have a clear commitment to action as a goal.

Behavioral approaches to counseling place a particular emphasis on action. Clear, observable goals are developed, accompanied by follow-up and evaluation. The cognitive-behavioral therapist often assigns specific "homework" so that ideas generated in the interview are taken home and practiced. Most approaches to psychotherapy are not this specific, but all therapeutic approaches encourage clients to look at their plans and the results of their actions.

As an example of the difficulty of establishing culturally appropriate goals, consider the treatment of eating disorders such as bulimia and anorexia. Generally, these are problems of women in North American culture, although male eating disorders are on the increase. Thinness is valued in the North American culture. Thus, in helping clients generate a more positive body image and accept their weight, the counselor often works against cultural imperatives. Therefore, cultural awareness and consciousness raising often need to be included in the treatment of bulimia and anorexia. Such awareness should include the fact that some cultures consider heaviness desirable, viewing thinness as less attractive. The therapist must be aware that what is successful adjustment and adaptation in one culture can result in serious problems in another.

For example, middle-class European-Americans are considered adjusted if they have accumulated private wealth. If they distributed their material possessions to friends and family, they would be considered to be suffering from a serious psychiatric problem. In South Pacific Fiji, the custom is that the individual must give away any material good if a friend or family member requests it—and give it away forever. The Native American potlatch in which wealth is given to others in an elaborate ceremony is another example of how individuals in some cultures gain status and prestige by sharing rather than acquiring. As can be seen, "mental health" depends on cultural perspective.

Learning about other cultural value systems and goals is a lifelong process. Whether we are talking about Canada, the United States, Australia, or Great Britain, all these societies are now recognized as multicultural. Whereas once the Eurocentric model was considered appropriate for all clients, this is no longer true. Our effort throughout this book is to provide examples of culture-specific issues that make the application of therapeutic theory and technique more relevant to individuals and families.

The Scientist-Practitioner

Counseling and psychotherapy draw heavily on the concept of the scientist-practitioner, a helping professional who draws on research for more effective practice and who uses information from clinical work to generate new research questions and plans. You personally may not be a researcher, but regardless of the therapeutic model you select, you will be affected by the scientific background of the field.

Kurt Lewin summarizes the relationship between practice and research succinctly: "No research without action; no action without research" (quoted in Marrow, 1969, p. 193). Exhibit 1.1 provides a summary of research on the effectiveness of therapy.

There are three avenues to major change and growth in the field: (1) new theoretical orientations, such as family therapy, and developmental and multicultural approaches; (2) research; and (3) clinical discoveries made through direct practice. All three methods are critical for effective practice, useful theory, and meaningful research. Currently, the field is moving toward accountability, for example, supporting theory with research and contracting with clients for specific results from therapy. With accountability as a goal, the scientist-practitioner model becomes of central importance. Ideas for case study research will be detailed in this book in the belief that most clients benefit from clear, jointly established objectives for the helping process. It is possible — and desirable — to integrate research on therapeutic action as part of the helping process.

Each chapter in this book includes a brief research exercise for practice in the belief that each of us can learn by (1) generating hypotheses about a client, (2) testing these hypotheses in the client's world, (3) evaluating the results, and then (4) modifying the hypotheses as a result of clinical and research findings. In many cases, you will want to work with your clients as coinvestigators conducting joint research on the human condition.

Ethics and the Counseling and Psychotherapy Process

Effective practice is not only scientific, it is also ethical. Professional helping organizations such as the American Association of Marriage and Family Therapy (AAMFT), the American Counseling Association (ACA), and the American Psychological Association (APA) stress the importance of ethics in the helping relationship.

The Multicultural Foundation of Ethics

At a major conference on the future of professional psychology, Korman (1973, p. 105) stated:

The provision of professional services to persons of culturally diverse backgrounds by persons not competent in understanding and providing professional services to such

=== **Exhibit 1.1** ===

Research Summary on the Effectiveness of Individual Counseling and Psychotherapy: Eysenck and Meta-analysis

Studying the extensive data on the effectiveness of psychotherapy, Hans J. Eysenck let loose a bombshell on the therapeutic profession in 1952:

> In general, certain conclusions are possible from these data. They fail to prove that psychotherapy, Freudian or otherwise, facilitates the recovery of neurotic patients. They show that roughly two-thirds of a group of neurotic patients will recover or improve to a marked extent within about two years of the onset of their illness, whether they are treated by means of psychotherapy or not. This figure appears to be remarkably stable from one investigation to another, regardless of type of patient treated, standard of recovery employed, or method of therapy used (cited in Eysenck, 1966, pp. 29–30).

Eysenck's claim has been ably and sharply rebutted in numerous articles, but he was pivotal in forcing the field to look at its work and evaluate its effectiveness more carefully. The claims for the effectiveness of therapy include the following:

- Eysenck considered only 20 of over 400 studies then available (Smith & Glass, 1977).

- Meta-analysis (a complex statistical procedure) of 375 studies of therapy effectiveness found that clients who experienced therapy were indeed better off than untreated control subjects (Smith & Glass, 1977).
- An updated meta-analysis of 475 controlled studies supported the earlier findings of Smith and Glass (1977). However, two years after treatment, the effectiveness of therapy had diminished (Glass & Kliegl, 1983).
- Looking at benefits provides another way to review effectiveness data:

	Less benefit	Greater benefit
Psychotherapy	34%	66%
No therapy	66	34

"We are doing considerably better in our softer, wilder sciences than we may have thought we were doing" (Rosenthal, 1990, p. 776).
- Finally, McNeilly and Howard (1991) reexamined Eysenck's original data and found a 50 percent improvement rate among his subjects in about fifteen sessions, as compared to a 2 percent rate among those not treated. They comment that "Eysenck's data reveal that psychotherapy is very effective" (p. 74).

group shall be considered unethical; . . . it shall be equally unethical to deny such persons professional services because the present staff is inadequately prepared; . . . it shall be the obligation of all service agencies to employ competent persons or to provide continuing education for the present staff to meet the service needs of the culturally diverse population it serves.

Despite the clarity of this statement, the field moved slowly to implement these recommendations. Pedersen and Marsella (1982) comment: "A serious moral vacuum exists in the delivery of cross-cultural counseling and therapy because the values of a dominant culture have been imposed on a culturally different consumer" (p. 498).

Finally, in 1987, the American Psychological Association provided the first formal recognition of the importance of multicultural issues in psychology. Their *General Guidelines for Providers of Psychological Services* define good practice for the field, stating as part of the preamble: "These *General Guidelines* have been developed with the understanding that psychological services must be planned and implemented so that they are sensitive to factors related to life in a pluralistic society such as age, gender, affectional orientation, culture, and ethnicity" (p. 1).

Ethical practice, then, requires a multicultural orientation. Most of the theories presented in this book are based on traditional Eurocentric perspectives. Although traditional theory continues to remain of great value, ethical practice requires us to move beyond present theory to new approaches to the field.

We indeed are facing a paradigm shift. As a counselor or therapist, you will be taking part in the increasing awareness of multicultural issues as they relate to the helping process. Thus, it is imperative that you challenge the theories presented in this text and shape them for more culturally relevant counseling and psychotherapy.

The Relational versus Individualistic Orientation

Counseling and psychotherapy have traditionally focused on individuals and their wishes and desires. The goals of counseling as they have generally been presented in the field have generally been drawn from middle-class Northern European and North American frameworks. At first glance, autonomy and self-actualization sound like wonderful ideas with which no one could truly disagree. However, an exclusive focus on the self would be considered selfish and even an indication of mental disorder in much of Asian, South Pacific, and African culture. As another example, American Indian culture has long focused on the relationship of the individual to the group and to the environment. The Sioux Nation talks of *mitakuge ogasin* — "all my relations."

On reviewing the scholarship and research paradigms suggested by the African-American scholar W.E.B. DuBois, one discovers that many, perhaps most, of the current "discoveries" in multicultural work can be found in his early writings. For example, in 1908 DuBois wrote:

The family group . . . harks back to the sheltered harem with the mother emerging at first as nurse and homemaker, while the man remains the sole breadwinner. Thus the Negro woman more than the women of any other group in America is the protagonist in the fight for an economically independent womanhood in modern countries. Her fight has not been willing or for the most part conscious but it has, nevertheless, been curiously effective in its influence on the working world. (cited in Stewart, 1990, p. 14)

Parham (1990) points out that many of today's issues in counseling and therapy were first noted by minority authors, but full integration of these ideas into the field had to wait until they were endorsed by European-American mainstream authorities. White and Parham (1990) detail some of the history of the relational orientation. Despite a constant emphasis by minority authorities, the validity of the relational orientation did not reach the helping field until Gilligan's work on gender issues.

Gilligan and the Relational Orientation

Gilligan (1982) pointed out that male and female constructions of and beliefs about the nature of reality are very different. Before her work, much important research and thinking about moral and cognitive development tended to be presented from the perspective of male moral and cognitive development.

Gilligan noted the obvious: men and women are different. Their varying patterns of psychosocial development result in different patterns of thinking. At the risk of oversimplifying a highly complex issue, men may be said to be "linear" thinkers. The male model of thinking tends to focus on results and achievement of a specific goal. Gilligan describes women as "relational" thinkers, individuals who think about possibilities and relationships among possibilities before taking action.

An Example from Early Adolescence.   Gilligan compares linear or hierarchical thinking to the more complex relational mode of being in the case of Jake and Amy, two eleven-year-olds. A typical problem faced in therapy and counseling is attribution of responsibility when clients feel interpersonal conflict. Upon asking each of the youngsters the question "When responsibility to oneself and responsibility to others conflict, how should one choose?" Gilligan (1982) received the following responses:

Jake: You go about one-fourth to others and three-fourths to yourself.

Amy: Well, it really depends on the situation. If you have a responsibility with somebody else, then you should keep it to a certain extent, but to the extent that it is really going to hurt you or stop you from doing something that you really want, then I think maybe you should put yourself first. But if it is your responsibility to somebody really close to you, you've just got to decide in that situation which is more important, yourself or that person, and like I said, it really depends on what kind of person you are and how you feel about the other persons involved. (pp. 35–36)

Although Jake's and Amy's answers seem stereotypically male (linear) and female (relational), these general points should be kept in mind:

1. Women tend to have different ways of thinking about the world than men.
2. In many cases the direct, straightforward approach of the male model may be insensitive to others.

3. When viewed from an alternative perspective, the relational female model may be more conceptually advanced.

4. From an African-American or Native American perspective, the relational orientation could be broadened to include the extended family, neighbors, the community, and perhaps even the total ethnic group as well.

The linear versus relational orientation is basic to an understanding of counseling and therapy. Although relational issues manifest differently from culture to culture, Gilligan's distinction is helpful in understanding not only male and female clients, but also those of differing cultural groups. The relational approach espoused so long by African-American authorities is beginning to receive the attention it deserves and may be more descriptive of Asian-American, Latina/o, Native American, and other cultures.

Ethics and Responsibility

The core of ethical responsibility is to *do nothing that will harm the client or society*. The bulk of ethical responsibility lies with you as the helper. A person who comes for help is vulnerable and open to destructive action by the counselor. Knowledge of psychological, counseling, social work, and family therapy guidelines is essential. Following are some simple guidelines for you to consider as you review ethical standards in more detail.

1. *Maintain confidentiality*. Counseling and psychotherapy depend on trust between counselor and client. You as the therapist are in a powerful relationship; the more trust you build, the more power you have. This book asks you to practice many basic strategies of counseling and therapy. It is essential that you maintain the confidence of your clients, but if you are a student, you do not have legal confidentiality, and your clients should be made aware of this. Confidentiality is designed to protect clients (not counselors), and only the courts, in the final analysis, can provide a guarantee of confidentiality.

2. *Recognize your limitations*. It is vital that you maintain an egalitarian atmosphere with your clients, classmates, or coworkers. Share beforehand with them the task you wish to work through. Inform them that they are free to stop the process at any time. Do not use the interview as a place to delve into the life of another person. The interview is for helping others, not examining them.

3. *Seek consultation*. As you practice the exercises presented throughout this text, remain in consultation with your professor, workshop leader, mentor, or coworker. Counseling and psychotherapy are often very private. It is important that you obtain supervision and/or consultation in your work. You may also find it helpful to discuss your own growth as a helper with others. At the same time, be very careful in discussing what you have learned about your clients.

4. *Treat the client as you would like to be treated*. Put yourself in the place of the client. Every person deserves to be treated with respect, dignity, kindness, and honesty.

5. *Be aware of individual and cultural differences*. This point has been stressed throughout this chapter. An emphasis on cultural issues can lead at times to stereotyping an individual. At the same time, an overemphasis on individuality may obscure multicultural issues.

6. *Review ethical standards constantly*. Read and reread ethical sections as you encounter new ideas in this text.

Overview

In part 1 we explore *foundational theories of psychotherapy*. Foundational theories are those that provide qualities and skills basic to the practice of all counseling and therapy and include empathy, counseling skills, decision making, multicultural understanding, and developmental issues.

Each of these foundational theories can be considered an alternative construction of the field and can be used as a basis for effective practice. Understanding of and competence in foundational theories will help you work more effectively with the traditional theories described.

Part 2 presents *major historical theories of counseling and psychotherapy* that have been vital to the field's development. Presented in chronological and historical order are psychodynamic theory (Freud, Bowlby, and Taub-Bynum), cognitive-behavioral theory (Cheek, Meichenbaum, Ellis, Beck, and Glasser), and existential-humanistic theory (Rogers, Frankl, and Perls).

These three theoretical areas are often called first force (psychodynamic), second force (cognitive-behavioral), and third force (existential-humanistic). A fourth force—multicultural counseling and therapy—is now changing the field (Cheatham, 1990; Pedersen, 1991).

Part 3, on *integrating family and multicultural issues in the practice of counseling and therapy*, presents the family systems approach and encourages you to think about your own integration of this complex, evolving field.

Taking Theory into Practice

Your task as a therapist and counselor is multiple. You must not only learn therapeutic theories at a cognitive level, but also you must practice them. Each chapter has a number of practical exercises that will give you an opportunity to take theory into direct practice and learn whether or not the theory "works" for you—that is, if it is applicable to your personal experience and if you wish to consider the issues in more detail.

Reading a text such as this should be considered at best a beginning. You will learn far more about the theories if you do the exercises seriously. We recommend that you develop a portfolio of your experiences with the ideas and theories presented in this book. A portfolio of clinical competencies will stay with you long after you have read this text.

We look forward to having you with us on the journey toward more effective, multiculturally aware counseling and therapy. As you take theory into practice, you will discover new questions and new ideas. We hope we will hear from some of you about your journey, and we welcome your suggestions for changes and additions to future additions of this book.

NOTES

1. Although the term *European-American* will be used frequently in this book, the authors also recognize that many Jewish-Americans would prefer to be recognized separately, as their past experience in Europe has not been positive.
2. The basic concept of immobility, the inability to act effectively and intentionally, will appear in many forms in this book among many types of clients. Words and phrases such as *stuckness, inability to respond, polarized emotions, frozen behavioral pattern, indecision, rigidity, fixated*, and many others all represent the loss of intentionality and resulting immobility.

REFERENCES

AMERICAN PSYCHOLOGICAL ASSOCIATION. (1987). *General Guidelines for Providers of Psychological Services*. Washington, DC: Author.

BUMPUS, G. (1991, October 25). Skin color doesn't determine culture. *Amherst Record*, p. 4.

CHEATHAM, H. (1990). Empowering Black families. In H. Cheatham & J. Stewart (Eds.), *Black families* (pp. 373–93). New Brunswick, NJ: Transaction Press.

ESCHER, M. (1960). *The graphic work of M. C. Escher.* New York: Ballantine.

EYSENCK, H. J. (1966). *The effects of psychotherapy*. New York: International Science.

GILLIGAN, C. (1982). *In a different voice*. Cambridge, MA: Harvard University Press.

GLASS, G., & KLIEGL, R. (1983). An apology for research integration in the study of psychotherapy. *Journal of Consulting and Clinical Psychology, 51*, 28–41.

KORMAN, M. (1973). *Levels and patterns of professional training in psychology*. Washington, DC: American Psychological Association.

MCNEILLY, C., & HOWARD, K. (1991). The effects of psychotherapy: A reevaluation based on dosage. *Psychotherapy Research, 1*, 74–78.

MARROW, A. (1969). *The practical theorist*. New York: Basic Books.

PARHAM, T. (1990, August). *White American researcher in multicultural counseling: Significant challenges and rewards*. Paper presented at the annual meeting of the American Psychological Association, Boston.

PEDERSEN, P. (1991). Multiculturalism as a fourth force in counseling. *Journal of Counseling and Development, 70*, entire issue.

PEDERSEN, P., & MARSELLA, T. (1982). The ethical crisis for cross-cultural counseling and therapy. *Professional Psychology, 13*, 492–500.

ROSENTHAL, R. (1990). How are we doing in soft psychology? *American Psychologist, 45*, 775–76.

SMITH, M., & GLASS, G. (1977). Meta-analysis of psychotherapy outcome studies. *American Psychologist, 32*, 752–60.

STEWART, J. (1990). Back to basics: The significance of Du Bois's and Frazier's contributions for contemporary research on black families. In H. Cheatham & J. Stewart (Eds.), *Black families* (pp. 3–30). New Brunswick, NJ: Transaction Press.

SUE, D. (1991). A diversity perspective on contextualism. *Journal of Counseling and Development, 70,* 300–301.

SUE, D., & SUE, S. (1990). *Counseling the culturally different* (2nd ed.). New York: Wiley.

WHITE, J., & PARHAM, T. (1990). *The psychology of Blacks* (2nd ed.). Englewood Cliffs, NJ: Prentice-Hall.

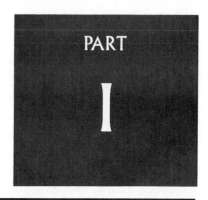

PART

I

FOUNDATIONAL THEORIES OF COUNSELING AND THERAPY

Foundational to counseling and psychotherapy are theories that focus on basic underlying dimensions of the helping process. These theories, discussed in part 1, have the following dimensions in common:

1. *A belief in multiple approaches to the helping process.* Each of the chapters presents a specific theoretical and practical orientation and also stresses the need to incorporate ideas from other theories into counseling and clinical practice.

2. *An emphasis on multicultural issues.* Each theoretical framework gives attention to issues related to client diversity.

3. *An ability to operate as a separate and distinct helping theory.* Each framework discussed emphasizes linkage. In addition, the ideas in each chapter provide a working set of theories and skills within which counseling and therapy can be conducted.

4. *An emphasis on those underlying processes believed important to all ap-*

proaches to helping. We believe that the empathic dimensions, listening skills, and developmental concepts are crucial to all forms of helping. Those committed to multicultural theory stress the need to support older theories as they become more culturally relevant.

The chapters in this part focus on five foundational theoretical and practical frameworks. Chapter 2 presents the basis of empathic theory, which is that each client is a unique individual who is intimately involved in the family experience. The family, in turn, is the primary place where culture is learned.

All counselors and therapists, whether they work at the individual, family, or multicultural level, use specific interviewing skills, which are discussed in chapter 3. However, different cultural groups tend to use the skills differently. In addition, the major historical forces of counseling and therapy can be considered from a skills perspective.

Chapter 4 explores the topic of decisional counseling. Counseling and therapy are about decisions, and an understanding of how decisions are made can be invaluable, regardless of the therapist's theoretical orientation. Decisional style varies from individual to individual, and different cultural groups may have different styles as well.

Multicultural counseling and therapy (MCT), as discussed in chapter 5, is becoming central to the field. MCT points up that all theory is generated within a cultural context. This chapter provides information on universal and focused approaches to MCT, cultural identity theory, and some examples of interviewing practice from this frame of reference.

Individual development can be considered the goal of counseling and psychotherapy. Developmental counseling and therapy (DCT) is presented in chapter 6 as an integrative model that is helpful in assessing client cognitive and emotional processes, matching interviewing style to client needs, and generating treatment plans.

The concepts presented in these chapters will prepare you to look to the future and integrate the complex precepts of the three major traditional theoretical forces in psychotherapy and counseling: psychodynamic, cognitive-behavioral, and existential-humanistic.

The Empathic Attitude:
Individual, Family, and Culture

CHAPTER GOALS

This chapter seeks to help you:

1. Define individual empathy and its personal meaning to you. You will also gain familiarity with a scale for rating empathic qualities.

2. Understand and use central empathic concepts, particularly positive regard, respect and warmth, concreteness, immediacy, and genuineness.

3. Determine the importance of family heritage and the role of the family as the primary transmitter of the culture in your own construction of the meaning of empathy.

4. Know key multicultural competencies and standards basic to individual, family, and cultural empathy.

Empathy and Empathic Approaches

Empathy is often described as seeing the world through another's eyes, hearing as they might hear, and feeling and experiencing their internal world. Native Americans called this "walking in another's moccasins." However, empathy does not involve mixing your thoughts and feelings with those of the client. Although the empathic attitude requires that you accept the client's being, as therapist and counselor you must remain separate, true to yourself and to your own beliefs.

Acceptance as the Foundation of Empathy

Acceptance may be described as the foundation of empathy. How would you define and experience acceptance? The following exercise may be helpful:

> Recall a time when you felt accepted by someone else just as you are or were. Recreate the situation in your mind. What is happening and what are you seeing? What is being said? What are your thoughts and feelings that go with the image? Focus on your body. Can you locate a specific place in your body for your feelings? If you are not as comfortable with visual images, use words, poetry, sounds, scents and odors, or bodily feelings.

Counseling and therapy ask you to accept[1] the client. It is easy to feel acceptance toward a small child suffering from an emotional hurt or toward a survivor of spousal abuse. However, it is far less easy to feel accepting of the bully on the playground or the perpetrator of family violence. The following exercise can help you explore your ability to be accepting:

> How do you imagine yourself if you were to work with a bully or an abuser? Take time to let this image arise. What do you see and hear? Most important, what do you feel? Can you locate that feeling in a specific place in your own body?

The feelings you experience in your own body may be the best indicator of your degree of acceptance and ability to be empathic. Most of us have difficulty when we work with those who hurt others. Yet the bully, the abuser, and the rapist need empathy and acceptance as much as the child, adolescent, or adult who has survived attack. At the same time, we should not use empathic understanding as a way to excuse the behavior of the perpetrator.

Empathic Understanding, Prevention, and the "Upstream Approach"

As counselors and therapists, we have a special responsibility to protect victims and survivors of attacks. One way to meet this responsibility is by working effectively with those who may harm others. Not only may empathic understanding help those who have been hurt, but it can also serve as a basis for prevention work with perpetrators.

An analogy can be drawn to illustrate this point. In a rural area, there was a swimming hole bordered by a warm sandy beach near a bend in the river. The local people enjoyed swimming and playing on the beach, but one day a drowning child came around the bend, and a strong swimmer pulled him to safety. The next day the same thing happened again; this time a woman was saved. Daily thereafter, drowning people came round the river's bend—men, women, and children, and sometimes whole families. The people decided to organize a life-saving club to rescue victims as they came downstream. One person disagreed and started walking up river around the bend, saying, "I think we need to go upstream to see who's throwing these people in!" As the story shows, empathy is not just the understanding of another's experience; it can also include action.

In the "downstream" approach you will primarily work with survivors. If you truly embrace the empathic challenge of acceptance, you can move "upstream" as well to work with perpetrators and abusers and prevent victimization. The real challenge of the empathic approach is to accept those who seem unacceptable and work with them to change their behavior, attitudes, and feelings.

Constructs of Empathy

In 1957 Carl Rogers produced a landmark paper, "The Necessary and Sufficient Conditions of Therapeutic Personality Change," which made a strong case that empathy and related constructs are all that is needed to produce change in a client. To help another person grow, Rogers said, requires an integrated congruent relationship with the client, unconditional positive regard for the client, and the communication of empathy from the counselor to the client—"No other conditions are necessary" (p. 27).

The influence of this article has continually expanded, and its tenets are now articles of faith for those of the existential-humanistic orientation. Moreover, cognitive-behavioral, psychodynamic, and most other orientations to counseling and therapy now accept the importance of empathy. Empathy and the accompanying empathic conditions, such as respect, warmth, and genuineness, are foundational to most helping theories.

What Is Empathy?

Rogers offers the following contemporary definition of empathy:

> This is not laying trips on people. . . . You only listen and say back the other person's thing, step by step, just as that person seems to have it at that moment. You never mix into it any of your own things or ideas, never lay on the other person anything that person didn't express. . . . To show that you understand exactly, make a sentence or two which gets exactly at the personal meaning this person wanted to put across. This might be in your own words, usually, but use that person's own words for the touchy main things. (Gendlin & Hendricks, 1978, p. 120)

This definition takes empathy beyond an attitude. Rogers suggests specific actions and skills of empathic attitude the counselor or therapist can use in the interview to communicate empathy and understanding to the client. A summary of research on the role of empathy in therapy can be found in exhibit 2.1.

=== **Exhibit 2.1** ===

 Research Summary on Empathy

Does empathy exist? Can it be measured? Does it make a difference? The answers to these questions seem to be affirmative. Following are some of the key findings over the years:

- A landmark series of studies by Fiedler (1950a, 1950b, 1951) is often considered foundational in the study of empathy. He discovered that expert therapists of varying theoretical orientations appear to have much in common. For example, psychodynamic, Adlerian, and client-centered experts have more in common with each other than they do with inexperienced therapists of their own theoretical orientation.

- An avalanche of research in the 1960s and 1970s supported Fiedler's conclusions (see Anthony & Carkhuff, 1977; Auerbach & Johnson, 1977).

- Some reviewers criticized the facilitative conditions studies as flawed (Lambert, DeJulio, & Stein, 1978; Rachman & Wilson, 1980.) Some of these reviews were written by behavioral researchers who at that time were seeking to prove the superior validity of behavioral methods.

- Pivotal to an integration and acceptance of the facilitative conditions outside the Rogerian and human resource development groups were the Sloane et al. (1975) and Sloane and Staples (1984) studies. These researchers found that behavioral therapists exhibited higher or equal levels of empathic conditions than did other psychotherapists. Successful patients in both therapies rated their personal interaction with the therapist as the single most important part of treatment.

- More recent reviews related to this area may be found in Bergin and Garfield (1986) and Goldfried, Greenberg, and Marmar (1990). The latter conclude their review by noting that "no orientation has consistently been found superior to any other" (p. 680), although they do indicate that research is beginning to reveal that clients who suffer from different types of problems (such as depression or personality disorder) may benefit from varying the style of relationship in the interview.

It is difficult to dismiss such powerful data, and the field has gradually come to accept the vital importance of counselor-client relationship as central to the helping process. Empathy and the facilitative techniques appear to have been accepted by the field as part of a generic approach to the helping process.

Positive Regard and the Empathic Attitude

Positive regard is part of the empathic attitude, and is aptly demonstrated by Rogers, whose positive attitude and hope for his clients have become legendary. Positive regard means that you as therapist are able to recognize values and strengths in clients, even when the client holds widely different attitudes from yours. Positive regard is a concept basic to all counseling and therapy theory. If you as therapist cannot believe there is something positive and valuable in the client, there is little hope for client change.

Leona Tyler, in her classic counseling text (1961), presents a concrete explanation of the importance of positive regard:

> The initial stages of . . . therapy include a process that might be called *exploration of resources*. The counselor pays little attention to personality weaknesses. . . . [He or she] is most persistent in trying to locate . . . ways of coping with anxiety and stress, already existing resources that may be enlarged and strengthened once their existence is recognized.

In essence, positive regard asks that you look at the client affirmatively, expecting that he or she has potential resources. By positively identifying the client's strengths, you build a base on which together you can build a working future. Tyler calls this "minimum change therapy," which is based on the assumption that if you can identify a strength or resource in the client and if you support it over time, it will grow and become more central to the client's life.

Positive resources can be a special talent of the client, a friend or family member of the client, or ways to help the client look at old negative situations in more positive ways. Family therapists, for example, talk about the *positive reframe* in which negative family interaction is viewed from more hopeful perspectives. In addition, the therapist's own empathic, positive, and respectful attitude toward the client may be the positive resource that makes change and growth possible.

Multicultural Considerations: Empathy and Positive Regard

The above constructs of empathy focus on individual counseling and therapy. The concept of respectfully entering the other person's world has profound implications for family work and multicultural relationships. Multicultural empathy requires that we respect worldviews different from our own. As we seek to understand those who have a different ethnic/racial, religious, or gender experience from our own, we will find ourselves in a lifelong learning process.

Positive regard asks that we find positives in the worldviews and attitudes of those who are different from us. The Mexican-American counselor working with a European-American client has a special responsibility to find positive meanings in the client's life experience. Similarly, the European-American counselor faces the same challenges with a Mexican-American client: the counselor must learn to respect, understand, and be able to work with different clients.

Facilitative Conditions

Human resource development (HRD) was conceptualized by Carkhuff (1981) as a way to expand the physical, emotional, and intellectual dimensions of human potential. Based on principles of empathy and understanding, HRD's influence has expanded beyond counseling and therapy to management, medical education, and other areas (Carkhuff, 1983, 1987). The very term *human resource development* reminds us of the importance of focusing on what human potential can achieve rather than emphasizing the negative.

The Empathy Rating Scale

One of Carkhuff's (1969) unique contributions was to point out that it is possible to identify whether or not the counselor or therapist is truly empathic. Exhibit 2.2 presents a seven-level adaptation of Carkhuff's original work.

The seven levels provide a way to measure the therapist's degree of empathy and acceptance. At some point, you will want to make an audiotape or videotape of yourself to examine your own positive and empathic abilities. Consider using this seven-level scale to rate yourself as you listen to one of your own interviews. This exercise will be particularly important when you are working with a difficult client or family and question whether some part of their inability to grow in counseling is related to your level of empathic understanding.

Testing Your Ability to Use the Scale

Imagine you are working with a parent in a family session. The reason the family has come for treatment is that they are concerned about their ten-year-old's lack of achievement. You observe the family to be cold and disconnected; the only apparent value they hold in common is that of academic success. In the following segment, all four family members are present. Assume that the short exchange is representative of what you have been hearing repeated in different words for the past ten minutes:

Parent 1: Billy just isn't measuring up to Esther. He's bright enough, but he just isn't trying hard enough. I think his stomachaches are just a way to get out of work.

Parent 2: Yes, when I was his age, I studied two hours every night. Esther does that even though she's younger than Billy.

Esther: (sits quietly looking down)

Billy: (squirms in his chair and appears sad)

Exhibit 2.2

The Empathy Rating Scale

Instructions: Before rating a counselor's statement for its degree of empathy, it is critical that the context of what the client has been saying be considered as well. Therefore, examine what the client has just said before determining how well the counselor is "tuned in." Rate each counselor statement on the following seven-point scale for degree of empathy. It is also possible to examine several counselor statements or an entire interview segment and rate that for empathy.

Level 1: The counselor or therapist is overtly destructive to the interviewing process. He or she fails to attend (sharp body shifts, major topic jumps) in a way that sharply disrupts client flow or attacks the client or discounts information.

Level 2: The counselor or therapist may be implicitly and subtly destructive, even though overtly trying to be helpful. The distinction between levels 1 and 2 is a matter of degree and sharpness. The disagreement or lack of attention doesn't seem as unusual here and is seen in the daily life of most people in some form. (Also see level 5.)

Level 3: At first glance, the session appears to be moving normally. However, on deeper analysis, one sees that the counselor or therapist is *detracting* slightly from what the client has been saying. The paraphrase is close, but still misses the client's meaning. Much of our daily conversation fits this pattern. As a result of the interaction, the client is not damaged and has been listened to minimally, but counselor responses take away from what the client says or minimizes statements.

Level 4: Considered by many the *minimal* level for counseling, level 4 responses are *interchangeable* with what the client is saying. An interchangeable response is best exemplified by an accurate reflection of feeling, paraphrase, or summary that catches the essence of what the client has said. An open question or a self-disclosure that aids client responding is another example of a level 4 response.

Level 5: At this point, counseling becomes truly additive in that the counselor or therapist is adding something beyond an interchangeable response. In addition to an accurate paraphrase or reflection of feeling, the therapist adds a mild interpretation or a probing question or interpretation that not only catches the major meanings of the client, but *adds* something new to facilitate growth and exploration. Generally speaking, level 5 requires the use of influencing skills or questioning techniques. Ineffective use of these skills at this point, however, may return the counselor or therapist to level 2. As one employs the influencing skills, the possibility for error increases.

Level 6:   The counselor is truly becoming an intentional person. Attending and influencing skills are used in combination with the many qualities of empathy (concreteness, immediacy, and so on) to provide a more effective and facilitating level of counseling. Patterns of movement synchrony and movement complementarity often are manifested.

Level 7:   The highest level of counseling is one that relatively few counselors and therapists attain. In addition to solid, effective intentional manifestation of the many microskills and qualities of empathy, the counselor is totally "with" the client, yet apart and distinct. For some, this can be termed a "peak experience" in a relationship. Direct mutual communication is shown at this stage in its full dimensions.

(Circle appropriate number for each below.)

Empathy (global impression)	1 2 3 4 5 6 7
Positive regard	1 2 3 4 5 6 7
Respect	1 2 3 4 5 6 7
Warmth	1 2 3 4 5 6 7
Concreteness	1 2 3 4 5 6 7
Immediacy	1 2 3 4 5 6 7
Confrontation	1 2 3 4 5 6 7
Genuineness	
in relation to self	1 2 3 4 5 6 7
in relation to others	1 2 3 4 5 6 7
Cultural empathy	1 2 3 4 5 6 7

How would you respond to this family? What would you say? Think about your own feelings about situations such as the above. What might you like to say if you could? Take a moment as you think this through. You might find it helpful to write your responses down.

How you respond to your client often says as much about you as it does about the client. Referring to exhibit 2.2, locate the point on the empathy scale that best represents your response. Also consider what you might feel tempted to say and where it ranks on the empathy scale. If your two self-ratings are markedly different—that is, if what you would say is much higher than what you would like to say—very likely you have not allowed yourself to respond authentically and it is likely that your client will pick up nonverbal clues of your anger and frustration.

In short, true empathy cannot be an act—it must be genuine. It is not impossible to respond positively to people who have negative behaviors and traits. Empathy can be learned, and with patience and understanding, you will find you can accept and help many types of difficult clients.

Applying the Empathy Scale to Sample Counselor Statements

Some other possible responses to the family presented in the above example follow. Rate each response on the seven-point scale in exhibit 2.2, and compare your ratings with those supplied at the end of the chapter.

1. It sounds as if achievement is very important in this family. Could you two parents talk to each other about achievement so I can understand its importance to you better?

2. (angrily) Stop it, I'm sick and tired of you sitting there so complacently while your two beautiful children are suffering in front of your eyes.

3. It's really important to you to have the children achieve. At the same time, I note that Billy and Esther haven't said a word and we've been here fifteen minutes. They look a bit sad and uncomfortable. What type of things work well in your family that involve you all together?

Classifying responses as to empathic level can be helpful in examining your own interviewing style. Generally speaking, an interview segment of from five to ten minutes is required for more accurate measures of empathy.

It is hard to imagine counseling or therapy being conducted without some minimal level of empathy. HRD has identified important constructs, such as respect and warmth, concreteness, immediacy, and congruence, that can help in communicating your feelings of understanding and empathy for the client.

Respect and Warmth

An impassive counselor or therapist can appear professional and competent, but underlying the façade of professionalism may be unconscious hostility toward and dislike of the client. The intentional counselor likes and respects other people and communicates these feelings to them.

Respect is close to positive regard and can be communicated verbally through a language of respect. Virtually all the comments concerning positive regard and exploration of resources discussed earlier communicate respect for another person. Enhancing statements might include such comments as "You express your opinion well" and "Good insight."

Respect is also communicated nonverbally through individually and culturally appropriate eye contact and body language. These dimensions will be explored in more depth in the following chapter.

It is important to remember that you do not have to support or respect the behavior to respect the client. It is especially important to sort out negative behaviors. At times, these behaviors must be forcefully stopped. Antisocial and borderline clients offer a particular challenge to your ability to respect. However, most clients so categorized have histories of extremely severe child abuse and/or multiple trauma. Thus, these are the very clients who most need your positive regard and respect.

Warmth as Related to Respect

It is possible to respect another person's point of view but still lack the critical dimension of personal warmth. Together, however, respect and warmth present a powerful combination.

Warmth of counselor response has been demonstrated to be an important factor underlying an empathic relationship. But what is warmth? Warmth may be defined as an emotional attitude toward the client expressed through nonverbal means. Vocal tone, posture, gestures, and facial expression are how the counselor's warmth and support are communicated to the client. Smiling has been found to be the best single predictor of warmth ratings in an interview (Bayes, 1973).

Delineating warmth, respect, and positive regard as separate categories is perhaps not really possible. Yet, one can imagine a person expressing positive feedback, respect, and positive regard to a client in a cold, distant fashion. The lack of warmth can negate the positive message. The communication of warmth through smiling, vocal tone, and other nonverbal means adds power and conviction to counselor comments.

Concreteness

Clients often come to therapy with vague, ambiguous complaints. A task of the intentional therapist is to clarify and understand vague ideas and problems expressed by the client. Effective interviews tend to move from vague descriptions of global issues to highly concrete discussions of what happened or is happening in the daily life of the client.

Through interviewing leads that focus on concrete client experience, the helper can move from generalization to a clear understanding of what actually happened. Becoming empathic and understanding is easier when you understand specific facts. Generally, most clients will welcome concreteness, as "objective facts" are less susceptible to distortion. Furthermore, specificity and concreteness will provide a more solid base for client and therapist problem solving.

The search for concreteness underlies many, perhaps even most helping interviews. The client lacks full understanding and often has labeled a situation incorrectly. Some clients are very abstract in their language and may talk in generalities. If you ask clients for an example of the general situation, they will often become more concrete.

Asking clients the open-ended question "Could you give me a specific example?" of the problem in question usually helps clients organize their thinking and become less abstract, thereby clarifying what was most likely a confusing interview.

Sometimes the emotional experience may have been too intense for immediate discussion of concrete specifics. In cases of rape and abuse, it may be wise to delay the search for concreteness. North Americans in general tend to prefer discussion of concrete specifics of a problem, but the concreteness and directness of this approach can put off many Europeans, Asians, or Africans whose culture may be oriented toward a more subtle approach.

Immediacy

There are two commonly used definitions of this term in counseling and therapy, one focused on the time dimensions and the other on the here-and-now nature of the interview.

Immediacy as Time Orientation

The English language divides time into past, present, and future. Generally speaking, the most powerful and immediate counseling leads are those couched in the present tense. Different theories discussed in this book give different emphasis to different time dimensions.

The tense of discussion in the helping interview heavily influences the nature of client-counselor interaction. The following are abbreviated examples of how therapists of varying theoretical orientations might use the time dimension differently:

Client: (trembling) I'm scared and worried about the possibility of being hit again. I don't intend to go back.

Psychodynamic therapist: Stay with that feeling . . . (pause) Locate it in your body . . . (pause) Now free associate to your earliest childhood experience when you had that same feeling in your body. [*Here-and-now experiencing related to the past*]

Humanistic therapist: I experience you as gaining strength in your decision to move on your own. At the same time, you're very scared and frightened right now. [*Here-and-now experiencing*]

Crisis counselor: You now know that going back won't work, but it's scary alone. Let me be with you a moment and then later we can handle the future. [*Here-and-now experiencing related to the future*]

Which of the above counseling leads is most effective will depend on the precise context of the client's comment and your own worldview. Immediacy is an important and potentially powerful factor in each orientation. We can experience anxiety deeply in the past, present, or future. At the same time, if emotional dimensions are not emphasized, past- or future-tense immediacy is likely to be less intense.

Immediacy as Here-and-Now Interpersonal Discussion

As you move toward a more present-tense helping orientation, you may find yourself focusing on the here-and-now experience of the interview and asking your client such questions as "What's going on with you, right now?" or "What are you feeling/experiencing at this moment?"

Egan (1990) talks about "self-involving statements" in which you share your own reactions to the client. For example, you might share your own feelings with the client who refuses to return home: "I'm glad you're taking your own direction and having faith in yourself. I'm impressed with your strength." Such statements tell clients where you are in relationship to them. At the same time, the primary focus in such statements is on the client rather than the therapist.

Egan also explores here-and-now immediacy in the counselor-client relationship. In the following example, the client and counselor talk directly about what is happening between them:

Counselor: I'd like to stop a moment and take a look at what's happening right now between you and me.

Agnes: I'm not sure what you mean?

Counselor: Well, our conversation today started out quite lively, and now it seems rather subdued to me. I've noticed that the muscles in my shoulders have become tense and I feel a little flush. I sense something's up that way when I feel I might have said something wrong. [*Note how the counselor uses awareness of his own body to facilitate communication*]

Agnes: What could that have been?

Counselor: Agnes, is it just me, or do you also feel that things are a bit strained between us right now?

Agnes: Well, a little.

Counselor: Last month you discussed how you control your friends with your emotions. This gets you what you want, but the price you pay can be too high. . . . Now all of a sudden you've gone a bit quiet, and I've been asking myself what I might have done wrong. To be truthful, I'm feeling a bit controlled too. What's your perspective on all this? (pp. 226–27)

This use of here-and-now immediacy in examining the client-counselor relationship can be very powerful and enlightening. At the same time, it obviously can be overdone and thus needs to be used sparingly, with care and a sense of ethics.

Congruence, Genuineness, and Authenticity

Rogers (1957) stated that the therapist in a counseling relationship should be a "congruent, integrated person. It means that within the relationship he is freely and deeply himself, with his actual experience represented by his awareness of himself. It is the opposite of presenting a facade either knowingly or unknowingly" (p. 97).

It is difficult to fault such a statement, as it is clear that openness and honesty on your part are central to your effectiveness as a counselor. There are times, however, when complete openness and spontaneity of expression may be damaging to the client. This point was brought home forcefully in Lieberman, Yalom, and Miles's 1972 study of encounter group casualties. They found that "open, authentic" group leaders produced more emotional casualties than did more conservative counselors who developed relationships with group members more slowly and naturally.

There are two types of authenticity to consider. The first is authenticity to yourself. Being authentic, truthful, and open may be a laudable stance, but your client may not be ready for such behavior. A more important type of authenticity rests in having a genuine, congruent relationship with your client. This means taking into account where your clients "are at," listening to them, and opening an empathic dialogue.

The following exchange illustrates some issues in regard to genuineness:

Client: Yes, I can't decide what to do about the bab . . . I mean abortion until I know where I stand with Ronnie. He used to treat me nice, especially when we were first dating. He came over and fixed my car and my stereo, he liked to run errands for me. Now if I ask him anything, he makes a big hassle out of it.

Helper: At this moment, I can sense some confusion. Let me check this out with you. When someone is nice to me, I get to trust them and feel comfortable. But then if they let me down, I get low and lost and really confused. Is my experience at all like yours?

Client: I guess I have felt like that. I know I blame him for getting me pregnant because he wouldn't do anything to prevent it. It makes me damn mad!

Helper: Right now, you really are angry with him.

The counselor shows genuineness in relationship to self through skillful self-disclosure and shares feelings and thoughts in a very real and personal manner. Self-disclosure does not necessarily have to be specific and detailed; it can be relatively vague and nonconcrete.

Suppose the counselor was thinking of a past event concerning his or her parents. If that concrete event had been presented, the counselor would still be genuine in relation to self, but the introduction of an example so different from the client's immediate personal experience could disturb the counseling relationship. Genuine and appropriate self-disclosure, on the other hand, can produce increased genuineness on the part of the client. Intentional counselors tend to produce intentional clients.

Empathy and Family and Multicultural Issues

How well are you equipped to be empathic with people of different races, ethnic groups, or affectional orientation, or with those facing physical issues, Vietnam veterans, or other populations? Are you ready to empathically understand their experiential world? There are several ways to prepare for a deeper understanding of the diverse clientele we as helpers encounter. The first involves a commitment to listen to and learn from and with a vast array of people different from yourself. If you listen effectively, your clients will eventually indicate to you how they feel comfortable.

Being a warm, empathic, skillful counselor is often not enough. As a helper, you will benefit by a program of lifelong study of key aspects of individual, family, and cultural differences. Then, you can apply that knowledge and examine which theories of therapy are likely to be helpful to those whose background may be different from yours. Such a program includes examining your own family and ethnic heritage. In a sense, all therapy and counseling is multicultural, for our family/cultural/historical self is always present in the interview.

Counseling Issues and Personal Multicultural History

As individuals, we all develop in a family system that itself develops in a cultural setting. It is in the family of origin that we learn the culture. McGoldrick, Pearce, and Giordano (1982) illustrate this important point, presenting varying cultural expectations of families and how these affect the way individuals represent the world.

To some people, a person with an Irish-Catholic heritage would be considered virtually identical to an individual with a British-American history. However, closer examination reveals that these two European-American cultural backgrounds result in very different types of belief systems. Furthermore, even the most cursory reading of history reveals centuries-long conflict between the United Kingdom and Ireland, which continues today. Thus the commonly used term *Anglo-Celtic* might be perceived by some Irish-Americans as an insult.

Exhibit 2.3 presents the work of one counseling student who examined his family background. One parent came from an Irish heritage, the other from a British background. Due to cultural differences, the parents gave the student differing messages and values. Of particular note is the perceived "fatalism" of his Irish heritage as contrasted to the belief in personal action represented by his British heritage. This type of cultural difference shows how intentionality can play out very differently among different cultures.

As you read the statements in exhibit 2.3, remember that this is the way this individual views the world. You do not have to agree with those views. Your goal is to empathically understand, not to judge.

Counseling Issues and Multicultural Factors

A client from a mixed Anglo-Celtic background seeking help about a possible divorce would likely express attitudes shaped by this mixed cultural background. If the client identified more strongly with British roots, the decision to divorce might not be as difficult as it would if the client identified more strongly with the Irish-Catholic prohibitions against divorce.

Since many people in the United States and Canada come from bicultural backgrounds, it is most likely that some conflict between the two value systems will appear

=== **Exhibit 2.3** ===

A Student Looks at His Mixed Family Heritage

The following discussion was generated by Mark Darling, a student in cross-cultural counseling. Mark comes from a family which most would consider "typically American." One parent is Irish, the other British-American. Mark, himself, is a third-generation American. Until the course in cross-cultural counseling, Mark saw himself solely as "American." With reading and study, he came to realize that many of his beliefs and values were not just American, but were the result of long-term Irish and British values. He also found that some internal conflicts within himself were not solely his own individual "problems," but were also the result of variant cultural messages he received from his parents.

The analysis below presents a summary of his personal observations plus reading in cross-cultural counseling and family therapy (McGoldrick, Pearce, and Giordano, 1982). It should be obvious that cultural intentionality on the part of the therapist requires empathy to the cultural background of the client, an empathy that can only be built through long study and effort on your part into the specifics of varying cultures. Then, armed with that knowledge, you still face a unique individual before you with unique personal syntheses of cultural background. Given this information, would you say that Mark is predominantly Irish, British, or American?

Irish-American Messages	*British-American Messages*

Life Expectations

People are basically evil; life is determined by fate. You are the victim or beneficiary of luck; you have no say in the matter.

Good and bad are an individual choice. You are responsible for your fate. Live by the rules and work hard. Therein lies success.

These two basic attitudes underlie the belief system of an English-Irish individual. One of these will probably be dominant, yet both will be present. The combined message could likely be "Win or lose, it's not your choice, but you are responsible for your failures." In this case, the individual would consider success to be luck, and failure to be a personal lack of initiative or ability. Thus the individual comes to feel like a failure with *certainty* of failing again, and *no expectation* of success.

Family Relations

The family is your source and your strength. Family is identity and your obligation. To leave is to be alone and powerless.

You are an individual, strong and self-reliant. Leave home to make your fortune; establish your own family. Your life is up to you.

The conflict created by these two attitudes is very important. One possible synthesis of these is "You are old enough to leave now, but you do not have the necessary strength to make it on your own." Thus the individual will feel a strong desire to set out on his own, but a corresponding inability to leave.

Gender Roles

Women are morally superior to men. Men are morally weak, given to uncontrollable weakness. The mother is the strength of the household.

Women are fragile and must be protected. The father is the strength of the household.

The conflict here becomes one of role in the household. This may be synthesized as "You are expected to be strong and virtuous, but you are incapable by nature of being so." In this way, individuals will feel the need to be something they cannot see themselves as being, and may experience a tremendous sense of inadequacy.

Marriage

Marriage is a necessity, and you are bound by it for life. If you have problems in your marriage, they are your due, and you must accept them.

Marriage is a social contract. Both parties are responsible to maintain the agreement. If one is in violation, divorce is acceptable.

These two messages are very hard to reconcile: "You made a bad contract, and you have the right to a divorce, but divorce is wrong." The practical result may be that the individual will get a divorce yet feel that action to be illegitimate and wrong.

Language

Words are poetry, an expression of emotion. They have beauty but no reality and may always be traded for better ones. Words are dreams through which you create an internal reality.

Language is law, the structure of reality. Words are specific and binding. Language is the means by which life is directed, and our plans are the key to growth and our gain. Through words you create your external reality.

In this conflict is the expression of a major source of misunderstanding between English and Irish culture. The English function by contracts, and contractual agreements demand that words be specific and binding. The Irish, on the other hand, see words as defined by the context in which they are used. These messages may be synthesized by the individual as "Your daydreaming is a waste of time. You never do what you say you are going to do. Plan for the future, but it's all idle dreaming." The result can be an individual who is unable to follow through on agreements and is not generally relied upon.

A common tendency today is to stereotype and condemn "white males," particularly those of "Anglo-Celtic" background. But, as may be clearly observed here, British and Irish backgrounds are very different. It is not possible to stereotype any one individual because of color or ethnicity. Mark Darling is a unique person, in some ways bicultural, who works his way through the maze of cultural messages uniquely. As a young white male, he does not suffer the problems of sexism, racism, or ageism. Yet, it should also be clear that every client comes from a cultural background with special implications. Understanding variations in ethnicity and religion, race and sex, and many other factors will enrich your understanding in the counseling interview.

in counseling. Often this conflict is an internal struggle that neither the client nor the counselor is aware of. One of the counselor's tasks is to facilitate awareness of the relationship between culture and individual consciousness.

In addition to cultural background is the factor of social values. For instance, North American society is influenced by materialism, television, and the enthusiasm for free choice emphasized in this culture. In a sense, North Americans are tricultural, usually having two cultural backgrounds, with an overlay of social values.

The Concept of a "White Culture"

Many in North America refer to the "White culture," and in truth, there is a general set of privileges extended to the White majority. The light-skinned European-American majority tends to discriminate against those with darker skin. Given this reality, the concept of White culture can be useful.

At the same time, the Anglo-Celtic example in exhibit 2.3 is a reminder that the idea of a single White culture is likely as much a myth as a single Asian-American or African-American culture. Just as Britain (predominantly Anglo) and Ireland (predominantly Celtic) represent widely varying worldviews, so do worldviews from other cultural groups have many facets.

Our Multicultural World

When we add together factors of race and ethnic heritage plus those of age, gender, religion, physical issues, and so forth, the need to expand one's understanding of cultural issues is readily apparent. If you are a Navaho or Yakima counselor, you need to be aware that Whites vary widely in their constructions of the world; Whites do not have a single worldview. If you are French-Canadian, you must be aware that the Cree, Mohawk, and Inuit nations of Quebec are as different from each other as you are from the English-speaking members of your province.

The Danger of Stereotyping

In the study of cultural differences, it is important to beware of stereotyping. Chances are that you as a *unique individual* have some beliefs in common with your family and broad culture as well as some significant differences. There is a great danger in assuming that every individual of a group has the same characteristics.

For example, a Jewish individual would not appreciate your assumption that she or he holds the same values toward education as other Jewish people, despite the fact that education is generally a value in Jewish culture (Herz & Rosen, 1982).

The individual in the counseling interview remains unique; group characteristics do not predict individual characteristics.

However, a basic understanding of group characteristics can help you understand your clients better. For instance, knowing that homosexuals often, though not always, suffer from job discrimination and may sometimes have families that reject them may help you be more empathic toward a particular gay male or lesbian client. Or knowing that many older people, but not all, face problems of loneliness can help you in working with this group.

The Role of Family Background

Much of our learning about culture occurs in our families of origin. Whether you agree or disagree with your family's attitudes about life, ethnic/racial heritage, or personal/cultural values, you are nonetheless influenced by these attitudes. Examining yourself and your family of origin is an important part of developing multicultural understanding.

Think about your own family. How does your family feel about issues such as where children are expected to live after they marry? How much emotional and financial support does your family offer? What is the attitude toward intellectual achievement? What are the expected roles of men and women? What are attitudes toward pain? About drinking? Then examine yourself and your life. How are your constructs similar to and different from those of your family? Exhibit 2.4 presents a framework within which you can examine your own cultural/ethnic heritage.

You may think it inappropriate that a young Italian couple lives with the parents and has a very close relationship if this is different from your own cultural background. Alternatively, an Italian-American therapist might view a Jewish-, Irish-, or British-American family as strange and different if they are not as closely knit as an Italian family. And an African-American, Asian-American, or Latina/o might see the situation differently still. Clients and counselors alike whose heritage can be traced to Colombia, Cuba, El Salvador, Haiti, Mexico, Puerto Rico, and other South or Latin American countries should not be grouped as having a single orientation; each is likely to have a unique worldview.

Toward Multicultural Empathy and Competence

We are indeed individuals, and we also all have our origins in families. These factors impact our empathic understanding, as do the influence of our peer groups and friends, the neighborhood and community, and the overall culture. Throughout this

An Exercise in Cultural Awareness

It is difficult to be understanding of others without an awareness of yourself as a cultural being. The following questions are designed to begin some thinking on your part about how your cultural/historical heritage may affect your work in the counseling and therapy interview.

1. *List your ethnic heritage.* With what ethnic background do you first identify? You may first identify your nationality—U.S. citizen, Canadian, Mexican, and so on. Beyond this first answer you may find the words *White, Native American, Black, Polish, Mormon, Jewish,* and others coming to your mind. Record those words.

   Then, where do your grandparents come from? Great-grandparents? Can you trace a family history, perhaps with different ethnic, religious, and racial backgrounds?

   Identify in list form or in a family tree your heritage. Do not forget your heritage from the country within which you live.

2. *Are you monocultural, bicultural, or more?* Review the list you developed and pick out the central cultural, ethnic, religious, or other types of groups that have been involved in your development.

3. *What messages do you receive from each cultural group you have listed?* Take time to list values, behaviors, and expectations that people in your group have come to emphasize over time. Exhibit 2.3 illustrates the process of how to list some key life messages given by your family or other cultural groups. How have you personally internalized these messages? If you are aware of the message, the chances are you have made some deviation from the family, ethnic, or religious value. If you are unaware, the values from outside may be so incorporated within yourself that you are a "culture bearer" without knowing it. Becoming aware of these obvious but unconscious culture-bearer messages may become the most difficult task of all.

4. *How might your cultural messages affect your counseling and therapeutic work?* This final question is the most important of all. If you believe in individuality as supreme, given your family history, you may tend to miss the relational, family orientation of many Asians, Blacks, and Italians. If you come from a relational orientation, you may have difficulty in likewise understanding individualistic WASPs (White Anglo-Saxon Protestants) and label them as "cold" and "calculating." As we all come from cultural histories, it is easy to think that our way of being in the world is the way things "are and should be."

   The development of empathy requires a deeper understanding of ourselves and our cultural heritage so that we do not unconsciously impose our beliefs on others.

book, we will explore issues relating to all of these areas, although the primary focus will be on *the individual developing in a family and multicultural context*.

The Professional Standards Committee of the Association for Multicultural Counseling and Development has generated a basic set of multicultural competencies and standards (Sue, Arrendondo, & McDavis, 1992). Table 2.1 outlines some challenging goals that may be useful as you conceptualize your personal goals as a helper. These goals are briefly discussed here:

Table 2.1   Multicultural Competencies and Standards

Goals	*Attitudes and Beliefs*	*Knowledge*	*Intervention Strategies*
Counselor awareness of own cultural values and beliefs	• Sensitive to one's own cultural heritage and how this influences thoughts, feelings, and behavior. • Recognizes limits of abilities. • Comfortable with differences in race, ethnicity, culture, and beliefs.	• Aware of how background affects the definition of "normality" and the process of counseling. • Understands concepts of racism, discrimination, and stereotyping. • Understands how one has benefited from above dimensions (for European-Americans). • Knows how one's own style may be inappropriate for culturally different clients.	• Seeks educational/ training experiences for continued learning, seeks consultation, and refers when necessary. • Seeks to understand oneself as racial/ cultural being and actively seeks a nonracist society.
Counselor awareness of client worldview	• Aware of negative emotional reactions and stereotypes relating to other groups; seeks to move to a nonjudgmental posture.	• Possesses specific knowledge of worldview, cultural style, and cultural identity levels of clients. • Understands how cultural issues relate to personal styles, help-seeking behaviors, and whether or not a particular helping intervention is suitable. • Familiar with what social and political influences such as poverty, racism, and powerlessness have on client development	• Skilled in latest research and theoretical findings on groups culturally different from self. • Seeks appropriate educational experiences. • Actively involved with minority individuals in projects, friendships, social/political functions, and celebrations so that perspective of minority experience is more than an academic or helping exercise.

Table 2.1   (continued)

Goals	Attitudes and Beliefs	Knowledge	Intervention Strategies
		and how these influence the counseling process.	
Culturally appropriate intervention strategies	• Respects clients' religious/spiritual beliefs and values and understands how these affect expressions of distress. • Respects indigenous helping practices and minority communities' natural help-giving networks. • Sees bilingualism as an asset rather than liability.	• Understands how Eurocentric tradition in counseling and therapy may conflict with cultural values of other traditions. • Aware of institutional barriers and bias in assessment instruments and techniques. • Aware of the influence of varying family and community structures on the counseling process. • Understands issues of racism, oppression, and so on.	• Sends verbal and nonverbal messages accurately and appropriately. • Able to determine if clients' "problems" result from external factors, such as racism and bias in others. • Uses institutional interventions on behalf of clients. • Works with traditional healers and spiritual leaders as culturally appropriate. • Refers to good sources when own linguistic skills are insufficient. • Conducts training/educational interventions to combat oppression. • Educates clients to their personal and legal rights for effective multicultural intervention.

SOURCE: Adapted from ACA Professional Standards, *Journal of Counseling and Development*, 1992. Reprinted with permission. No further reproduction authorized without written permission of the American Counseling Association.

1. *Counselor awareness of own cultural values and beliefs.* If you are to be empathic with those of different backgrounds, it is essential that you become self-aware. The exercise in this chapter exploring your relation to your family of origin can be a step toward developing sensitivity about yourself as a cultural being. Other exercises in this book will focus on helping you develop this type of self-awareness.

2. *Counselor awareness of client worldview.* Chapter 1 focused on this important concept, but it is critical that you enhance this brief introduction by further reading and study. Being aware that worldviews and family experiences vary is a helpful beginning, but the next task is an in-depth study of the culture and worldviews of many other groups, including your own.

3. *Culturally appropriate intervention strategies.* This book is about theory and practice of counseling and therapy. Thus the authors have a special responsibility to present a variety of intervention possibilities and their appropriateness for various cultural groups. This book gives extensive attention to new work in multicultural counseling and therapy and feminist theory. We also attempt to provide a more culturally relevant portrayal of empathy, the microskills of listening and attending, and other dimensions.

Using Individual, Family, and Multicultural Empathy in the Interview

Your empathic response to one type of client may be insensitive with another. How can you cope with the variety of clients and their many diverse cultures when no formula or theory provides an unfailingly reliable — that is, "correct" — response or action? The following three-step model of empathy provides you with a summary framework for balancing the uniqueness of the individual client with your own general knowledge and with counseling and therapy theory.

1. *Listen to and observe your clients' comments.* As you listen, recall that family and multicultural constructs may be an important part of their verbal or nonverbal behavior. As you listen, you can begin learning how your clients wish to be related to.

2. *Respond to clients' main words and constructs.* When in doubt, use attending and listening skills. When culturally and individually appropriate, add approaches based on your own experience, knowledge, and intuition. Also listen for and consider family and cultural issues.

3. *Check out your statements or interventions.* Ask, "How does that sound?" "Is that close?" or some other statement that allows the client to respond to you. You may also indicate such a check of your perceptions by raising your voice at the end of your response in a questioning tone.

By checking out your approach with the client, you open the way for a more mutual, egalitarian dialogue. Although this is a good generic approach, some clients may prefer a more authoritative style.

Use the perception check as a way to learn how to be with your client more empathically.

Then return to the first step and change your style and comments as necessary until you and the client are both comfortable. Empathy is best cultivated as a process in which counselor and client together explore the nature of the client's worldview and beliefs about the problem. There is no final standard of "correct" empathy; rather, empathy requires that you constantly attune yourself to the wide variety of individual clients with whom you will work.

The importance of the perception check in building a solid, empathic counselor-client relationship cannot be stressed enough. By asking "Have I heard you correctly?" you show your empathy and respect for your client. Your client, in turn, will provide you with concrete data as to the effectiveness of your comment or intervention. If you respond accurately, your client will likely smile, say yes, and continue. If you are off target, your client will correct you, and you can use your new understanding to proceed with the session.

NOTE

1. This exercise on acceptance is derived from the work of Gladys Lam of Hong Kong Polytechnic.

REFERENCES

ANTHONY, W., & CARKHUFF, R. (1977). The functional professional therapeutic agent. In A. Gurman & A. Razin (Eds.), *Effective psychotherapy* (pp. 103–19). Elmsford, NY: Pergamon Press.

AUERBACH, A. & JOHNSON, M. (1977). Research on the therapist's level of experience. In A. Gurman & A. Razin (Eds.), *Effective psychotherapy* (pp. 84–102). Elmsford, NY: Pergamon Press.

BAYES, M. (1973). Behavioral cues of interpersonal warmth. *Journal of Counseling Psychology, 39,* 333–39.

BERGIN, A., & GARFIELD, S. (1986). *Handbook of psychotherapy and behavior change.* New York: Wiley.

CARKHUFF, R. (1969). *Helping and human relations* (Vols. 1 & 2). Troy, MO: Holt, Rinehart & Winston.

CARKHUFF, R. (1981). *Toward actualizing human potential.* Amherst, MA: Human Resource Development Press.

CARKHUFF, R. (1983). *Interpersonal skills and human productivity.* Amherst, MA: Human Resource Development Press.

CARKHUFF, R. (1987). *Learning and thinking in the age of information.* Amherst, MA: Human Resource Development Press.

EGAN, G. (1990). *The skilled helper.* Pacific Grove, CA: Brooks/Cole.

FIEDLER, F. (1950a). A comparison of therapeutic relationships in psychoanalytic, nondirective, and Adlerian therapy. *Journal of Consulting Psychology, 14,* 435–36.

FIEDLER, F. (1950b). The concept of an ideal therapeutic relationship. *Journal of Consulting Psychology, 14,* 239–45.

FIEDLER, F. (1951). Factor analysis of psychoanalytic, nondirective, and Adlerian therapeutic relationships. *Journal of Consulting Psychology, 15,* 32–38.

GENDLIN, E., & HENDRICKS, M. (1978). Changes. In E. Gendlin, *Focusing* (pp. 118–44). New York: Everest House.

GOLDFRIED, M., GREENBERG, L. & MARMAR, C. (1990). Individual psychotherapy: Process and outcome. In M. Rosenweig & L. Porter (Eds.), *Annual review of psychology* (pp. 659–88). Palo Alto, CA: Annual Reviews.

HERZ, F., & ROSEN, E. (1982). Jewish families. In M. McGoldrick, J. Pearce, & J. Giordano (Eds.), *Ethnicity and family therapy* (pp. 364–92). New York: Guilford.

LAMBERT, M., DeJULIO, S., & STEIN, D. (1978). Therapist interpersonal skills. *Psychological Bulletin, 85*, 467–89.

LIEBERMAN, M., YALOM, I., & MILES, M. (1972). *Encounter groups: First facts.* New York: Basic Books.

McGOLDRICK, M., PEARCE, J., & GIORDANO, J. (Eds.). (1982). *Ethnicity and family therapy.* New York: Guilford.

RACHMAN, S., & WILSON, G. (1980). *The effects of psychological therapy.* New York: Wiley.

ROGERS, C. (1957). The necessary and sufficient conditions of therapeutic personality change. *Journal of Consulting Psychology, 21*, 95–103.

SLOANE, R., & STAPLES, F. (1984). Psychotherapy versus behavior therapy: Implications for future psychotherapy research. In J. Williams & R. Spitzer (Eds.), *Psychotherapy research: Where are we and where should we go?* (pp. 203–15). New York: Guilford.

SLOANE, R., STAPLES, F., CRISTOL, A., YORKSTON, N., & WHIPPLE, K. (1975). *Psychotherapy versus behavior therapy.* Cambridge, MA: Harvard University Press, 1975.

SUE, D., ARRENDONDO, P., & McDAVIS, R. (1992). Multicultural counseling competencies and standards. *Journal of Counseling and Development, 70*, 447–86.

TYLER, L. (1961). *The work of the counselor* (2nd ed.). East Norwalk, CT: Appleton & Lange.

RESPONSES TO SAMPLE COUNSELOR STATEMENTS (p. 29)

1. Level 4, interchangeable response. This response has the advantage of enabling the parents to feel heard. It builds trust and prompts further discussion of the issue.

2. Level 1, attacking response. (A level 2 response might appear similar, but would be more subtle.)

3. Level 6, the counselor has listened accurately, but is adding a useful family therapy technique in which positive assets and strengths of the family are noted. If this response is successful, the family later may use these strengths in working on their problems.

Developing Intentional Interviewing Skills

CHAPTER GOALS

This chapter identifies key microskills critical to the counseling and psychotherapy process. By using these microskills, you can examine your own interview behavior, with the aim of modifying your interaction to make a significant difference in the life of your client.

This chapter seeks to help you:

1. Identify key nonverbal factors for yourself and your client.

2. Understand the basic interview microskills of attending, listening, and influencing and their potential impact on the client for change.

3. Examine the microskills of focus and selective attention, which are basic to family and multicultural issues in counseling and therapy.

4. Know how and when to use the microskill of confrontation.

5. See the importance of teaching skills to the client as a counseling and psychotherapy strategy.

6. View interviewing skills from a multicultural frame of reference.

The Microskills Approach

The process of identification and selection of specific skills of counseling is called the microskills approach. Using the microskills approach, we can break down the complex interaction of the counseling interview into manageable and learnable dimensions. Basic microskills include the skills of attending, listening, and influencing.

Other important skills are focus, selective attention, and confrontation. Underlying and shaping these skills are the nonverbal factors the helper brings to the interview.

For instance, through body language and facial expression, the counselor expresses an attitude toward the client. Figures 3.1 shows a counselor listening to a client in two different ways.

Before reading further, take a moment to list on a separate sheet the specific nonverbal attitudes expressed in each photo. Be as precise as possible in identifying observable aspects of nonverbal behavior. Also note which counselor style would be more inviting to you if you were the client.

In the first photo in the figure, the counselor's forward stance, direct eye contact, and relaxed body style communicate interest and assurance. In the second photo, the counselor's poor eye contact, slouched body position, and closed arms and legs communicate a lack of interest.

How to communicate nonverbally as you practice microskills is a complex challenge that can be further complicated by multicultural issues. For example, for clients of some cultures, the body language of the counselor in the first picture may be considered intrusive instead of inviting. As you learn more about microskills and their application in multicultural settings, you will become more adept at choosing the appropriate nonverbal mode for the particular client.

Attending Skills

When you interview or counsel another person, it seems obvious that you should look at them and maintain natural eye contact. Further, your body should communicate

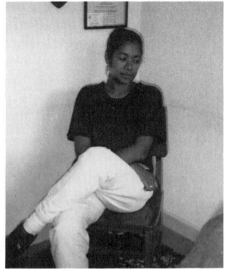

Figure 3.1   Counselor Listening Styles

interest. It was once believed that counseling was solely a verbal occupation, but with the advent of videotaping and the increased use of filming in interview training, it has become apparent that nonverbal communication is basic in any interviewing, counseling, or therapy session.

Eye contact and body language are the physical fundamentals of attending behavior.

Another basic aspect of attending behavior is vocal tone. Does your voice communicate warmth and interest or boredom and lack of caring? Even though you may be physically attending, your voice often indicates the quality of your willingness and interest in listening.

Moreover, if you are to attend to someone, you must "listen" to them. Listening, however, is not an observable behavior. Intentional therapists not only maintain attentive body posture and facial expression, they also stay on the topic with the client and seldom interrupt or change topics abruptly. A major mistake of beginning counselors is to change the topic of discussion and ignore or fail to hear what the client has to say. For example:

> *Client:* I've been downtown this afternoon, and I really got anxious. I even wanted to run when I saw a friend. I broke out in a sweat and felt I couldn't move. I've been in my room until just now.
>
> *Nonattending counselor:*   Let's see now, you're a sophomore this year?
>
> *Attending counselor:*   You say you wanted to run when you saw your friend. Could you describe the situation and what was happening in more detail?

It is seldom necessary or desirable to change the client's topic, particularly when a client such as the above is describing what most likely was a panic attack. Attend carefully, and the client will tell you all you need to know.

Attending and Cultural Differences

Attending behavior varies from culture to culture and from individual to individual (see table 3.1). Data show clearly that individual differences among clients may be as important as cultural patterns. When reviewing such summaries of cultural patterns, do not assume that one pattern of attending (or influencing) is appropriate for every individual of that cultural group you might interview.

Sue (1990) presents a framework for culture-specific strategies in counseling. He cites research showing that many minority clients terminate counseling early and suggests that more culturally sensitive approaches are needed. He summarizes literature demonstrating the vital importance of including spacial, nonverbal, and related dimensions in the helping process. He supports this by quoting a saying common among African-Americans: "If you really want to know what White folks are thinking or feeling, don't listen to what they say, but how they say it" (p. 427).

Original microskills research and theoretical conceptions were generated from a Eurocentric frame of reference (Ivey et al., 1968; Ivey, 1971). Since that time, however, continuous attempts have been made to correct the original constructions and

Table 3.1   Nonverbal Attending Patterns in European–North American Culture Compared with Patterns of Other Cultures

Nonverbal Dimension	European–North American Pattern	Contrasting Example from Another Culture
Eye contact	When listening to a person, direct eye contact is appropriate. When talking, eye contact is often less frequent.	Some African-Americans may have patterns directly opposite and demonstrate more eye contact when talking and less when listening.
Body language	Slight forward trunk lean facing the person. Handshake a general sign of welcome.	Certain Eskimo and Inuit groups in the Arctic sit side by side when working on personal issues. A male giving a female a firm handshake may be seen as giving a sexual invitation.
Vocal tone and speech rate	A varied vocal tone is favored, with some emotionality shown. Speech rate is moderate.	Many Latina/o groups have a more extensive and expressive vocal tone and may consider European–North American styles unemotional and "flat."
Physical space	Conversation distance is ordinarily "arm's length" or more for comfort.	Common in Arab and Middle-Eastern cultures is a six- to twelve-inch conversational distance, a point at which the European-American becomes uncomfortable.
Time	Highly structured, linear view of time. Generally "on time" for appointments.	Several South American countries operate on a more casual view of time and do not plan that specified, previously agreed-upon times for meetings will necessarily hold.

NOTE: It is critical to remember that individuals within a single cultural group vary extensively.

recognize cultural difference (Ivey & Authier, 1978; Ivey, 1988a, b; Ivey, Gluckstern, & Ivey, 1992). It is critical that attempts be made to update counseling theory as the field discovers more about multicultural influences. Multicultural perspectives are frequently omitted from theories and models of counseling and therapy, and it is good to be alert to old, outmoded methods that are still used in counseling and psychotherapy theory and practice. Exhibit 3.1 details the development and findings of microskills research.

Mirroring Nonverbal Behavior

Examination of films and videotapes of interview sessions reveals fascinating patterns of nonverbal communication. In a successful, smoothly flowing interview, movement complementarity or movement symmetry often occurs between counselor and client. Movement complementarity is represented by a "passing" of movement back and forth between client and counselor. For example, the client pauses in the middle of a sentence, the counselor nods, and the client then finishes the sentence. Movements between counselor and client pass back and forth in a rhythm.

In movement symmetry, counselor and client unconsciously assume the same physical posture; their eye contact is usually direct; and their hands and feet may move in unison as if they were dancing or following a programmed script. Movement symmetry can be achieved in a rudimentary fashion by deliberately assuming the posture and "mirroring" the gestures of the client. This mirroring of nonverbal behavior often brings the therapist to a closer and more complete understanding of the client. The series of photographs in Figure 3.2 show a client and counselor discussing an issue of mutual interest. The time for the completion of this series of movements is about one second. Careful examination of helping interviews reveals many examples of movement symmetry as well as dissynchronous movement that often indicates failure to communicate effectively.

This lack of complementarity and symmetry is an important factor in counselor-client communication. For instance, the counselor may say something, and the client's head may jerk noticeably in the opposite direction. Dissynchronous body movements that occur between counselor and client can indicate that the interview is on the wrong track. A solid knowledge and awareness of body language is necessary to consistently observe dissynchronous behavior.

Once you become skilled in observing and practicing mirroring, it can be a valuable tool. If you note the general pattern of body language of your client and then deliberately assume the same posture, you will find yourself in better synchrony and harmony with the client. Through mirroring, new understandings and communication can develop. This tool should not be used manipulatively, but rather to develop increased awareness and new levels of insight.[1]

Listening Skills

Attending skills can be organized into a coherent and systematic framework called the basic listening sequence. Table 3.2 identifies the specific microskills of listening: open and closed questions, encouraging, paraphrasing, reflection of feeling, and summarization. All these skills are intended to bring out the client's story. The aim of listening skills is to discover how the client presents his or her story, with minimal intrusion on the part of the counselor or therapist.

The microskills of listening have been part of counseling and therapy for twenty-

≡ Exhibit 3.1 ≡

Research on Attending Behavior and Interviewing Microskills

Prior to approaches such as microskills, counseling and therapy were considered almost mystical, and the idea of systematic definition of interview behavior did not exist. Where does a basic construct such as attending behavior come from? In their 1968 study, Ivey and colleagues Normington, Miller, Morrill, and Haase sought to identify foundational, specific skills of helping. After months of study and experimentation led only to failure, a simple experiment, described below, laid the foundation for the microskills approach discussed in this chapter. (The original work on microskills occurred in a European-American context. The findings would have been different had multicultural issues been considered.)

> The basic breakthrough which resulted in the concepts of attending behavior and microcounseling occurred with one of our secretaries. The process consisted of five minutes of videotaping when she was interviewing a student volunteer. This was followed by a replay of the tape in which her behaviors, which reflected lapses of attending, were pointed out, and direction was given in how to increase identified attending behaviors. She returned to reinterview the student, and, after a moment of artificiality, began to respond in highly impactful ways. In fact, she performed like a highly skilled, highly experienced counselor. The

change was not only dramatic, but, when we began to consider the twenty minutes of training, almost shocking! We have had less change of behavior in practicum students in an entire year.

When a hiatus was reached, the lack of training in counseling skills became apparent. The hiatus called for initiation of new areas, and the secretary did not follow one of our counseling traditions. If she had, she would have either waited for the client to respond (nondirective), initiated an expression of her own feeling state (recent client-centered), directed attention to early experience (analytic), presented a discriminative stimulus to elicit verbal responses which could be reinforced (learning theory), induced a trance state (hypnoanalysis), or brought out a Strong Vocational Interest Blank (vocational counseling).

The secretary actually began to talk about an interesting experience in her own immediate past (standard social behavior). However, since she still was attempting to engage in attending behaviors, this led rapidly to a new topic for the student, and she again resembled the highly skilled counselor.

As an indication of the relevance of attending and related constructs to behavior beyond the interview, our secretary entered the office on Monday and could not wait to tell us about attending to people over the weekend. She had developed an entirely new behavioral repertoire which was reinforced by a new kind of excitement and involvement with other people. The impact even on her husband was apparent. (Hackney, Ivey, & Oetting, 1970, p. 344).

This process of identification of researchable dimensions in counseling is cited in detail because it illustrates the sometimes whimsical nature of the research process in which discoveries are often made by chance rather than by choice. Since the original 1968 study on attending behavior, over 250 studies on the microskill of attending behavior have been completed (see Ivey, 1971; Ivey & Authier, 1978; Daniels, 1985; Baker & Daniels, 1989; Baker, Daniels, & Greeley, 1990).

Following are some of the more important findings of microskills research:

1. Clients respond better and more positively, are more likely to verbalize at greater length, and indicate a greater willingness to return to attending counselors and therapists.
2. Experienced and sophisticated therapists and counselors seem to have good attending skills, whereas many beginning counselors score poorly on these dimensions.
3. Clients and therapists from varying cultures use microskills, but in a different fashion than presented in the original Eurocentric framework.
4. Different counseling theories use microskills, but focus on varying dimensions of client experience.
5. Training clients in microskills can be a useful part of a broader treatment program.

---

five years but were not presented as an integrated sequence and theory until relatively recently (Ivey, 1988b). The *basic listening sequence* was first identified through direct observation by a skilled manager at Digital Computer Corporation. When an employee came up to the manager with a problem on the production line, the manager engaged in good attending behavior. His responses to the employee included the following listening skills:

> Could you tell me about the problem on the production line? [*open question*]
> The zenos chip? [*encouraging*]
> You say the supply department hasn't given you enough computer chips to keep your group moving smoothly? [*paraphrasing*]
> Sounds like the situation really makes you angry. [*reflection of feeling*]

The manager then *summarized* the employee's view of the problem, and only then did he start to move toward action.

Subsequent work has revealed the importance of the basic listening sequence in a multitude of helping settings. Many counseling and therapy theories use the basic listening sequence to draw out information from the client. Although the skills are not always sequenced as clearly as they are in the following example, most therapists

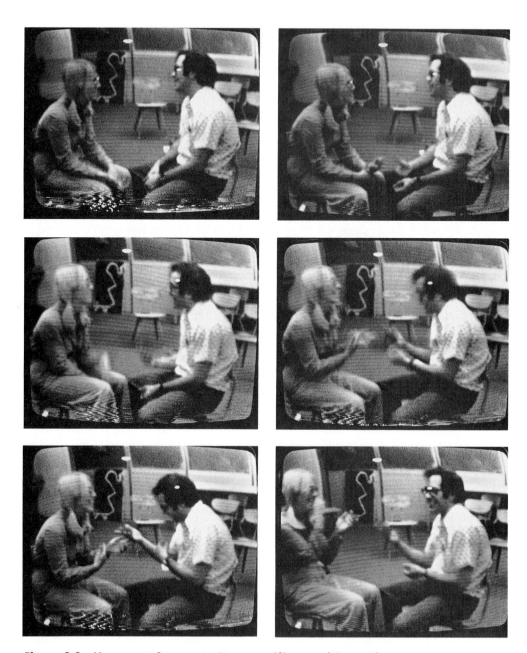

Figure 3.2   Movement Symmetry Between Client and Counselor

SOURCE: Photos from A. Ivey and J. Authier, *Microcounseling: Innovations in Interviewing, Counseling, Psychotherapy, and Psychoeducation* (Springfield, IL: Thomas, 1978). Used by permission.

Table 3.2 The Basic Listening Sequence

Skill	Description	Function in Interview
Open questions	"What": facts "How": process or feelings "Why": reasons "Could": general picture	Used to bring out major data and facilitate conversation.
Closed questions	Usually begin with "do," "is," "are" and can be answered in a few words.	Used to quickly obtain specific data, close off lengthy answers.
Encouraging	Repeating back to client a few of the client's main words.	Encourages detailed elaboration of the specific words and their meanings.
Paraphrasing	Repeating back the essence of a client's words and thoughts using the client's own main words.	Acts as promoter for discussion; shows understanding; checks on clarity of counselor understanding.
Reflection of feeling	Selective attention to emotional content of interview.	Results in clarification of emotion underlying key facts; promotes discussion of feelings.
Summarization	Repeating back of client's facts and feelings (and reasons) to client in an organized form.	Useful in beginning interview; periodically used in session to clarify where the interview has come to date and to close the session.

and counselors use variations of this basic model as they get to know their client and the client's life concerns.

Could you tell me about your family and how they react to your fear of going out in public? [*Open question—leads to drawing out how client organizes the problem*]

Protect you? [*Encourager—leads to exploring client's key words and underlying meanings*]

So, when you find yourself not wanting to go outside, the family goes out for you? [*Paraphrase—client knows she or he is heard*]

Is that right? [*Perception check—helps client know whether or not hearing has been accurate*]

And you seem to be feeling very sad/frightened/inadequate right now. [*Reflection of feeling—leads client to explore emotion*]

So this is what I'm hearing you say . . . [*Summarization—counselor emphasizes main points of the client's story to enhance understanding of the problem in a more organized fashion*]

The basic listening sequence has specific goals. It is vital that we bring out the client's story by using these skills. In doing this we need to know the *main facts* as described by the client, how the client *feels about those facts,* and how the client *organizes the story.*

In approaching these goals, it is good to take into account multicultural and gender issues. Men tend to ask more questions than women (and they also tend to interrupt more often). Women tend to use the techniques of paraphrase and reflection of feeling more often than men. Then too, a European-American therapist working with a minority client may appear too intrusive if too many direct questions are used. Although it is vital that you draw out the client's story and the key facts, feelings, and organization of the story, the basic listening sequence must be modified in the here and now of the interview.

Whether you are helping a client with a vocational decision, negotiating a divorce, or conducting a psychodynamic dream analysis, you will need to know the facts and how the client feels about those facts and then organize them for further analysis. The basic listening sequence and its accompanying microskills can be very useful when you employ the different therapeutic approaches discussed later. Whether you are a behavioral counselor, a reality therapist, or a family counselor, the basic listening sequence is a critical therapeutic tool.

Using Listening Skills with Children

The basic listening sequence and all the microskills are helpful in working with young children, with some modification. If you have a highly verbal child, perhaps even as young as five or six, listening skills work very effectively and you can follow the general rules presented here. But most children will need help in expressing information.

Many children will respond to an open question with confusion, looking puzzled and saying perhaps only a few words. Closed questions, phrased gently, often are useful in helping children express themselves. The danger, of course, is leading the child to a conclusion. The child may be anxious to please you as the counselor and follow your lead too easily. The danger closed questions pose for leading the child is especially critical when a child is being interviewed on issues of child abuse.

Paraphrasing can be especially useful in helping children talk. Effective classroom teachers constantly paraphrase comments of their students. Paraphrasing helps children keep on the topic, acts as a reinforcer, and indicates that you have heard them. Each child generates a unique construction, and if you use the key words of the child, you are more likely to learn how that child sees the situation.

MacFarlane and Feldmeth (1988, pp. 8–9) outline some key aspects of interviewing children. They point out that children's cognitive processes are different from adults' and that it is necessary to gear comments to the language and cognitive level of the child. These researchers provide several useful guidelines for communicating with young children, which are summarized and paraphrased as follows:

1. Use short sentences and simple words.
2. Use concrete language and avoid abstractions. "Did he touch you?" is clearer

than "Did he do something naughty?" The specifics of the touch may need to be clarified as well, perhaps through the use of anatomically correct dolls.

3.   Avoid double negatives. Say "Did the teacher tell you not to do that?" rather than "Didn't the teacher tell you not to do that?"

4.   Causal reasoning can cause some children difficulty. Say "Don't do that. You will get in trouble" rather than "If you do that, then you will get in trouble." The if/then reasoning of logical consequences (see the influencing skills in the next section) requires late concrete operational thinking, which many young children are not able to master.

5.   Use names rather than pronouns. Children (and adults) under stress may confuse people and situations.

6.   Be careful with closed questions that can be answered yes or no. This poses a challenge for many interviewers of children, as children's verbal skills may be quite limited. When you must ask such questions, follow up with paraphrasing and encouragers such as "Tell me more" to facilitate conversation. If you are called to court to testify in a case of child abuse, expect the attorney to quiz you thoroughly on whether or not you acted in a leading fashion in your interview procedure.

Beyond these guidelines, your personal ability to establish rapport and trust is essential. A pleasant office, small children's furniture, and suitable pictures and games can be helpful. Warmth and a cheerful smile are important to children. Most children talk more easily while playing games such as checkers or cards, molding clay with their hands, or drawing pictures. Children can readily do two things at once, so you can move easily between the game and your interview goals.

Influencing Skills and Strategies

Clients can profit and grow even if you use only attending skills. A basic competency to achieve is the ability to conduct a full interview using only basic listening sequence skills. Many clients can often work through problems and concerns very effectively if you avoid giving advice, direction, or suggestions. The early theories of nondirective counseling as presented by Rogers advocated using only listening skills and even went so far as to severely criticize the use of questions.

However, solely using attending and listening skills can make growth slow and arduous. When you become an active participant in the interview, you can influence and speed the change process. Through your knowledge of theory and skills, personal life experience, and specific understanding of the unique client and his or her culture, you can share more of yourself and your knowledge to the benefit of your client.

Influencing skills and their functions are summarized in table 3.3. Influencing skills are complex and often are more effective if used sparingly and in careful concert with listening skills.

The *interpretation*, or *reframe*, may be considered the central influencing skill. It provides clients with a new and alternative way in which to view their problems and

Table 3.3   Influencing Skills

Skill	Description	Function in Interview
Interpretation/reframe	Provides an alternative frame of reference from which the client may view a situation. May be drawn from a theory or from one's own personal observations. *Interpretation may be viewed as the core influencing skill.*	Attempts to provide the client with a new way to view the situation. The interpretation provides the client with a clear-cut alternative perception of "reality." This perception may enable a change of view which in turn may result in changes in thoughts, constructs, or behaviors.
Directive	Tells the client what action to take. May be a simple suggestion stated in command form or may be a sophisticated technique from a specific theory.	Clearly indicates to clients what action counselors or therapists wish them to take. The prediction with a directive is that the client will do what is suggested. Table 3.4 lists several specific directives drawn from different theories that will have differing anticipated results with clients.
Advice/information/other	Provides suggestions, instructional ideas, homework, advice on how to act, think, or behave.	Used sparingly, may provide client with new and useful information. Specific vocational information is an example of necessary use of this skill.
Self-disclosure	The interviewer shares personal experience from the past or may share present reactions to the client.	Emphasizes counselor "I" statements. This skill is closely allied to feedback and may build trust and openness, leading to a more mutual relationship with the client.
Feedback	Provides clients with specific data on how they are seen by the counselor or by others.	Provides concrete data that may help clients realize how others perceive behavior and thinking patterns, thus enabling an alternative self-perception.
Logical consequences	Interviewer explains to the client the logical outcome of thinking and behavior—if/then.	Provides an alternative frame of reference for the client. This skill helps clients anticipate the consequences or results of their actions.
Influencing summary	Often used at or near the end of a session to summarize counselor comments; most often used in combination with the attending summarization.	Clarifies what has happened in the interview and summarizes what the therapist has said. This skill is designed to help generalization from the interview to daily life.

themselves, which can lead to a change in worldview. The frame of reference for a paraphrase or reflection of feeling is the client's way of making sense of the world. The frame of reference for an interpretation (and the remainder of the influencing skills) is primarily that of the therapist.

The reframe is used sparingly by most effective therapists and counselors. Two or three skillful reframes are usually the maximum for a session. Clients can only accommodate so much challenging of their existing frame of reference, and overuse of interpretation will result in a client rejecting your wisdom or, perhaps, leaving the interview completely.

In the following example, the counselor reframes the client's concept that she should be trying harder as "enabler behavior," which actually may support her husband's drinking problem.

Client: (tearfully) Well, I think that Chuck would be OK and stop drinking if only I did a better job. I really should keep the house better. A lot of our troubles are my fault.

Counselor: (interpreting/reframing) You're feeling responsibility for his drinking. You've been to AA family groups, and you're taking the enabler role again. The more you rescue Chuck and take responsibility for his actions, the more he will be likely to continue drinking. You can only take care of yourself.

Theoretical orientation plays an important role in the use of interpretations, as it does for most influencing skills (see table 3.4). The above intervention might be expected from an alcohol counselor working within an AA twelve-step orientation. A counselor working from a family systems orientation might have a somewhat similar approach but might focus more on the family system, saying, "Suzanne, it's the classic system. Chuck gripes at what you do; you try harder, but can never match his expectations. You miss one detail, and then he starts hitting you. After he hits you, you make up, and then the cycle starts again."

For a client in long-term psychoanalytic therapy, the counselor might relate childhood patterns to actions in the present by saying, "Your problem with Chuck goes back to your own father. You're trying to please Chuck as you never were able to please your Dad." A behavioral therapist might interpret the same situation in still another way by commenting, "Suzanne, you're always reinforcing Chuck's gripes by trying harder."

Which interpretation or reframe is correct? Most likely, all of them. Each theoretical orientation has a useful way of constructing and making sense of the world. The effective interpretation is one that the client can use to make a difference in her or his own life. Each alternative interpretation of life experience encouraged by the counselor lays the groundwork for the later change in client behavior and illustrates how cognitions can lead to behavior change.

The *directive* is the most actively "influencing" of the influencing skills. Despite extensive belief to the contrary, counselors often tell their clients what to do. Directives are therapist statements that direct a client to do something, say something, or act in a certain way. The counselor may provide a directive by guiding a client through a fantasy (humanistic counseling), suggesting specific behavioral changes (assertiveness training), or making focused free association suggestions (psychodynamic therapy). Asking a client to complete an action homework assignment is a directive.

A useful, but potentially dangerous, set of influencing skills centers around *advice* and *information giving.* In this mode, the counselor makes suggestions, provides instructional information, and may even say, "If I were you, I would . . ." At times, counselors must give advice because they have important information the client needs. Vocational counselors give advice or provide vocational information. Transactional analysts sometimes acquaint their clients with the theoretical basis of the therapy. Reality therapists teach clients skills and knowledge necessary for practical coping in the world.

However, advice and instruction can be overused. Advice must be given carefully and mainly at the request of the client, otherwise the client likely will say, "Yes, but . . ." Anytime the client responds with "Yes, but . . ." it is generally time to change your style and move to an attending skill such as questioning or paraphrasing. For example, you might say, "You feel that suggestion isn't helpful. What might be more useful to you?" With clients like Suzanne in the foregoing example, advice must be given carefully, as people stuck in alcoholic systems have real difficulty in accepting and listening to advice.

Self-disclosure occurs when you share your own life experience with the client, as when you say, "I've been there too. My father was an alcoholic, and I married an alcoholic. It took years for me to realize that I was an enabler myself."

Feedback is closely related to self-disclosure in that you share your impressions of the client with the client, as, for example: "We've been talking for a half hour now, and I'm impressed with your ability to hang on through these problems. You've got a lot of strength in you. I can see it. How do you react to that?" In this example, the counselor uses the perception check after providing feedback. This can be especially helpful in giving back the conversational lead to the client and learning if your influencing skill was helpful or not.

Both feedback and self-disclosure are useful for helping clients know how they are coming across to others. Distinctions between the two skills are obviously somewhat arbitrary, but both can help clients feel more comfortable and more willing to self-disclose. Too much personal feedback and self-disclosure may close off client interchange. For some clients, an open counselor is helpful and reassuring; for others, such an approach can be more intrusive than a barrage of questions.

For instance, self-disclosing your own experience, as did the counselor with the enabler background, can be useful if correctly done in an appropriate context. If the timing or context is wrong, however, self-disclosure can be destructive to the interview. Self-disclosure of your feelings to the client is often considered helpful if you are working from any of several multicultural orientations or in a modern Rogerian theoretical framework. Many therapists who work with complex clients, such as those diagnosed as multiple or borderline personalities, would argue that self-disclosure is inappropriate. Self-disclosure must be employed with some caution with all clients.

Feedback is basic to encounter groups and to other group experiences. With feedback from group members, the client learns how others perceive him or her. Feedback also may be an important skill to use in the family therapy treatment program. In family therapy, the client may need to learn how other family members view his or her behavior.

Employing *logical consequences,* a complex skill, involves leading clients to understand the possible consequences of their actions. For instance, the counselor may say, "Suzanne, as I listen to you, I hear that *if* you try to meet Chuck's needs, *then* you are likely to up the ante, and he only demands more. The consequence of your trying harder is that he asks ever more of you. How does that sound?"

The structure of a logical consequence statement is basically one of paraphrase and reflection of feeling, with the addition of the logical consequences of continuing the behavior. The logical if/then structure underlies this influencing skill. It is important to include a perception check to give the client room to react and lessen the imposition associated with this skill.

The influencing summary often is used by therapists at the end of the interview. In this instance, what the therapist has said and introduced during the session is reviewed. Influencing summaries usually appear in combination with listening summarization. The critical distinction between the two lies in which data are being summarized — the client's (attending summarization) or the counselor's (influencing summary).

Focus and Selective Attention

Beginning counselors and therapists often focus on problems instead of the people in front of them. It is generally (but not always) wiser to first focus on the client and later on the problem. The temptation is to focus on the problem and solve it, perhaps even disregarding the thoughts and feelings of the client in the process. This course should be avoided — for example:

Client: Yes, you've got it. I've got to cope with so many things, and it seems endless. I don't know where to turn. I've tried to get Chuck to Alcoholics Anonymous, but he only goes for a session or two and then quits. The school guidance counselor called me in because Joss got into trouble on the playground. They said he was bullying a smaller boy. How can I solve all these problems?

Counselor: I hear you as overwhelmed by it all. Let's start first with *you* and what's happening with *Suzanne.*

The counselor uses two personal pronouns and the client's name. Such naming of the client is an important personalizing technique seldom stressed sufficiently in the helping profession. By focusing on Suzanne, the counselor indicates an interest in the person and what that person feels and thinks. *Counseling is, after all, for the client.*

Although focus should usually be on the client, it can be invaluable to broaden the focus in a balanced fashion to include several additional dimensions. In working with a complex case such as Suzanne's, it should be clear that focusing just on Suzanne will not be sufficient in the long run. This client needs to work out her relationship with her husband, help her children, and resolve a wide variety of pragmatic problems. Thus, although counseling is indeed for the client, the ability to look beyond the client and focus the interview more broadly is also crucial.

Client-centered Rogerian theory and psychoanalytic theory treat the issue of focus differently. These systems of helping focus their interviewing leads almost totally on the client and give minimal attention to family issues or context. However, family, feminist, and multicultural theories hold that it is important to consider situational and contextual variables. It is also the case that some clients can best be reached by first focusing on the problem; only then will they be able to focus on themselves and their feelings.

Focus Analysis

It is apparent that focus can be approached in different ways. Thus it is useful that we ensure that we have considered all possible aspects of a client's problem. The seven dimensions of microskill focus analysis listed below are vital for understanding what is happening in any therapy session. Consider the following client statement:

> *Client:*   Yes, you've got it. I've got to cope with so many things, and it seems endless. I don't know where to turn. I've tried to get Chuck to Alcoholics Anonymous, but he only goes for a session or two and then quits. The school guidance counselor called me in because Joss got into trouble on the playground. They said he was bullying a smaller boy. How can I solve all these problems?

It is possible to respond to the client's statement in any of several ways:

1. *Client focus:* "Suzanne, you feel confused and lonely. You're unsure of what you want to do." This response contains four personal references to the client. Although counseling generally recommends a client focus, this may be culturally inappropriate in some situations. The client focus approach puts the problem squarely on Suzanne and tends to ignore family factors and gender issues.

2. *Other focus:* "Tell me more about your husband." In this case, the client likely will start telling about her husband and his drinking. The question "What's going on with Joss?" would result in a focus on the son. Both of these questions may lead to valuable information, but they do not tell us about the client and her reaction to the situation. For some clients, however, an other focus may be more appropriate than a client focus, as they may feel uncomfortable talking about themselves in the early stages of the helping process.

3. *Family focus:* Therapists are beginning to understand the importance of family history and family interaction and how these are played out in therapy with the individual client. A child who bullies on the playground may be acting out an abusive pattern at home. Responses that focus on the family include: "How would your son's bullying relate to what's going on in the family?" or "Family issues often reflect what happens in the individual. Tell me more about what's happening in your family" or (more historically oriented) "Let's go back to your own family of origin. Could you tell me what role alcohol played in your family while you were growing up?"

4. *Problem/main theme focus:* The presenting problem or main theme of the session could be said to be the general issue of how alcohol affects the client and her family. More specifically, this client seems to be nearing a crisis. Sample responses focusing on the problem and its solution would include: "What can I do to help you find housing so you could move out?" or "The situation sounds like an emergency. I'll call the women's shelter right now. You'll be safe there." or "Let's talk about how we could help your husband become more involved with AA." Clients often need concrete problems solved, particularly in times of crisis, and a focus on the individual client could be inappropriate at times.

5. *Interviewer focus:* "I grew up in an alcoholic family too. I can sense some of your issues." Focusing on your own experience may be useful as a self-disclosure or feedback technique, and it may help develop mutuality with the client. As rapport develops, such responses may be increasingly helpful. However, they must not be overdone. Counseling is for the client, not for the counselor.

6. *"We" focus:* "Right now we seem to be getting somewhere. The two of us ought to be able to generate some good ideas using what we know." This type of mutual sharing frequently appears in humanistically oriented interviews. It is also characteristic of feminist counseling and therapy in which the helper frequently joins the client as an advocate. This particular type of mutual focus leads toward a more egalitarian relationship between helper and helpee.

7. *Cultural/environmental/contextual focus:* "This is a concern facing many women. Society and its limited support systems do not always make things easy." Undergirding our client problems are long histories of interaction with sociopolitical systems. With some clients, this can become an important focus for discussion. Helpers with a multicultural or feminist orientation often effectively use this focus to produce change. Sample responses might include: "Many African-Americans feel a sense of rage because of discrimination. Racism is a fact of our society" or "You say that you can't speak assertively for yourself. This is a problem that many women have in our culture due to sexist conditioning." Most counseling theories, particularly the major ones, often overlook the cultural/environmental context and the historical background of the individual.

Focus analysis is concerned with the subject or main theme of the client-counselor interchange. Analyzing the grammatical subject of the client's sentences indicates the focus for the counseling intervention. Counseling is centrally concerned with getting clients to make "I" statements—statements in which they discuss themselves and their concerns. Counselors elicit "I" statements from their clients by using personal pronouns such as "you" and "your" and by using clients' names. It must again be emphasized that the other types of interview focus remain appropriate at times and, in fact, must be included if counseling is to be relevant to life experience.

Confrontation

We often think of confrontation as a hostile and aggressive act. In counseling and therapy, confrontation is usually a far more gentle process in which we point out to the client discrepancies between or among attitudes, thoughts, or behaviors. In a confrontation, individuals are faced directly with the fact that they may be saying other than what they mean, or doing other than what they say.

Double messages, incongruities, and discrepancies appear constantly in counseling interviews. A client may present an open right hand and smile while the left hand is closed in a fist. The counselor may be sitting with an open posture while covering the genital area with both hands. The client may say, "I really like my parents" while sitting in a closed posture with arms crossed over the chest.

One of the main tasks of counseling is to assist clients to work through, resolve, or learn to live with incongruities. Most counseling theories have as their main focus the resolution of incongruities. Freudians talk about resolving polarities and unconscious conflicts; Gestaltists, about integrating splits; client-centered therapists, about working through mixed feelings; rational-emotive therapists, about the need to attack incongruent irrational thinking; vocational counselors, about the distinction between unreal and real goals . . . the list could continue. The importance of identifying and resolving incongruities cannot be overemphasized.

Examples of ways to confront Suzanne, the client in the above examples, include:

Counselor: You're laughing, but I sense from the tone of your voice and the look on your face that underneath it isn't a laughing matter. [*Confrontation of discrepancy between verbal behavior and nonverbals*]

Counselor: On one hand, you say you want to get out of this relationship with Chuck, but on the other hand, you've been saying this for several months and you're still staying. How do you put that together? [*Confrontation of discrepancy between what is said and what is done*]

A useful model sentence for confrontation is: "On one hand, you think/feel/behave . . . but on the other hand, you think/feel/behave . . ." This model sentence provides the essence of the confrontation statement. It is nonjudgmental and helps clarify the confusing situation faced by the client. Using your hands in a gesture as if weighing the two alternatives can be very useful in emphasizing the contradiction.

An overly confronting, charismatic therapist can retard client growth, as can an overly cautious therapist. Intentional counseling requires a careful balance of confrontation with supporting qualities of warmth, positive regard, and respect. The empathic therapist is one who can maintain a balance, a "push-pull," of confrontation and support by utilizing a wide variety of counseling skills and theories.

Different Skill Patterns for Different Theories

Microskills theory holds that all systems of counseling and therapy employ various patterns of skills. Most systems give particular attention to the basic listening sequence. By mastering the specific skills presented here, you can "mix and match" these foundational patterns and achieve mastery of many alternative theories of therapy.

Table 3.4 summarizes theoretical orientations in terms of their differential usage of

Table 3.4   Microskill Usage According to Theoretical Orientation

Microskill Category	Client-Centered Theory	Psychodynamic Theory	Multicultural Theory
Focus	*Primarily on individual client.* The problem will often be conceptualized as one of understanding one's own unique needs and wishes. A major goal is self-actualization.	*Primarily on individual client.* The problem is understanding how past experience affects what occurs in the present. A major goal is understanding unconscious mental functioning.	*Balance between the individual, family, and multicultural issues.* The problem is thought of as developed in a context. A major goal is helping the client understand self in relation to context and taking action for self and others.
Listening skills	*Central use of listening skills to facilitate client expression;* minimum use of questions. The therapist attempts to minimize influence on client constructions and meaning making. Major emphasis is on reflecting feelings.	*Basic listening sequence used to draw out data relating to psychodynamic theory.* Questions and encouragers are especially important to facilitate exploration of unconscious processes.	*Basic listening sequence used to facilitate client understanding of self-in-system.* The therapist will tend to listen for family and contextual issues that affect client expression of self.
Influencing skills	*Feedback and reflection of meaning most commonly used.* Interpretation and reframes are avoided. There is little or no attempt to lead the client to behavioral action.	*Interpretation is central skill.* In later stages of therapy, interpretations/reframes may be the only skill used. There is little or no attempt to lead the client to behavioral action.	*Varying use of the influencing skills depending on client's cultural context.* In general, there will be a greater emphasis on feedback and self-disclosure to build a more egalitarian relationship. Reframes will often focus on family and cultural issues. There may be an attempt to encourage the client to act on issues and to also consider action in the community and society as well.

microskills. In this table, it can be seen that client-centered theory primarily uses attending skills and very few questions. Psychodynamic theory makes extensive use of interpretation. Both tend to focus on individual issues. By way of contrast, multicultural therapy focuses on self-in-context and takes a more action-orientated approach.

Each therapeutic system has varying patterns that must be mastered if you are to work within that orientation. However, all systems use the basic listening skills to some extent, and once you have mastered these skills, it is easier to move across theoretical orientations into new ways of functioning. When you learn new methods of therapy, you then can build on these skills and frame them into a wide variety of techniques and strategies appropriate to the system you are studying.

Using Microskills as a
Treatment Supplement

Following our identification of attending behavior (see exhibit 3.1), we brought the concepts into clinical use. Our first subject was a depressed college student who complained that he had no friends and was unable to talk to people. In the here and now of the interview, the counselor taught the student the four main dimensions of attending behavior and then role-played a conversation. The immediate change in the student was dramatic. He was able to take the skills home and practice them. He returned the following week greatly improved. Like most depressed people, this client tended to talk too much about himself and his problems. This self-focus led to a continuous cycle of depression. Learning listening skills, particularly attending behavior and open questioning, helped him focus outwardly and gave him less time to focus narrowly on his own problems. Another benefit was that by listening to others, he was better able to build a solid base for friendships.

This first experience with microskills therapy was followed by several studies on teaching psychiatric patients listening skills (Donk, 1972; Ivey, 1973, 1991). The findings in each of these clinical evaluative studies were that patients could learn the skills and that the skills resulted in changes in ward behavior and were useful in learning job-related skills. This early work also included a major emphasis on family and multicultural issues (Ivey, 1973, p. 342):

> The more important issue in generalization of behavior, however, lies in transfer of the newly learned behavior to society at large. . . . Many families really don't want the behavior of psychiatric patients changed. Change simply disrupts the reinforcement balance within the home. Similarly, society does not necessarily want behavior change. One patient, for example, who had shown marked improvement from depression commented that he really couldn't see any meaning in his routine assembly job. . . . To meet this patient's needs, one can work on cognitive restructuring . . . or, better yet, work on changing the society that helped bring about the psychotic break.

Based on these and other findings, microskills theory holds that individual change is insufficient. It is also necessary to do therapy, to educate, and to organize change in the family, the community, the workplace, and the broader cultural context. Training as a treatment modality in this broader change context can be an important part of counseling and therapy.

Applying Microskills in the Multicultural Domain

The most recent innovation in microskills is multicultural application, with the goal being to provide some direction in generating more culturally relevant theory and practice. One way to approach this objective has been to start with an examination of a specific country's culture and then examine how these findings relate to North American cultural groups.

The first step in theory development is awareness that theories are drawn from cultural perspectives. For example, the individualism inherent in Rogers's person-centered and Freud's psychodynamic theories represents the male, Western worldview, which is reflected in the entire structure of the therapy and counseling process. White and Parham (1990) endorse the need to generate new theories based on the real experiences of each cultural group.

Uchenna Nwachuku, a Nigerian Igbo, explored this direction and generated the beginnings of a specifically Afrocentric theory and method of helping (Nwachuku, 1989, 1990; Nwachuku & Ivey, 1991). Nwachuku's methods are highly instructive for those who seek to make broad concepts of multicultural helping applicable in practice.

Drawing on his personal experience and knowledge of Western helping methods, Nwachuku evolved several specific steps to generate an Afrocentric theory of helping. The steps that follow provide ideas for generating culturally relevant theory and practice:

1. *Examine the culture itself. What are important personal and interpersonal characteristics in this culture?*

This goal entails field research, interviews with informants, and reading from an anthropological frame of reference. Out of this examination, Nwachuku notes six key characteristics of the Igbo he believes to be important foundations of his Afrocentric theory (see exhibit 3.2).

Nwachuku, reflecting on his own developmental history, talks about going for walks with his mother as a child. Rather than running ahead or holding his mother's hand as a Western child might, Nwachuku recalls walking with his hand held close under his mother's armpit and feeling the beat of her heart. He talks about that beat still being with him. This particular vignette provides an interesting example of how a relational African culture uses the developmental process to foster cultural goals.

Although the Igbo have much in common with other African cultures, they also have much that is distinctive to their own group. For instance, we cannot generalize or draw stereotypes from the Igbo and then apply these to the Nigerian Yoruba. African

Exhibit 3.2

 ## Cultural Values and Culturally Relevant Theories of Helping

1. *What is the cultural attitude toward individual and relational issues?* Traditional European theories tend to focus on the individual. The African Igbo are both individualistic and oriented to the group; thus both individual and relational issues must be considered in helping approaches. Similar issues play themselves out for African-Americans, Asian-Americans, Latina/os, and Native Americans, and each group has its unique pattern.

2. *How are decisions made and who are the natural helpers?* The attitudes and wishes of extended family and the entire community are central to individual decision making in Igbo culture. This suggests that decisions need to focus not only on the client, but also on these other influencers as well. This is in direct contrast to the locus of individualistic decision stressed in European-American theories. Native American culture, in particular, is more similar to that of the Igbo than to that of European-Americans.

3. *What are the developmental progressions?* Igbo childrearing is balanced between the nuclear family, the extended family, and the community, as contrasted with the nuclear family tradition of European-

American culture. Developmental theory and the definition of healthy adjustment in one culture cannot be generalized easily to another.

4. *What is the attitude toward change?* The Igbo are receptive to change, but they also value age and respect elders. For counseling purposes, this suggests that some Western techniques and ideas may be appropriate, but also that the age of the counselor may be important. Attitudes toward change vary among groups. For instance, South Pacific Islanders and many Native American nations value harmony with the environment, which is not usually a European-American value.

5. *How is language used?* The Igbo frequently use figures of speech, proverbs, quotations, and other forms of complex communication. Such language usage suggests that Igbo clients would respond well to metaphorical orientations but that the straightforward style of European-American counseling approaches might be resisted. For an Igbo client, it may be better to tell a story or have them join you in storytelling. Cheek (1976) and White and Parham (1990) stress the importance of bidialectic communication with African-Americans.

cultures are different, just as the French and German, Haitian and Cuban cultures are different.

    2. Identify concrete skills and strategies that can be used in modern helping relationships. Organize these strategies into patterns and test them in clinical practice.

    Drawing out the client's story through empathic listening is an integral part of the Igbo theory of helping. However, in traditional Igbo helping, personal problems were also addressed through storytelling or metaphor. The task of the Igbo helper was to "help," which traditionally meant taking an authoritative, directive approach to helping once the client's issues were understood.

    The microskill of focus is particularly important in Nwachuku's theory and practice. Whereas most counseling theory focuses on the individual client, Afrocentric counseling theory recommends a focus on the extended family and the community, with a secondary focus on the individual and the nuclear family.

    Applications of the Igbo model to African-Americans and other nonmajority populations should be considered. Berman (1979) found that a "we" focus was used in counseling sessions among Blacks considerably more often than with Whites, which suggests more mutuality between client and therapist than is usually recommended by traditional counseling theory. Roberts (1982) replicated these findings among African-American managers. Working with culturally distinct Arabian groups in Lebanon, Kikoski (1980) also found a more mutual focus and an orientation to a more directive approach to helping.

    3. Test the new helping theory and its skills in action.

    Nwachuku used the microtraining format to generate Eurocentric and Afrocentric videotape examples of culturally appropriate helping. Both videotaped examples focused on the same problem: Should an African student return home from graduate school in the United States and meet family responsibilities?

    In the Eurocentric model, the helper focused immediately on the problem, and, using an "I" focus, encouraged the client to make an independent autonomous decision. As excellent listening skills were demonstrated, most counseling experts would consider this model a fine example of how counseling should be approached, pointing out that the client was supported in finding his own, independent decision.

    The Afrocentric Igbo model of helping was quite different. More time was spent at the beginning of the session, as the counselor helped the client feel comfortable. Although a "we" focus was used, it was also clear that the Igbo helper was establishing himself as an authority who expected to take charge of the session.

    The client's story was drawn out by the Igbo helper through questioning. After briefly probing the client's personal thoughts about the issue, the interviewer then focused on the extended family and asked questions about the client's uncle. (Paternal uncles are important figures in Igbo culture.) It soon was apparent that a broader network of decision makers was involved. This client had been influenced by North American individualism and needed a reminder from the counselor that more people than just himself were involved in this important life decision.

The counselor told the client a traditional Igbo story about family values and then looked at the client. The client understood the meaning of the story, acknowledged that he had lost track of some of his traditional values in the more individualistic United States, and accepted the necessity of returning to Nigeria.

Implications for the Future of Nwachuku's Model

Many therapists may feel uncomfortable with the idea that the family and the counselor so directly influence the decision of the client. Such an approach may seem directly antagonistic to the traditional goals of counseling and therapy. This is a type of dilemma inherent in working with multicultural groups.

Counseling theory is in a time of change and revision. Nwachuku's framework can be applied to a variety of cultural contexts and can help generate a new view of European-American helping theory and practice. Understanding worldviews from Afrocentric, Eurocentric, Native American, Asian-American, and other perspectives can bring about new levels of communication that will change the practice of counseling and therapy.

Limitations and Practical Implications of the Microskills Approach

The microskills approach is noted for its precision and clear description of behavior. Although early presentations of the model did not take cultural issues into account, the precision of the approach led to its current, hopefully more culturally sensitive, presentation. It is now an axiom of the microskills approach that all interviews must take into account both individual and multicultural differences.

The microskills of attending and listening "work," and they are clear and teachable. They should, however, be used in a culturally and individually appropriate fashion. There is a danger in teaching culturally inappropriate skills to trainees, particularly those skills that are effective and precise in description.

The first author of this book worked with a highly skilled Aboriginal social worker in Australia in jointly examining the multicultural implications of attending. The social worker was videotaped interviewing a client in the "Aboriginal way," which involved limited eye contact and a more self-disclosing and participative style of interviewing. On reviewing the tape, the social worker commented, "You mean it's OK to do counseling in our people's way?" Despite his obvious skill, the social worker had come to believe that only the European-Australian style of listening was appropriate. Needless to say, he was encouraged to maintain and sharpen his traditional ways of listening.

And at the present time, people in Australia, Canada, and the United States continue to teach and use the earlier microskills approach. Needless to say, this gap between theory and practice is not solely associated with the microskills approach. Individualistic psychodynamic and client-centered theories are also transported to relational cultures and presented as "the way to conduct interviewing and therapy." Powerful and intrusive Gestalt techniques may be highly effective in North America, but they can be highly inappropriate in other settings. Cognitive-behavioral techniques, like microskills, are often useful in other cultural settings, but require serious cultural modification to ensure that they are appropriate.

The experience in Australia illustrates (1) the danger of taking a helping theory to a new setting and imposing it directly without consideration of the culture and participation of its people; and (2) the need for all of us to update our practice and thinking about counseling and therapy theory. What we learn in the university or workshop today often will need to be modified as the field generates new research and knowledge.

NOTE

1. The issue of manipulation works two ways. The importance and power of nonverbal communication and mirroring are now part of the popular culture. A case was recently presented to one of the authors in which the client deliberately assumed nonsynchronous movement each time the therapist tried to match the client. Fortunately, the therapist decided to ignore body movement. Later, the client commented, "I know what you therapists do—you try to mirror my body language. But I want my own space." Needless to say, this type of experience again suggests the importance of authenticity and of recognizing the uniqueness of the individual with whom you work. This example also indicates the need for a more egalitarian and less hierarchical form of helping.

REFERENCES

BAKER, S., & DANIELS, T. (1989). Integrating research on the microcounseling program: A meta-analysis. *Journal of Counseling Psychology, 35,* 213–22.

BAKER, S., DANIELS, T., & GREELEY, A. (1990). Systematic training of graduate-level counselors: Narrative and meta-analytic reviews of three major programs. *Counseling Psychologist, 18,* 355–421.

BERMAN, J. (1979). Counseling skills used by black and white and male and female counselors. *Journal of Counseling Psychology, 26,* 81–84.

CHEEK, D. (1976). *Assertive Black, puzzled White.* San Luis Obispo, CA: Impact.

DANIELS, T. (1985). *Microcounseling: Training in skills of therapeutic communication with R.N. department program nursing students.* Unpublished doctoral dissertation, Dalhousie University, Halifax, Nova Scotia.

DONK, L. (1972). *Attending behavior in mental patients. Dissertation Abstracts International, 33* (Ord. No. 72-22,569).

HACKNEY, R., IVEY, A., & OETTING, E. (1970). Attending, island, and hiatus behavior: A process conception of counselor and client interaction. *Journal of Counseling Psychology, 17,* 342–46.

IVEY, A. (1971). *Microcounseling: Innovations in interviewing training.* Springfield, IL: Thomas.

IVEY, A. (1973). Media therapy: Educational change planning for psychiatric patients. *Journal of Counseling Psychology, 20,* 338–43.

IVEY, A. (1988a). *Intentional interviewing and counseling.* Pacific Grove, CA: Brooks/Cole.

IVEY, A. (1988b). *Managing face-to-face communication.* Lund, Sweden: Studentlitteratur, Chartwell Bratt.

IVEY, A. (1991, October). *Media therapy reconsidered.* Paper presented at Veterans Administration Conference, Orlando, FLA.

IVEY, A., & AUTHIER, J. (1978). *Microcounseling: Innovations in interviewing, counseling, psychotherapy, and psychoeducation* (2nd ed.). Springfield, IL: Thomas.

IVEY, A., GLUCKSTERN, N., & IVEY, M. (1992). *Basic attending skills* (3rd ed.). North Amherst, MA: Microtraining.

IVEY, A., NORMINGTON, C., MILLER, C., MORRILL, W., & HAASE, R. (1968). Microcounseling and attending behavior: An approach to pre-practicum counselor training. *Journal of Counseling Psychology, 15,* 1–12.

KIKOSKI, K. (1980). *A study of cross-cultural communication, Arabs and Americans: Paradigms and skills.* Unpublished doctoral dissertation, University of Massachusetts, Amherst.

MACFARLANE, K., & FELDMETH, J. (1988). *Child sexual abuse: The clinical interview.* New York: Guilford.

NWACHUKU, U. (1989). *Culture-specific counseling: The Igbo case.* Unpublished doctoral dissertation, University of Massachusetts, Amherst.

NWACHUKU, U. (1990, July). *Translating multicultural theory into direct action: Culture-specific counseling.* Paper presented at the International Roundtable for the Advancement of Counseling, Helsinki, Finland.

NWACHUKU, U., & IVEY, A. (1991). Culture specific counseling: An alternative approach. *Journal of Counseling and Development, 70,* 106–11.

ROBERTS, W. (1982). *Black and white managers in helping: Interaction effects of managers in responding to culturally varied subordinate vignettes.* Unpublished doctoral dissertation, University of Massachusetts, Amherst.

SUE, D. (1990). Culture-specific strategies in counseling: A conceptual framework. *Professional Psychology, 21,* 424–33.

WHITE, J., & PARHAM, T. (1990). *The psychology of Blacks.* Englewood Cliffs, NJ: Prentice-Hall.

Decisional Counseling:
The Basis of All Counseling and Therapy

CHAPTER GOALS

This chapter seeks to help you:

1. Understand trait and factor theory, the first systematic decisional model, from a more current and more relational frame of reference.

2. Explore the five-stage model of the interview and see how this model can be useful not only for decisional counseling, but also for other theories of helping.

3. Apply the decisional model in practice through three important dimensions: the balance sheet, creativity and intuition, and relapse prevention.

4. Examine single-case evaluation research and its implications for counseling and therapy practice.

5. Increase your awareness that decisions are always made in a relational, multicultural context, even when the decisional frame is highly personal and individualistic.

Decisional Style

Take a moment to think about an important decision—choosing a life partner, selecting a career, buying a house, or any other important personal decision—you have made in the past or are in the process of making.

Once you have a specific situation in mind, think about the following questions as they relate to that decision and your general decision-making style.

- Is your decisional style rational and logical, or is it more intuitive and creative? Do you make lists of factors involved in important decisions and weigh the decision carefully, or do you have some inner sense of what made that decision "feel" right?
- How much are you influenced by others when you make a decision? Do you make the decision alone or in relationship to other key individuals or family members?
- How does creativity relate to your decisional process? Can you generate something new in terms of a product or how you and others behave, think, or feel?

Each of us has differing decisional styles, and your client's way of making decisions will likely be different from your own. How patient and understanding will you be with clients and families who have very different decisional styles from your own?

Clients constantly come to counselors for help making key decisions involving such concerns as choice of college; financial planning; how to get along with a lover or mate, parents, or in-laws; finding a new job; and dealing with issues of drug and alcohol abuse.

A knowledge of the decisional process and how it relates to counseling and psychotherapy theory is basic to effective counseling. The psychodynamic, client-centered, and behavioral traditions are all influenced by decisional issues. Furthermore, decisional counseling is a theoretical frame of reference in its own right.

The Decisional Counseling Worldview

Decisional counseling is most often oriented toward practical thought and action. This practical, empirical bent links it to the pragmatic North American tradition associated with the philosophers C.S. Pierce and William James. *Pragmatism* is concerned with a practical approach to life matters and ignores "why" questions that philosophically are often unanswerable. Inventors such as Thomas Edison, Eli Whitney, or Henry Ford exemplify the pragmatic tradition of thinking things through logically and then testing the ideas to see if they work. This North American tradition historically has been interested in reasons and results.

Many clients seek pragmatic action and become impatient with complex theorizing. They want to get help and then move on. Much of counseling and clinical practice involves such pragmatic decision making; it is the bulk of the practice of employment counselors, vocational counselors, and many of those who work at the front line in crisis centers. In addition, many complex decisions in longer-term therapy can be facilitated by using decisional theory and decisional models.

Benjamin Franklin is often credited as being the first to outline the basic steps of the pragmatic model of decision making, as follows:

1. Define the problem or concern clearly.[1]
2. Generate alternative possibilities for solution.

3.   Weigh the positives and negatives of each alternative in a simple *balance sheet.*
4.   Select one alternative for action and see how it works.

Franklin's system is perhaps the ultimate expression of the pragmatic worldview. His discovery of electricity by flying a kite is a particularly apt example of how logic and creativity interplay in the decisional process.

A variety of decision-making models exist in counseling and therapy, and all contain basic elements of Franklin's logical system, most use some variation of his original balance sheet, and all have a natural respect for the creative process (Brammer, 1990; Carkhuff, 1987; D'Zurilla, 1986; Ivey, 1988; Janis & Mann, 1977).

Multicultural Issues and Decisional Counseling

The decisional style of most White male European-North Americans tends to be individualistic, with the locus of decision making in the individual. This style often implicitly dominates decisional work, even though it may not always be appropriate.

The decisional style of women is more relational in orientation. Hansen (1990) stresses that decisions need to be made in context, with special attention given not only to individual needs, but also to the needs of important others. Needless to say, many women would feel more comfortable with Hansen's decisional frame. Men might also profit from the relational orientation. Ben Franklin's model is elegant in its simplicity, but misses some of the complexity of the decisional domain.

As discussed in the preceding chapter, the central locus of decision for the Nigerian Igbo culture is in the extended family and community, not in the individual. Solely individualistic decision making also may be inappropriate for clients of African-American, Latina/o, and Japanese-American cultures. For such individuals, trait and factor theory, with its history of emphasizing the relationship of the individual in context, can offer an alternative decisional approach.

Trait and Factor Theory

Trait and factor theory can be best summarized as rational decisional counseling in which the task of the counselor or therapist is to assist the client in making better choices for living more effectively. In making a decision, it is good to consider as many *traits and factors* as possible.

Historically, the roots of trait and factor counseling can be traced to Frank Parsons, who founded the Boston Vocational Bureau in 1908. Undergirding the practice of most vocational counseling, as well as much personal counseling, Parsons's (1909/1967) model for vocational choice is simple:

In the wise choice of a vocation there are three broad factors: (1) a clear understanding of yourself, your aptitudes, abilities, interests, ambitions, resources, limitations, and their causes; (2) a knowledge of the requirements and conditions of success, advantages and disadvantages, compensation, opportunities, and prospects in different lines of work; (3) true reasoning on the relations of these two groups of facts. (p. 5)

Parsons's model may be paraphrased and expanded to take into account a wide range of personal issues as well. For example:

> In any decision there are three main issues: (1) a clear understanding of the client and the client's ability and perceptions; (2) a clear understanding of the environment important to the client's decision; and (3) true reasoning on the relationship of the client to the environment.

Despite errors of analysis of both the person and environment, trait and factor counseling has survived and been critical to the formulation of decisional counseling. Perhaps this is because Parsons's logic is virtually impossible to fault — and because the decisional process does "work," thus meeting the pragmatic test.

Rational and cognitive dimensions predominate in the trait and factor model, but what about emotion? It is obvious that even the most rational of decisions will be unsatisfactory if the client does not feel good about what is decided and if people important to the client are not satisfied as well. This often-missing facet of decisional theory will be explored later in this chapter.

The Importance of Environmental Action

Trait and factor theory exhibits a particular awareness of the environment and its impact on the individual. The emphasis on person-environment interaction stands in contrast to person-centered theories, such as client-centered and psychodynamic, that predominate in most counseling and therapy.

In Parsons's framework, the environment is as important as the individual. In fact, when possible the counselor is encouraged to act to change that environment. Cheatham (1990), focusing on the African-American client, urges such action, observing that "traditional concepts of psychological intervention ignore the cultural and contextual specificity of Black families and their members and thus are inadequate to serve these clients" (p. 388).

The Career Resource Center of Rochester, New York, provides an example of an environmentally oriented counseling approach. Developed originally as a "grassroots" women's center, the counselors found that clients could not take charge of their lives if they had to continue in a less-than-satisfactory work setting. Thus, a major effort of the Career Resource Center focuses on consultation with management: "We believe employers will provide as a matter of course, employee career development, spouse employment relocation and retirement/life work assistance because it makes sense to do so. Everyone will win — the organization, the supervisor, the employee, the dual-career couple, and, in general, our work force" (Neece & Harrison, 1990, p. 1).

The earliest and most important trait and factor theorists (Williamson, 1939; Paterson & Darley, 1936) have been criticized for failing to take into account the full complexity of the human condition. Nevertheless, their insights into people and their environments are impressive. Paterson and Darley's work at the Minnesota Stabilization Institute reveals a deep awareness of how social and environmental conditions were considered central to any type of counseling and therapy, and Williamson's work with counseling students in the college environment led to the field now called student development.

Chartrand (1991) reviews the current status of trait and factor theory, pointing out that person-environment interaction remains a key focus. She points out that Williamson's 1939 book, often roundly criticized in the profession, was culturally in tune with the times and included a highly advanced systematic decisional model not unlike those presented in this chapter. The "Minnesota tradition," led by Williamson and Paterson and Darley, has had great influence on the helping field, and its most recent advances are evident in Sunny Hansen's work on integrated life patterns.

The Integrative Life Patterns Model

Hansen's (1990) integrated life patterns (ILP) model points out that decisional counseling operates in a complex web of relationships over the life span. Hansen's framework is more relational and more comprehensive than most decisional theory and provides a useful framework in which to expand ideas about the importance and place of the decisional process in professional counseling and therapy. The ILP model expands the scope of the trait and factor tradition. More relational in nature, ILP tends to be accepted more readily by women, Latina/os, and Asian-Americans, among other groups.

The concept of life patterns or patterning as presented in the ILP model is particularly important. Formerly, ILP was defined as "integrative life planning" and focused on decision making. The concept of patterning allows for more emphasis on relationships and life-span issues. Decision making tends to focus on outcomes, whereas patterning helps us recall that decisions are a process and are made contextually in relation to others in the family, community, and society.

Hansen (1990) defines ILP as the "lifelong process of identifying our primary needs, roles, and goals and the consequent integration of these within ourselves, our work, and our family" (p. 10). ILP is a comprehensive model of decisional counseling in which each individual makes decisions about his or her total development — physical, intellectual, social/emotional, vocational/career, sexual, and spiritual.

Major Life Patterns

ILP focuses on four major life roles — loving, learning, labor, and leisure — as the expression of life patterns. Each of these life areas requires us to make decisions. A decision about labor affects present and future decisions in other areas. For example, a decision to undertake a particularly demanding career might allow less time for relationships, learning, and leisure. ILP expands traditional trait and factor theory by pointing up the systemic impact of any one decision.

A problem with trait and factor counseling and decisional theories is their emphasis on a linear decisional process. Hansen, while working within the decisional tradition, explores a more comprehensive developmental view. Although individual decisions are clearly important, counselors and therapists need to help their clients consider the impact of their decisions on important relationships.

Decisions in Relationship

ILP suggests the need for planning and making decisions about *life roles,* to focus not only on achievement and success, but also on *achievement in relationship to others.* In the ILP model, life patterns of both women and men, individually and in relationship, are examined, and the importance of self-sufficiency and connectedness for both is stressed.

The ILP model encourages decisions that move from dominant-subordinate to *equal partner relationships* and also supports *intuitive decision making* as well as rational thought. (The importance of this dimension is discussed later in this chapter in the subsection on creativity.) ILP attempts to avoid decisional counseling that leads to making decisions out of context, emphasizing the importance of taking into account changing life contexts in work, family, education, and the larger society.

Hansen (1991) suggests a variety of individual, group, and workshop strategies appropriate for implementing the ILP model, including the use of lifelines in which one examines one's past history and future situation; exercises in risk taking, visualization and imagery, and life role identification; and client journal work to record decisional experiences.

The Circle of Life

In figure 4.1, a lifetime of decision making is presented as a circle. Varying decisional styles that have been useful over the life span are influenced by internal factors—the "core" you—and by external factors—messages about family, education, and so on—and result in life decisions. The circle of life example illustrates how integrated life patterns take place in relationship to others. The circle of life concept provides a more holistic framework for considering person-environment counseling and action, reflecting "the deep integration, wholeness, a source of the interrelatedness of all life" (Hansen, 1991).

Decisional Theory in the Interview: The Five-Stage Model

The five-stage decisional counseling model presented in this chapter is an extension of trait and factor theory and Benjamin Franklin's work (Ivey & Matthews, 1984; Ivey, 1988). The central theoretical point of the five-stage model is that *counseling and therapy are not only about decisions, but the interview itself also may be structured using a decision-making framework.* Mastering the five-stage interview, gaining an understanding of key empathic dimensions, and developing competence in interviewing microskills will give you a framework for understanding many different approaches to helping theory.

You can structure a very effective interview using the following five stages as a model or checklist:

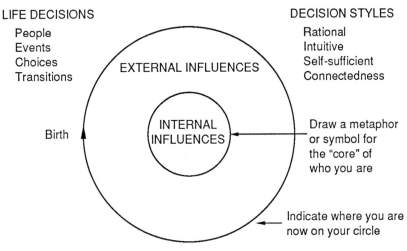

LIFE DECISIONS
People
Events
Choices
Transitions

Birth

DECISION STYLES
Rational
Intuitive
Self-sufficient
Connectedness

EXTERNAL INFLUENCES

INTERNAL INFLUENCES

Draw a metaphor
or symbol for
the "core" of
who you are

Indicate where you are
now on your circle

SIGNIFICANT MESSAGES
Family
Education
Work
Leisure
Gender roles

Figure 4.1 Circle of Life: An Integrated Life Patterns Example

SOURCE: Adapted from S. Hansen's Integrative Life Planning Exercise, 1991. Used with permission.

1. Establishing rapport and structure ("Hello" and "This is what we'll be doing today.")
2. Gathering data and identifying assets ("What's the problem or concern?" and "What are your strengths?")
3. Determining outcomes ("What do you want to have happen?")
4. Generating alternative solutions ("What are we going to do to generate new ideas?")
5. Generalizing and transferring learning ("Will you do it?")

These five stages and their functions are explored in more detail in table 4.1. Different cultural groups will likely work through the five stages in differing manners. Think of these five stages as a checklist, and use it flexibly to meet the needs of your particular client.

In figure 4.2, the five stages are represented as five parts of a circle. Not all clients will profit from a linear use of the five-stage model. The circle of decision making shows that all five stages are part of a totality. Different clients will want to work with the decisional model from alternative perspectives. In such cases, the decisional model can serve as a useful checklist to ensure that all dimensions of decision making have been covered.

Table 4.1   The Five-Stage Structure of the Interview

Definition of Stage	Function and Purpose of Stage	Cultural and Individual Issues
1. Establishing rapport and structure "Hello. This is what we'll be doing today."	To build a working alliance with the client and to enable the client to feel comfortable with the interviewer. Structuring may be needed to explain the purpose of the interview. Structuring functions to help keep the session on task and to inform the client what the counselor can and cannot do.	With some clients and some cultural groups, rapport development may take a long time so that trust can grow. Methods of rapport development and decision making will vary with individuals and cultures.
2. Gathering data and identifying assets "What's your concern?" "What are your strengths?"	To find out why the client has come to the interview and how he or she views the concern. Skillful problem definition will help avoid aimless topic jumping and give the interview purpose and direction. Also to identify clearly positive strengths of the client.	Not all clients appreciate the careful delineation of issues typical of middle-class helping. Moreover, once goals are clearly established, it may be helpful to return to this stage.
3. Determining outcomes "What do you want to have happen?"	To find out the ideal world of the client. How would the client like to be? How would things be if the "problem" were solved? This stage is important in that it enables the interviewer to know what the client wants. The desired direction of the client and counselor should be reasonably harmonious. With some clients, skip stage 2 and define goals first.	If work is clear and concrete here, specific resolutions may be immediately apparent. Many cultural groups and individuals prefer to start here. If we know goals, the concern may be clear and we can move to stage 4.
4. Generating alternative solutions "What are we going to do to generate new ideas?"	To work toward resolution of the client's issue. This may involve the creative problem-solving model of generating alternatives (to remove stuckness) and deciding among those alternatives. It also may involve lengthy exploration of personal dynamics. This phase of the interview may be the longest.	It is critical that individual and cultural differences in decisional style be acknowledged. What is the "correct" decision from your point of view may be highly inappropriate to another. With some groups, a highly directive style on the counselor's part may be appropriate. In general, listen and let the client decide.
5. Generalizing and transferring learning "Will you do it?"	To enable changes in thoughts, feelings, and behaviors in the client's daily life.	The degree of generalization will also relate highly to how effectively you took cultural

Table 4.1   Continued

Definition of Stage	Function and Purpose of Stage	Cultural and Individual Issues
	Many clients go through an interview and then do nothing to change their behavior, remaining in the same world they came from.	and individual differences into account in the early stages of the session(s).

Interviewing Children Using the Five-Stage Model

Children are often a bit random in their thinking, and it is your task as a counselor to help them structure their ideas. Most early elementary children simply do not have the words or concepts for our traditional theories. Thus, in working with children, your intuitive style and questioning skills become especially important. Generally, children tend to be very trusting of adults. As you help them tell their stories, seek to avoid leading or biasing them in any way.

Developing the basic five-stage structure of the interview may take as many as ten sessions with a child. It may take several weeks just to establish rapport, but, alternatively, you may find yourself going through all five steps in ten minutes. The following guidelines can help in working with children:

1. *Establishing rapport.* Establish rapport in your own way. A smile may be enough, or you may want to play a game first. Most children like to do artwork,

Figure 4.2   The Circle of Decision Making

play with clay, and do something with their hands while they talk. Traditional "talk therapy" is slow and boring for many children.

2. *Data gathering emphasizing strengths.* If the child comes directly from the playground and is all excited, he or she will likely be "off and running" ahead of you. Children often talk in short, random, concrete segments. Allow them to talk in their own fashion, while you paraphrase, reflect feelings, and summarize frequently. You can help them organize their stories. With a less talkative child, closed questions are important, but be sure you do not lead the child. Keep your questions and concepts very concrete and avoid abstract talk.

Identifying positive assets and strengths must be part of every interview. If you cannot find something right with the child, do not attempt the interview or treatment. If you find yourself feeling impatient, bored, or frustrated, seek personal supervision. This point, of course, holds for work with adults as well, but children may be particularly vulnerable to your lack of understanding.

3. *Determining goals.* Ask the child "What do you want to have happen?" Allow the child to explore an ideal world and discover fantasies and desires. Children whose parents are going through divorce may express impossible goals. Accept their goals but help them focus on a concrete goal that will be useful here and now. For example, "What if you play with your friend Jamie after school, or when you feel sad go skating or play basketball?" Playing with a friend or physical activities are helpful for avoiding depression.

4. *Generating alternative solutions and actions.* Many children may be in tears at one minute and then happily playing the next. Children respond well to creative brainstorming ("How many different ways could your problem be solved?"). Break the problem down into workable small steps. Often, listing solution alternatives can be helpful. The five-stage model is also useful in group work. For example, if you bring together three to five children who have experienced divorce, they can often help another child who is experiencing the same difficulties. At this point, imagining the future and the emotional consequences of alternatives can be especially helpful.

5. *Generalizing.* Try not to leave a child without a concrete goal for the day or evening. Homework assignments work well. Observe their behavior in the classroom or with friends if possible. Systematic behavioral programs that have the support of teachers or parents can be helpful.

Alternative Theories and the Five-Stage Model

Ivey and Matthews (1984) describe the five-stage decisional framework as a *metatheoretical model* in that decisional counseling draws on a multitude of other theories as it seeks to facilitate the creative client decisional process. Furthermore, they argue that effective counseling and therapy, regardless of theoretical orientation, tends to cover the five major points over time. The timing and style of work, of course, vary with theoretical orientation, but the five-stage interview format seems to be a consistent decisional model.

The five-stage decisional model also provides an outline for what occurs in much of traditional counseling and psychotherapy. By mastering the five-stage interview structure, you will find it easier to work with many differing types of theoretical approaches ranging from client-centered interviewing to psychodynamic dream analysis.

The Five Stages in Dreamwork

For example, in applying the five-stage model to an egalitarian dream analysis, you might start the interview by first establishing rapport and sharing with the client what is likely to happen. If the client agrees, you might then move to the data-gathering phase, drawing out information (facts, thoughts, and feelings) about the client's dream using the basic listening sequence of microskills. In the third stage, your goal might be to discover how the dream relates to the client's past and/or present experience. Here again you could elicit client goals using the basic listening sequence. Decisional theory suggests that shared goal setting can facilitate the solution phase.

In the fourth stage of the interview, you might ask the client to identify an important feeling from the dream and locate that feeling in a specific part of the body. The client can be directed to free associate to an earlier or current life experience. Free associations from feeling or body experiences often are quite powerful, and the therapist should be ready and able to deal with strong emotions. (Chapter 6 identifies additional concepts and techniques for therapy at this stage of the interview.)

Psychodynamic theory typically gives little attention to generalization or taking concepts home. However, you can encourage your client at this fifth stage of the session to think about specific things that can be done to promote transfer of new learning. The foregoing is but one example of how mastery of empathic concepts, microskills, and decisional theory can serve as a foundation for effective work in other theoretical orientations.

Summary

The five-stage decisional counseling model may be useful in many different approaches to counseling and therapy. You will find that it helps you and your client structure your relationship. At the same time, you can see that the model needs to be adapted to meet individual client needs, that moving through the five stages can take greatly varying lengths of time (from ten minutes to six months or more), and that the basic model may need to be changed to fit different multicultural situations.

The Practice of Decisional Counseling

This section presents some additional specifics on the practice of decisional counseling. The following material on decisional style, the balance sheet, creativity in the counseling process, and relapse prevention are all useful constructs in decisional counseling and psychotherapy.

Individual Decisional Style and the Balance Sheet

Each individual has a different style of making decisions. Consider your own decisional style—how do you make decisions? Some of us make decisions rationally, drawing up careful lists of the pros and cons. Others of us simply "go with the flow" and let decisions happen to us. Still others find decisions traumatic and may procrastinate endlessly on even the smallest decision.

Five basic styles of decision making have been identified by Janis and Mann (1977):

1. *Vigilant* (intentional and purposive)
2. *Hypervigilant* (anxious emotional arousal, with limited search for alternatives)
3. *Defensive avoidance* (procrastination)
4. *Unconflicted adherence* (staying with the decision regardless of consequences)
5. *Unconflicted change* (often controlled by emotion, constant vacillation)

At issue for most clients is finding a balanced intentional, or vigilant, style in which alternatives are considered and a decision is made within a reasonable emotional climate.

Decisional Theory in Psychoeducational Practice

Mann and his colleagues at Flinders University in Australia have used decisional theory in many settings and with particular success in groups (Mann et al., 1982, 1989; Mann, Harmoni, & Power, 1990). Their psychoeducational sessions start with presentations of alternative methods of decision making, and clients are encouraged to identify their typical decisional style. Vigilant decision making is emphasized as a desired goal.

The *decisional balance sheet,* developed by Mann and his colleagues, is a sophisticated version of Benjamin Franklin's early model (see figure 4.3). When the client has an important decision to make, working carefully and systematically through the gains and losses associated with the decision is helpful in clarifying issues. The client completes one of these grid sheets for each alternative for action under consideration. The first two items focus on the facts of the decision; the last two on how the client and others would feel about that decision.

The balance sheet gives as much attention to the impact of the decision on others as it does to the impact on the person making a decision. In this way it helps clients develop greater sensitivity and empathy in their decisional process. The decisional balance sheet offers a simple, but very useful, process that can help clients think of themselves in relationship to others. In some ways, this represents a major advance for decisional theory.

Another decision-making tool is the *future diary.* Decisions are not just rational,

ALTERNATIVE # _____

GAINS	LOSSES
Material gains for me	Material losses for me
Material gains for others	Material losses for others
Gains in self-approval	Losses in self-approval
Approval by others	Disapproval by others

Figure 4.3   The Balance Sheet Grid

SOURCE: L. Mann et al., *Decision workshops for the improvement of decision making skills.* Flinders University of S. Australia, Adelaide, © 1982. Used by permission.

they are also deeply linked to emotions. Keeping a future diary helps clients think through the *emotional aspects of decision making.* In the diary, clients describe a typical day one year in the future, based on the circumstances that might evolve from a particular decision. Future diaries often bring out feeling issues that were not brought out by the more cognitive decisional balance sheet.

These emotional issues can be more easily identified by helping clients generate visual, auditory, or kinesthetic images of their futures. Guided imagery works well as a supplement to decisional counseling, particularly in aiding clients to think ahead to the future.

Creativity, Intuition, and Magic

Creativity may be described as a primarily emotional process that underlies decision making in the interview. *Any client change requires some creativity — the generation of something new.* You will need theoretical knowledge, imagination, practice — and some magic — to help your clients become creative.

Most of the decision frameworks presented in this chapter are oriented toward a "rational" decision-making style. However, when you think of your own life, are your best decisions always rational and planned? Whether you are a careful deliberate decision maker or work more from intuition, it should be clear that emotional satisfaction is the ultimate deciding factor on whether a decision "works."

You cannot force creativity, intuition, or new ideas—they seem to appear out of nowhere. A person may have been wrestling with a seemingly unsolvable problem, and then, in frustration, leave it for a time. On returning to it, the "bell rings" or the "light dawns," and a new answer pops to mind. Creativity depends on spontaneity and a willingness to "let go." The classic alternating goblet/face from Gestalt psychology (figure 4.4) shows the spontaneous—the "aha"—nature of creative thought.

In looking at the figure, some individuals have considerable difficulty seeing both the goblet and the face. These clients are, in effect, immobilized and frozen in one view of the world. Given time and prompting, they can become freed to see the alternatives existing in the figure. This moment of "letting loose" and the accompanying insight (the "aha!" experience) are the essence of creativity—the ability to generate something new out of old pieces.

Something similar happens with the Necker cube (figure 4.5). Most people immediately see a cube, then another cube, and with further examination, the two cubes "moving" from one to the other. However, with further study it is possible to generate many more physical images (flat plane figures, triangles, and so on).

The "magic" in creativity is the spontaneous generation of something new out of already existing pieces. By analogy, consider the client who enters the counseling relationship. He or she may have the pieces, the traits and factors of the problem,

Figure 4.4 Alternating Goblet/Face

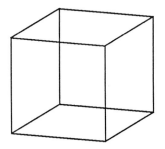

Figure 4.5   The Necker Cube

fairly clear in mind but be unable to loosen up and generate new ideas. With rigidity, immobility, and fixation comes the loss of magic or creativity. The task of the therapist is to help the client create new alternatives for being.

Using Microskills to Facilitate Creativity

Two of the most valuable tools for facilitating creativity are the basic listening sequence and the confrontation skills discussed in chapter 3. If you listen carefully to clients' confused thoughts and feelings and then summarize what they have said, you can often help them organize their thinking in useful new ways.

Calling clients' attention to discrepancies in nonverbal and verbal behaviors and statements can also aid in perturbing clients' cognitions and emotions. The dissonance this facilitative confrontation creates may propel clients toward new ways of being. An interpretation or reframe may produce similar effects.

Theoretical Orientation and Creativity

Of the various therapeutic orientations, psychoanalytic theory particularly allows room for the creative process by creative interpretations, dream analysis, linking present with past influences, and constructing new ways of thinking and feeling about issues. The ability to create new ways of thinking with clients is also important in cognitive-behavioral, existential-humanistic, and multicultural approaches.

Creativity involves trusting to intuition at times and practicing careful systematic thought at other times. As counselor and facilitator, you can do much to "prime the creative pump" to help your clients find new ways to think, feel, and behave. But new ways of thinking and behaving are relatively useless if the client is unable to take them out of the interview and use them in real life. Relapse prevention provides a method of transferring learning from the interview to real life.

Relapse Prevention

Relapse prevention (RP) is a set of cognitive-behavioral techniques and strategies developed by Marlatt and Gordon (1985) that have become foundational to counseling and therapy. It is an axiom of therapy that clients often will lose insights, behaviors, and new skills gained from therapy if the counselor does not take specific action to help clients maintain these gains.

In your one-hour session each week with your client, you may see some changes taking place. Then the client returns to the home environment and faces the same problems that led to therapy. For example, an alcohol abuser or a teenager suffering from bulimia must live with the same family and/or job circumstances that likely played an important part in generating the client's difficulties. Your task in relapse prevention is to work with clients to help them find workable strategies for the future.

Research on Relapse Prevention

General findings on relapse prevention show that single efforts at maintaining client behavior change are weaker than more broad-based comprehensive programs. The RP model is a comprehensive program based on Marlatt's work with alcohol addiction (Daley, 1989; Marlatt & Gordon, 1985) that was later extended to weight control (Rosenthal & Marx, 1979) and to the maintenance of skills training (Marx, 1982, 1984).

Research on relapse has shown that the initial lapse in treatment is particularly important in the likelihood of future and continued lapses. For example, in weight control therapy, the way the overeater handles the first failure to stay on the diet is highly predictive of what will happen in the future. Because skills developed in therapy have not yet been tested in real-life situations, we can expect relapse in nearly 100 percent of our clients in some form. Our task as therapists is to help our clients construct relapse prevention programs (generalization programs in the fifth stage of the interview) to ensure that newly learned behavior and insights are not lost shortly after the interview. Research in RP clearly indicates that a systematic program can help clients learn more from their therapy and training programs and maintain their behavioral change for a longer time.

Helping the Client Cope with the Environment

Environmental realities (family, job, the availability of cigarettes, drugs, and so on) often conspire to make long-term behavioral maintenance almost impossible. To combat the difficulties of the environment, Marx developed a four-point program to help clients become more prepared to manage the postcounseling environment.

1. *Anticipate difficult situations.* Clients can often predict the circumstances likely to be threatening to their resolve to maintain their behavioral change program. Clients, with the counselor's assistance, can identify high-risk situations that might sabotage new learning and serve as an early warning system so that they will be on guard against relapse.

2. *Regulate thoughts and feelings.* Emotions can sometimes get out of control

and make us feel incompetent, upset, or temporarily irrational. Relapses are less likely to occur if clients expect these temporary responses and then return to a rational approach and learn from their mistakes.

3. *Diagnose necessary support skills.* Although we may help clients change behavior, their old patterns may reemerge when they are in a hurry or when faced with other stressors. Techniques such as assertiveness training, time management, or key cognitive skills may be useful in helping clients avoid eventual relapse.

4. *Regulate consequences.* A key behavioral concern is to provide appropriate consequences for behavior. When a client maintains a new behavior, there will be no thunderous applause. That support must come from the client, who must learn how to create meaningful rewards for good actions and behavioral maintenance.

Making RP Work for You

Exhibit 4.1 summarizes the RP program in the form of an exercise you can use with a real or role-played client. Note that RP is skill specific. For example, a client may want to stop overeating. The task of the therapist is to help the client understand the several strategies that are available for controlling overeating. Once clients have learned the behavioral techniques to slow down the rate of eating (that is, eat only in specified places and times, monitor calories, understand how emotions affect eating, and eliminate discretionary eating), they are ready to begin preparing for the hurdles in the environment once counseling is over and they must manage on their own.

Adding Evaluation Research to RP

Setting goals with the client can help you integrate research planning in your interview. Many argue that such evaluation research should be part of every treatment plan. Exhibit 4.2 presents a goal-setting exercise you can use to integrate some basic elements of evaluation research and accountability into your own clinical and counseling practice.

Limitations and Practical Implications of Decisional Counseling

The limitations of the decisional model center around its historical basis in linear, cause-and-effect thinking. Not everyone makes decisions in a step-by-step fashion. The use of creativity concepts and the integrated life patterns model can loosen the sometimes overly tight constructs of the decisional model.

Cultural considerations are important and pose a serious potential limitation for the decisional model. As has been stressed throughout this chapter, individuals, families, and cultural groups may have widely varying decisional styles. At the same time, decisional counseling as presented here does attempt to consider the place of others

══════ **Exhibit 4.1** ══════

 Relapse Prevention Worksheet

Self-Management Strategies for Skill Retention

By Robert Marx

_____

(Go through this worksheet by yourself perhaps using one of the microskills of this text or a behavior you have difficulty in maintaining. Alternatively, use the form to go through the danger or relapse with a real or role-played client.)

I. Choosing an Appropriate Behavior to Retain

Describe in detail the behavior you intend to retain:

_____
_____
How often will you use it? _____
How will you know when a slip occurs? _____
_____

II. Relapse Prevention Strategies

A. Strategies to help you anticipate and monitor potential difficulties—regulating stimuli.

Strategy	Assessing Your Situation
1. Do you understand the relapse process? What is it?	_____ _____
2. What are the differences between learning the behavioral skill or thought and using it in a difficult situation?	_____ _____ _____
3. Support network? Who can help you maintain the skill?	_____ _____
4. High-risk situations? What kind of people, places, or things will make retention especially difficult?	_____ _____ _____ _____

B. Strategies to increase rational thinking—regulating thoughts and feelings.

5. What might be an unreasonable emotional response to a temporary slip or relapse?	_____ _____ _____

6. What can you do to think more effectively in tempting situations or after a
relapse?

_____

_____

_____

C. Strategies to diagnose and practice related support skills—regulating behaviors.

7. What additional support skills do you
need to retain the skill? Assertiveness?
Relaxation? Microskills?

_____

_____

_____

D. Strategies to provide appropriate outcomes for behavior—regulating consequences.

8. Can you identify some likely outcomes of your succeeding with your
new behavior?

9. How can you reward yourself for a
job well done? Generate specific rewards and satisfactions.

_____

_____

_____

_____

_____

_____

Predicting the Circumstance of the First Lapse

Describe the details of how the first lapse might occur, including people, places,
times, emotional states.

SOURCE: R. Marx, University of Massachusetts. Used by permission.

Exhibit 4.2

Single-Case Evaluation Research Exercise

Decisional therapists have a maxim: No counseling and therapy without follow-up research and evaluation. Decisional counselors believe that research and evaluation techniques need to be integrated into every counseling and therapy case, whether individual or family. The basic technique is to establish a clear goal for therapy and counseling with the assistance of the client and then to determine if the goal (or goals) has been achieved.

Your evaluative research task is to compare how the client is behaving, thinking, and feeling now and prior to counseling (time A) and to compare client status at the close of sessions (time B) and at a prearranged follow-up time of perhaps three to six months (time C).

For example, a client at time A may think that he or she is not getting along on the job, that coworkers are condescending. Client feelings about the situation are focused on anger. The only behavior and feelings available to the client at time A is anger, which is expressed by acting out through yelling.

At the close of counseling (time B), client and therapist might generate the goals of (1) having alternative behaviors to use when stressed on the job, (2) feeling more positive about the working situation, and (3) generating some positive interchanges with coworkers. If these three goals are achieved, counseling very likely has been effective. Hopefully, at follow-up time C, positive thoughts, feelings, and behavior will continue.

Decisional counseling recommends this, or a similar, evaluation research design for each of your clients. Apply these simple evaluation research concepts to your own behavior first using the following exercise: Select one of your own behaviors you would like to improve (perhaps procrastination, eating junk food, smoking, and so on). Having decided on a behavior, do as follows:

- Time A—Identify your thoughts, feelings, and behaviors. Make them as clear and specific as possible. Attempt to change these thoughts, feelings, and behaviors in your own way.
- Time B—At a later point, perhaps one week to one month, review where your thoughts, feelings, and behaviors are at this point.

- Time C—At a still later point in time, again review your thoughts, feelings, and behaviors.

You may find that reviewing and using the techniques of relapse prevention are helpful in this process. RP provides clarity and is especially important in helping maintain change at time C.

There are an immense array of possibilities for single-case evaluation research. In addition to the above suggestions, you can request another person to observe your target changes, ask your client to keep a journal, use weekly homework/relapse prevention exercises as an ongoing treatment/evaluative plan, assign a standardized test at various points in therapy, utilize personality tests, and more. At issue here is using simple single-case research techniques so that you can look at your own effectiveness as a counselor and therapist.

Over time, this single-case study design can be built into longer-term program evaluation. It is important to note that many crucial aspects of traditional research design, such as control groups, larger sample sizes, and your own involvement in the evaluation process, can cloud the meaning of findings and observations.

in the decisional process. Again, the ILP model is a good illustration of how decision making can be more relational and culturally sensitive.

The strengths of the systemic five-stage model are relatively obvious. Most clients can benefit from some variation of the decisional balance sheet. The decisional framework is considered by many to be an important part of the cognitive-behavioral tradition. However, the framework existed prior to cognitive-behavioral models of decision making and represents a theoretical structure in itself.

NOTE

1. Lanier (personal communication, Sangamon University, Springfield, IL, November 1991) comments that the word *problem* may be inappropriate for many clients. He finds that when many African-American youth are asked "What's your problem?" they often say that they don't have a "problem," but they do have "concerns." Lanier's point is well taken. Many clients will object to the "problem" language and orientation of our field. It seems important to use the language constructions of your client rather than impose the conventions of our textbooks.

REFERENCES

BRAMMER, L. (1990). *The helping relationship*. Englewood Cliffs, NJ: Prentice-Hall.

CARKHUFF, R. (1987). *The art of helping VI*. Amherst, MA: Human Resource Development Press.

CHARTRAND, J. (1991). The evolution of trait and factor career counseling: A person × environment fit approach. *Journal of Counseling and Development, 69,* 518–24.

CHEATHAM, H. (1990). Empowering Black families. In H. Cheatham & J. Stewart (Eds.), *Black families* (pp. 373–93). New Brunswick, NJ: Transaction Press.

DALEY, D. (Ed.). (1989). *Relapse: Conceptual, research, and clinical perspectives*. New York: Haworth.

D'ZURILLA, T. (1986). *Problem-solving therapy: A social competence approach to clinical intervention*. New York: Springer.

HANSEN, S. (1990, July). *Work and family roles: An integrated context for career planning*. Paper presented at the International Roundtable for the Advancement of Counseling, Helsinki, Finland.

HANSEN, S. (1991). Integrative life planning: Work, family, community. *Futurics, 15,* 80–86.

IVEY, A. (1988). *Intentional interviewing and counseling*. Pacific Grove, CA: Brooks/Cole.

IVEY, A., & MATTHEWS, W. (1984). A meta-model for structuring the clinical interview. *Journal of Counseling and Development, 63,* 237–43.

JANIS, I., & MANN, L. (1977). *Decision making: A psychological analysis of conflict, choice, and commitment*. New York: Free Press.

MANN, L., BESWICK, G., ALLOUACHE, P., & IVEY, M. (1982). *Decision workshops for the improvement of decision making skills*. Flinders University, Adelaide, South Australia.

MANN, L., BESWICK, G., ALLOUACHE, P., & IVEY, M. (1989). Decision workshops for the improvement of decision making: Skills and confidence. *Journal of Counseling and Development, 67,* 478–81.

MANN, L., HARMONI, R., & POWER, C. (1990). The gofer course in decision making. In J. Baron & R. Brown (Eds.), *Teaching decision making to adolescents*. New York: Erlbaum.

MARLATT, G., & GORDON, J. (1985). *Relapse prevention: Maintenance strategies in the treatment of addictive behaviors*. New York: Guilford.

MARX, R. (1982). Relapse prevention for managerial training: A model for maintenance of behavior change. *Academy of Management Review, 7,* 433–41.

MARX, R. (1984, August). *Self-control strategies in management training: Skill maintenance despite organizational realities*. Symposium chaired at the annual meeting of the American Psychological Association, Toronto, Canada.

NEECE, E., & HARRISON, B. (1990). *Career development services annual report: Career planning for the future*. Rochester, NY: Career Resource Center.

PARSONS, F. (1967). *Choosing a vocation*. New York: Agathon. (Original work published 1909)

PATERSON, D., & DARLEY, J. (1936). *Men, women, and jobs.* Minneapolis: University of Minnesota.

ROSENTHAL, B., & MARX, R. (1979, December). *A comparison of standard behavior and relapse prevention weight reduction programs.* Paper presented at the meeting of the Association for the Advancement of Behavior Therapy, San Francisco.

WILLIAMSON, E. (1939). *How to counsel students.* New York: McGraw-Hill.

Multicultural Counseling and Therapy: Changing the Foundations of the Field

Harold E. Cheatham, Allen E. Ivey,
Mary Bradford Ivey, Lynn Simek-Morgan

CHAPTER GOALS

This chapter seeks to help you:

1. Define multicultural counseling and therapy (MCT) from both a universal and culture-specific focused frame of reference.

2. Understand some basic constructs of the multicultural orientation, the distinctions between the Afrocentric and Eurocentric worldviews, and cultural identity theory.

3. Examine your own level of cultural identity development and awareness of cultural issues in the helping process.

4. Examine some concrete examples of practice in multicultural counseling and therapy. Special attention will be paid to MCT's contribution to an integrated practice of counseling and therapy. In addition, the network treatment, as set forth by Native American Carolyn Attneave, will receive special consideration.

The Multicultural Counseling and
Therapy Frame of Reference

Multicultural counseling and therapy (MCT)—referred to as the fourth force of counseling theory—starts with awareness of differences among clients and the importance of the effects of family and cultural factors on the way clients view the world. MCT challenges counselors and therapists to rethink the very meaning of our work.

Cheek (1976) was one of the first to note the multicultural limitations of traditional counseling and psychotherapy:

> I am advocating treating one segment of our population quite differently from another. This is implicit in my statement that Blacks do not benefit from many therapeutic approaches to which Whites respond. And I have referred to some of these approaches of counselors and therapists as "White techniques." (p. 23)

In the following years, attention to the need to generate culturally appropriate theory slowly increased. Cheatham (1990) comments first on the dangers of culturally insensitive therapy and then goes on to suggest fundamental changes needed for truly multicultural counseling and therapy:

> The helping professional doubtless will violate the Black client's sense of integrity or "world view." . . . Blacks are products of their distinct sociocultural and sociohistorical experience. Counseling and therapy are specific, contractual events and thus must proceed on the basis of understanding of the client's cultural context. (pp. 380–81)

Cheatham argues that the role of the therapist is not just to work with an individual, but also with the family *and* extended networks that may be important for the client. An African-American client who suffers from depression should not be treated just as an individual; the cultural context of racism that often contributes to such depression must also be addressed. White and Parham (1990) also agree that multicultural counseling and therapy will not be effective until counselors focus on and intervene in issues of racism, sexism, and oppressive societal elements.

Other researchers maintain that traditional therapy can be harmful for clients of other cultures. According to Sue (1992):

> Counseling has been used as an instrument of oppression as it has been designed to transmit a certain set of individualistic cultural values. Traditional counseling has *harmed* minorities and women. Counseling and therapy have been the handmaiden of the status quo and as such, represent a political statement. (p. 6)

Freire (1972) uses the term *conscientização,* meaning a consciousness of self in relation to contextual and cultural issues. *Conscientização* is focused on the liberation of the individual from personal, social, and economic oppression. Freire believes that such cultural awareness should be a general goal of education—and, by extension, of counseling and therapy as well. Many clients blame themselves for their condition. The counselor's task is to liberate these clients from self-blame, encourage them to see their issues in a social context, and facilitate personal action to improve their condition.

The MCT frame is concerned with counseling and psychotherapy as liberation — the viewing of self in relation to others and to social and cultural context. Interdependence is basic to philosophy and action in MCT. MCT advocates working *with* the individual and family in an egalitarian fashion. MCT further encourages client and therapist to cooperatively work together in the community and society to alleviate and prevent future concerns and problems.

The Multicultural Worldview

If we fail to understand the unique clients before us and their cultural surrounds, particularly as manifested in their families of origin, even the most well-intentioned counseling and therapy effort is likely to fail. Pedersen (1985) summarizes the issue:

> To some extent, all mental health counseling is multicultural. If we consider age, lifestyle, socioeconomic status, and gender differences, it quickly becomes apparent that there is a multicultural dimension in every counseling relationship. (p. 94)

Multicultural counseling and therapy starts with cultural awareness — *conscientização*. In client-centered, psychodynamic, or cognitive-behavioral theories, culture is often considered important but typically remains in the background. In MCT, culture takes the foreground. Freire (1972) points out that when people learn to discuss their issues in cultural context, they learn to balance what was previously seen as "their problem" with what may indeed be "society's problem" (p. 117).

Wrenn (1962, 1985) talks about the "culturally encapsulated counselor." As the women's movement has helped demonstrate, personal and individual issues are better understood in the context of an often sexist society. *Conscientização* is the process of learning a balance of individual and societal responsibility and acting on that knowledge. This chapter seeks to answer some of the important questions raised by multicultural theoreticians over the years. The fourth force — multicultural counseling and therapy — is likely to be critical in helping the entire field move out of encapsulation toward *conscientização*.

The Universal Approach to MCT

There are two distinct trends in the multicultural field: the *universal*, which states that every session contains multicultural issues, and the *focused*, which emphasizes the importance of culture-specific understanding.

Traditional counseling theory has been historically unaware of culture. There is a tendency for these theories to focus on values of individualism, rationalism, and self-determination. In research on counseling and therapy, the typical client is European-American, educated, middle-class, and female (even though theories were predominantly generated by European-American males[1]).

Client-centered, psychodynamic, and cognitive-behavioral theories all have tended to focus on the individual, giving minimal attention to contextual issues. The decisional counseling frame makes an effort to include environmental action, but remains focused primarily on individual issues.

Fukuyama (1990) argues for a transcultural, universal approach to MCT, maintaining that certain factors are important regardless of culture. The universal approach recommended by Fukuyama challenges all counselors and therapists to become aware of multicultural issues and to recall that all counseling and therapy is culturally based. Fukuyuama argues for a counseling curriculum that:

1. Defines culture broadly (including gender, affectional orientation, age, and so on, as well as ethnic/racial issues).
2. Teaches the danger of stereotyping.
3. Emphasizes the importance of language as the vehicle of counseling and therapy.
4. Encourages loyalty and pride in one's own culture and family ties.
5. Provides information on the processes of acculturation and oppression.
6. Discusses the importance of gender roles.
7. Facilitates each individual's identity development as a member of a culture.
8. Builds self-esteem and awareness.
9. Facilitates the understanding of one's own worldview and how it relates to family and cultural history.

The MCT universal approach requires that cultural issues are considered in each counseling contact. Rather than starting with the individual, it is important to start with the multicultural context and environment of each person. Treatment may require more than individual therapy, possibly involving a network of interventions and even community action. Fukuyama believes that the universal approach has the capacity to change the field in that it challenges the foundations of traditional counseling and therapy.

The Focused Culture-Specific Approach to MCT

Locke (1990) challenges the universal approach to MCT and advocates a more focused approach that would emphasize the specialness of critical cultural groups. He supports his case with an example from his personal experience. He was invited to teach a session on multicultural issues to a class studying special education. The students were told to read any article on a culturally different group before Locke arrived to make his presentation. As Locke relates the story:

> I went to the class and made a formal presentation about culturally different students focusing primarily on African-Americans. Finally, I asked the students about what they had read. To my chagrin I discovered that not one student in the class had selected an

article about African-American students or any other group likely to be in their special education classes. (p. 22)

Locke stresses that it is incumbent on you to gain cultural expertise on specific groups that you are likely to encounter in practice. If the multicultural approach becomes too general, specific cultural groups will suffer, and inefficient and oppressive methods of counseling and therapy will result. A strictly universal approach also can weaken and dilute efforts for change in the field. Given the history of racism in North America, Locke and many others argue that multicultural counseling needs to focus primarily on African-American, Asian-American, Latina/o, and Native American cultures.

Locke argues for what he terms a "focused approach" in which it is important "to see people *both* as individuals and members of a culturally different group" (p. 23). This approach obligates us to:

1. Examine our own racial beliefs and attitudes as they relate to culturally different individuals and groups;
2. Discuss racially relevant topics at an institutional level and be willing to work on issues of oppression beyond the individual and family session; and
3. View our clients both as individuals and members of groups.

The universal versus focused MCT debate is becoming increasingly heated. Some authorities feel that concerns of women, gays/lesbians, and other special populations are used to dilute what is the central issue in society—racism. On the other hand, those of a feminist, gay/lesbian, or religious orientation have criticized a multiculturalist approach that focuses primarily on racial/ethnic differences. Still others wish to avoid a multicultural orientation, arguing that "people are people" and that a discussion of cultural differences is irrelevant and unimportant.

Central Constructs of Multicultural Counseling and Therapy

Some key constructs of multicultural counseling and therapy are presented in this section. First, the field of multicultural counseling and therapy will be defined, followed by a review of key elements of Afrocentric theory and how this theory exemplifies some key issues of multicultural theory. The section concludes with a review of cultural identity development theory.

Definition and Assumptions of MCT

The position on MCT taken in this book represents a midpoint between the focused and universal orientations. If we define gender, age, physical issues, and other characteristics as dimensions of multiculturalism, all counseling and therapy includes multicultural issues, and thus the universal orientation has relevance. However, the focused position is more immediately practical, draws attention to underserved groups, and provides clearer guidelines for action.

Given this, multicultural counseling and therapy has the following defining characteristics:

1. MCT is *both* a general, or metatheoretical, orientation to all theories as well as a specific set of theories for practice.

2. All counseling and therapy theory is derived from a cultural base. Traditional theories discussed in this book, for the most part, have been predominantly generated by male European-North Americans. There is a need to reconsider each of these theories and examine each for possible contributions to a reconstructed broad metatheoretical multicultural theory of counseling and therapy.

3. The Black consciousness-raising movement of the 1960s established the base of multicultural helping by pointing out the importance of cultural awareness and respect for one's cultural group. This movement, in turn, influenced the growth of feminist, gay/lesbian, disabled, and other group awareness movements. At times, the African-American influence has been insufficiently recognized.

4. It is possible to develop new theories and methods of helping by starting from a cultural frame of reference. Examples of this are Afrocentric theory and feminist theory.

5. MCT operates on the assumption that a network of culturally appropriate interventions, including individual, family, group, and neighborhood, may be a necessary part of any treatment plan. These interventions must meet the needs of the specific group with which you are working.

The above list should be considered a beginning. The difficulty of balancing the broadly based universal view of MCT with the focused frame of reference should be clear. In the following section, the focus is on an African-American worldview. Nonetheless, the following discussion attempts to illustrate some broadly based universal issues of MCT.

The Afrocentric and the North American European Worldviews

The Afrocentric worldview proposes that African-American experience in the United States continues African history and culture. Years of slavery and racism have not dimmed the African intergenerational legacy of family relationship and group solidarity. Molefi Kete Asante's controversial and influential book, *The Afrocentric Idea* (1987), has brought this view to national prominence, and many other authors have also emphasized these ideas (for example, Blassingame, 1972; Gutman, 1976; and Myers, 1988).

Cheatham (1990) elaborates on the Afrocentric idea:

Unlike the Western philosophic system, the African tradition has no heavy emphasis on the individual; the individual's being is authenticated only in terms of others. Nobles writes that there is a sense of corporate responsibility and collective destiny as epitomized in the traditional African self-concept: "I am because we are; and because we are, there I am." (p. 375)

Synthesizing available sources, Cheatham argues that African philosophic linkages were retained even with transplantation to America, that the South's particular physical features facilitated retention of African ethos, and that rigidly enforced isolation of Blacks allowed (perhaps even required) retention of their orientation.

Contrasting the Afrocentric and Eurocentric Frameworks

The Afrocentric or African worldview is holistic, emotionally vital, interdependent, and oriented to collective survival. In addition, it emphasizes an oral tradition, uses a "being" time orientation, emphasizes harmonious blending and cooperation, and is highly respectful of the role of the elderly (White & Parham, 1990).

In contrast, the North American Eurocentric view tends to divide the world into discrete "knowable" parts, handles emotion somewhat carefully (even to the point of emotional repression), focuses on self-actualization and independence as a goal of life, emphasizes the clarity and precision of the written word, is oriented toward a linear "doing" view of time, stresses individuation and difference rather than collaboration, and places more value on youth than on age. In different ways, traditional counseling theories support this orientation.

The purpose here is not to point to either frame of reference or worldview as "right" or "wrong." Rather, each represents a way of constructing the world and making meaning. The point is that it can be harmful either to impose an Afrocentric frame on a Franco-American or to impose a Eurocentric frame on an African-American.

The Afrocentric Worldview and Other Cultures

The children of southern Italian, Chinese, Japanese, Puerto Rican, or Mexican origin often have a life orientation closer to that of the Afrocentric worldview than to the European-North American worldview. Sue and Sue (1990) provide an important summary of key issues in multicultural counseling and development. They point out that constructions of the world are very different among Asian, African-American, European-American, and Native American populations, and that issues of relationship are often more important in non-Eurocentric cultures. Although present counseling theory can help in the counseling of multicultural individuals, it will be most effective if the therapist is aware of some of the key aspects of the Afrocentric tradition.

Each individual who comes for help is likely to be some mixture of cultural frames of reference. For example, many African-Americans or Japanese-Americans have been influenced by North American culture and have incorporated Eurocentric values. *What is most important is to not expect your client to construct the individual or family in the same fashion you do.* What is pathological in your frame of reference may be highly functional and normal for your culturally different client. This holds true whether you are a Jewish-American, Italian-American, African-American, or Native American therapist.

Each individual is unique and special. One African-American client may be more like a farmer from Idaho than like his or her ethnically related brothers and sisters. Or a White Mormon client may have a more relational and family centered orientation than do some African-Americans. *Again, it is crucial to never stereotype your clients.* You must structure your interviews to learn from clients, or your "culturally aware" helping may be oppressive rather than facilitating.

Cultural Identity Development Theory

The issue of cultural identity is made more complex by the fact that the degree of clients' awareness of their cultural frame of reference varies. Cultural identity development theory identifies these levels of cultural awareness and stresses the importance of counselors and therapists recognizing clients' cultural identity or awareness level. It is considered helpful to match interviewing style to the level of client awareness. The most highly developed models of cultural identity have been generated by African-Americans (Cross, 1971, 1991; Helms, 1990; Jackson, 1975) and Asian-Americans (Sue & Sue, 1990). Myers and colleagues (1991) present a comprehensive universalist approach to these issues.

Jackson (1975, 1990; Jackson & Hardiman, 1983) has proposed a five-stage[2] developmental theory describing how cultural consciousness grows and changes for African-Americans. He suggests that diagnosis of consciousness level is essential if a counselor is to work effectively with any client, whether they are of similar race or not. What clearly is implied by Jackson's theory is that many non-Blacks likely will be ineffective in working with some African-Americans. Furthermore, African-American therapists can be expected to have some difficulties with African-American clients who have differing worldviews from their own.

The five stages of Black identity development are presented in exhibit 5.1. Note the *movement of consciousness,* from naive lack of awareness to action and awareness of self-in-relation to society. Jackson's model provides two key dimensions for working with the Black client. The first is to assess worldview and then match helping style to meet client special needs. The second is to understand the *evolution of consciousness*—the growing awareness of oneself in relationship to others and society. This second point will be stressed in more detail in the next section as a generic foundation of not only multicultural counseling and therapy but also of helping in general.

Jackson is quick to point out that each stage has a special value in personal development. He would argue that all but the first and second stages are valuable places for an African-American to spend her or his entire life. Even so, Jackson points out that for any individual subject to oppression, denial or acceptance at times may be

Exhibit 5.1

Jackson's Black Identity Development Theory

Stage 1. Naivete. The individual has no awareness of self as African-American. This is most clearly represented by children who do not distinguish skin color as an important feature. It can also be manifested by an individual who fails to see that on some specific issue, skin color is important. Jackson points out that many White individuals lack awareness that they are White and of the meaning this has in our society.

Stage 2. Acceptance. At this stage, the African-American individual thinks of him- or herself as non-White. Personal identity is defined by the "other." White may be construed as the correct way of being. The client at this stage is likely to be subservient and highly cooperative when working with a Eurocentric counselor. However, it is at this stage that referral to an African-American counselor may be most needed and useful. The stereotype of the Uncle Tom who pleases Whites is sometimes used to describe this now very rare form of Black consciousness. Acceptance can be passive or active.

Stage 3. Resistance and Naming. The African-American goes through a critical transformation and recognizes (names the fact) that being African-American is an identity in itself. The individual encounters Blackness and its full meaning in an often racist society. At this stage, some individuals experience much anger and may actively or passively refuse to work with a White European-North American counselor.

Stage 4. Redefinition and Reflection. The development of awareness of being an African-American continues. At stage 2, this awareness focused on separation of African-Americans from predominantly White society. Also at stage 2, personal identity is still formed by reaction against Whiteness rather than through a truly pro-African-American orientation. At stage 3, the Black individual may turn more fully away from White culture and become totally immersed in reflecting on African-American history and the Black community. At this point, European-American society is somewhat irrelevant. The developmental task is to establish a firm African-American consciousness in its own right.

Stage 5. Multiperspective Internalization. The individual becomes an African-American person with pride in self and awareness of others. This individual makes use of the important dimensions of all stages of development and thus recognizes and accepts the worthwhile dimensions of the predominant culture, fights those aspects that represent racism and oppression, and integrates all the stages in a transcendent consciousness. The individual is able to view the world through multiple frames of reference.

Entry, Adoption, and Exit Phases. Each of the five stages is further divided into entry, adoption, and exit phases. For example, stage 2 (resistance and naming) starts with a relatively unstable entry that then turns into full adoption of the ideas and beliefs around the stage. Later in stage 2, the individual begins to see the limitations of this type of consciousness and begins the exit process.

necessary for survival and sanity. The second level of consciousness is one of action, whereas the third is one of reflection.

Although there may be seeming advantages to the fifth level of consciousness, this level involves a multiperspectival division of consciousness that sometimes makes action in a racist society more difficult. Furthermore, this level of critical consciousness may be emotionally and cognitively exhausting at times.

Cultural Identity Issues and Developmental Task

Jackson emphasizes that Black identity development is task specific. Thus an individual may recycle to earlier stages of consciousness again and again as new issues are encountered. For example, African-Americans and other minorities often spend considerable time in therapy talking about how they have handled a particular incident of racism or oppression. These experiences often lead to a recycling of the anger associated with the resistance stage and the need for reflection before these individuals can integrate the experiences.

Table 5.1 presents Jackson's model as it relates to first women's and then Vietnam veterans' identity theory. It should be pointed out that survivors of trauma experiences, such as Vietnam veterans, comprise a special culture, and such individuals need highly sensitive treatment designed to their level of awareness.

Any individual we work with may have more than one set of multicultural issues. For example, suppose you are working with a Chinese-American nurse who suffered posttraumatic stress disorder from working in Vietnam. This woman not only has issues around posttraumatic stress disorder, but also will have been treated differently by the bureaucracy, colleagues, and others because she is a woman and a minority person. Her level of consciousness may be high in terms of her Asian-American identity, but she may also be at different levels on awareness of women's issues and the meaning of the Vietnam war.

Identity Development Theory for European-North American Counselors and Therapists

Ponterotto's (1988) model of identity development for White counselor trainees is similar to others described above, particularly that of Jackson. According to Ponterotto, the European-North American counselor trainee often works through the following stages when confronted with multicultural concerns:

Stage 1. Preexposure. The White counselor trainee has not thought about counseling and therapy as multicultural phenomena. He or she may say that "people are just people" and in counseling practice may engage in unconscious racism and sexism or, more positively, try to treat all clients the same.

Stage 2. Exposure. When multicultural issues are brought to his or her attention, the White therapist trainee (or experienced professional) learns about cul-

Table 5.1   Cultural Identity Developmental Theory Related to Women and Vietnam Veterans

Jackson's Stage of Development	Women's Developmental Identity Theory	Vietnam Veterans' Developmental Identity Theory
Naivete	Not aware of issues.	Not aware of issues.
Acceptance (passive and active)	Lacks awareness of system; "buys into" status quo.	Feels guilty and at fault for participation in war; frequent physical/emotional concerns.
Naming and resistance (passive and active)	Becomes aware of women's oppression; often becomes angry and takes action to produce change.	Becomes aware that he or she is not "at fault." May become angry at being a tool for the system. Becomes angry with governmental agencies and society in general for their lack of support and sensitivity.
Redefinition and reflection	Pride in being a woman; often separates from men to find self and self-in-relation to other women.	Generates increased pride for role in defending country. Often, with the help of other veterans, develops an understanding of self-in-relation to others and the war.
Multiperspective internalization	Views male/female relationships in cultural/historical perspective. Values aspects of maleness, sees men selectively. Able to accept parts of women's identity theory interchangeably and accept, act, and reflect as the situation warrants.	Multiperspective and sees war and participation in war as both individual and social phenomena. Able to accept the status quo at times; able to become angry and use action when appropriate. Can reflect on both self and situation from multiple perspectives.

tural differences and discrimination and oppression and realizes that previous educational experiences have been incomplete. The trainee at this stage may become perturbed and confused by the many apparent incongruities.

Stage 3. Zealotry or defensiveness. Faced with the challenge of multicultural issues, counselor trainees and professionals may move in one of two directions. Some become angry and active proponents of multiculturalism—even to the point of offending some of their colleagues. Others retreat into quiet defensiveness, taking criticisms of Eurocentric culture, "the system," and therapeutic theory personally. These individuals become passive recipients of information and "retreat back into the predictability of the White culture" (Helms, 1985, p. 156).

Stage 4. Integration. The counselor acquires a respect and awareness of cultural differences, understanding how personal family and cultural history might affect the interview and treatment plan. There is an acceptance that one cannot know all dimensions of multicultural counseling and therapy all at once, and plans are made for a lifetime of learning.

Although the above model was generated for White European-Americans, it also has implications for counselor and therapy trainees of other cultural backgrounds. For example, a Lakota Sioux counselor may be quite aware of his or her own cultural issues and those of midwestern European-Americans but may not have had contact with Mexican-Americans and African-Americans. This counselor will likely face issues of multicultural awareness regarding these groups as presented in Ponterotto's model. It is important to think about where you are in your cultural identity development as a counselor or therapist. Exhibit 5.2 provides an exercise that can facilitate your personal awareness of your cultural identity as a counselor and therapist.

The Multicultural Cube

Regardless of the problem the client presents, it is important to remain aware of specific multicultural issues that apply to clients and their level of awareness of these issues. *Many clients who seek counseling and therapy have suffered some personal insult around multicultural issues.*

Exhibit 5.2

Identifying Personal Cultural Identity

Following are some questions for you to consider as you think about the role of multicultural counseling and therapy in your own practice:

Ethnic/Racial Identity

1. From your personal ethnic/racial background, where are you in Jackson's five-stage model?
2. At earlier stages of your life, was your ethnic/racial identity different from what it is now? How did you think then? What led you to change?

Counselor/Therapist Identity and Multiculturalism

1. Trace your personal path in your counseling and therapy training program.
2. Identify dimensions of preexposure, exposure, zealotry, defensiveness, and integration in your way of being and thinking.

Locke's focused culture-specific orientation to MCT constantly reminds us that for African-American, Asian-American, Latina/o, and Native American clients, cultural oppression will likely play a role in whatever problem they present. Universal MCT theory holds that failing to recognize clients' cultural issues can be a serious problem in therapy.

From Fukuyama's universal frame of reference, the White male European-American is unlikely to suffer discrimination and personal injury for cultural reasons. This is not the case for White female European-Americans or for White male European-Americans who are of gay or bisexual orientation, for these individuals often encounter some sort of discrimination. It is well to remember, as those in the men's movement remind us, that European-American males do face many concerns and issues surrounding cultural demands and expectations (Osherton, 1986).

Figure 5.1 presents a cube model illustrating the various types of multicultural concerns clients can present in therapy. All clients are combinations of many multicultural issues, and differing ones may be prepotent at different times. A range of multicultural issues affecting the counseling relationship make up one side of the multicultural cube.

Along the left side of the cube is the locus of the issue. Although therapists traditionally tend to locate the concern in the individual, an individual issue may actually be derivative of the family, and the family issue may derive from problems in the group, community, state, or even country. This points to the need to engage in family therapy, group work, or even community and political action to promote change.

Clients also have differing levels of awareness of multicultural issues. Four stages of cultural identity are listed in the figure. Although Jackson's terminology has been adapted and used here, other models (such as those proposed by Atkinson, Morten, and Sue or Ponterotto) would also apply.

Consider, as an example, the following use of the multicultural cube: A Hawaiian-American may have a keen level 3 or 4 awareness of self as Hawaiian but a limited (stage 1 or 2) gender awareness. As a World War II veteran, this individual's awareness of personal trauma may range from very limited to full awareness. Each of these multicultural dimensions may be vitally important in establishing a working interview and treatment plan.

The same procedure would apply to a family or group, which could have multiple issues on multiple levels of awareness, thereby requiring a multifaceted treatment approach.

The multicultural cube can also be viewed over linear time. Thus a client, family, group, or even community might change in awareness of issues over the time of counseling and therapy or a group/community intervention.

Although most of the multicultural issues listed in figure 5.1 should be self-evident, further elaboration on some issues is provided in the following subsections.

Language and Translation Issues

Language is one of the most powerful, yet most often ignored, multicultural issues. Good language skills are usually essential for social and economic success. Thus cli-

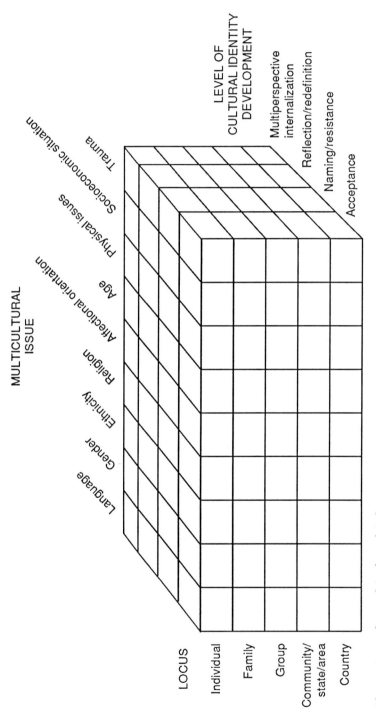

Figure 5.1   The Multicultural Cube

ents who are not yet fully proficient in English may be seen by some as "disadvantaged." Consider, instead, the alternative view that clients who have English as their second language should be viewed as intellectually advantaged—that is, if you cannot talk to your clients in their natural language, you are the one lacking in skills.

If you must talk to clients in a language with which they are less familiar, it is important that they be encouraged to discuss particularly important issues and feelings in their own language, even though you may not understand them. After they have expressed their ideas, they then may translate for you. Clients come closer to their deeper experiences when expressing themselves in their own language.

Nowhere does language become more of an issue than when counselors and therapists work with translators. Marcos (1979, p. 173) offers the following example, in which interpreter-to-patient and patient responses are translated back into English:

> *Clinician to Chinese-speaking patient:*   What kinds of moods have you been in recently?
>
> *Interpreter to patient:*   How have you been feeling?
>
> *Patient's response:*   No, I don't have any more pain, my stomach is fine, and I can eat much better since I take the medication.
>
> *Interpreter to clinician:*   He says that he feels fine, no problem. . . .
>
> *Clinician to patient:*   What about worries, do you have many worries?
>
> *Interpreter to patient:*   Is there anything that bothers you?
>
> *Patient's response:*   I know, I know that God is with me. I'm not afraid, they cannot get me. (pause) I'm wearing these new pants and I feel protected. I feel good. I don't get headaches anymore.
>
> *Interpreter to clinician:*   He says that he is not afraid, he feels good, he doesn't have headaches anymore.

Obviously, effective practice with non-English-speaking clients is greatly enhanced by counselor facility in language issues.

Age

Children are perhaps the most oppressed of all groups. They are treated as property and have limited legal rights. In addition, they frequently suffer emotional and physical abuse and neglect. Although each age group has its special issues and concerns, children and the elderly are separate cultural groupings, each with their own separate issues.

Socioeconomic and Class Differences

These are the least-discussed multicultural issues. Economic deprivation, the absence of adequate health care, and discrimination are only some of the issues faced by those of less advantaged status. Ortiz (1978) quotes Domitila, a woman of the Bolivian mines who attended a conference on women's issues, as she addresses a wealthy woman at the conference:

Señora, I've known you for a week. Every morning you show up in a different outfit and on the other hand, I don't. Every day you show up all made up and combed like someone who has time to spend in an elegant beauty parlor and who can spend money on that, and yet I don't. . . . I'm sure you live in a really elegant home, in an elegant neighborhood, no? And yet we miners' wives only have a small house on loan to us, and when our husbands die or get sick or are fired from the company, we have ninety days to leave the house and then we're in the street. Now señora, tell me: is your situation at all similar to mine? Is my situation at all similar to yours? . . . We can't, at this moment, be equal, even as women. (pp. 202–3)

Trauma

As a distinct culture, trauma has tended to be ignored. Rape and sexual exploitation traumatize a large number of women each year. Gavey (1991) cites data indicating that 24 percent of San Francisco women and 27.5 percent of U.S. college students have experienced rape. A large number of Vietnam veterans suffer from posttraumatic stress disorder. Those who find themselves HIV infected and face the ordeal of AIDS experience initial and continuing trauma.

Brassard, Germain, and Hart (1987) document that there were over 1.7 million cases of *reported* child maltreatment in 1984, suggesting that actual abuse and neglect may be much more extensive. Many of these children live in alcoholic homes in which spousal abuse is common. In one study, nineteen of twenty diagnosed female borderline clients had been subjected to sexual abuse (Flaherty, 1989). A study of clinically depressed inpatients revealed that seventeen of twenty had clear histories of trauma or abuse (Rigazio-DiGilio, 1989).

If all the above groups are accepted as separate cultures, it is clear that every session we have with clients will be a multicultural encounter. However, the warning of both Fukuyama (1990) and Locke (1990) must always remain before us: *If we define culture too broadly, we may miss significant issues.* Cultural expertise demands continuing and expanding awareness, knowledge, and skills for culture-specific counseling and therapy.

The Practice of Multicultural Counseling and Therapy

In 1972, Bailey Jackson and the first author of this book conducted a workshop on listening skills and multicultural issues at a predominantly Black college in the state of Georgia. During a lunch break, we visited the campus bookstore and examined the counseling texts in use. *Not one textbook focused on the African-American experience nor did they contain any information on multicultural issues.*

In 1992, the situation has improved, but what exists now still can best be considered but a promising beginning. There is as yet no comprehensive framework for a universal approach to counseling and therapy such as that suggested by Fukuyama (1990). What does exist is an increasingly specific array of focused approaches to counseling and therapy that we can call the "evolving multicultural tradition." Some broad conceptual frames that may eventually represent the context of a universal approach to MCT may be found in Baruth and Manning (1991), Cheatham and Stewart (1990), White and Parham (1990, 1991), Pedersen, Draguns, Lonner, and Trimble (1989), Sue (1990), and Sue and Sue (1990).

This section presents four issues important in concretizing MCT theory into clinical practice: internal and external locus of responsibility, feminist counseling, *conscientização* as an organizing framework for counseling and therapy, and the network treatment conceptions of the Native American therapist Carolyn Attneave.

Internal and External Locus of Responsibility and Cultural Identity

Sue and Sue (1990) give special attention to internal and external locus of responsibility. Does the client attribute his or her problem or concern to the "individual" or to "society" and the environment? Research clearly indicates that many ethnic minority and female clients attribute their difficulties externally; they are keenly aware of problems that society creates for them. Exhibit 5.3 presents a survey of two decades of research findings on psychotherapeutic services for ethnic minorities.

The concept of focus (chapter 3) as a microskill is helpful in understanding and dealing with the issue of locus of responsibility. For example, Berman (1979) asked Black and White counselor trainees viewing video examples of client concerns to indicate what they would say next to the client. White males tended to ask questions; White females, to reflect feelings and paraphrase; and African-Americans, to give advice and directions.

Berman found that African-Americans identified the problem as being in society rather than in the individual, whereas Whites attributed the problem to the individual. Each tended to use the microskill of focusing differently. Whites tended to focus on individuals, whereas African-Americans focused on the cultural-environmental context. Atkinson, Marujama, and Matsui (1978) replicated these findings with Asian clients.

Sue and Sue (1990) make a simple point, the importance of which cannot be overstressed. In traditional counseling theory, we learn to make "I" statements and help the client focus on what the individual person can do to change the situation. But if a client is suffering from external oppression, using the word *I* and focusing on the individual continues the oppression. The woman suffering from sexism, the Navajo suffering from a poor educational system, and the Vietnam veteran need more than an "I"-focused approach.

In the interview you can show your understanding of the client's situation by balancing the focus between the situation and the individual. Since much counseling training focuses on individual work, you may find this change initially stressful. But, as you develop increasing awareness and skill, you will find that just working at the individual level is limiting. Considering family, environment, and multicultural issues will enrich your practice.

Exhibit 5.3

Research Survey on Psychotherapeutic Services for Ethnic Minorities

In his review of the literature on helping services for ethnic minorities, Sue (1988) found that services for minorities are frequently considered ineffective. His summary of the multiple studies on this topic follows:

1. *There are important differences in conceptualization of psychological issues.* Many minority groups conceptualize psychological difficulties as organic in nature, feeling that "mental health is enhanced by will power and the avoidance of morbid thinking" (p. 302). Thus it seems likely an understanding of cultural differences is important for counseling and therapy.

2. *Majority counselors often have negative stereotypes of the ethnically different.* "These stereotypes tend to reflect the nature of race or ethnic relations in our society" (p. 302). The Afrocentric and Eurocentric worldviews illustrate how very differently reality is viewed by these two groups. If we consider these differences as constructions rather than labeling one view "correct" compared to the other, we will have an important beginning toward multicultural understanding.

3. *Despite these considerations, there is some evidence that minority clients do benefit from therapy, even with European-American helpers.* Sue cites the work of Jones (1978, 1985)

and others to support this encouraging finding.

African-American clients were likely to discuss issues surrounding race during the therapy process. Griffith and Jones (1978) comment: "Unquestionably, race makes a difference in psychotherapy. Still, this is not to say that the skillful and experienced White therapist cannot effectively treat the Black client. Rather the critical requisite is that the White therapist is sensitive to the unique ways in which . . . race affects the course of treatment" (p. 230).

4. *The degree of acculturation is important in client-therapist matching.* Sue (1988) presents extensive research that reveals that many minority group members prefer a counselor of their racial/ethnic background. Clearly, some minorities will not be willing to consult with majority counselors. However, data also exist that a highly acculturated minority counselor may be ineffective with a less acculturated client of the same race or ethnic group.

Cultural identity theory may help explain these seemingly contradictory findings. If clients are matched with therapists who have similar cultural awareness (and the therapists are competent), a good result may be expected. A sensitive, European-American therapist may be equally effective *if the cli-*

ent is at a level of cultural identity development that makes seeing a White counselor a viable alternative. As Sue (1988) summarizes the point: "Ethnicity is important, but what is more important is its meaning" (p. 307).

Internal and External Locus of Control in Clinical Settings

Focusing on external versus internal attribution can create difficulties for students in practicum and internship settings. Counselor and therapist trainees who focus on external issues may help their clients find housing or deal with finance companies and state agencies. Such actions may come under fire from internally oriented supervisors of these programs. Ivey (1992) documents several cases in which doctoral and master's practicum/internship candidates have suffered severe pressure to forgo an external focus with clients.

Traditionally trained agency workers and therapist supervisors often feel that trainees can develop serious "countertransferential" problems if they focus on external issues. Existential-humanistic and psychodynamic theories, in particular, have historically emphasized the importance of the individual while simultaneously devaluing contextual issues. Thus supervisors often discourage student therapists from pursuing multicultural issues involving a focus beyond the individual. An effort in this book is made to balance the sometimes overly individualistic orientation of the field.

Feminist Therapy

According to Ballou and Gabalac (1984):

> Feminist therapy holds that traditional systems of psychotherapy are in serious error which stems from traditional sexist assumptions about women. Therefore, research paradigms, personality theory, clinical practices . . . are all suspect. . . . The feminist orientation to therapy is eclectic, endorsing theoretical positions which postulate external factors as causative in the client's problems. . . . The client's strengths rather than her weaknesses are emphasized. . . . An egalitarian relationship between therapist and client is demanded by feminist therapy.

The *self-in-relation* (Miller, 1991) is a particularly important construct to consider in the counseling and therapy of women. Miller conceptualizes relationship as understanding and being understood by another. The self does not exist except in relationship. It could be said that a woman's sense of self is constructed in a relationship between the individual and the other. A self is articulated through relationships with others and exists only in a web of relationships. According to Miller, the patriarchal world often incorrectly considers a woman's way of being as less than complete.

Kaplan (1984) builds on the notions of Miller, pointing out that women experience a sense of loss due to their relational orientation and that they are denied the opportunity to express anger and aggression, with a consequent loss of self-esteem. As a result, women suffer more from clinical depression than do men.

Miller reminds us that the self-in-relation requires another person for fulfillment. Moving from dependency to independence sounds, at first glance, like a positive move. However, *interdependence* is likely a more appropriate goal for the helping process. There exist some parallels between this line of thinking and the Afrocentric frame of reference presented earlier in this chapter.

Major Themes

Ballou and Gabalac (1984) have summarized the major content areas of feminist therapy, which are also important to multicultural counseling and therapy, as follows:

1. *Egalitarian relationship.* The feminist therapist considers herself a partner with the client and values women and their need for mutual support and exploration. Self-disclosure of one's own personal experiences as a woman is a particularly important part of the therapeutic process.

2. *Use of community resources.* Therapy does not end with the completion of the interview. Many clients are referred to women's support groups, community action work, legal aid, and other relevant community services.

3. *An active, participatory counseling style.* The feminist therapist works with a conflicted client to understand her emotions but also confronts the client with the need for growth and resolution. Although the therapist may be warm and supportive, she gradually moves the client toward independent thought. The therapist is likely to use most of the techniques discussed in this book (such as assertiveness training, Frankl's dereflection, dream analysis, and so forth) but does so with an awareness of the feminist context of the helping process.

4. *Information giving.* A strong educational component exists in feminist counseling. The client may be instructed in social/historical facts concerning sexism and the impact of cultural conditioning. Sex-role analysis (Carter & Rawlins, 1977) may be used to help clients understand how they have become culturally conditioned to respond in certain ways.

5. *Personal validation.* Many women come from oppressed situations in which they have little or no awareness of their own inherent personal worth. Feminist therapy seeks to validate the individual as a unique and valuable person.

6. *Use of traditional theories with awareness of their multicultural implications.* Brown and Ballou (1992) bring together a highly useful feminist critique of traditional counseling and therapy theory and of personality development and show how to use and shape traditional theories in a fashion that is more gender and culturally sensitive.

A particular value conflict within feminist theory focuses on the issue of when and how women should be confronted with issues of sexism. Clearly, a fragile individual at stage 1 of feminist cultural identity could be overwhelmed and disturbed if suddenly confronted with the social facts of her life. Marriages can be destroyed by the anger that is often released as a client moves from lower to higher levels of feminist identity. Given the egalitarian orientation, most feminist theorists would generally support providing the stage 1 client with some information and then letting her make the choice as to whether or not to continue exploration of issues.

Although feminist theorists may differ on specific social issues, all would agree that helping clients understand how gender issues relate to individual concerns is a vital part of counseling and therapy.

In summary, feminist therapists would hold that it is not sufficient to help a woman work through a depressive episode. It is critical to help this woman develop consciousness of how society's expectations of her gender relate to her depression. Does responsibility for change exist in the individual or society? Feminist therapy would suggest that each client needs to achieve a balance of self and environment.

Conscientização and the Liberation of Consciousness

As discussed earlier, the concept of *conscientização* focuses on liberating clients from self-blame and helping them see themselves in relationship to others and to their culture. The goal of *conscientização* is critical consciousness. The client experiences self, perhaps for the first time, and then begins to see how self was constructed in a sociocultural relationship. Paulo Freire's seminal *Pedagogy of the Oppressed* (1972), when combined with cultural identity theory (Jackson, 1975, 1990),[3] provides a concrete and highly specific set of goals and practices useful for MCT as well as for therapy in general in designing and assessing the effectiveness of helping interventions.

As discussed in chapter 2, empathy is the foundation for all effective interventions. The three aspects of counselor empathy—empathy with the individual, empathy with how that individual developed in the family of origin, and empathy with the cultural background of the family—are vital to maintain in the helping interview. Your empathic understanding will enable clients to see themselves in their cultural context and free themselves from self-blame.

Conscientização can be considered a metagoal of therapy. Specifically, MCT seeks to enable clients to see themselves and their development in a cultural context. This is illustrated by Rivera-Arzola (1991), who studied low-income Puerto Rican women suffering from *ataques de nervios* (fainting spells) common in that cultural context.[4] She found that the more poverty and abusive trauma that low-income women experienced, the more likely they were to suffer these spells. Rivera-Arzola's findings suggest that responsibility for the problem of *ataques de nervios* is not "in the client" but rather in the client's response to multiple societal oppression—sexism, racism, economic deprivation. The *ataques de nervios* are actually an understandable response to an impossible situation.

Conscientização: A Case Example of MCT Practice

This section presents an example of how multicultural counseling and therapy might use cultural identity development theory to facilitate *conscientização* and the generation of critical consciousness.

You are working with a low-income Puerto Rican woman who suffers from *ataques de nervios*. She is a single parent, twenty-five years of age with two children. She has been sterilized, with only minimal information given to her before she gave consent, and she has suffered physical abuse both as a child and in more recent relationships. Using Jackson's stages as a basis, an eight-stage model of cultural identity can be developed with this client, as follows:

1. *Acceptance — diagnostic signs.* The client enters counseling hesitatingly; her *ataques de nervios* have been increasing in frequency. A physician has referred the client to you believing that the fainting spells are psychological in origin, as no physical basis can be found. As you talk with the client, you discover that she blames herself for the failures in her life. She comments that she is "always choosing the wrong man," and she states she should have been sterilized sooner so that she would have had fewer children.

2. *Acceptance — interventions to help and to produce dissonance.* Your intervention at this stage is to listen, but following Freire (1972), you seek to help her codify or make sense of her present experience. You use guided imagery as you help her review critical life events — the scenes around sterilization, the difficulties of economic survival when surrounded by others who have wealth, and discrimination against Puerto Ricans in nearby factories. Through listening and perturbing with dissonant images, you move the client toward a more critical consciousness. But at the same time, your client needs practical help. You help her obtain sufficient food and shelter and find a job. You may teach her basic stress management and relaxation, but most important, you listen to and learn from her.

3. *Naming and resistance — diagnostic signs.* At this point, your client becomes very angry when she sees that the responsibility, or "fault," she believed was hers lies almost totally with her oppressive environment. Her eyes flash as she talks about "them." She experiences an emotional release as she realizes that the decision for sterilization was not truly hers but was imposed by an authoritarian physician. She seems likely to seek to strike back wherever possible against those she feels have oppressed her. In the early stages of naming, she fails to separate people who have truly victimized her from those who have "merely" stood by and said nothing.[5]

4. *Naming and resistance — interventions to help and to produce dissonance.* Early in this stage, you do a lot of listening. You find it helpful to teach the client culturally appropriate assertiveness training and anger management. There is a delayed anger reaction to traditional sex roles. Although she may profit from reality therapy, you know you must tailor the therapy to her relational Puerto Rican

heritage. You support constructive action on her part to change oppressive situations. Later in this stage, you help her see that much of her consciousness and being depends on her *opposition* to the status quo and that she has given little attention to her own real needs and wishes.

5. *Reflection and redefinition — diagnostic signs.* It is tiring to spend all one's emotional energy in total anger toward society and others. Consciousness-raising theorists note that at this stage, clients often retreat to their own gender and/or cultural community to reflect on what has happened to them and to others. Responsibility becomes more internal in nature, but there remains a keen awareness of external issues. At this stage, your client is less interested in action and more interested in understanding self and culture. She shows a great interest in understanding and appreciating her Puerto Rican heritage and how it plays itself out in North America.

6. *Reflection and redefinition — interventions to help and to produce dissonance.* At this stage, you teach your client cultural identity development theory, which can be useful because it helps explain issues of development in culture. Culturally appropriate theories, such as those of Nwachuku (see chapter 3) or feminist theory, may be especially helpful, although they are not useful at all consciousness levels. Cognitive-behavioral, psychodynamic, and person-centered theories can be used if adapted to the culture and needs of the person.

7. *Multiperspective integration — diagnostic signs.* Your client draws from all previous stages as appropriate to her situation. At times, she accepts situations; at other times, she is appropriately aggressive and angry, later withdrawing to reflect on herself and her relationships to others and society. She is aware of how her physical symptoms — her *ataques de nervios* — were a logical result of the oppression of women in her culture. She is able to balance responsibility between herself and society. At the same time, she does not see her level of *conscientização* as "higher" than others. She respects alternative frames of reference.

8. *Multiperspective integration — interventions to help and to produce dissonance.* You ask your client to join with you and your group to attack some of the issues that "cause" emotional, personal, and financial difficulty. Your client establishes a family planning clinic that provides accurate information on the long-term effects of sterilization, and she lobbies to establish a day-care center. She is clearly aware of how her difficulties developed in a system of relationships, and she balances internal and external responsibility for action. In terms of introducing dissonance, you see your task as helping your client to manage time and stress and to balance the many possible actions she encounters. You also arrange to see that she has accurate feedback from others about her own life and work.

Summary

MCT, as presented in the foregoing case example, provides specific actions that can lead to clients' critical consciousness and *conscientização*. The eight-stage model can be used with many clients—a middle-class woman, a gay male, or any of a variety of culturally distinct clients. Particularly relevant for broader practice of counseling and therapy is Pfefferle's (1989) developmental concepts of long-term psychological problems. She states that depressed clients typically see themselves as responsible for their problems in the early stages and only gradually move to awareness that depression was generated in a systemic context. Rigazio-DiGilio (1989) and Rigazio-DiGilio and Ivey (1990) found that systematic questioning of depressed clients moved them toward critical consciousness. In this new state of awareness, clients were able to balance responsibility for self and others in a more constructive fashion.

MCT and *conscientização* seem to offer an important direction for the future—a future in which clients are far better able to see themselves in relation to their families and to cultural influences on their development.

Network Therapy

From a multicultural therapeutic orientation, there is something paradoxical about working with the individual alone when that person comes from a relational culture. Carolyn Attneave originated network therapy as a way to integrate Native American conceptions of relationship and community with family therapy (Attneave, 1969, 1982; Speck & Attneave, 1973).

Attneave was not satisfied to limit her interventions to the individual. For example, if the presenting problem was alcoholism, Attneave brought the individual together with the family and community network, which included the nuclear family, the extended family, important neighbors, and key figures from the community such as the priest, the teacher, the police, and perhaps even the local bartender. These group meetings generated a network of helpers who were aware of the individual alcoholic's problem. Alcoholism is often a hidden behavior, and family and community members often remain silent, even if they suspect the problem. Attneave's network approach brings group awareness and help for the individual's issues.

Attneave's community interventions inevitably changed the way the community thought about themselves and their relationships. For example, the bar owner could not sell drinks to the alcoholic without awareness that the priest or a neighbor might observe this and inquire. The teacher, now aware of the family difficulty, could not simply dismiss the acting-out child. The police would be more aware of their responsibility as community support agents and might be motivated to work more closely with the community.

Network therapy addresses the individual and the family, but it also relates the community and the environment. Underlying the network approach are Native American conceptions of interdependence as the basis of therapy, as contrasted with the independent orientation. La Fromboise and Low (1989) explain the Native American traditions underlying network therapy:

> Traditionally, Indian people live in relational networks that serve to support and nurture strong bonds of mutual assistance and affection. Many tribes still engage in a traditional system of collective interdependence, with family members responsible not only to one

another but also to the clan and tribe to which they belong. The Lakota Sioux use the term *tiospaye* to describe a traditional, community way of life in which an individual's well-being remains the responsibility of the extended family. . . . When problems arise among Indian youth, they become problems of the community as well. The family, kin, and friends join together to observe the youth's behavior, draw the youth out of isolation, and integrate that person back into the activities of the group. (p. 121)

Like Afrocentric and feminist orientations, the network approach stresses the importance of interdependence and self-in-relation (Cheatham & Stewart, 1990). This multilevel intervention approach to change has been applied to the treatment of child abuse by Ivey and Ivey (1990). Individually focused counseling and therapy interventions tend to be ineffective, especially when working with children, and a network approach can make a difference. Although it is not always possible to bring together a full network, several types of intervention with children can be used to produce change, as explored in exhibit 5.4.

Exhibit 5.4

 Adaptations of Network Intervention Treatment with Children

Multilevel network interventions may make a difference in the life of a child, adolescent, or adult. The following specific interventions have been combined in an overall treatment plan.

1. *Individual therapy.* Individual sessions allow children to tell and/or enact their stories. Interviews are conducted with an awareness of self-in-relation to others, family, and culture.

2. *Small group work.* Friendship, social skills, and sharing groups can be useful for children, such as groups of children who all experience alcoholism in the home or self-esteem groups focused on the values of varying cultural groups.

3. *Classroom observation and teacher consultation.* Children spend much of their day in the classroom. Unless behavioral programs and teacher support are provided, the results of small group work and individual therapy will be lost. Classroom instruction is often European-American in orientation. A vital helping intervention may be to change the curriculum to a more balanced, culturally sensitive approach.

4. *Educational support team.* Children in counseling often also have academic difficulties. Many schools now have special education and treatment teams available to support the overall treatment plan for the child. Special education efforts, of course, need to be undertaken in concert with family and cultural expectations.

5. *Family therapy and counseling.* If a child has difficulties, the family often

has multigenerational difficulties as well. For example, in a case of child abuse, members of the abusing family may themselves have been abused in their own family of origin.

6. *State and government intervention.* It is legally mandated that state agencies must be involved with abused children and their families. At times, economic support may be required, as financial issues often bring about abuse in the family.

7. *Community/multicultural intervention.* Some children need mentors or older friends from the community to give them attention that has been unavailable at home. In addition, the family may be refugees, and children may have suffered multiple traumas before entering the school situation. In addition, they may face

discrimination and prejudice in the community. In such cases, action to institute better housing options and to change community attitudes may be necessary.

8. *Large group/network meetings.* In some cases, it is possible to assemble network meetings of many individuals in the community. In these sessions, the approach is very similar to that endorsed by Attneave in that a general "community plan" is agreed to by participants. When it is not feasible for the full network to meet, bringing together the extended family, the employer, a religious figure, and perhaps some key friends and neighbors can be a powerful supplement to individual and group work.

For those of us oriented toward individual intervention, Attneave's network therapy approach seems almost overwhelming. However, with children and many adult clients, taking the time to establish multiple levels of intervention early will be more efficient than long-term one-on-one or family work. It is crucial that the key interventions discussed in exhibit 5.4 be in place and coordinated; otherwise change will occur more slowly.

Where to Start with Network Therapy

When you work with a European-American child, it is likely that you can start network therapy with the individual and the family, later expanding to larger networks. However, if you are working with a Laotian or Cambodian child, for example, you may want to start by going into the community and learning about the customs of the group. You may find that developing an understanding relationship with a Buddhist monk is more important in helping you understand how to help the child solve problems than doing play therapy.

Similarly, with African-American clients, there will likely be some measure of distrust if you are of a different cultural group (Solomon, 1990; White & Parham, 1990). Working in the community to combat racism may be a step you can take that will aid you in developing a meaningful counseling relationship with a child or adolescent. Cooperation is often best developed by framing your intervention in terms of a "we" egalitarian relationship with the African-American client or family.

The following guidelines can be helpful when using the network approach:

1. *Don't expect to do it all by yourself.* As a counselor or therapist, you cannot personally be expected to do all that is involved in the network approach on your own. Network therapy relies on a treatment team working together. Case management skills and the ability to work with organizations can be as important as your individual helping skills.

2. *Use multiple theoretical approaches.* Also implied in the network approach is that different theories may be useful at different times with different clients. At one time a child may need art therapy to work out certain issues, play therapy at another, and traditional talk therapy at still another. Surprisingly, most adult therapy techniques work well with children if you use appropriate language.

3. *Consider the value of network treatment for all clients.* If you work with a traumatized individual, you can expect that the family is also traumatized in some way. In addition, anticipate that the extended family as well as the neighborhood and community are influenced as well by your client. Network therapy has value for adult European-American clients just as it does for Native American and other groups.

Limitations and Practical Implications of Multicultural Counseling and Therapy

The most important implication of MCT is that it now stands as a distinct and building theoretical orientation in itself, with as much or more potential than the traditional therapies. The concepts of cultural identity theory suggest that many of our present systems of therapy are incomplete and perhaps more limited than we would like to admit.

MCT is a highly diverse approach to the field, and no fully clear direction can be defined at this time. Whereas it once appeared that MCT was in opposition to traditional theory, it now seems that we can begin to build bridges to connect with therapeutic tradition. Multicultural issues act to challenge and change traditional theory and practice. MCT, in turn, can draw on many ideas from existing theory.

Perhaps the major limitation of this newest approach to therapy is that it challenges so much of what we find in traditional approaches to helping. MCT concepts will be particularly difficult to assimilate for established professionals, who already have concepts and methods that "work." MCT suggests that sometimes what "works" actually may be harmful for some clients.

There is a danger that these new theories will be forcefully imposed by overly convinced and visionary practitioners on unsuspecting clients. Yet the very nature of these theories suggests that forcefulness is alien to the goals and purposes of the orientation. As a newly developing orientation, MCT will continue to be defined by further theory, research, and practice, and its contributions will become increasingly important over time.

NOTES

1. Grosskurth (1991) states that many ideas generated by women have been incorporated by men. In the psychoanalytic field, for example, the ideas of Melanie Klein, Helene Deutsch, Anna Freud, and Karen Horney preceded the constructs of D. W. Winnicott, Otto Kernberg, and Heinz Kohut.

In the same vein, Parham (1990) points out that African-American scholars generated many concepts of multicultural counseling but were ignored until White males started presenting similar ideas, often without recognizing African-American contributions.

2. Jackson's theory has been selected for presentation here as it was the source of inspiration for the first model of White identity development (Hardiman, 1982) and a variety of other models, including the long-term mentally ill (Pfefferle, 1989). In addition, the Jackson model was important in the construction of the developmental counseling and therapy paradigm (Ivey, 1986), as presented in the following chapter.

Other stage theorists in identity development often list five or even six stages. Stage 1 is often followed by a time in which the individual becomes aware of the inadequacies of this first level. This is termed a stage of dissonance by Atkinson, Morten, and Sue (1989) and Myers et al. (1991). This concept of dissonance is helpful, as it is this very perturbation and confrontation in the inadequacies of thinking at stage 1 that lead to the transformation in stage 2, as Jackson defines it. Jackson, however, points out that each of the following stages includes awareness of dissonance as the individual matures at that stage. Personal awareness of the inadequacies of each stage leads the individual to be able to move to the next. As such, Jackson's theory would allow room at the end of each stage for dissonance, in effect laying the groundwork for an eight-level model.

3. Following from Jackson, the authors believe that each cognitive-developmental stage has useful qualities, but also that some produce dissonance and the desire to move onward to more complete development of consciousness.

4. Many other cultures manifest variations of *ataques de nervios*. *Susto* in Guatemala and *espanto* in Mexico closely parallel the Puerto Rican syndrome. Variations of the fainting spells exist in India, Newfoundland, eastern Kentucky, and many other settings (Rivera, 1991).

5. "Not to decide is to decide." This was a popular poster of the 1960s attributed to the theologian Harvey Cox. MCT raises difficult issues about responsibility for change. Many good people have not victimized directly, but by their silence they may also share a responsibility for the hurt of others. Reparation for one's inaction may at times be as important as confessing complicity in direct hurts.

REFERENCES

ASANTE, M. (1987). *The Afrocentric idea*. Philadelphia: Temple University Press.

ATKINSON, D., MARUJAMA, M., AND MATSUI, S. (1978). The effects of counselor race and counseling approach on Asian Americans' perception of counselor credibility and utility. *Journal of Counseling Psychology, 25,* 76–83.

ATKINSON, D., MORTEN, G., & SUE, D. (1989). *Counseling American minorities: A cross-cultural perspective* (2nd ed.). Dubuque, IA: Brown.

ATTNEAVE, C. (1969). Therapy in tribal settings and urban network interventions. *Family Process, 8,* 192–210.

ATTNEAVE, C. (1982). American Indian and Alaskan native families: Emigrants in their own homeland. In M. McGoldrick, J. Pearce, & J. Giordano (Eds.), *Ethnicity and family therapy* (pp. 55–83). New York: Guilford.

BALLOU, M., & GABALAC, N. (1984). *A feminist position on mental health.* Springfield, IL: Thomas.

BARUTH, L., & MANNING, M. (1991). *Multicultural counseling and psychotherapy.* New York: Merrill.

BERMAN, J. (1979). Counseling skills used by Black and White male and female counselors. *Journal of Counseling Psychology, 26,* 81–84.

BLASSINGAME, J. (1972). *The slave community.* New York: Oxford University Press.

BRASSARD, M., GERMAIN, R., & HART, S. (1987). *Psychological maltreatment of children and youth.* New York: Pergamon Press.

BROWN, L., & BALLOU, M. (1992). *Theories of personality and psychopathology.* New York: Guilford.

CARTER, D., & RAWLINS, E. (Eds.). (1977). *Psychotherapy for women.* Springfield, IL: Thomas.

CHEATHAM, H. (1990). Empowering Black families. In H. Cheatham & J. Stewart (Eds.), *Black families* (pp. 373–93). New Brunswick, NJ: Transaction Press.

CHEATHAM, H., & STEWART, J. (Eds.). (1990). *Black families.* New Brunswick, NJ: Transaction Press.

CHEEK, D. (1976). *Assertive Black . . . puzzled White.* San Luis Obispo, CA: Impact.

CROSS, W. (1971). The Negro to Black conversion experience. *Black World, 20,* 13–25.

CROSS, W. (1991). *Shades of Black.* Philadelphia: Temple University Press.

FLAHERTY, M. (1989). *Perceived differences in early family relationships and parent/child relations between adults diagnosed as borderline personality or bipolar disorder.* Unpublished doctoral dissertation, School of Education, University of Massachusetts, Amherst.

FREIRE, P. (1972). *Pedagogy of the oppressed.* New York: Herder & Herder.

FUKUYAMA, M. (1990). Taking a universal approach to multicultural counseling. *Counselor Education and Supervision, 30,* 6–17.

GAVEY, N. (1991). Sexual victimization prevalence among New Zealand university students. *Journal of Consulting and Clinical Psychology, 59,* 464–66.

GRIFFITH, M., & JONES, E. (1978). Race and psychotherapy: Changing perspectives. In J. Masserman (Ed.), *Current psychiatric therapies* (Vol. 18) (pp. 225–35). Orlando, FL: Grune & Stratton.

GROSSKURTH, P. (1991, September 29). Mothers of psychoanalysis. *New York Times Book Review,* p. 12.

GUTMAN, H. (1976). *The Black family in slavery and freedom: 1750–1925.* New York: Harper-Collins.

HARDIMAN, R. (1982). *White identity development: A process oriented model for describing the racial consciousness of White Americans.* Unpublished doctoral dissertation, University of Massachusetts, Amherst.

HELMS, J. (1985). Toward a theoretical explanation of the effects of race on counseling: A Black and White model. *Counseling Psychologist, 12,* 153–65.

HELMS, J. (1990). *Black and White racial identity.* Westport, CT: Greenwood.

IVEY, A. (1986). *Developmental therapy: Theory into practice.* San Francisco: Jossey-Bass.

IVEY, A. (1992, February). Caring and commitment: Are we up to the challenge of multicultural counseling and therapy? *Guidepost,* p. 16.

IVEY, A., & IVEY, M. (1990). Assessing and facilitating children's cognitive development: Developmental counseling and therapy in a case of child abuse. *Journal of Counseling and Development, 68,* 299–306.

JACKSON, B. (1975). Black identity development. *Journal of Educational Diversity and Innovation, 2,* 19–25.

JACKSON, B. (1990, September). *Building a multicultural school.* Paper presented to the Amherst Regional School System, Amherst, MA.

JACKSON, B., & HARDIMAN, R. (1983). Racial identity development: Implications for managing the multiracial work force. In R. Vitvo & A. Sargent (Eds.), *The NTL managers' handbook* (pp. 107–19). Arlington, VA: NTL Institute.

JONES, E. (1978). Effects of race on psychotherapy process and outcome. *Psychotherapy Theory, Research, and Practice, 15,* 226–36.

JONES, E. (1985). Psychotherapy and counseling with Black clients. In P. Pedersen (Ed.), *Handbook of cross-cultural counseling and therapy* (pp. 173–79). Westport, CT: Greenwood.

KAPLAN, A. (1984). The self-in-relation: Implications for depression in women. *Work in Progress* (Monograph, Stone Center for Developmental Services and Studies). Wellesley, MA: Wellesley College.

LaFROMBOISE, T., & LOW, K. (1989). American Indian adolescents. In J. Gibbs & L. Hwang (Eds.), *Children of color* (pp. 114–47). San Francisco: Jossey-Bass.

LOCKE, D. (1990). A not so provincial view of multicultural counseling. *Counselor Education and Supervision, 30,* 18–25.

MARCOS, L. (1979). Effects of interpreters on the evaluation of psychopathology in non-English-speaking persons. *American Journal of Psychiatry, 136,* 171–74.

MILLER, J. (1991). The development of women's sense of self. In J. Jordan, A. Kaplan, J. B. Miller, I. Stiver, & J. Surrey (Eds.), *Women's growth in connection* (pp. 11–26). New York: Guilford.

MYERS, L. (1988). *Understanding an Afrocentric world view: Introduction to an optimal psychology.* Dubuque, IA: Kendall/Hunt.

MYERS, L., SPEIGHT, S., HIGHLEN, P., COX, C., REYNOLDS, A., ADAMS, E., & HANLEY, P. (1991). Identity development and worldview: Toward an optimal conceptualization. *Journal of Counseling and Development, 54,* 54–55.

ORTIZ, V. (1978). *Let me speak! Testimony of Domitila, a woman of the Bolivian mines.* New York: Monthly Review Press.

OSHERTON, S. (1986). *Finding our fathers.* New York: Free Press.

PARHAM, T. (1990). *Do the right thing: Racial discussion in counseling psychology.* Paper presented at the American Psychological Association Convention, Boston.

PEDERSEN, P. (Ed.). (1985). *Handbook of cross-cultural counseling and therapy.* Westport, CT: Greenwood.

PEDERSEN, P., DRAGUNS, J., LONNER, J., & TRIMBLE, J. (1989). *Counseling across cultures* (3rd ed.). Honolulu: University of Hawaii Press.

PETERSON, P. (1990). The multicultural perspective as a fourth force in counseling. *Journal of Mental Health Counseling, 12,* 93–95.

PFEFFERLE, S. (1989). *Developmental identity theory for the long-term mentally ill.* Unpublished paper, University of Massachusetts, Amherst.

PONTEROTTO, J. (1988). Racial consciousness development among White counselor trainees. *Journal of Multicultural Counseling and Development, 16,* 146–56.

RIGAZIO-DIGILIO, S. (1989). *Developmental theory and therapy: A preliminary investigation of reliability and predictive validity using an inpatient depressive population sample.* Unpublished doctoral dissertation, University of Massachusetts, Amherst.

RIGAZIO-DIGILIO, S., & IVEY, A. (1990). Developmental therapy and depressive disorders:

Measuring cognitive levels through patient natural language. *Professional Psychology: Research and Practice, 21,* 470–75.

RIVERA, M. (1991). *Ataques de nervios.* Unpublished comprehensive paper, University of Massachusetts, Amherst.

RIVERA-ARZOLA, M. (1991). *Differences between Puerto Rican women with and without* ataques de nervios. Unpublished doctoral dissertation, University of Massachusetts, Amherst.

SOLOMAN, B. (1990). Counseling Black families at inner-city church sites. In H. Cheatham & J. Stewart (Eds.), *Black families* (pp. 353–73). New Brunswick, NJ: Transaction Press.

SPECK, R., & ATTNEAVE, C. (1973). *Family process.* New York: Pantheon.

SUE, D. (1990). Culture-specific strategies in counseling: A conceptual framework. *Professional Psychology, 21,* 424–33.

SUE, D. (1992). Derald Wing Sue on multicultural issues: An interview. *Microtraining Newsletter* (North Amherst, MA), p. 6.

SUE, D., & SUE, D. (1990). *Counseling the culturally different* (2nd ed.). New York: Wiley.

SUE, S. (1988). Psychotherapeutic services for ethnic minorities: Two decades of research findings. *American Psychologist, 43,* 301–8.

WHITE, J., & PARHAM, T. (1991). *The psychology of Blacks: An African-American perspective* (2nd ed.). Englewood Cliffs, NJ: Prentice-Hall.

WRENN, C. (1962). The culturally encapsulated counselor. *Harvard Educational Review, 32,* 444–49.

WRENN, C. (1985). The culturally encapsulated counselor revisited. In P. Pedersen (Ed.), *Handbook of cross-cultural counseling and therapy* (pp. 323–29). Westport, CT: Greenwood.

6

Developmental Counseling and Therapy: Integrating Alternative Perspectives

CHAPTER GOALS

This chapter seeks to help you:

1. Define the multiple perspective world of developmental counseling and therapy and see how this approach relates to a multicultural frame of reference.

2. Outline the central constructs of a developmental metatheory that integrates the many theories of this book in a coherent frame of reference.

3. Learn some basic techniques of DCT, including specifics of cognitive-developmental assessment, emotion in the interview, and ways to facilitate client growth.

4. Become familiar with life-span review theory and see the multicultural extensions of DCT.

5. Understand how DCT integrates the multiple perspectives of counseling and therapy via a case presentation.

Multiple Seeing: What Is Your Perspective?

Consider the image, often used in Gestalt work, in figure 6.1. What occurs for you when you focus on this drawing? Take a moment and record your perspective. This drawing is usually described as containing both an old and a young woman. At first glance, some see the old woman, whereas others see the young. There are multi-cultural implications inherent in the drawing. Why is the woman with the large nose often considered "ugly" or "old," whereas the woman with a small nose is considered "young and beautiful"? There is no particular reason why a person with a large nose is older or less beautiful than one whose nose is smaller. Our perceptions and interpretations often come from our cultural perspective. We think we "see what we see," but we often fail to realize that our surrounding environment affects the very way data enter our minds.

If you continue looking at the figure, you may see both women. Some individuals

Figure 6.1   A Figure to Figure

SOURCE: Originally drawn by W. E. Hill and published in *Puck,* November 6, 1905. First used for psychological purposes by E. G. Boring, "A New Ambiguous Figure," *American Journal of Psychology,* 1930.

find it difficult to see the second woman. This form of "stuckness" could be described as a lack of intentionality—an inability to take a new perspective. If you continue to focus on the drawing, you will find that the two images alternate; you can see them move from one to another as if in a motion picture. With further concentration, you can obtain a "still photo" in which you see *both women at once.* When this happens, you are experiencing multiple seeing—the ability to find multiple perspectives simultaneously.

This chapter is about *multiple seeing*—or the ability to take several perspectives—in the counseling and therapy process. Seeing clients from multiple perspectives is the basis of developmental counseling and therapy (DCT) and also of multicultural counseling and therapy (MCT). Whether you commit yourself to a single theory, become an eclectic, or outline your own metatheoretical integrative approach, the ability to use theories and see clients from multiple perspectives and points of view is invaluable.

The Developmental Counseling and Therapy Integrative Worldview

Developmental counseling and therapy (DCT) is based on an adaptation and reinterpretation of the thinking of the Swiss epistemologist/psychologist/biologist Jean Piaget (1926/1963, 1965). Through observation, Piaget found that children constructed knowledge at four different levels. Piaget's observations have been useful with children, but have had only limited use in adolescent and adult clinical and counseling situations. The last decade, however, has seen a gradual burgeoning of new conceptual work with adults based on Piaget's stage concept (Basseches, 1984; Ivey, 1986, 1991b; Kegan, 1982; Rosen, 1985).

DCT's central assumption is that whether child, adolescent, or adult, we *metaphorically* repeat the well-known developmental stages of sensorimotor, concrete, formal, and postformal operations again and again. Piaget's strategies can be used throughout the full life span. However, Piaget stressed the importance of moving to higher, more complex forms of thinking. DCT, on the other hand, values multiperspective thought, holding that there can be as much value in experiencing the world directly at the sensorimotor level as at the most complex, abstract levels. The basic tenet of DCT is: *Higher is not better; each perspective is different and clarifies the whole.*

As a holistic framework, DCT depends on multiple seeing and multiple theories. The following summarizes DCT's integrative view of foundational skills: (1) for effective counseling and therapy, *an empathic relationship with a skilled counselor is essential;* (2) most sessions will involve *decisional counseling issues;* (3) *multicultural factors* modify these dimensions and offer additional perspectives. DCT suggests that it is important for you to be skilled and knowledgeable in these foundational dimensions so that you can meet the needs of a highly diverse clientele.

Furthermore, DCT's holistic frame of reference finds value in approaches to the helping process the worldviews of which at times may seem even antagonistic. For example, DCT finds value in individualistic approaches to theory such as Freudian psychodynamic thought, Skinner's radical behaviorism, and Rogers's humanism. Although the Native American, Afrocentric, and feminist therapy conceptions of interdependence and self-in-relation are central to the DCT frame, with some clients, values of autonomy and independence may be more immediately helpful. Multiple seeing demands multiple realities if we are to maintain a holistic view.

The Relationship of Multicultural Counseling and Therapy to DCT

Basic to the DCT worldview is that multicultural issues deeply influence the way we think about and construct reality. All counseling and therapy are multicultural experiences. In particular, the theories that have traditionally been presented in texts such as this are culturally embedded Eurocentric theories. This fact does not discount the value of these theories, but merely shows that they are incomplete and need to be balanced with new theories from the evolving multicultural counseling and therapy tradition. In addition, the MCT framework helps modify and make traditional theory more relevant to a multicultural world.

Counseling and therapy are usually thought of as a two-person relationship — specifically the relationship between a counselor and the client. There is now reason to believe that the concept of relationship in the interview requires a broader understanding. Some theorists suggest that the interview is not just a relationship between the two people physically present in the session (see Clement, 1983; Lacan, 1966/1977). There are actually four "participants" in the interview (see Ivey, 1987). Figure 6.2 provides a schematic of this four-factor relationship. The individual or family before you brings their specific cultural and historical backgrounds that may affect the session powerfully, and you as therapist bring your own unique cultural background to the interview. As the figure shows, the client and therapist are what we see and hear communicating in the interview. But neither can escape the cultural and family heritage from which they come.

Some theories of counseling and therapy tend to be ahistorical and give little at-

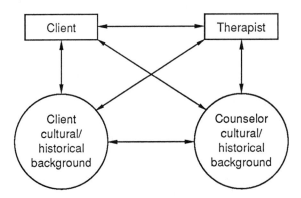

Figure 6.2 The Influence of Cultural/Historical Background on the Interview

tention to the power of history, family, and culture on the client. They focus solely on the client-therapist interaction and omit the importance of broader factors. Schneiderman (1983) states that "those who attempt to erase cultural differences, who wish to create a society in which Otherness is nonexistent, come to be alienated. . . . The moral condemnation of Otherness is racist; of this there is little doubt" (p. 174).

DCT has been coconstructed by a multicultural team[1] and influenced by multicultural thought, particularly that of Jackson's (1975) cultural identity developmental theory. There are marked parallels between DCT's four-level description of cognitive development and the tenets of cultural identity theory and of Freire (1972) outlined in chapter 5. The network ideas of Attneave (1969) have been particularly influential in DCT's view of the treatment plan.

Central Constructs of Developmental Metatheory: Integrating Skills and Theory

Drawing from a holistic worldview that is developmental and focusing on self-in-relation, DCT uses three major theoretical foundations: (1) coconstruction of relationships between counselor/therapist and client, (2) a reformulation of Piagetian cognitive stages for use in counseling and therapy, and (3) a spherical metatheory integrating the multiple theories of counseling and therapy.

Coconstruction of Knowledge, Assimilation, and Accommodation

DCT emphasizes that clients and counselors learn together. The term *coconstruction* is similar to the self-in-relation concepts of feminist therapy and holistic Afrocentric theory. The term emphasizes the importance of interdependence of counselor and client and is a specific attempt to move toward a less hierarchical, more egalitarian therapist-client relationship.

The Problem of Imposing Therapist Constructions on the Client

Traditionally, therapeutic theory starts with the worldview of the theorist; the counselor/therapist then assumes that view and applies the corresponding techniques to the client. For example, when a client goes through psychoanalysis, the Freudian worldview will most likely provide the framework for what happens in therapy. Through free association, dream analysis, and related techniques, the client will gradually learn to talk about his or her problems in the language of Freudian analysis and may eventually come to accept the Freudian worldview as truth.

As therapist you must be aware of the danger of superimposing your perceptions or worldview on the client. You are in a powerful position, and clients are vulnerable and may likely take your words very seriously, even to the point of learning your language. In a famous and highly influential film, a client named Gloria is interviewed by three therapists of different orientations—Carl Rogers, Fritz Perls, and Albert Ellis (Shostrum, 1966). In a series of classic studies, researchers examined this film in detail (Meara, Shannon, & Pepinsky, 1979; Meara, Pepinsky, Shannon, & Murray, 1981). Through linguistic analysis, they found that Gloria tended to assume the language pattern of each different therapist, using client-centered language with Rogers, Gestalt language with Perls, and rational-emotive language with Ellis.

In the filmed session, Gloria talks about her difficulties with men and her own father. Each therapist focuses on the *individual issues* faced by Gloria but fails to take into account how her problems may be the result of being a woman in a predominantly male world or developmental and family influences—issues that would be addressed by a multicultural approach. An additional advantage to DCT and the multicultural approach is that counselors may be less likely to impose their language or frameworks on clients. There is some evidence that effective White counselors tend to join their African-American clients in language patterns rather than imposing their own frames either consciously or unconsciously (Fry, Knopf, & Coe, 1980).

Coconstruction of Knowledge in the Interview

The Fry, Knopf, and Coe study cited above reminds us that not only does the counselor influence the client, but if they are flexible, *counselors are also influenced by the client.* The theory behind a dialectic coconstructivist approach is complex (Ivey, 1986), but may be summarized as follows:

1. Client and therapist exist in a dialectical relationship. Each has a unique family and cultural developmental history that affects their perceptions and the meanings they make. (This can be seen in figure 6.2.)

2. In the therapeutic relationship, each person acts on the other and learns from the other. Reality is *coconstructed* between counselor and therapist.

3. In turn, counselor and client are each molded by their dialectical relationship with the culture. As we found with the Gestalt illustration of the "young" and "old" women in figure 6.1, what we see and the meanings we make are influenced by our developmental history in a multicultural setting.

4. We are not just culture bearers, we also have the capability to create and change culture. Just as therapist and client can change each other, so can both affect the environment and culture that led to our perceptions. We are part of a "multiplicity in One."[2]

The coconstructive process may become a bit clearer when we examine some interpretations of Piagetian theory.

Basic Schema Theory and Assimilation and Accommodation

Schema theory is basic to Piagetian thinking (Piaget, 1985). Our minds through interaction with the world build structures or theories—*schema*—about the world.[3] Thus each client has developed theories or schema about the world as he or she has developed in relation to others, family, and culture. From DCT's cognitive/emotional-developmental theory, the task of the therapist or counselor is to understand the client's schema and how these schema were developed in a family and cultural context. In addition, when necessary, the counselor's function is to help the client generate new, more workable schema or theories for more effective thinking, feeling, and behavior.

Assimilation and accommodation are processes identified by Piaget to explain how schema are developed.

> Assimilation and accommodation are different ways to describe a single process. In accommodation, the individual receives (and possibly transforms) a stimulus from the environment; in assimilation, the individual acts on and imposes his or her perspectives on the environment. One aspect is impossible without the other. Like yin and yang, they are inseparable, even though one may be prepotent and primarily operative at a particular time of development. Together these constructions represent the adaptive process of development. (Ivey, 1986, p. 42)

In *assimilation* we use our constructions of knowledge and information (schema or theories about the world) to act on the world. For example, Freud and Skinner both had very tightly organized theories/schema that they used to explain virtually all human behavior. For another example, an abused child has assimilated schema/theories about the world that he or she may use throughout life in relationships with others. Assimilated knowledge may be described as what we have internalized over time as the result of our interactions with the world.

One task of counseling and therapy is to help the client find new more workable schema/theories through *accommodating* new views of the world. When we encounter a new event or stimulus in our lives, we first try to assimilate it into our existing schema or theories about the world. Sometimes the new data does not fit, and the person or client simply cannot or will not take new information in. This situation represents rigid schema/theories. Accommodation occurs when the person either uses new data to modify old schema or builds entirely new schema.

The empathic approach described in chapter 2 and the microskills presented in chapter 3 are intended to help the counselor/therapist enter the constructed worldview of the client. Simply listening to and hearing how the client sees, hears, and feels the world may be sufficient to effect change. In these cases, the therapist has succeeded in focusing on accommodating to and learning from the client. Moreover, when the counselor repeats back to the client what has been said (encouraging, paraphrasing, reflecting feeling, summarizing), the client is able to accommodate to this clearer vision and change old cognitive structures. Rogerian client-centered therapy, for example, may be described as a primarily accommodative theory, as the focus is on the client's constructions of the world.

Some theories and therapists, however, use a primarily assimilative approach in which the therapeutic task is seen as encouraging the client to enter the worldview of the therapist. For example, many clients in psychodynamic therapy tend to talk about their lives using the language of psychoanalysis. There is more than one learner in the counseling and therapy process. Given this, DCT argues for a balance between accommodative and assimilative approaches to human change. Figure 6.3 is a visual representation of the interweaving of assimilation and accommodation between therapist and client.

Reformulating Piagetian Stage Theory for Adolescent and Adult Cognitions and Emotions

Learning how to recognize client cognitive and emotional developmental level in the here and now of the clinical interview can facilitate your understanding and choice of appropriate interventions. There are two major issues in assessing cognitive/emotional-developmental level: (1) identifying the level of clients as they describe their

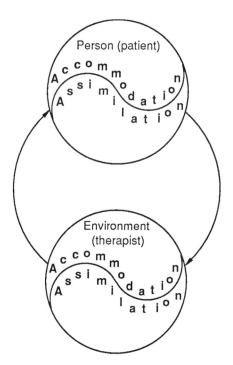

Figure 6.3   Accommodation and Assimilation between Client and Therapist

SOURCE: A. Ivey, *Developmental therapy: Theory into practice.* (San Francisco: Jossey-Bass, 1986), p. 48. Used with permission.

problems at multiple levels; and (2) utilizing these data in interview and treatment planning.

Identifying Client
Cognitive-Developmental Level

Piaget talks of four major stages of cognitive development. DCT treats Piagetian thinking as a metaphor, posing four major cognitive/emotional-developmental levels that appear and reappear constantly in clients. We meet clients who come to us at sensorimotor, concrete, formal, and dialectic/systemic levels of thinking and emotion.

DCT states that an important task for the counselor/therapist is to enter the world of the client as the client makes sense of that world. Clients make meaning at four major cognitive-developmental levels, which are presented in some detail in table 6.1.[4] Each level involves a different complexity of language and meaning. If you observe your clients carefully, you will find that they do indeed talk about their experience at different cognitive-developmental levels.

For example, a client who is going through a divorce may talk about the divorce from different cognitive and emotional levels. It is good to remember that such a client is highly likely to need varying types of counseling and therapy. Following are examples of how a client might work through the divorce issue at the four cognitive-developmental levels:

1. *Sensorimotor:* The client may talk in a random, confused fashion but may simultaneously deny feelings of hurt and anger. At times, the client is able to experience the hurt and confusion fully at a body level and allow tears to come.

2. *Concrete:* The client may relate many details and stories about the divorce. Feelings about specific situations may be named, but there may be an absence of self-reflection and considerable blame and anger directed toward the spouse.

3. *Formal:* The client talks more abstractly. If you listen carefully, you will find that specifics of what happened between the couple are seldom discussed. Rather, the client discusses repeating patterns of interaction. The client is able to reflect on the self and feelings.

4. *Dialectic/systemic:* The client takes multiple perspectives on the divorce and is even able to see the spouse's frame of reference. The client may see how patterns learned in the family of origin were repeated in the couple's relationship. Multicultural issues of gender, ethnicity, and religion may be included in the awareness.

DCT operates on the assumption that one task of the therapist/counselor is to match language and treatment techniques with the cognitive/emotional level of the client. It does little good to try to get clients who are at the sensorimotor or concrete levels of cognition and feeling to reflect on patterns or think about how they were involved in the divorce. DCT argues that it is imperative to join the client where he or she is emotionally or cognitively. As table 6.1 shows, each level (or stage) has strengths and weaknesses. Full development of human potential suggests the validity of expanding client awareness and potential at each cognitive-developmental level.

As we have seen, *clients present their problems at multiple levels.*[5] To continue with the above example, the client may start the interview with a dialectic/systemic analysis of issues and very quickly move on to a formal operational discussion about the damage to his or her view of self. As the counselor, you may note that this person is unable to experience affect at the sensorimotor level, although he or she may reflect on feelings and talk about being hurt.

For another example, a teenager suffering from bulimia, although enmeshed in the sensory world of food and the body, nevertheless may be a very successful gymnast or ballet dancer quite capable of acting on the world. This same teen may be skilled in formal operations and be an excellent student while simultaneously having a very low self-concept. Very often, the family will blame the teenager and deny that the family system in some way affects what is happening.

At the dialectic/systemic level, the teenager's family usually requires assistance. Furthermore, feminist and multicultural theory reminds us that attitudes of society toward food and thinness are an important influence on women becoming bulimics. Network theory would involve the gymnastics or ballet teacher, as these teachers may at times encourage abnormal eating patterns to facilitate performance and physical appearance (Kurtzman et al., 1989; Thelan et al., 1987). Exhibit 6.1 provides further discussion of DCT and cultural identity theory.

The Developmental Sphere: DCT's Metatheoretical Integration of Counseling and Psychotherapy

Anderson (1983), in describing "style-shift counseling," emphasizes that we need to accommodate to the client's assimilated schema, choose a counseling approach that matches the cognitive-developmental level of the client, evaluate its effectiveness, and "shift style" to another approach if the client has grown or the chosen intervention is ineffective. Once we have assessed client cognitive-emotional style or level, we first need to match and later mismatch interventions to facilitate growth. Generally, clients need to expand their functioning at more than one level.

Given that clients are likely to be at different levels, and that the counselor/therapist needs to shift helping style accordingly, DCT argues that counselors and therapists should be equipped with multiple theories and multiple skills. DCT is based on the idea that development is holistic; it identifies four basic types of counseling style. In Figure 6.4, the client's developmental journey is represented by the spiral of cognitive and emotional development. Along the journey, four levels or planes of therapeutic style are presented—all of which can facilitate the client journey.

No form of knowledge is considered superior. Rather, all four levels are considered important for full cultural intentionality. And, once having developed cultural intentionality on any one developmental task, the client often returns to the beginning to start anew on another task. This is the paradox of development: to arrive where we started and to know the place for the first time. Life is simultaneously a journey, a destination, and a state of being.

═══ **Exhibit 6.1** ═══

Cultural Identity Development Theory Related to DCT Levels

The four levels of cognitive/emotional development can be related to Jackson's Black identity development theory (discussed in chapter 5). The embedded consciousness of Jackson's stage 2 (active and passive acceptance) is parallel to many of the cognitions at the sensorimotor level. Stage 3 (resistance and naming) and its frequent association with anger and action have parallels with concrete operational thought. Stage 4 (redefinition and reflection) has much in common with formal operational thought patterns. Finally, the multiperspective stage 5 internalization contains many of the same descriptive words as the dialectic/systemic level.

Identity developmental theory tends to describe anger as a feature of Jackson's stage 3. Anger is manifested at each level, Brooks (1990) maintains, but it plays itself out differently. At stage 2, for example, anger is repressed or denied and may play itself out in physical symptoms such as high blood pressure, which is a typical problem of many African-Americans. Anger is acted out at stage 3, often through direct action. At stage 4, anger is more reflective, and African-Americans may share feelings and thoughts about anger and issues of oppression. Finally, at stage 5, anger is experienced in a more complex multiperspective form. The individual may recognize the need to deny or hold back anger at times, will use anger to motivate action in certain situations, and certainly will reflect on the meaning of anger for both self and others.

Brooks provides useful bridges between DCT and the multicultural approach. DCT's theory of emotion is founded on a similar basis and holds that the way emotion plays itself out in life varies with the level of developmental consciousness. DCT, like multicultural counseling and therapy, holds that a major goal of counseling and therapy is the liberation of consciousness—and acting on that new consciousness.

There are many other routes toward development in addition to the four therapeutic environments shown in figure 6.4 and listed in table 6.1. Many techniques and theories are also multilevel. You may, for example, want to devise your own list of theories and interventions that for you are most appropriate for each developmental level.

Following style-shift theory, the first task is to assess client developmental level and match our interventions to the cognitions of the client. *Horizontal development* occurs when we help a client explore further issues at the entering cognitive/emotional-developmental level. An African-American female, for example, may enter counseling with an Afrocentric therapist at a level 3 consciousness (concrete resistance

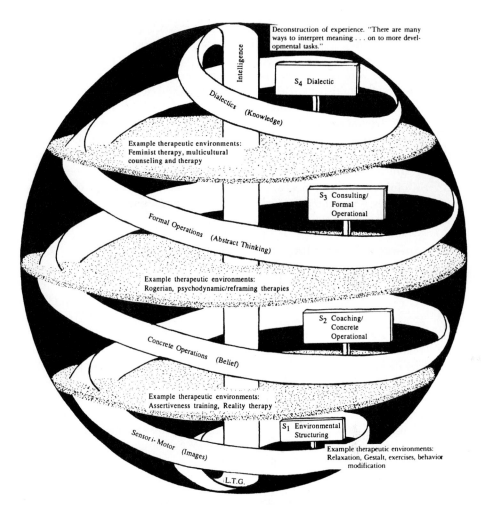

Deconstruction of experience. "There are many
ways to interpret meaning . . . on to more developmental tasks."

Intelligence

S₄ Dialectic

Dialectics   (Knowledge)

Example therapeutic environments:
Feminist therapy, multicultural
counseling and therapy

S₃ Consulting/
     Formal
     Operational

Formal Operations   (Abstract Thinking)

Example therapeutic environments:
Rogerian, psychodynamic/reframing therapies

S₂ Coaching/
     Concrete
     Operational

Concrete Operations   (Belief)

Example therapeutic environments:
Assertiveness training, Reality therapy

S₁ Environmental
     Structuring

Sensori-Motor   (Images)

Example therapeutic environments:
Relaxation, Gestalt, exercises, behavior
modification

L.T.G.

**Figure 6.4   The Developmental Sphere: A Holistic View of Four DCT
Therapeutic Environmental Styles**

SOURCE: Originally conceived and drawn by Lois T. Grady, this figure is used here with her
permission.

and anger). The first task is to help the client expand awareness and competence at
that level. Cheek's (1976) culturally aware cognitive-behavioral approach (see chapter
9) may be especially appropriate. A formal operational European-American male
may enter counseling with doubts about the self and might profit from horizontal
development with a counselor using a client-centered or psychodynamic frame of
reference.

Vertical development, within the DCT spherical frame, can be either up or down.
Since all dimensions of consciousness are considered important for holistic development, higher is not better. Both the African-American female and European-American male client might benefit from imaging, relaxation training, and other

sensorimotor techniques at the sensorimotor level. For the African-American, the techniques might be useful in helping her get in better touch with her hurt and outraged feelings surrounding racism. The European-American male client might be helped by sensorimotor imaging to better understand the roots of his self-doubt. In turn, both might benefit from further horizontal development at the sensorimotor level on personal and cultural issues.

DCT recommends both horizontal and vertical development on as many cognitive-developmental and emotional issues as feasible for each client. DCT draws on Attneave's network therapy in stressing that each individual client can benefit from a treatment plan that is multidimensional and involves more than one helping theory. In addition, network therapy reminds us that individual therapy can often work more effectively if also integrated with family and community interventions.

Developmental Counseling and Therapy in Applied Practice

As a metatheoretical approach, DCT draws from all the theories and strategies presented in this book. With Jackson (1975) and Cross (1991), DCT argues for an integrated theory and practice in which expanding consciousness and action based on that expanded awareness are major goals of all counseling and therapy. Cultural identity development theory and DCT appear to support changing intervention style to match the cognitive and developmental needs of the client.

DCT also has generated some additional constructions and techniques of its own that appear to be useful as part of the process of therapy and counseling. Three dimensions will be focused on in this section: developmental questioning strategies, Gonçalves's integration of assessment and treatment planning, and DCT as a counseling and therapy action framework.

DCT Questioning Strategies

We all like others to listen to us. When you accommodate to clients through the use of listening skills, not only are you better able to understand their perspective on things, but you also have given them a rare gift. Through the simple act of listening, clients can see and understand themselves more clearly. If you listen well to a client, that may be enough to promote change.

At the same time, you as a counselor or therapist have an immense amount of power. Research shows that clients tend to take on the language and perhaps even the way of thinking of their therapist. We all selectively attend to what our clients and others say. Some of us focus only on negative things that clients talk about, whereas others of us focus on the positive. A Rogerian counselor will tend to focus on individual issues; a family therapist, on family concerns; and a feminist therapist, on issues related to women's role in society. Each therapist, with the best of intentions, inevitably leads the client to certain emphases.

Not only will clients talk about what you listen to, they will also talk and act at the cognitive-developmental level at which you listen, ask questions, and conduct your interventions. It is not enough to discover that you have a concrete client who is most likely telling you highly detailed stories. Your interviewing task is dual.

First, you need to encourage horizontal development by asking concrete questions and conducting interventions (for example, concrete decision making, assertiveness training). Second, you need to mismatch and encourage vertical development at the sensorimotor level (imaging, body work), formal operational level (self-examination of repeating patterns), and dialectic/systemic level (how the problem may be affected by multicultural, family, or systemic issues).

Using Specific Questions to Help Clients Talk at Multiple Levels

Your style of selective listening and focusing plus the questions you ask impact how the client presents his or her issues. If a female client talks about her difficulties on the job and you listen and ask questions at the concrete level, the client will give you specific information. If you focus on formal thoughts, the client may examine patterns in the self or situation. Moreover, if you focus on the possible issues of job discrimination or other gender issues, the client may talk to you at the dialectic/systemic level.

DCT has found that using specific questions can help clients explore their issues at each cognitive/emotional level in more depth. Exhibit 6.2 provides an abbreviated summary of example questions, and exhibit 6.3 explores how developmental level classification works in practice. Experienced practitioners will note that the questions are, for the most part, familiar. Many counselors and therapists of differing theoretical persuasions often use neo-Piagetian questions as a natural way to interview. DCT points out that consciousness of developmental questions can facilitate understanding of naturally occurring events in the session, leading to more intentionality.

Ethics and Care in Questioning Clients

On a sensitive topic, many clients are moved easily to tears by the simple and direct here-and-now orientation of sensorimotor questions. Both of you may be surprised at the strength and easy accessibility of these deeper emotions. If your client is fragile or "on edge," you may want to use safer concrete and formal questioning procedures.

DCT recommends that you share the purpose of your questions with your clients and let them know ahead of time what may happen. If you have shared what will happen with your clients in a coconstructive fashion, the surprise will be less and you can make a joint decision as to where to move next. Your own comfort level with emotion will be important as to how clients cope with the situation. Rather than staying with the immediacy of the emotion, you can say in an empathic fashion, "Tell me what happened when you were feeling that" (concrete) or "Is that way of feeling a pattern for you?" (formal).

Exhibit 6.2

 **Developmental Strategies
Questioning Sequence**

A useful practice exercise is to take a volunteer "client" through the four cognitive/emotional-developmental levels. Begin your exercise by informing your client of what you are planning to do and share the following list with her or him. Once you and your client have selected a practice topic, ask the first question and assess the client's cognitive/emotional-developmental level at the start of the session.

Then, slowly work through each of the phases of the DCT questioning sequence, giving your client time to experience each level fully. Use particular care at the sensorimotor level, showing respect for your client's privacy.

Identifying Cognitive/Emotional-Developmental Level

What occurs for you when you focus on your family, your difficulty at work, your divorce, or your harassment on the job? (Obtain story of from 50 to 100 words and assess overall functioning of client on varying cognitive-developmental levels.)

Sensorimotor Questions

Get a single image in your mind involving your family, difficulty at work, your divorce, or a harassment. What are you seeing? Hearing? Feeling? (It is helpful to locate the feeling in the body.)

Concrete Questions

Could you give me a specific example of the situation, issue, or problem? Describe what happened. Can you describe your feelings in the situation?

Formal Questions

Does this happen in other situations? (or) Is this a pattern for you? Do you feel that way in other situations? Have you felt that way before?

Dialectic/Systemic/Integrative Questions

How do you put together or organize all we've been talking about? How might your thoughts and feelings about the concern have taken form in your family of origin? How do you see sex stereotyping and/or multicultural issues influencing your thoughts and feelings about the concern? How could we describe this from the point of view of some other person or using another framework?

NOTE: A more comprehensive eight-level Standard Cognitive-Developmental Interview is available (Ivey, Rigazio-DiGilio, & Ivey, 1990), as is a research-oriented classification system (Ivey & Rigazio-DiGilio, 1990).

Exhibit 6.3

Defining Cognitive-Developmental Level in Research and Practice

Do the constructions of DCT really exist? Can they be identified and measured reliably? Does the claim that clients talk at cognitive-developmental levels suggested by the theory hold true in practice?

All of these questions were answered in the affirmative in work with inpatient depressed clients (Rigazio-DiGilio & Ivey, 1990). Raters were able to classify patient cognitive-developmental levels with high reliability (.98, kappa = .87). When answering standard questions from the DCT model, both short- and long-term clients responded consistently with the theory (99 percent). Informal clinical data now being followed up revealed cognitive and behavioral changes after the brief treatment. Mailler (1991) found that instruction in the DCT model was useful with students preparing for the workplace. He used variations of the systematic questioning model to conceptualize a program for burnout prevention, personal growth, and organizational change.

Rigazio-DiGilio and Ivey (1990) offer the following exercise as an example of how raters were trained in DCT classification, which will give you an opportunity to test your own ability to rate client statements:

Define the *predominant* cognitive-developmental level of the depressed client in each of the following four statements. There will

be dimensions of other levels, but determine whether the client talks in a *primarily* sensorimotor, concrete, formal, or dialectic/systemic fashion. The depressed inpatient here is talking about the death of his sister. The information is randomized from varying parts of the interview.

1. I'm reacting this time very similarly, as I did to my sister's death. I guess everyone saw her as ill but me. I didn't see anything wrong. And when she died I was completely shocked. I fell apart just like I'm falling apart now. Everyone else had to take care of things.

2. I feel paralyzed . . . petrified. I feel like my legs are stiff and still . . . great weights keeping me stuck. . . . I feel empty . . . dead inside.

3. What I learned when I was growing up has not prepared me for dealing with loss. My parents did everything to protect me and my sister. . . . We were never taught to look for problems and try to fix them, or that natural things would occur, and we would have to adjust. This talk is making it clear that I don't know what to do, so I completely pull into myself and become paralyzed.

4. She came home from work and rather than having diner on the table, she was sitting at the table looking distraught . . . upset. She said, "We have to talk," and I thought maybe someone died. Then she told me she wanted to leave . . . she was unhappy for five years. I collapsed. I didn't see

it coming. I didn't know what to do. That's why I'm here . . . she brought me to the hospital 'cause I didn't know what to do. (p. 474)

Statement 1 is formal. The client is reflecting on himself and contrasting his reactions with others. A concrete client would have real difficulty with this cognitive task. Statement 2 is considered predominantly sensorimotor, although there are concrete elements in which the patient at times names emotions— "I feel paralyzed"—as contrasted to experiencing them at a fuller sensorimotor level—"great weights keeping me stuck," "dead inside." Statement 3 is dialectic/systemic. Statement 4 is a fairly straightforward example of concrete description.

You will find that if you take clients through the standard questions listed in exhibit 6.2, you and your clients will gain new perspectives on the issues. Things seem very different when viewed from sensorimotor, concrete, formal, and dialectic/systemic perspectives. You will find that integrating questions about the family of origin with the standard series is particularly valuable.

The Questioning Sequence and Other Theoretical Orientations

The DCT questioning sequence can be altered; it is not necessary to follow the standard sequence. Building on the points made clear by Cheek (1976) many years ago, it may be more useful when working with African-American clients to focus first on the dialectic/systemic level and follow up with more individually oriented questions and interventions. MCT theory might go so far as to turn the question sequences of DCT "upside down," putting a far greater emphasis on cultural and systemic issues.

Knowledge of the Piagetian sequences inherent in the questions will likely be helpful as you work in other theoretical orientations. For example, therapists of many orientations appear to follow the Piagetian sequences in their work, although they do not describe what they do from this orientation.

For example, the cognitive-behaviorist Aaron Beck often asks clients to picture images from earlier in life (sensorimotor). Clients are then encouraged to describe happenings at that time (concrete) and then to observe patterns in later life derived from these images. Finally, Beck asks clients to step back from this sequence and reflect on the systems of operations. Through this process, clients obtain a new integration that can lead to new thoughts and behaviors. Beck, however, tends not to discuss multicultural issues as an inherent part of his systematic procedures. Rogers and Perls have been observed to follow similar sequences in their work, but they also maintain an individual focus similar to Beck (Ivey, 1986, 112–16).

Gonçalves's Integrated Assessment and Treatment Plan

Given the complex model of DCT, how can you assemble all this information into a comprehensive plan for treatment? Recall that DCT asks you to (1) be aware of client cognitive-emotional processes; (2) use multiple theories with a single client, changing theory appropriately with varying client needs; and (3) maintain multicultural awareness.

Gonçalves has generated a comprehensive integration of the therapy process (1989, 1990; Gonçalves & Craine, 1990; Gonçalves & Machado, 1989), which is built on DCT and Guidano's (1991) postrationalist cognitive therapy. Gonçalves discusses his adaptation of DCT, illustrating the discussion with a clinical case of agoraphobia (Gonçalves & Ivey, 1992).

Client Assessment

The first step in Gonçalves's model is to assess the client cognitive-developmental level using an extended version of the DCT questions presented in exhibit 6.2. This assessment permits the identification of the client's predominant level of functioning and how skilled the client is in looking at the problem from various cognitive-emotional perspectives. This permits the establishment of a "firing order" (Lazarus, 1976), which helps determine the sequence of client treatment.

If this assessment reveals deeper-level problems, a more comprehensive assessment plan is called for and may require the administration of psychological tests. As part of this phase of assessment, a life-span review is conducted, with an emphasis on client history. The therapist and client examine how developmental history relates to present functioning (see Tamase & Kato, 1990; Guidano, 1991; see also later in this chapter).

An integrated assessment is produced in which the therapist evaluates the client's modes of experiencing the world at the sensorimotor level, ability to engage in concrete operations, formal patterns of cognitions and self-statements, and dialectic/systemic context such as intergenerational family issues and culture. At the dialectic/systemic level, Gonçalves gives special attention to the client's cognitive ability to examine self-in-system. Major attention is given to person-environment and multicultural issues and to placing the client in a context of "no blame." Throughout this assessment process, it is important to recall the concepts of coconstruction—*therapist and client constructing together the nature of the relationship* they will share in counseling and therapy.

Treatment Planning

Treatment planning within DCT closely follows Attneave's (1969) network therapy model presented in chapter 5. DCT treatment can be aimed at a single issue and may be completed in one or two sessions. Or DCT treatment may be highly complex and involve multiple network interventions. Deeper levels of DCT treatment may run from eight sessions to a year or more. We tend to think of deep therapy as long-term therapy. Gonçalves points out the naivete of such thinking. Deep therapy, if constructed developmentally, with a solid array of multiple interventions, need not be long-term.

The assessment and treatment model is elaborated through presentation of a complex case example of the treatment of agoraphobia (Gonçalves & Ivey, 1992). An agoraphobic male client had developed increasing problems which were virtually incapacitating him. Gonçalves established a developmental treatment plan that attacked the agoraphobia at multiple levels with substantial success.

Given this background, let us turn to a clinical example of integrative developmental counseling and therapy in action.

DCT Treatment Example: Coping with Injury and Depression

Kenney and Law (1991) used the DCT model in conceptualizing and treating a forty-seven-year-old secretary who was injured in a fall at work. She had major back problems, lost her job, was without insurance, and on medication for depression.

Sensorimotor/Concrete Presentation and Treatment

In the first session, the client, Leana, was asked to describe details of her injury. Her difficulty in presenting issues suggested that she was functioning primarily at the sensorimotor level as well as engaging in considerable denial. Treatment was therefore initiated at those two levels.

> When asked to describe whatever image came to her mind when she thought of her injury, Leana broke into tears. Leana and the counselor focused on the sensorimotor components of her injury, with an emphasis on pain and feelings of fear during and immediately after the fall. (p. 36)

The counselor continued using a balance of sensorimotor imaging and concrete description of the painful experiences. Needless to say, mere discussion of the sensitive concrete details led Leana back to the sensorimotor mode, where she talked about fears of losing her mind, inability to work as a secretary, and a general loss of self-esteem and self-respect.

Moving between Concrete and Formal Exploration

As treatment evolved, Leana was able to start to identify patterns of anger, withdrawal, and "submitting to her symptoms." The counselor found that attempts to encourage Leana to find meaning in her symptoms (formal) or to seek another job (concrete) again resulted in her regression to a sensorimotor mode of behavior—namely, tears.

Over the next few sessions, the counselor encouraged her to talk about behavior rather than feelings at the concrete level. The following is an example of negative self-talk that can sometimes occur at the formal level after sufficient concrete work.

Leana gradually developed the ability to separate her sense of self from environmental events. When asked what basic rule of life she was operating under, she replied "I can't do anything right! I'll never work again. I'm a failure." (p. 36)

Given this difficulty, the counselor focused in highly concrete terms on Leana's past success experiences. This focus on concrete positive dimensions led to a more balanced formal operational picture of self.

Leana was eventually able to understand the pattern of failure-frustration-withdrawal-low self-esteem which she had enacted in her life. . . . Leana sought and found comfort in her religious faith. She joined a support group and a church volunteer group. . . . She had learned to think about her experiences more objectively and was developing personal goals, other than employment, which were meaningful to her. (p. 37)

Dialectic/Systemic Implications

DCT would point out that many of Leana's responses to illness and loss of job were generated in her family of origin and that being a woman led to certain expectations of self and others. Leana could be helped by being encouraged to become active in promoting rights of employees and in seeking a safer work setting. Many times clients find meaning in their lives through helping others avoid the problems they have suffered themselves.

Depression is an area that has been important in DCT treatment and practice. Ivey (1991a) reviews microtraining/media therapy treatment practices (see chapter 3) and comments that (1) sensorimotor and body work are essential parts of the treatment of depression, (2) concrete skills training facilitates communication and helps depressed clients discover feelings of competence, (3) formal work with self-esteem and recognizing patterns of depression seem essential for transfer of training and for evaluating mood, and (4) at the dialectic/systemic level, it is important to focus on helping clients examine the family and social system that brought them to therapy in the first place. As Ivey (1973) notes:

Many families really don't want the behavior of psychiatric patients changed. Change simply disrupts the reinforcement balance within the home. Similarly, society does not necessarily want behavior change. One patient, for example, who had shown marked improvement from depression commented that he really couldn't see any meaning in his routine assembly job. Although his behavior had changed, he still saw the futility of much of his efforts. To meet this patient's needs, one can work on cognitive restructuring . . . or, better yet, work on changing the society that helped bring about the psychotic break.

. . . Perhaps an additional goal of the psychiatric facility should be to train patients as change agents. Each patient might be encouraged to develop changes in the society that sent him to a psychiatric setting. Examples of such change activities would be teaching one's own family how to relax systematically or to listen more effectively to one another. The change might be at a societal level and require involvement in community action programs such as work with the poor or disadvantaged. One of the most successful programs for helping some individuals fight drug addiction is working to fight drug addiction in others. (p. 342)

DCT argues that clients can benefit from dialectic/systemic action with the family and society. This point is similar to that stressed by the multicultural counseling and therapy movement. Cheatham (1990), for example, emphasizes the importance of starting treatment with awareness of societal influences on the individual and family. By so doing, it is possible to avoid "blaming the victim."

Multicultural Extensions of DCT: Life-Span Review and Process/Outcome Research Issues

DCT, generated by a multicultural, multinational group of men and women, has given special attention to opening the model to constant change and review. Two Japanese scholars, Machiko Fukuhara and Koji Tamase, have been instrumental in DCT's conception of life-span events and in process/outcome research understandings.

Life-Span Review: Introspective-Developmental Counseling

Introspective-developmental counseling (IDC) seeks to learn how the client's life history affects present experiencing (Tamase, 1991). With that knowledge, counselor and client can draw on strengths in the past and present to work on and resolve problematic life issues. IDC is Tamase's integration of Japanese Naikan therapy (Reynolds, 1990), Erik Erikson's life-span theory (1950/1963), and DCT questioning concepts discussed above.

Let us build toward Tamase's theory by first examining some concepts of Japanese therapy. Then, his framework will be presented in more detail.

Naikan Therapy

Naikan therapy is aimed at assisting clients to discover meaning in life and to repair damaged relationships with others (Reynolds, 1990). Naikan therapy seeks to help clients move from narrow self-centeredness to awareness of how the individual was and is formed by important relationships. Naikan therapy points out that a narrow focus on the self leads to neurotic pain.

For example, in North American culture most depressed clients focus very much on themselves. They could benefit from focusing outward and seeing themselves in a relational context. Rigazio-DiGilio and Ivey (1990) found that DCT questions helped inpatient depressed clients see themselves more in context. This approach proved to be therapeutic and resulted in better feelings toward self and others—that is, *the self-in-relation.*

Modifying Erikson's Life-Span Framework

Tamase's work is unique in that it combines Eastern and Western frameworks. Erikson's life-span theory (summarized in table 6.2) has been severely criticized on grounds that he derived his ideas primarily from ideas about White males in Northern European and U.S. societies (Gilligan, 1982). Nonetheless, it provides a useful framework, which is modified by Tamase.

As a multicultural perspective reveals, *different cultures move through the life span differently.* For example, Erikson defines the developmental task of early childhood (ages 2–4) as focused on developing a sense of autonomy. If you think back on the Afrocentric idea or the nature of childhood in Japan and in many South American cultures, the goal of this period is not autonomy but rather a sense of connectedness to the caregiver. Too much autonomy and separation is considered pathological in many cultures. At the same time, too much dependence on others can occur in any culture. Natane (1984) analyzes this issue in detail.

IDC's Integrative Framework

Tamase avoids labeling any developmental period as being focused on particular tasks. He observes that different cultures will focus on different issues and have different crises and issues from those proposed by Erikson. He points out that each individual uniquely finds her or his own life path, but always within a network of relationships. Furthermore, as life experience expands and contracts through accommodation and assimilation processes, each individual makes different meanings.

Tamase talks about age-related developmental phases in IDC, such as birth through preschool, elementary school, adolescence, and present-day life. Tamase's framework offers some advantages over Eriksonian life stages, as he does not impose a set of culturally bound expectations such as "autonomy versus shame and doubt," or "identity versus role confusion." By emphasizing age periods without prior constructions of meaning, Tamase seeks to offer a more multiculturally viable life-span review process.

Making Meaning from the Past

Drawing from Naikan therapy values, the goals of IDC are in some ways similar to psychodynamic formulations in that the past is believed to affect the present. However, Tamase attempts to avoid giving theoretical interpretations for the client. Rather, the IDC interviewer simply listens and helps the client review the past. Not too surprisingly, if you listen to past events carefully, clients begin to discover repeating patterns and make their own interpretations. When the interviewer adds the sensorimotor, concrete, formal, and dialectic/systemic DCT questions discussed earlier, IDC becomes a powerful therapeutic tool. Thus, whereas Erikson's work is solely descriptive, Tamase's provides room for specific action and treatment.

Tamase has thus far focused his work primarily on the early life stages. As the model expands, additional questions need to be raised about later life stages. Early

Table 6.2   Erikson's Developmental Stages throughout the Life Span

Life Stage, Approximate Age, and Major Developmental Crises (derived from Eurocentric norms)	Key Environmental Systems (Eurocentric perspective)	Developmental Tasks (primarily Eurocentric perspective)	How Life Stages Differ among Multicultural Groups
Infancy (birth–2): Balancing trust vs. mistrust	Caregiver and nuclear family. Families may be traditional, single-parent, blended, grandparents, adoptive, gay or lesbian, rich or poor. The nature of the family will have an important impact on children's growth and development.	Attachment to family. Sensorimotor intelligence. Basic motor coordination.	Attachment patterns in some African-American and Latina/o cultures focus more on extended family than in typical middle-class families. The "holding environment" of Japan may produce closer attachments than in Eurocentric cultures.
Early childhood (2–4): Autonomy vs. shame and doubt	Family, extended family, preschool playgroup. The nature of family varies in different cultural groups. In many cultures, the extended family is more important than the nuclear family.	Self control. Language learning. Walking and play activities central. Attachment to family is basis for developing a beginning sense of self.	Autonomy is a Eurocentric construct. In Japan, for example, the child is often encouraged to develop a sense of closeness and dependence on others. Too much autonomy is viewed as selfishness in some cultures.
Middle childhood (5–7): Initiative vs. guilt	Family, neighborhood, school.	Gender identity. First stages of moral development. Concrete mental operations.	Boys and girls have been taught since infancy to behave differently, dress differently, and are rewarded for different types of behaviors in virtually all cultures. Initiative may be defined as aggressiveness in some groups.
Late childhood (8–12): Industry vs. inferiority	Family, neighborhood, school, and peer group.	Basic time of learning social relationships through work and play, building self-esteem and feelings of competence (ego-centric learning),	Children of poverty are not surrounded by a stimulating middle-class environment and may have little chance to learn self-esteem and many

Table 6.2   (continued)

Life Stage, Approximate Age, and Major Developmental Crises (derived from Eurocentric norms)	Key Environmental Systems (Eurocentric perspective)	Developmental Tasks (primarily Eurocentric perspective)	How Life Stages Differ among Multicultural Groups
		learning of many basic life skills in the culture; team membership; late concrete mental operations (if/then reasoning); moral development in terms of right vs. wrong.	basic skills considered natural to children of a more advantaged background. The word *industry* is related to a "doing orientation" of Eurocentric culture, as contrasted with Afrocentric and Arabic ideas of "being."
Puberty and adolescence (12–18): Identity vs. role confusion	Peer group, school, family, neighborhood, work setting.	Sexual maturation. Formal operational thought. Generation of self-concept and awareness of personal identity. Movement toward independent living.	Piagetian theorists estimate that between 25 and 40 percent of the population never reaches full formal operations. Gay or lesbian adolescents may have a particularly difficult time at this stage due to cultural expectations.
Young adulthood (20–30): Intimacy vs. isolation	New family and living mate(s) become central. Friendship network may move away from family of origin. Work setting becomes central.	Finding one's own sense of self in a family relationship of love and commitment. Initial parenting. Detachment from parents and extended family. Major career and financial decisions.	Adolescent women in U.S. culture work on issues of intimacy during adolescence, perhaps even more so than identity. In some African and Italian cultures, the extended family remains especially important in living and decision-making arrangements.
Adulthood (30–65): Generativity vs. stagnation	Family and children, friendship network, work setting, community.	Reworking of all the issues above from a new perspective of maturity. Special emphasis on career and family changes. Particularly important	Women's career and life patterns do not easily fit into Erikson's framework. Rather than move systematically through the stages

Table 6.2   (continued)

Life Stage, Approximate Age, and Major Developmental Crises (derived from Eurocentric norms)	Key Environmental Systems (Eurocentric perspective)	Developmental Tasks (primarily Eurocentric perspective)	How Life Stages Differ among Multicultural Groups
		are the physical, cognitive, and emotional changes that come with each new decade.	one by one as suggested by Erikson, some women work on many stages simultaneously. Maturity may be flexibility in the use of all stages, and each culture will define maturity differently. The thirty years of adulthood are more complex than allowed for in the Eriksonian time frame.
Old age (65–death): Ego integrity vs. despair	Family, friendship network, community. Caring and health agencies as one faces illness and nears death.	Reworking all previous developmental crises once again. Life review and finding meaning in what one has done. Coping with physical changes and illness. Dealing with the death of family and friends. Financial/living concerns and decisions.	Experts now concede that many are still in middle age at 70. A new, rapidly increasing category is the "old-old" who are age 85 and over, many of whom still have good health and enjoy full lives, contrary to cultural stereotypes. Age is valued far more in Native American Indian culture.

SOURCE: Developmental tasks adapted and extended from Egan and Cowen (1979).

research and clinical practice, however, reveal that the four phases produce a substantial base of information and insight in about four hours of interviewing (Tamase & Kato, 1990; Tamase, 1991). Tamase has developed specific questions for each life period, which may be viewed in more detail in Ivey (1991b).

Making Meaning from Life History

In response to developmental questions at the birth-to-preschool period, Tamase finds that clients tend to discuss random, disconnected images and events in fragments. At the elementary school age, concrete stories are obtained, whereas adolescents demonstrate self-examination and the beginnings of pattern recognition. In the final session on current life clients become quite aware that their present mode of functioning is deeply related to their past developmental history. Exhibit 6.4 presents a shortened version of IDC with a multicultural focus. The exercise is useful in helping you think about your clients more developmentally and from a multicultural perspective.

Exhibit 6.4

 ## Exercise in Developmental Mapping and Storytelling

This exercise will help you understand how you or your client generated key construct systems and beliefs about the world. The exercise can be quite lengthy, and a review of each life stage could take an hour or more. Alternatively, writing a simple brief story from each stage may help you understand how some life patterns have developed.

Review one life stage or more, asking yourself or your client the following questions. If you wish to work through the framework at a deeper level, add the four-level questioning framework of DCT in exhibit 6.2 to your interview. For example, in discussing the family situation in the first question, ask for an image and what is seen/heard/felt, then for a concrete situation, then for patterns, and end with a systematic multicultural examination of the family system.

1. *Key environmental systems.* What was the family situation during this life stage? What important life events or stressors affected your family or caregivers during this period? What is the nature of family or extended family in your personal history? Where did you obtain your support at that life stage? (The focus here is on the individual and key environmental support systems.)

2. *Life stage developmental story.* Tell me one story and/or significant event that stands out for you from this life stage. (Examples might be a birth story, a fragment of a childhood memory, a family story repeated again and again. As time permits, solicit aditional stories from the life stage. The focus here is on individual recollections, although recollections are usually in a context.)

3. *Multicultural issues.* How did gender, religion, ethnic/racial status, or other multicultural issues affect your development during this period? Tell me a story you recall from that time period about the role of men or women, a religious figure, or an ethnic/racial figure. Who were your heroes? To whom did you look up? (The

focus here is on the individual and how he or she relates to multicultural issues.)

4. *How does the past relate to the present?* How do the data you've discussed during this time period relate to your present life experience? Do you see any patterns that relate to

how you are now and/or how you relate to others? What do you see as the influence of family and culture on where you are now? (The focus here is on the individual, with secondary emphasis on how family and multicultural issues influence being.)

Process/Outcome Research: A Case Example

Fukuhara (1984) utilized DCT assessment and treatment in a successful seven-interview series of sessions with a young female university student in Japan. The case is interesting, as it suggests that emotional/cognitive development may be a universal phenomenon, but that it may play itself out differently among men and women and those of varying cultures.

Client Assessment and Therapeutic Approach

The young woman client in this case was age 18 at the time of counseling and was self-referred. Early in the first interview (as translated from Japanese), she introduced her problem as follows:

> This spring, I met this boy . . . and thought our love would last a long time. However, when I returned from summer vacation, he did not even seem to want to talk to me. This finally made me so angry that I became aggressive and we had a fight. Surprisingly, my boyfriend seemed to like being told off. Still, he doesn't ask me out and the only time I see him is at the activity club. . . . I project into the future and think that if I continue to love him, we would eventually get married. What would my life be then? Would I have to make sacrifices to his will? . . . Would this eventually destroy my love for him? Should I give up on him now? (p. 1)

The issue this woman faced seemed to be one of intimacy, but this issue manifests itself differently in Japanese culture — that is, the level of involvement would not typically appear among North American clients. In terms of DCT cognitive-emotional assessment, there is a good deal of sensorimotor emotion, while the client's words are concrete and descriptive.

Client Cognitive-Emotional Movement through Interventions

The concrete/sensorimotor description of the problem required Fukuhara to use listening skills in a concrete fashion. The client needed to tell her stories, especially her emotional story, in great detail. Fukuhara utilized the skill of reflection of feeling almost exclusively in the first session. The reflections were focused on naming and clarifying specific feelings, and problem solving was avoided. The reflections were concrete ("You felt angry when your friend didn't call you," "We are sad when that happens"[6]). Patterns of emotions associated with formal operations were not explored until later in the interview series ("We seem to feel anger about many situations").

In the first interview, the client's perception of the relationship with her boyfriend was "He is mine; I am his" despite the realities of a relationship that had clearly ended. The client's cognition was "stuck" or immobilized by an unrealistic sensorimotor perception that influenced much of her thinking and behavior and interfered with performance in other areas as well.

The first three sessions focused on person-centered listening during which the client moved toward a conceptual frame that allowed for more distinctions between herself and her former boyfriend. For example, in session 3, the client was able to express "He should be different from me, but I cannot admit it." The interview plan at this point called for Fukuhara to enter the client's frame as fully as possible. This close relationship between therapist and client allowed the young woman to start the process of truly separating from her "loved one."

Table 6.3 presents the client's perception of her relationship with her boyfriend from the beginning of the interview series to the conclusion. The client gradually moved from an overly attached, embedded relational orientation to one in which she

Table 6.3   Client Descriptions of Relationship and External Evaluations of Reality Testing over a Seven-Interview Series

Interview Session	Client Perception of Relationship[a]	Client Reality Testing (evaluated by three counselors)		
		Co. A	Co. B	Co. C[b]
1	He is mine; I am his.	xx	xx	x
2	His whole existence is for me; my whole existence is for him; I should come up to his expectations.	xx	x	Δ
3	He should be different from me; but I cannot admit it.	x	Δ	Δ
4	I can keep my identity only when I am away from him.	Δ	Δ	o
5	I have come to understand his own behavior, which is different from mine.	Δ	o	o
6	I am myself; he is himself.	o	o	O
7	I have to do something for my own good.	O	O	O

[a]As the measure of reality testing, this I-Thou relation was used.

[b]xx = very poor   x = poor   Δ = average   o = good   O = very good   Co. = counselor

was appropriately separated and independent. Three external counselors observed the interview series and rated the client's reality testing — that is, how realistic was the client's frame of reference toward the world. The client became more realistic as therapy progressed.

By interview session 4, the client was able to engage in more formal thought and developed a stronger sense of self-in-relation. Fukuhara then returned to the sensorimotor level for more in-depth experiencing of emotion, using Gestalt techniques to "activate" client thinking and action. Sessions 4 and 5 used some of the concepts of Ellis's rational disputation.

The client at interview 6 was able to separate herself fully: "I am myself; he is himself." The final session focused around plans for the future: "I have to do something for my own good." In these final interviews, the client was able to step back and look at herself in a *system of operations.* She was able to reflect on herself and her patterns both as a person and as a woman in Japanese society.

Case Summary

Fukuhara's case is particularly interesting as it illustrates the cognitive growth and development that can occur in a client in the brief course of counseling and therapy. The client's language at both surface and deep structure levels has clearly changed.

This case illustrates the cross-cultural similarity of a basic male-female issue of love and relationship, separation and attachment. Nonetheless, in different cultures the script of the interview and the degree of attachment or separation may play out differently. Fukuhara comments that despite cultural differences, much of "counseling theory is basically applicable to individuals whatever their problems . . . or background" (p. 6).

Limitations and Practical Implications of an Integrative Approach to Counseling and Therapy

The DCT framework presents a special challenge to the therapist/counselor, as it demands expertise in multiple theories and interventions. Very few of us can be equally expert in all modes of helping. The network conceptions of treatment planning endorsed by DCT provide a partial answer to this problem in that working with a team of intervention specialists often may be more effective than attempting to do all the work yourself. Only the rare counselor or therapist can be equally effective as individual, family, and community intervention specialists.

The DCT framework is the newest of the theories described in this book. Although early clinical and research findings have been promising, clearly much study and experience will be needed to verify the framework more fully. Fortunately, DCT was designed as an open system and, as such, is constantly subject to change and modification over time. Furthermore, DCT is only one integrated approach to counseling and therapy. Lazarus's multimodal therapy (1981, 1986) and Assagioli's (1976) psychosynthesis are other important metatheoretical models.

On the positive side of the DCT orientation are the multicultural, multinational origins of the framework in theory, research, and practice. DCT's reliance on cultural identity theory as well as its orientation toward Afrocentric, feminist, and Native American approaches to helping may give it multicultural relevance. In addition, DCT does not reject any form of therapy. Rather, it seeks to find what is best in each therapy and, more than that, how each therapy might be beneficial to some individual client or family.

DCT also offers a theoretical framework for integrating seemingly diverse approaches to the field. The developmental roots in Piagetian thinking lead to a focus on client cognition and emotion, which, in turn, leads to an attempt to move away from imposing an external frame of reference on the client and toward a more egalitarian coconstructive relationship. DCT hopes that the counselors and therapists will work "with the client" rather than "on the client."

NOTES

1. The multicultural team who have coconstructed the central concepts of DCT include Machiko Fukuhara, Tokiwa University, Japan; Oscar Gonçalves, University of Minho, Portugal; Allen Ivey and Mary Bradford Ivey, University of Massachusetts; Koji Tamase, Nara University of Education, Japan; and Sandra Rigazio-DiGilio, University of Connecticut. In addition, Jay Carey, University of Massachusetts, has adapted and extended the ideas here in his theories of cognitive-developmental supervision. Evelyn Brooks, University of Massachusetts, recently has furthered DCT's understanding of emotion in the interview and helped provide new connections between the framework and multicultural issues. Dianne Kenney and Joseph Law, University of South Alabama, and William Mailler, University of Massachusetts, have extended the DCT model to vocational counseling. Mary Brodhead, Ottawa, has utilized the model in teacher education.

2. Modern philosophers related to these ideas include the founder of the concepts of intentionality, Franz Brentano (1874/1984), and the central existential/humanist and author of *Being and Time* (1926), Martin Heidegger.

3. Varying grammatical forms of *schema* and *schemata* (the plural of *schema*) are used by different authors, including *scheme, schemes,* and *schemas.* Here the word *schema* will be used as both singular and plural.

4. The four levels of client cognitive development are further divided into eight levels. The Standard Cognitive-Developmental Interview and Standard Cognitive-Developmental Classification System may be viewed in Ivey (1991b). The eight levels have many parallels to the Jackson/Freire integration presented in chapter 5.

5. A further set of fine distinctions is made by DCT—*each of the four cognitive-developmental levels contains all of the other levels within.* This is a rather esoteric and difficult aspect of DCT theory. The ideas of "relational holism" are outlined in detail in the chapter "Development as a Holistic Enterprise" in Ivey (1986, pp. 261–303). There the theories of the theologian Paul Tillich, Carol Gilligan, and French psychoanalyst Jacques Lacan (1977) are presented as varying models of Oneness.

6. Note that Japanese counselors in a more relational culture will often use the word *we,* whereas European-American counselors might focus more on the individual.

REFERENCES

ANDERSON, T. (1983). *Style-shift counseling.* [Internal government publication.] Ottawa: Staff Training and Development Branch, Correctional Service of Canada.

ASSAGIOLI, R. (1976). *Psychosynthesis.* New York: Penguin.

ATTNEAVE, C. (1969). Therapy in tribal settings and urban network interventions. *Family Process, 8,* 192–210.

BASSECHES, M. (1984). *Dialectical thinking and adult development.* Norwood, NJ: Ablex.

BRENTANO, F. (1984). *Psycholgie vom Empirischen Standpunkt [Psychology from an empirical standpoint.]* (Original work published 1874) Cited in R. Chisholm, Intentionality, in P. Edward (Ed.), *The encyclopedia of philosophy* (Vol. 4) (pp. 201–4). New York: Macmillan.

BROOKS, E. (1990). *Emotions and identity.* Unpublished paper, University of Massachusetts, Amherst.

CHEATHAM, H. (1990). Empowering Black families. In H. Cheatham & J. Stewart (Eds.), *Black families* (pp. 373–93). New Brunswick, NJ: Transaction Press.

CHEEK, D. (1976). *Assertive Black . . . puzzled White.* San Luis Obispo, CA: Impact.

CLEMENT, C. (1983). *The lives and legends of Jacques Lacan.* New York: Columbia University Press.

CROSS, W. (1991). *Shades of Black.* Philadelphia: Temple University Press.

EGAN, G., & COWEN, E. (1979). *People in systems.* Pacific Grove, CA: Brooks/Cole.

ERIKSON, E. (1963). *Childhood and society* (2nd ed.). New York: Norton. (Original work published 1950)

FREIRE, P. (1972). *Pedagogy of the oppressed.* New York: Herder & Herder.

FRY, P., KNOPF, G., & COE, K. (1980). Effects of counselor and client racial similarity on the counselor's response patterns and skills. *Journal of Counseling Psychology, 27,* 130–37.

FUKUHARA, M. (1984). *Is love universal? — From the viewpoint of counseling adolescents.* Paper presented at the forty-second annual conference of the International Association of Psychologists, Mexico City.

GILLIGAN, C. (1982). *In a different voice.* Cambridge, MA: Harvard University Press.

GONÇALVES, O. F. (1989). The constructive-developmental trend in cognitive therapies. In O. F. Gonçalves (Ed.), *Advances in the cognitive therapies: The constructive-developmental approach.* Porto, Portugal: APPORT.

GONÇALVES, O. F. (1990). *Terapia comportamental: modelos teóricos e manuais terepêuticos [Behavior therapy: Theoretical models and therapeutic manuals].* Porto, Portugal: Edições Jornal de Psicologia.

GONÇALVES, O. F., & CRAINE, M. (1990). The use of metaphors in cognitive therapy. *Journal of Cognitive Therapy, 4,* 135–50.

GONÇALVES, O. F., & IVEY, A. (1992). Developmental therapy: Clinical applications. In K. T. Kuehlwein & H. Rosen (Eds.), *Cognitive therapy in action: Evolving innovative practice.* San Francisco: Jossey-Bass.

GONÇALVES, O. F., & MACHADO, P. P. (1989). Do pensamento absolutista ao pensamento dialéctico através da terapia cognitiva [From absolutist to dialectical thought through cognitive therapy]. In J. F. Cruz, R. A. Gonçalves, & P. P. Machado (Eds.), *Psicologia e educação.* Porto, Portugal: APPORT.

GUIDANO, V. (1991). *The self in process: Toward a post-rationalist cognitive therapy.* New York: Guilford.

HEIDEGGER, M. (1926). *Being and time.* New York: HarperCollins.

IVEY, A. (1973). Media therapy: Educational change planning for psychiatric patients. *Journal of Counseling Psychology, 20,* 338–43.

IVEY, A. (1986). *Developmental therapy: Theory into practice.* San Francisco: Jossey-Bass.

IVEY, A. (1987). The multicultural practice of therapy: Ethics, empathy, and dialectics. *Journal of Social and Clinical Psychology, 5,* 195–204.

IVEY, A. (1991a, October). *Developmental counseling and therapy: A review of the 1971–73 microtraining/media therapy psychoeducational project with psychiatric inpatients.* Paper presented at the Veterans Administration Conference, Orlando, FL.

IVEY, A. (1991b). *Developmental strategies for helpers: Individual, family and network interventions.* Pacific Grove, CA: Brooks/Cole.

IVEY, A., & GONÇALVES, O. F. (1988). Developmental therapy: Integrating developmental processes into the clinical practice. *Journal of Counseling and Development, 66,* 406–13.

IVEY, A., GONÇALVES, O. F., & IVEY, M. (1989). Developmental therapy: Theory and practice. In O. F. Gonçalves (Ed.), *Advances in the cognitive therapies: The constructive-developmental approach.* Porto, Portugal: APPORT.

IVEY, A., & IVEY, M. (1990). Assessing and facilitating children's cognitive development: Developmental counseling and therapy in a case of child abuse. *Journal of Counseling and Development, 68,* 299–305.

IVEY, A., & IVEY, M. (1991). Network interventions and DCT. In A. Ivey (Ed.), *Developmental strategies for helpers: Individual, family and network interventions* (pp. 228–59). Pacific Grove, CA: Brooks/Cole.

IVEY, A., & RIGAZIO-DIGILIO, S. (1990). The standard cognitive-developmental classification system. In A. Ivey (Ed.), *Developmental strategies for helpers: Individual, family and network interventions* (pp. 289–99). Pacific Grove, CA: Brooks/Cole.

IVEY, A., RIGAZIO-DIGILIO, S., & IVEY, M. (1990). The standard cognitive-developmental interview. In A. Ivey (Ed.), *Developmental strategies for helpers: Individual, family and network interventions* (pp. 289–99). Pacific Grove, CA: Brooks/Cole.

JACKSON, B. (1975). Black identity development. *Journal of Educational Diversity and Innovation, 2,* 19–25.

KEGAN, R. (1982). *The evolving self: Problem and process in human development.* Cambridge, MA: Harvard University Press.

KELLY, G. A. (1955). *The psychology of personal constructs* (Vols. 1 & 2). New York: Norton.

KENNEY, D., & LAW, J. (1991). Developmental counseling and therapy with involuntary midlife career changers. *Journal of Young Adulthood and Middle Age, 3,* 25–39.

KURTZMAN, F., YEAGER, J., LANDSVERK, J., WEISMIER, E., & BODURKURKA, D. (1989). Eating disorders among selected female student populations at UCLA. *Journal of the American Dietetic Association, 89,* 45–53.

LACAN, J. (1977). *Ecrits: A selection.* New York: Norton. (Original work published 1966).

LAZARUS, A. (1976). Multimodal assessment. In A. Lazarus (Ed.), *Multi-modal behavior therapy.* New York: Springer.

LAZARUS, A. (1981). *The practice of multimodal therapy.* New York: McGraw-Hill.

LAZARUS, A. (1986). Multimodal therapy. In J. Norcross (Ed.), *Handbook of eclectic psychotherapy* (pp. 65–93). New York: Brunner/Mazel.

MAILLER, W. (1991, October). *Preparing students for the workplace: Personal growth and organizational change.* Paper presented at the North Atlantic Regional Association for Counselor Education and Supervision, Albany, NY.

MEARA, N., PEPINSKY, H., SHANNON, J., & MURRAY, W. (1981). Semantic communication and expectations for counseling across three theoretical orientations. *Journal of Counseling Psychology, 28,* 110–18.

MEARA, N., SHANNON, J., & PEPINSKY, H. (1979). Comparisons of stylistic complexity of the language of counselor and client across three theoretical orientations. *Journal of Counseling Psychology, 26,* 181–89.

NATANE, C. (1984). *Japanese society*. Rutland, VT: Tuttle.

PIAGET, J. (1963). *The origins of intelligence in children*. New York: Norton. (Original work published 1926)

PIAGET, J. (1965). *The moral judgment of the child*. New York: Free Press.

PIAGET, J. (1985). The equilibration of cognitive structures. Chicago: University of Chicago Press.

REYNOLDS, D. (1990). Morita and Naikan therapies — similarities. *Journal of Morita Therapy, 1*, 159–63.

RIGAZIO-DiGILIO, S., & IVEY, A. (1990). Developmental therapy and depressive disorders: Measuring cognitive levels through patient natural language. *Professional Psychology: Research and Practice, 21*, 470–75.

ROSEN, H. (1985). *Piagetian dimensions of clinical relevance*. New York: Columbia University Press.

SCHNEIDERMAN, S. (1983). *Jacques Lacan: The death of an intellectual book hero*. Cambridge, MA: Harvard University Press.

SHOSTRUM, E. (Producer). (1966). *Three approaches to psychotherapy* [Film]. Santa Ana, CA: Psychological Films.

TAMASE, K. (1991, April). *The effects of introspective-developmental counseling*. Paper presented at the American Association of Counseling and Development, Reno, NV.

TAMASE, K., & KATO, M. (1990). Effect of questions about factual and affective aspects of life events in an introspective interview. *Bulletin of Nara University of Education, 24*, 153–63.

THELAN, M., MANN, L., PRUITT, J., & SMITH, M. (1987). Bulimia: Prevalence and component factors in college women. *Journal of Psychosomatic Residents, 33*, 73–78.

HISTORICAL THEORIES OF COUNSELING AND PSYCHOTHERAPY
The First, Second, and Third Forces

Three major historical theoretical trends mark the field of counseling and psychotherapy. These major theories are often called "forces" in that the ideas have had such an immense impact on the field. Although somewhere between 250 and 500 theories of change can be identified, psychodynamic, cognitive-behavioral, and existential-humanistic theories remain the most influential. In this section, two chapters are devoted to each of the major historical forces.

The first force—psychodynamic theory— is primarily associated with its founder, Sigmund Freud. Although Freudian theory remains influential, derivatives of this theory have the most immediate impact on practice today. At this time, the work of John Bowlby, as supported by the researcher Mary Ainsworth, on attachment theory is especially important. Understanding the basic concepts of attachment theory

presented here will give you a solid foundation on which to study object relations theory, ego psychology, and the many permutations of psychoanalytic thought.

The second force—cognitive-behavioral theory— has long been associated with B. F. Skinner. Again, the concepts have been extended and modified. Skinner preferred to identify himself as a behaviorist rather than a cognitive-behaviorist. He considered the "mind" and "cognition" to be relatively unimportant constructs. Such authorities as Donald Meichenbaum, Albert Ellis, Aaron Beck, and William Glasser have extended Skinner's foundational work in important ways, demonstrating the importance of "mind" as well as behavior. The cognitive-behavioral tradition is currently the most frequently practiced of all orientations.

The third force—existential-humanistic theory— has its origins in European philosophy but achieved its maximum influence in counseling and therapy through the seminal work of Carl Rogers. The work of Viktor Frankl and of Frederick (Fritz) Perls is presented in detail as representing two important extensions of the third-force orientation. The existential-humanistic conception has deeply influenced the way all other theories are practiced.

The fourth force — multicultural counseling and therapy — relates to these historical theories. MCT recognizes that traditional theories of helping developed in a predominantly Northern European and North American context. As such, these traditional theories are relevant for working with clients from those cultures but have some limitations with clients of other cultures. For example, most historical theories of helping have been generated by European-American White males and, as such, tend to have gender and cultural limitations. Moreover, there is relatively little consideration of family issues in the first-, second-, and third-force orientations.

The multicultural counseling and therapy approach may be described as unifying in that it seeks to respect multiple perspectives and use different approaches in individually and culturally appropriate treatment. MCT draws heavily on first-, second-, and third-force theory in its actual practice but constantly adapts the constructs to meet diverse needs of clients. The United States and Canada, as culturally diverse nations, increasingly are finding it necessary to find new ways to think about delivery of counseling and therapy services. In this process, MCT recognizes the value of traditional approaches.

In addition to integrating and utilizing these historical theories of counseling and psychotherapy, MCT is generating its own conceptions. The case example applying cultural identity developmental theory to a Puerto Rican woman (chapter 5) illustrates how MCT theory can be used with first-, second-, and third-force ideas. Moreover, those oriented to MCT have initiated new explorations in psychodynamic, cognitive-behavioral, and existential-humanistic theory. These ventures are extending traditional theory and making it alive and relevant in new ways.

The following six chapters, then, focus on description of psychodynamic, cognitive-behavioral, and existential-humanistic thinking. At the same time, an effort is made both to critique this approach and to recognize innovations that are extending the value and influence of these basic theories of counseling and psychotherapy.

Psychodynamic Counseling and Therapy: Conception and Theory

CHAPTER GOALS

This chapter seeks to:

1. Summarize the worldview of psychodynamic theory and illustrate that it is far from a single orthodox framework.

2. Give special attention to multicultural issues and the psychodynamic frame of reference.

3. Present some central theoretical constructs, giving special attention to the object relations developmental framework and focusing on the work of Bowlby and Ainsworth.

4. Extend this framework through consideration of Taub-Bynum's view of the family unconscious, a theory and practice that help relate psychodynamic theory to current multicultural trends.

The Psychodynamic Frame of Reference

Freud brought order out of chaos. Until his brilliant and insightful work was publicized, mental operations and behavior seemed unknowable and almost mystical. His place in history ranks with the major influences of Darwin, Einstein, and Marx. While discussions of his legacy sometimes bring more heat than light, there can be no disputing his importance in the development of Western psychological thought.

What does Freud offer us today? First, his extensive writings organize human functioning and conceptualize the emotional and irrational feelings underlying behavior. Second, his many disciples provide a constant impetus for change in psychotherapy through addition to and modification of his concepts. Those who started from a Freudian orientation include close followers such as Ernest Jones and revisionists and neo-Freudians such as Alfred Adler, Eric Erikson, Karen Horney, Melanie Klein, and Harry Stack Sullivan. When names such as Fritz Perls (Gestalt therapy), Alexander Lowen (bioenergetics), and Eric Berne (transactional analysis) are added, it is easy to see how profound Freud's influence remains.

The psychodynamic frame of reference presented in this chapter starts with Freud but then moves to the more multiculturally relevant attachment theory of John Bowlby, which is supported by the research of Mary Ainsworth. The innovative work of Bruce Taub-Bynum is then presented, as it shows how family and multicultural influences can be made more explicit in the psychodynamic model. Just as the entire field of counseling and therapy is changing, so can we anticipate major new constructions of psychodynamic theory in the future.

The Psychodynamic Worldview

"If Freud's discovery had to be summed up in a single word, that word would without a doubt have to be 'unconscious,' " wrote Laplanche and Pontalis (1973, p. 474). The word *unconscious* means lack of awareness of one's own mental functioning. More broadly, it also means all things of which we are not aware at a given moment — both biological and psychological. Individuals are unaware (unconscious) of what is impelling and motivating them toward action.

Psychodynamic theory needs to be contrasted with *psychoanalytic theory*. As used here, the term *psychoanalytic* refers specifically to Freud's theory and orientation. Psychodynamic theory is a broader set of constructs that includes psychoanalytic theory as an important foundation. Some key aspects of the definition of psychodynamic theory used in this chapter follow:

1. *Client developmental history is important and needs to be considered for full client understanding.* Freud is often considered the first developmental psychologist. Basic to his orientation and the psychodynamic frame of reference is the importance of childhood experience in determining how we act and behave in the present.

2. *Important in our developmental history are the key people we have related with over time — our object relations.* In psychodynamic language, *object relations*

is the term given to relationships with people and important objects in our life. We develop in relationship to people — our family, friends, and peers.

3. *We are unaware (unconscious) of the impact of biological needs, of past developmental object relations, and of cultural determinants on our present behavior.* The unconscious is the reservoir of our memories and biological drives, most of which we are unaware of.

4. *We constantly act out in our daily lives our developmental history and our unconscious biological drives.* From the psychodynamic frame of reference, we are heavily ruled, sometimes even completely determined, by forces outside our awareness. However, some psychodynamic theories claim biology is central in unconscious development, whereas others focus more on life-span developmental issues. Increasingly, the influence of multicultural factors in unconscious development is being recognized.

5. *The task of counseling and therapy is to help the client discover the unconscious roots of present behavior.* Through psychodynamic techniques and concepts, such as free association, interpretation, and analysis of transference, we can help the client discover and understand the background of present behavior, thoughts, and feelings.

Each of the above points would be modified greatly if one were to assume an ego psychology position (Freud, 1982; Erikson, 1950/1963; Hartmann, 1958), a more classic object relations orientation (Guntrip, 1968; Klein, 1975; Winnicott, 1988), a linguistic interpretation (Lacan, 1966/1977), a feminist orientation (Chodorow, 1978; Baker Miller, 1976; Okun, 1992), or a family/multicultural orientation (Taub-Bynum, 1980, 1992). Within each of the groups, there are sharp differences, and the authorities just listed are but a small part of a vast array of scholars and clinicians whose opinions vary widely.

Clearly, there exist differences of opinion within the psychodynamic establishment, but all in the field agree on the central importance of the unconscious. The position emphasized in this chapter is basically that of Bowlby's (1969, 1973, 1988) attachment theory, a variation of the object relations orientation. Attachment theory takes an ecological person-environment approach to psychodynamic thought and is currently rapidly increasing in influence. Ainsworth has conducted the basic research supporting the theory, and she and Bowlby (1991) won the American Psychological Association Award for Distinguished Scientific Contributions.

The chapter will close with consideration of Taub-Bynum's psychodynamically oriented work (1984, 1992), which builds on Jungian theory and shows how family and multicultural forces are in action at the conscious and unconscious levels.

Multicultural Issues and the Psychodynamic Tradition

Psychodynamic theory has received a great deal of criticism,[1] much of it from women and minority groups. Psychoanalytic theory tends to be seen as male and elitist in origin. Many still think of psychoanalytic theory as a monolith, with orthodox inter-pretations based on libido theory and unconscious sexuality. With sexist concepts such as penis envy, a highly verbal intellectualized orientation, and a reputation for long periods of treatment, psychodynamic theory has been viewed by many as ther-apy only for the wealthy.

Integrating Multicultural and Feminist Issues with a Psychodynamic Approach

Comas-Diaz and Minrath (1985) urge that issues of ethnicity and race become part of the psychodynamic treatment process. Rather than separate multicultural issues from therapy, the modern psychodynamic approach encourages you as a counselor to use these issues as part of therapy. If there is some form of prejudice in your background, it will show in countertransferential form in the interview. If you have done work on multicultural issues, you may be able to use multicultural factors as part of the free association and insight processes, which is effective psychodynamic therapy.

Taub-Bynum (1984, 1992) makes the above general points more explicit. He points out that we learn about ourselves and our culture in the family and proposes, in his complex extension of the psychodynamic model, that we need to focus on the *family unconscious.* From the family unconscious perspective, each individual is a specific focus of experience in the family and culture, but much of that experience is also shared with others. Family experience is implicated in the inner landscape of *each person who shares the same family,* both unconsciously and consciously.

Jean Baker Miller's *Toward a New Psychology of Women* (1976) has been particu-larly influential as what could be termed psychodynamic criticism from a women's frame of reference (also see Baker Miller, 1991). Women's sense of self has been gener-ated in a family and cultural context, and Baker Miller argues that many women "do good" while "feeling bad." Society has placed conscious and unconscious roles on women that restrict their ability to cope with conflict. In terms of therapeutic work with women, Baker Miller would point out that the psychodynamic techniques are dangerous unless issues of gender are considered.

Psychodynamic Theory and Insight

Psychodynamic approaches are oriented to understanding and insight. Sue and Sue (1990) comment:

> We need to realize that insight is not highly valued by many culturally different clients. There are also major class differences as well. People from lower socioeconomic classes frequently do not perceive insight as appropriate to their life situations and circum-stances. . . . Insight assumes that one has time to sit back, to reflect and contemplate about motivation and behavior. . . .
>
>   Likewise, many cultural groups do not value insight. In traditional Chinese society, psychology is not well understood. . . . Many Asian elders believe that thinking too much about something can cause problems. . . . "Think about the family and not about

yourself" is advice given to many Asians as a way of dealing with negative affective elements. *This is totally contradictory to Western notions of mental health—that it is best to get things out in the open in order to deal with them.* (pp. 38–39) (Emphasis added)

Psychodynamic approaches are indeed focused on insight. The required self-disclosure and interpersonal openness are sometimes seen as immaturity by Asian cultures. Many African-Americans, Native Americans, and other minority members would strongly endorse variations of these statements. Sue and Sue's comments should give us all reason to pause as we review some central constructs of psychodynamic theory.

Central Constructs of Psychodynamic Theory

Psychodynamic methods have been described as an "uncovering therapy," in that the goals of therapy are focused on discovering the unconscious processes governing behavior. Once these unconscious processes are discovered in their full complexity, the individual is believed able to reconstruct the personality.

Id, Ego, Superego, and the Role of Anxiety

The Id

Imperative for uncovering unconscious functioning is an understanding of id, ego, and superego functioning. As Laplanche and Pontalis (1973) observe: "The id constitutes the instinctual pole of the personality; its contents, as an expression of the instincts, are unconscious, a portion of them being hereditary and innate, a portion repressed and acquired" (p. 197). It may be noted that the id is almost totally unconscious and may be either playful and creative or destructive. Biological drive theory is important for those who focus on the id.

Superego

By way of contrast, the superego is totally learned as the child matures in the family and society. Conscience, ideals, and values are within the realm of the superego. Whereas the id is uncontrolled, the superego may seek to control.

In the superego may be found internalized rules of the family and cultural history. It is in superego functioning that issues of gender roles, attitudes toward one's affectional orientation, and other multicultural issues are most relevantly explored. For example, the homeless, the Vietnam veteran suffering from posttraumatic stress disorder, or the gay male afraid to "come out of the closet" may have incorporated society's discriminatory attitudes at an unconscious level and blame themselves for their problems.

The Ego

The ego serves as a mediator between the superego (conscious rules from family and society) and the id (unconscious rebellion or playful storehouse). In traditional Freudian theory, the ego is sometimes seen as being at the mercy of these two competing forces. Modern ego psychology theorists, such as Erikson, talk about increasing ego functioning and giving the person more power to control her or his own life.

Ego strength may be increased through assisting the client to understand the interplay of ego with id and superego. The ego operates at conscious, preconscious, and unconscious levels of experience, although it is primarily manifested in counseling at the conscious level.

The Role of Anxiety

Anxiety and tension may result from the conflicts between the id, ego, and superego; from fear caused by conscious or unconscious memories of past experiences from childhood development; from dangerous impulses of the id, such as sexual desires that may be taboo; from superego-derived guilt; or from the inadequacies of the ego to resolve conflict.

Anxiety may be attached to a specific object or cause so that the reason for anxiety may be clear, or anxiety may be "free floating," in that the reason for anxiety is lost in the unconscious. A sense of free-floating anxiety without rational explanation is particularly threatening and may be repressed into the ego defense mechanisms described in the following subsection. The complex task of the therapist or counselor is to uncover the structure of anxiety so that personal reconstruction can begin.

Balancing Id, Ego, and Superego

If you work psychodynamically, you will have to take a position on the respective roles and importance of id, ego, and superego dimensions. If you place the id as central in importance, you will find orthodox, traditional analytic theory most helpful to you in uncovering the roots of anxiety. If you take an id or drive-oriented position, you may be more interested in and supportive of medication. If you place the ego as central to your theory, you will find ego theorists such as Erikson or Hartmann most helpful,

The position stressed in this chapter is that of Bowlby and Taub-Bynam, who recognize the importance of id and ego functioning but are more oriented to the superego and environmental/contextual issues. This balance of person and environment is likely to be more in accord with evolving fourth-force multicultural counseling and therapy.

The Ego Defense Mechanisms

What is the ego defending itself from? Generally speaking, the answer is anxiety. But where does the anxiety come from? It tends to come from conflicts between internal biological drives and wishes (id) and demands of the environment (superego). Thus ego defense mechanisms are oriented to protecting and strengthening the ego, which somehow has to balance these competing demands.

How Defense Mechanisms Arise

The specific role of defense mechanisms is well illustrated through Bowlby's (1940, 1951, 1988) observations of British children separated from their parents during World War II. The children were taken from their homes in London to protect them from the intense German bombing and placed in homes in the countryside. Needless to say, this was a highly anxiety-provoking time for the children.

Bowlby observed that the young children who were separated from their parents became depressed and morose but gradually learned to cope and to behave more "normally." When their parents visited them, most children did not greet them enthusiastically; rather, they edged toward their parents carefully. Some might display anger and even seek to hurt their parents.

Bowlby points out that the anxiety associated with the loss of the caregiver was so intense that the children *defended* themselves against another loss. *Avoidant behavior* and *acting-out* behavior are two types of defense mechanisms that protect not only children but also adults from deeper internal conflicts and the experience of anxiety. Bowlby notes that it was functional for the children to defend themselves against further anxiety—specifically a reexperience of loss when the parents returned to London. The defense mechanisms worked effectively to protect against emotional pain.

Bowlby may be considered a *developmental ecologist* in that he recognizes that each unique individual develops in relationship to the environment. Bowlby takes biology as a given but provides clear evidence that environmental factors shape the nature of individual uniqueness.

A family and multicultural view would extend the concepts of defense mechanism, maintaining that varying family backgrounds and varying cultural issues will have relevance to the type of defense mechanism selected (Taub-Bynum, 1992). For example, an older child taken from London might use the more positive defense mechanism of sublimation (discussed in exhibit 7.1) and survive the emotional trauma by taking care of and supporting other younger children. This child may have learned such behavior and thinking patterns in the family of origin. Family-of-origin patterns, then, are transferred as survival defense mechanisms in later life.

Imagine you are a therapist working with one of these children years later. As an adult, the individual may be suffering from deep anxiety that may play itself out in many ways (defense mechanisms and an array of pathologies such as depression, phobias, and so on). The client may talk to you about "not caring about the loss of parental support and nurturing" years ago. One of your therapeutic tasks, according to psychodynamic theory, is to *uncover the historic roots* of present anxiety, depression, or other ineffective current behavior.

The Antisocial Personality as a Defensive Structure

Nowhere is the importance of underlying mechanisms of defense more key than in your understanding of the antisocial personality. This diagnostic classification is often considered the most difficult to treat. Following from Bowlby, it is important to think of such behavior as a set of defense mechanisms used to protect the individual from harm.

Underlying the antisocial client's bravado and manipulation is a person whose dependency needs were never met. Although there is evidence that some antisocial behavior has a genetic foundation, family environments of antisocial individuals frequently are full of neglect and abuse (Brassard, Germain, & Hart, 1987). When you do establish a relationship with an antisocial client, he or she unconsciously fears the loss of this relationship and thus strives to avoid or to destroy it.

The child diagnosed with conduct disorder often reappears in later life as the antisocial personality. You can safely assume that many children who are difficult to manage experience abusive and assaultive home lives. The conduct disorder and/or antisocial client has learned that the "best defense is a good offense." Thus when you work with difficult clients, recall that you are working with defensive structures (their offensive behavior) that cover up underlying issues.

The Existence of Multiple Defense Mechanisms

The antisocial's attempts to leave a healthy therapy relationship can be considered a defense mechanism, which might be termed a reaction formation (doing the opposite of the desired) to the client's own underlying dependency needs. When you confront such clients, they will often use denial as a major way to protect themselves. Their repressed behavior is a continuation of past issues.

Your difficult task as a psychodynamic therapist is to break through the defensive structure and work for understanding of how the present situation was influenced by past history. *More than one defense mechanism may be represented by a single episode of behavior, feeling, or thought.* Exhibit 7.1 lists examples of defense mechanisms.

Counselors and therapists tend to think about defense mechanisms as abstract ideas. In truth, clients indicate again and again in very concrete ways their defensive style. Bowlby's attachment theory provides some very concrete ways in which you can use defense mechanisms to assist in understanding clients and in helping them break out of inefficient patterns of thinking, feeling, and behaving. These defense mechanisms are learned through our developmental history in the culture.

Developmental Roots of Behavior, Emotion, and Thought

Freud has been termed the first developmental psychologist because he made sense out of childhood by pointing out that distinct patterns and problems can be associated with each developmental stage. One of Freud's tenets is that each stage of development requires us to face key developmental tasks, as illustrated in the following subsections.

Exhibit 7.1

Examples of Defense Mechanisms

Following are examples of defense mechanisms, how these might be employed by varying types of clients, and possible positive benefits of each defensive structure. These interpretations are derived from Laplanche and Pontalis (1973).

1. *Repression and continuation.* An underemphasized generic concept of the defense mechanism is that our behavior, thoughts, and actions are repressed developmental continuations from the past. Winnicott (1988) maintains that all defense mechanisms are methods the child (and adult) uses to repress pain. These mechanisms stem either from denial of internal drives (id wishes) or hurts from external reality (superego pressures).

Therefore, in a broad sense defense mechanisms are all repressed continuations of past biological and environmental issues and stressors. Many, perhaps even most, of your clients will be continuing old behavior, thoughts, and emotions in some form from their developmental past.

The remainder of the defense mechanisms are elaborations of this basic point. Your task as a therapist, as both Winnicott and Bowlby imply, is to find the underlying structure of the anxiety and the purpose of particular defense mechanisms used by the client.

2. *Denial.* This is the most difficult and troublesome defense mechanism. Many of your clients will refuse to recognize their traumatic and troublesome past. Vietnam war veterans often split off and deny the origins of their distress in combat; the antisocial client will deny needs for dependency and attachment; and the survivor of abuse or rape may unconsciously forget (deny) that he or she was abused.

Denial, at the same time, can be healthy. If we allow ourselves to be in touch with our past and present pain all the time, we can only become depressed. From this frame of reference, then, depression is at least a partial failure of the positive aspects of the defense mechanism of denial.

3. *Projection.* When a client refuses to recognize behavior or thoughts in the self and sees, or projects, this behavior onto someone else, the defense mechanism of projection is likely to be in operation. One is most often troubled by behavior in others that is similar to one's own behavior.

At an extreme level, you will find projection in the paranoid client. The person with a paranoid style often has a history of real persecution in the family of origin or developmental past. He or she has learned to project onto others anticipated persecution. As it happens, anticipating persecution often results in a self-fulfilling prophecy. However, there can be positives to paranoia. For example, when buying a used car, it might help to be a bit paranoid.

Similarly, one of the most important helping skills may be related to projection. In empathy, we try to see the world as others see it and project ourselves into the client's worldview. Some of us become so empathic and entwined with others that we literally project ourselves into the client and fail to see the client. This relates closely to the Kleinian concept of projective identification, which is discussed in detail in chapter 8.

4. *Displacement.* This defense mechanism is a variety of transference in that the client's feelings or thoughts are transferred or directed toward a person other than the originating source. The worker who has a bad day on the job and then treats her or his spouse badly is a common example of displacement. If your antisocial client acts out against you for no apparent reason, he or she is likely to be displacing anger and aggression around past maltreatment onto you.

You may notice that each of the defense mechanisms relates to others. In a sense, displacement is behavior *repressed and continued* from the past. Displacement *denies* what is really happening and often *projects* onto others the events of the day or the past. The displacement may enact itself in an opposite form of the conscious intent—that is, *reaction-formation.* These defense mechanisms are not clearly distinct entities. Rather, defense mechanisms are simply alternative constructions of the same continued event from the past. You will find that one defense mechanism construction is more useful at times, and that another, at first seemingly totally different, mechanism is useful at others.

5. *Sublimation.* A more positive defense mechanism, sublimation takes repressed instinctual energy and unconscious continuations from the past and channels them to constructive work such as artistic, physical, or intellectual endeavor. A person who is frustrated sexually or a survivor of abuse may turn to movie making, athletics, or creative writing and be rewarded well by society for these efforts.

Sublimation, however, may fail in the long term as repressed anger and hurt well up in surprising places. Many survivors of child abuse sublimate past hurt and become counselors and therapists (see Miller, 1981). The danger here is that wounded helpers who have denied or sublimated their own history of abuse may unconsciously prevent clients who have been abused from looking at their own past history.

6. *Other Mechanisms.* The five mechanisms here represent only a beginning. Other mechanisms include: *fixation* (being immobilized at an earlier level of development), *rationalization* (the making up of rational reasons for irrational or inconsistent behavior), *regression* (returning to early childhood behavior when faced with a life event somehow resembling an old traumatic injury), *conversion* (translating unconscious mental functioning into physical symptoms such as headaches), *identification* (acting and behaving like someone else), *reaction-formation* (doing the opposite of unconscious wishes), and *provocative behavior* (acting in a way such that others are provoked to do to one what one is unable to do to oneself, such as showing anger or love), among other mechanisms.

The Issue of Trust

The child in the oral period (roughly 0–2 years) must learn how to be dependent, trust, and relate with the primary caregiver, usually the mother. If the child does not accomplish age-related developmental tasks adequately, interpersonal relationships will likely be disturbed and appear as adult problems.

The Issue of Control

The developmental task of the anal period (2–4 years) is that of control. The child must move away from the primary caregiver, take control over his or her own life, and become a separate, eventually individuated person. The "terrible two's," with characteristic strife and temper tantrums, are illustrative of the child's struggle to become her or his "own person." Freud (1925/1964) points out that the individual is often constituted in negativity or opposition. A child may have developed the capacity for relationships in the oral period, but unless separation occurs at this age, the individual may remain overly fused or overly distant from others as an adult.

It is a vast oversimplification to talk about the control of feces as the major issue of this period. This type of conceptualization is naive and makes it easy for many to reject the Freudian framework. The task of this period focuses on control and becoming a separate human being. This separateness is built on the earlier attachments of the oral stage.

Sex Role Development

The Oedipal period (4–7 years) is the time at which the child learns to understand the sex role he or she is to undertake. As can be seen in the oral and anal periods, the child has already received considerable training in sex roles through the holding environment and the manner in which the control issues of the anal period have been handled by the culture. What is distinctive about the Oedipal period is that the child develops awareness of the meaning and importance of sex roles themselves and brings together all previous learnings in a total gestalt.

The Oedipal Controversy

It is over the interpretation of the Oedipal period that most controversy has arisen. Chodorow (1978) has been particularly critical of the overly male interpretation of this period. Bragg and colleagues (1987) criticize traditional Oedipal theory from a lesbian frame of reference. Erikson's (1950/1963) formulations have been presented in the preceding chapter and have been an important influence on the way development has been viewed. But his framework, like Freud's, has been generated from a predominantly Eurocentric, White male frame of reference (see, for example, Neugarten, 1979).

Limitations of the Freudian View

Freud first pointed out the importance of early life stages and human development. His framework, however, is basically biological, and he gave relatively little attention to issues of caregiving, mothering, and the family. If something goes wrong with the child in the developmental process, the fault is seen in the child rather than in the system of interpersonal relationships.

One example of the limitation of the Freudian view is seen in the Oedipal drama. Freud talks about Oedipal issues as if the five-year-old is the most pivotal and influential family member. The role of possibly oppressive and immature parents tends to be minimized in classical Freudian drive theory. Traditional id-oriented drive theory has historically tended to minimize child abuse and child assault.

The developmental stages above and the key tasks associated with each are Eurocentric in origin and therefore do not address variations in gender and culture. *What is needed is a culturally relevant developmental framework* similar to that proposed by Tamase (1991), described in chapter 6, that allows for the fact that different cultures have differing needs at differing times in the developmental process.

Object Relations Theory

Object relations theory, an offshoot of psychoanalytic theory, leads to a new precision invaluable to all counselors and therapists in understanding the key word *relationship*.[2] Object relations (OR) could be translated as "people relations." OR theory is concerned with examining the relations between and among people and how the history of interpersonal relationships is transferred from the past to present behavior. The major object or person in a client's history is the caregiver, most often the mother.

However, depending on social, economic, and cultural considerations, the caregiver may be the father, a couple, or a grandmother. In traditional rural Puerto Rican culture, the caregiver is really the entire extended family. In Africa and Aboriginal Australia, the primary caregiver may be anyone in the extended family or the whole community. Issues of single parenthood, adoption (especially when the birth mother remains involved with the adoptive parents), and same-sex parents further change the concept of caregiver. Some would even argue that day-care workers need to be considered part of the caregiver complex. Regardless of terminology, all are important objects in the development of the child.

OR theory shows us how to study the *relationship* we have with our clients. With that developmental knowledge and the multiple frameworks of the family/cultural perspective, it is often possible to assess client developmental history. With this knowledge, you can predict with more accuracy how your intervention will be received by your client.

John Bowlby and Developmental Ecology

John Bowlby (1969, 1973, 1988) presents one of the clearest expositions of object relations theory, although he does not follow the traditional individualistic points of view. Bowlby (personal communication, January 1987) describes his ideas as having developed in opposition to Melanie Klein, the first major OR theorist. Bowlby is also interested in information-processing theory, social ecology, and psychological science. He may be construed as a developmental ecologist, as he stresses the importance of the child developing in relation to context and environment.

Attachment

Bowlby's concepts are often described as *attachment theory.* The primary task in the mother-child relationship[3] is for the child to learn how to become securely attached. If the child can become attached, it has a secure base for exploring. Using an attachment framework clarifies the developmental tasks specified in Freud's oral stage.

As a developmental ecologist, Bowlby emphasizes the joint construction of the mother-child relationship: the child is not only affected by the environment, but the child also impacts that same environmental context. For example, some children seem to be neurologically equipped for closer relationships than others. Moreover, Bowlby points out that the child's natural biological endowment develops in relationship with the mother. Child and caregiver grow (or deteriorate) in an ecological process of mutual social influence.

Bowlby points out that three major patterns of attachment exist: securely attached, anxious resistant (generated by an ambivalent and alternating accepting-and-rejecting mother-child relationship), and anxious avoidant (generated by a rejecting and impoverished relationship). Research by Ainsworth and others (Ainsworth, 1985; Ainsworth & Bowlby, 1991) has verified these attachment patterns.

Most important in supporting Bowlby's theories, however, is longitudinal research that shows that children's pattern of attachment assessed in the early months is highly predictive of later adjustment. Some specific examples follow:

1. The pattern of attachment identified at twelve months is still present at six years (Main & Solomon, 1986).

2. Children identified as securely attached are found to be described in nursery school three and a half years later as cheerful, cooperative, and popular, whereas anxious avoidant and anxious resistant patterns of attachment are described as emotionally insulated, hostile, and antisocial (Bowlby, 1988).

3. Children who are securely attached in early life are later found to respond to failure with increased effort, whereas the less securely attached do the opposite (Lütkenhaus, Grossman, & Grossman, 1985).

These are but a few examples, and a strong base of research literature supporting Bowlby's theories is developing (see exhibit 7.2).

Separation

There is also a second task related to attachment, that of separation. A securely attached child is able to separate and individuate. The task of separation may be con-

Exhibit 7.2

The Ainsworth-Bowlby Connection: How Research Validates a Theory

John Bowlby's theory has had immense influence. However, it is Mary Ainsworth who has verified Bowlby's work in a variety of cultural situations, including Africa (1967) and Europe (1977). Currently, Bowlby's attachment theory has more direct empirical validation than any other psychodynamic theory.

Essentially, what Ainsworth has verified is that children need secure attachments with the caregiver if they are to develop and eventually become separate human beings in accord with cultural expectations.

The Ainsworth Strange Situation Procedure (Ainsworth, Blehar, Waters, & Wall, 1978) provides a laboratory situation for testing the nature of a child's attachment. The child is videotaped with toys in situations in which the mother is first present and then absent. The focus is on how the child responds when the mother returns.

Securely attached children tend to smile and hug the returning parent. *Anxious resistant* children tend to show angry resistance on the mother's return. *Anxious/avoidant attached* children ignore or even back away from the mother and may show as much interest in a stranger as they do their own mothers. (These patterns of child interaction are similar to those observed by Bowlby in his work with children during World War II and discussed earlier in this chapter.)

Using the Strange Situation as a baseline, researchers have found that securely attached infants are (1) more cooperative, enthusiastic, and compliant at two years (Main, 1973; Matas, Arend, & Sroufe, 1978); (2) more competent with peers at age 3 (Waters, Wippman, & Sroufe, 1979); and (3) in better self-control in preschool (Egelund, 1983).

Bowlby (1988) cites research in Germany replicating these findings (Wärtner, 1986) and indicating that patterns of attachment tend to remain stable over time. A wide variety of studies exist that lend increasing support for Bowlby's descriptions. Needless to say, the data are not yet complete that will prove that the tenets drawn from Bowlby's early work will hold true through adulthood.

Ainsworth and Bowlby (1991) update these findings and provide an overview of the development of their theory and research.

sidered roughly analogous to the sense of autonomy and personal control associated with Freud's anal period. Other object relations theorists, particularly Margaret Mahler (1975), give detailed attention to this aspect of development. It is particularly important to note that Freud, Erikson, Mahler, and Klein tend to focus on individuation and separation. Bowlby recognizes the importance of these concepts but stresses attachment and a stable base in the family as critical for human development.

In summary, Bowlby's ecological/ethological position contrasts rather markedly with that of Freud but does not deny the validity of much of Freud's biological determinism. It can be argued that Freud did not give adequate attention to the fact that the child develops in a person-environment social context and that Freud and many of his followers have failed to consider the very real and demonstrated impact of the mother, the father, and other significant caregivers, such as the extended family, nursery school, child care providers, and so on. All these caregivers can and do affect children's growth and development.

Practical Implications

The practical implications for the counselor and therapist from Bowlby's work include:

1. Helping us become aware of the importance of early child relationships for later development;
2. Suggesting that psychoeducational interventions in terms of family education are critically important;
3. Indicating the importance of infant child care (including extended family, babysitters, and infant school) as important areas of counseling intervention;
4. Enabling us to identify likely early childhood experiences of our clients, thus underlining the importance of varying our style of therapeutic interaction and relationship according to the developmental history of our client. (For example, an adult who was insufficiently attached as a child may need more support and empathy from us, whereas an adult who was overly attached now may need encouragement to individuate and separate.)

This introduction to the complex, and sometimes esoteric, world of object relations is but a beginning. Although focused on a self-in-relation to other context and of demonstrated cultural relevance, Bowlby's framework may still give insufficient attention to multicultural issues. The following discussion adds a family and multicultural focus to understanding and treatment from a psychodynamic perspective.

The Family Unconscious and Multicultural Psychodynamic Theory

Taub-Bynum (1984) talks about three interrelated levels of unconscious functioning—the individual, the family, and the collective or multicultural unconscious. The individual unconscious is similar to that described in earlier portions of this chapter and is characteristic of most individualistic, Eurocentric approaches to psychodynamic thought.

The Family and
the Multicultural Unconscious

According to Taub-Bynum (1984), "The Family Unconscious is composed of extremely powerful affective (emotional) energies from the earliest life of the individual" (p. 11). This statement is in accord with object relations theory but reframes and extends these concepts. Essentially, our life experience in our family of origin enters our being in both positive and negative ways. Experience *in the family* (as contrasted with experience solely with a single caregiver) is transmitted to the child and becomes very much a part of the child's being (and later, of course, the adolescent and adult being).

Thus, the construction, development, and recognition of the family of origin become of key importance in understanding the individual's development. There is a marked relationship between these formulations and those of Tamase (1991; Tamase and Kato, 1990) presented in chapter 6. Both are telling the field that many of the social and environmental constructions of reality the individual absorbs come from the family, which itself is located in a cultural context.

Taub-Bynum draws from Jungian psychology for his concept of the multicultural or collective unconscious (see Jung, 1935). Jung talks of the collective unconscious as drawing on all the thought and behavior patterns over time. Jung's constructs have been clarified by Fordham (1957), who points out that much of the collective unconscious is the repository of client experience in the family. As indicated in chapter 2, when you work with an individual, the family and the culture are also present. From this frame of reference, this construct of the collective unconscious becomes closely allied with issues of multicultural empathy and understanding.

Family and Culture

The family is where we first experience and learn the culture. The family unit is the culture bearer—and we need to recall that the nature of the family and its functions vary widely among cultures. Taub-Bynum speaks of the "powerful affective . . . energies" we experience in the family. The interplay between individual and family affective experience is the formative dialectic of culture. It is not really possible to separate individuals, families, and culture, for their interplay is so powerful and persistent.

The interaction of family and culture is also reflected in the composition and dynamic life of the individual. Furthermore, when that individual is considered within the expanded context of the family unconscious, we readily see how each person's dynamic functioning is implicated in the functioning of significant others who share the same field of consciousness, energy, and experience. This interrelationship can be seen in the choice of symptoms and behavior, both somatic and psychological.

A hologram provides a useful analogy. In a hologram, each image and area in the overall field reflects and dynamically enfolds each other area but from a slightly different angle. That different angle significantly can be seen as the perception and experience of "individuality" in the interdependent family system. Each family member contains the experience of the family and the culture, but each member has vary-ing perceptions and experiences.

Unconscious mental functioning and constructs are heavily influenced by culture. For example, at birth the Japanese child is immediately placed on the mother's body, and the two mold—or bond—together as one. In European cultures, the newborn traditionally has been taken from the mother and held separately. Emotional body attachments and relational thinking are thereby reinforced in Japanese childrearing practices, whereas the focus in European societies is on separation and autonomy. This small example illustrates that individual constructions of self (or self-in-relation) depend very much on family and cultural conditions.

The Unconscious as the Discourse of the Other

Taub-Bynum's family and multicultural constructions are in some ways similar to those of the French psychoanalyst Jacques Lacan (1966/1977). Lacan disagrees with ego psychologists, whom he considers naive in their interpretations of Freud. Lacan argues for interdependence as the goal of psychotherapy rather than the traditional autonomy so often associated with ego psychology.

A classic statement of Lacan is that we do not even own our personal unconscious. Rather, we are the "discourse of the Other." The Lacanian view of development and ego psychology stresses that influences of the family and the culture are so profound that the ego itself is "very feeble." A major goal of Lacanian-style psychoanalysis is to help the client discover how much of the so-called self is indeed the result of a life-time of interactions in the family and the culture.

Therapeutic Implications of the Family and Multicultural Unconscious

You as counselor or therapist can assume that the client is in some way acting out the family and multicultural unconscious. In some cases, the client will present a unique personal construction of the problem, but in others, family or cultural influences are more powerful and important than are individual forces.

The microskill of focus is a simple introduction to a very complex issue. If a client presents an issue and you focus on the issue by emphasizing personal pronouns (*"You* seem to feel . . ."*) and "I" statements, the client will talk about the problem on an individual basis. If you focus on the family in connection with the individual, the process of therapy changes ("How did *you* learn that in your *family?*" "How does that experience relate to *your family of origin?*"), and the client will talk about issues from a family orientation.

At the multicultural level, the focus changes to the impact of the context and culture on the client's development and present worldview ("How does the *Irish* expe-rience of Yankee oppression in Boston relate to how *your* family generated its ideas in the world and how does that play itself out in *you?*" "What does being *African-*

American [or other minority group] have to do with your *family* experience and *your* own view of *yourself?*"). (These example questions are designed to be illustrative of the interrelationship of the individual, the family, and the cultural context; specific questions and clarifications should be appropriate to the context of the interview.)

Cheatham (1990), however, would challenge the above constructions, suggesting that we not only need to understand what is happening in the client's family and multicultural context, but we also need to take action. We as therapists need to work to help the family deal with the culture, and even more important, we as therapists need to work to change a culture that often is more responsible for problems and pathology than are individuals or families.[4]

Generation of Family Symptoms over Time

At a more complex level, Taub-Bynum talks about the intergenerational transmission of symptoms in a family. If you construct a family history/genogram of an alcoholic client, you often find several alcoholics in the family over the generations. Family theory (see chapter 13) gives central attention to this dynamic.

The story of Kunta Kinta in Alex Haley's popular book *Roots* (1977) illustrates the above point. Kunta Kinta, taken into slavery from Africa, provided his family with an image that played itself out over the generations, right to the time when Haley wrote his famous book. Family members acted out this story over the generations in differing ways, but much of their thinking and behavior could be traced to this ancestor. For example, an upstanding member of the family might be acting out the positive intergenerational family script, whereas another family member might be in trouble with the law and acting out the negative family script. Each of these family members could be said to be engaging in a set of defense mechanisms that could be explained by tracing individual, family, and cultural history.

The Family Dream

Dreamwork is an important part of psychodynamic practice (see chapter 8), and Taub-Bynum's (1980) conception of the family dream adds an important and interesting dimension. Traditionally, dream interpretation focuses on the meaning of the dream in the individual life context, with minimal attention given to family and cultural issues.

In family dreamwork, the focus is on how the dream represents not just individual life experience, but also family intergenerational themes. For example, a client may have an anxious dream about the loss of some object—perhaps in the dream the client searches for the holy grail. A common interpretation that focuses on the individual would be that the client fears loss of important attachments, perhaps through the parents' old age and impending death. This interpretation might be useful, but it would also be important to explore the meaning of loss in the client's family over the years.

To continue the example, loss to a Jewish-American client might be much more than an individual issue, perhaps representing broader intergenerational issues around the holocaust. It is clear that those who survived the holocaust experienced considerable trauma that shows up in unconscious grief reactions. These experiences do not end with the immediate survivor, but also are transmitted to the children and grandchildren (for example, see Rosenthal & Rosenthal, 1980).

Family dreamwork with German holocaust survivors would include individual interpretations but would also focus on complex intergenerational family issues. Furthermore, the cultural symbol of Jewish loss and persecution over time might be stressed as well. Therapy includes individual, family, and cultural grieving and appreciation work. Appreciations might include the strengths of the Jewish family over the generations, pride in religious heritage and symbolism, and values of cultural cooperation as represented by the kibbutz.

In traditional psychodynamic theory, dream analysis is only one technique and area of consideration. Daily life issues and traumas are open to analysis and discussion just as are dreams. Clients live their lives as they have learned to live them in their attachment histories in their families of origin.

Multicultural and Gender-Related Implications of Family Unconscious Theory

A system as complex as that of Taub-Bynum's is difficult to summarize in a few words in a text such as this. What he is saying is that the basic ideas of Freud (and Bowlby and others) have immense relevance in a multicultural practice of counseling and therapy. The limitation of traditional psychodynamic practice is that it has not gone far enough nor has it focused on positive cultural dimensions and issues that can help clients face their lives more courageously and with a greater sense of pride.

An African-American, Puerto Rican, or Chinese-American client who seeks therapy needs help in handling day-to-day issues. Taub-Bynum would endorse humanistic and concrete cognitive-behavioral approaches as most immediately practical to the client. However, if clients are dealing with more complex and long-term issues, psychodynamic techniques can be highly beneficial as part of a general treatment plan. It is important to help clients look at themselves from the perspectives of their developmental history and the influence of family and culture on present-day life. Developing this perspective will help many clients move to the fourth level of multiperspective awareness suggested by cultural identity developmental theory.

Okun's (1992) review of object relations theory and psychodynamic practice raises many similar issues from a feminist frame of reference. She particularly stresses the need to look at issues of development and object relations from a perspective of gender roles and women's development in an often sexist society. She points out that "object relations and self-psychology are too dependent on inference and confuse data with interpretation" (p. 37) and that insufficient attention is given to the father's role. The latter point is one that Taub-Bynum's family-oriented orientation speaks to directly. Rather than place responsibility for the child's psyche on one person (the mother), this approach shows us how the individual and a variety of family possibilities are generated in a multicultural context.

Limitations and Practical Implications of Psychodynamic Approaches

Psychodynamic approaches require and demand extensive study, reading, and supervised practice by carefully trained individuals who have completed years of study. Full-blown psychodynamic practice is not for the beginner in that psychodynamic training requires the most rigorous intellectual discipline of all methods. The ideas presented in this chapter represent the most complex organization of human experience of any set of theories.

Nonetheless, this approach can be helpful to counselors and therapists in that it can create an awareness that what a client presents as a surface problem, concern, or behavior may not be the issue. Underlying the description of a problem may be a vast array of unconscious or unknown forces, ideas, and thoughts. As John Bowlby and Mary Ainsworth, Jean Baker Miller, and Jacques Lacan remind us, the force of unconscious experience is extremely powerful and should not be overlooked.

Psychodynamic approaches have been criticized as antithetical to and irrelevant for any other than highly verbal middle-class clients. Furthermore, there are many practicing psychodynamic therapists who have yet to come to terms with the family and multicultural challenge. Focusing solely on the individual, they may miss issues critical for client change and growth. Miller (1981) has pointed out the pitfall of failing to be aware of the therapist's own issues, and Taub-Bynum reminds us that cultural and family roots must be part of an overall treatment conceptualization.

NOTES

1. Psychodynamic theory has long been criticized as self-referential and tautological—a needless repetition of the same thoughts in different words. However, it is a holistic framework, and each alternative language frame gives a new perspective on the client and the client's developmental framework. Examination of the important book *The Language of Psychoanalysis* (Laplanche & Pontalis, 1973) helps explain this basic, but often misunderstood, point. Start with any basic psychoanalytic construct (repression, Oedipal complex, transference, projective identification) and read the definition carefully. Starting with transference, for example, you will be referred to countertransference and projective identification for further information. Moving there, you will be referred back to transference, but also to new concepts that will ultimately enlarge your understanding of the place you started. Psychodynamic theory is like a dictionary: every word defines other words. In the process of studying the psychoanalytic "dictionary," you begin to understand the complex whole of psychodynamic thinking.

One is reminded of the story of the blind men and the elephant. How one defines the elephant depends on which piece of the elephant you touch. The world is a totality, but we can only grasp a piece of its complexity. The more ways we look at the elephant, the better we can understand the whole, which, in truth, is beyond language.

2. The presentation here is based on A. Ivey (1989). A general model of object relations is

proposed. The focus is on the work of John Bowlby and Alice Miller in the belief that these two theorists provide the clearest, most multiculturally relevant, and most available introduction to what is a very complex set of theories (such as Klein, 1975; Guntrip, 1968; Kernberg, 1980; Mahler, 1968; Masterson, 1981).

3. Bowlby and his colleague Ainsworth have both been criticized severely by some in the women's movement as focusing almost solely on the mother as caregiver. This criticism has some merit. For example, Bowlby's 1958 article was entitled "The Nature of the Child's Tie to His Mother." More recently, however, Bowlby seems to have come to terms with a broader definition of caregiver. For example, in 1988 he said, "Looking after babies and young children is no job for a single person. If the job is to be well done, the caregiver herself (or himself) needs a great deal of assistance. From whom that comes will vary: very often it is the other parent; in many societies, including more often than is realized, it comes from a grandmother" (p. 2). Bowlby goes on to point out that the concept of caregiver varies from culture to culture.

4. Cheatham's comment is challenging to the field. The first author of this book has worked with a number of minority students who have had difficulty in practicum or internship settings. The cause of the difficulty was that these students often spend time outside the clinical or counseling settings helping troubled individuals or families find shelter, work through financial difficulties, and so on. Many practicum and internship settings consider the act of "doing something" to be an inappropriate professional role. They have criticized minority clinicians severely for "countertransference."

This, of course, is a reasonable construction if one takes the traditional psychodynamic ego psychology model. If one assumes the broader frames of Miller, Taub-Bynum, and Cheatham, then community action is relevant, and it is the ego psychologists and practica/internship supervisors who suffer the pains of "countertransference" owing to their blindness to obvious family and cultural contextual issues. It may be anticipated that such issues will be debated more openly in the next decade.

REFERENCES

AINSWORTH, M. (1967). *Infancy in Uganda: Infant care and the growth of love.* Baltimore: Johns Hopkins University Press.

AINSWORTH, M. (1977). Social development in the first year of life. In J. Tanner (Ed.), *Developments in psychiatric research.* London: Hodder & Stoughton.

AINSWORTH, M. (1979). Attachment theory and its utility in cross-cultural research. In P. Leiderman, S. Tulkin, & A. Rosenfeld (Eds.), *Culture and infancy: Variations in the human experience* (pp. 47–67). San Diego: Academic Press.

AINSWORTH, M. (1985). I. Patterns of infant-mother attachment; II. Attachments across the life-span. *Bulletin of the New York Academy of Medicine, 61,* 771–812.

AINSWORTH, M., BLEHAR, M., WATERS, E., & WALL, S. (1978). *Patterns of attachment.* Hillsdale, NJ: Erlbaum.

AINSWORTH, M., & BOWLBY, J. (1991). An ethological approach to personality development. *American Psychologist, 46,* 333–41.

BAKER MILLER, J. (1976). *Toward a new psychology of women.* Boston: Beacon.

BAKER MILLER, J. (1991). The development of women's sense of self. In J. Jordan, A. Kaplan, J. Baker Miller, I. Stiver, & J. Surry (Eds.), *Women's growth in connection.* (pp. 11–26). New York: Guilford.

BOWLBY, J. (1940). The influence of early environment in the development of neurosis and neurotic character. *International Journal of Psycho-Analysis, 21,* 154–78.

BOWLBY, J. (1951). *Maternal care and mental health.* Geneva: World Health Organization.

BOWLBY, J. (1958). The nature of a child's tie to his mother. *International Journal of Psycho-Analysis, 39,* 350–73.

BOWLBY, J. (1969). *Attachment.* New York: Basic Books.

BOWLBY, J. (1973). *Separation.* New York: Basic Books.

BOWLBY, J. (1988). *A secure base.* New York: Basic Books.

BRAGG, M., DALTON, R., DUNKER, B., FISHER, P., GARCIA, N., OBLER, L., ORWOLL, L., PAISER, P., & PEARLMAN, S. (1987). *Lesbian psychologies.* Urbana: University of Illinois Press.

BRASSARD, M., GERMAIN, R., & HART, S. (1987). *Psychological maltreatment of children and youth.* New York: Pergamon Press.

CHEATHAM, H. (1990). Empowering Black families. In H. Cheatham and J. Stewart (Eds.), *Black families* (pp. 373–93). New Brunswick, NJ: Transaction Press.

CHODOROW, N. (1978). *The reproduction of mothering: Psychoanalysis and the sociology of gender.* Berkeley: University of California Press.

COMAS-DIAZ, L., & MINRATH, M. (1985). Psychotherapy with ethnic minority borderline clients. *Psychotherapy, 22,* 418–26.

EGELUND, B. (1983). Comments on Kopp, Krakow, and Vaughn's chapter. In M. Perlmatter (Ed.), *The Minnesota symposia on child psychology* (Vol. 16, pp. 129–85). Hillsdale, NJ: Erlbaum.

ERIKSON, E. (1963). *Childhood and society* (2nd ed.). New York: Norton. (Original work published 1950)

FORDHAM, M. (1957). *New developments in analytical psychology.* London: Routledge.

FREUD, A. (1982). *Psychoanalytic psychology of normal development: 1970–80.* London: Hogarth.

FREUD, S. (1964). Negation. In S. Freud, *On metapsychology* (pp. 435–42). London: Penguin. (Original work published 1925)

GUNTRIP, H. (1968). *Schizoid phenomena, object relations, and the self.* New York: International Universities Press.

HALEY, A. (1977). *Roots: Saga of an American family.* New York: Doubleday.

HARTMANN, H. (1958). *Ego psychology and the problem of adaptation.* New York: International Universities Press.

IVEY, A. (1989). *Object relations: An introduction.* Unpublished manuscript, University of Massachusetts, Amherst.

IVEY, A. (1991). *Developmental strategies for helpers: Individual, family and network interventions.* Pacific Grove, CA: Brooks/Cole.

JUNG, C. (1935). The personal and collective unconscious. In C. Jung, *Collected works* (Vol. 7, pp. 87–110).

KERNBERG, O. (1980). Developmental theory, structural organization and psychoanalytic technique. In *Rapprochement.* New York: Aronson.

KLEIN, M. (1975). *Envy and gratitude and other works, 1946/1963.* London: Hogarth.

LACAN, J. (1977). *Écrits: A selection.* New York: Norton. (Original work published 1966)

LAPLANCHE, J., & PONTALIS, J. (1973). *The language of psychoanalysis.* New York: Norton.

LÜTKENHAUS, P., GROSSMAN, K. E., & GROSSMAN, K. (1985). Infant-mother attachment at twelve months and style of interaction with a stranger at the age of three years. *Child Development, 56,* 1538–42.

MAHLER, M. (1968). *On human symbiosis and the vicissitudes of individual* (Vol. 1). New York: International Universities Press.

MAHLER, M. (1975). *The psychological birth of the human infant.* New York: Basic Books.

MAIN, M. (1973). *Play, exploration and competence as related to child-adult attachment.* Unpublished doctoral dissertation, Johns Hopkins University, Baltimore.

MAIN, M., & SOLOMON, J. (1986). Procedure for identifying infants as disorganized/disoriented during the Ainsworth Strange Situation. In M. Greenberg, D. Cicchetti, & M. Cummings (Eds.), *Attachment in the preschool years.* Chicago: University of Chicago Press.

MASTERSON, J. (1981). *The narcissistic and borderline disorders.* New York: Brunner/Mazel.

MATAS, L., AREND, R., & SROUFE, L. (1978). Continuity of adaptation in the second year: The relationship between quality of attachment and later competence. *Child Development, 49,* 547–56.

MILLER, A. (1981). *The drama of the gifted child.* New York: Basic Books.

NEUGARTEN, B. (1979). Time, age, and the life cycle. *American Journal of Psychiatry, 136,* 887–94.

OKUN, B. (1992). Object relations and self-psychology: Overview and feminist perspective. In L. Brown & M. Ballou (Eds.), *Theories of personality and psychopathology: Feminist reappraisals* (pp. 20–45). New York: Guilford.

ROSENTHAL, P., & ROSENTHAL, S. (1980). Holocaust effect in the third generation. *American Journal of Psychotherapy, 34,* 572–79.

SUE, D., & SUE, D. (1990). *Counseling the culturally different* (2nd ed.). New York: Wiley.

TAMASE, K. (1991, April). *The effects of introspective-developmental counseling.* Paper presented at the American Association of Counseling and Development, Reno, NV.

TAMASE, K., & KATO, M. (1990). Effect of questions about factual and affective aspects of life events in an introspective interview. *Bulletin of Nara University of Education, 24,* 153–63.

TAUB-BYNUM, E. B. (1980). The use of dreams in family therapy. *Psychotherapy: Theory, Research, and Practice, 17,* 227–31.

TAUB-BYNUM, E. B. (1984). *The family unconscious.* Wheaton, IL: Quest.

TAUB-BYNUM, E. B. (1992). *Family dreams: The intimate web.* Ithaca, NY: Haworth Press.

WÄRTNER, U. (1986). *Attachment in infancy and at age six, and children's self-concept.* Unpublished doctoral dissertation, University of Virginia.

WATERS, E., WIPPMAN, J., & SROUFE, L. (1979). Attachment, positive affect, and competence in the peer group. *Child Development, 50,* 821–29.

WINNICOTT, D. (1988). *Human nature.* New York: Schocken.

Psychodynamic Counseling and Therapy: Applications for Practice

CHAPTER GOALS

This chapter seeks to help you:

1. Realize the value of psychodynamic theory for case conceptualization. Effective client analysis may result in a more effective treatment plan, enabling you to use client-centered, cognitive-behavioral, and other techniques that relate to client unconscious needs.

2. Learn some central techniques from this theory through practice exercises.

3. Engage in a beginning psychodynamic interview using the five stages of decisional counseling.

4. Establish some guidelines for a more multiculturally oriented psychodynamic practice.

The complexities of the psychodynamic frame of reference are virtually infinite, yet these chapters will give you a solid foundation. Some of the exercises in this chapter can be quite powerful, particularly if you magnify them using the techniques of developmental counseling and therapy (chapter 6). As such, use the techniques with a sense of ethics and under appropriate supervision.

Free Association: The Past Repeats in the Present

Free association is the basic technique and strategy of the psychodynamic approach. Free association is the "method according to which voice must be given to all thoughts without exception which enter the mind, whether such thoughts are based on a specific element (word, number, dream-image, or any kind of idea at all) or produced spontaneously" (Laplanche & Pontalis, 1973, p. 169).

The following exercise uses *focused free association*. By engaging in the exercise, the material and concepts of this chapter will be more useful and understandable. Consider each item and think about it before moving on to the next.

1. Focus now on a current concern or issue for yourself. Take time and consider it fully. (It sometimes helps to visualize an image of the problem. What do you see, hear, and, *especially,* feel as you think about the issue?)

2. What emotions do you have around that problem? Focus now on your feelings. Locate that feeling physically in your body and really focus on it.

3. Allow your mind to drift to an earlier time in your life (the earlier the better) associated with that feeling. What comes to your mind? You may experience visual images, fragments of feelings, or remember a specific situation. Allow yourself to experience those old thoughts and feelings once again.

4. How do you connect your present concern with the past? How are the two similar? Does the association between them give you some new thoughts about the meaning of the present concern?

5. Think about your gender, family of origin, and cultural/ethnic identification. How do these factors relate to your experience?

This simple, but often very powerful, exercise encapsulates both the theory and practice of the psychodynamic approach to counseling and therapy. Psychodynamic theory holds the technique of free association important in the belief that whatever comes to mind from the past is significant and somehow is connected to current life issues. The sequence in this exercise started with an issue of concern for you. Then, using imagining and sensorimotor experiencing techniques, you were asked to locate the feeling physically in the body. Free association can often be much more powerful and understandable if conducted in a sensorimotor fashion and images are used.

The concrete description of both present issues and past free association is important in making connections between or patterns from the two. The making of connections or formal operational patterns is vital to psychodynamic thought and requires that one be able to engage in verbal work of this type. It also requires a highly trusting relationship between therapist and client.

From a multicultural frame, psychodynamic thought has been roundly criticized as overlooking issues of social justice and as "alien" to cultures that may not wish to disclose personal feelings and issues (Ponterotto & Casas, 1991). The fifth point in the above exercise, although not usually associated with psychodynamic theory, leads the client to talk at the level of systems in which the individual developed and therefore can add a multicultural dimension to the psychodynamic approach.

Using Psychodynamic Theory for Case Conceptualization

When asked how he worked with clients in therapy, Bowlby (personal communication, January 1987) replied clearly and directly: "Clients treat us as they were treated—this is our guide for treatment." What Bowlby is saying is that you can expect clients to repeat their developmental history with you. Their developmental history in their family of origin is particularly important, and you can anticipate that many client behaviors with you in the here and now of the interview may be traced back to past experience.

For example, if the client is narcissistic and attention seeking, you can anticipate that somehow this behavior relates to what happened in the family. Most likely, as children narcissistic clients were rewarded by parents for certain types of behavior. In therapy, this client will likely seek the same type of admiration from you, even though you and many others in the client's life find such behavior undesirable. Moreover, the narcissistic client often has a developmental history wherein he or she was only rewarded by parents and others for certain types of achievement; the child's very real need for admiration and support for just being a child was not met.

Miller (1981) talks about the importance of meeting the healthy narcissistic needs of the child. If these needs are met, the child will have a secure, attached base as described by Bowlby and Ainsworth in chapter 7. However, many children become instruments of their parents' desire. Narcissistic, obsessive-compulsive, and many other types of clients are often in varying ways trying to meet unmet needs from the past, as can be seen in the following discussion of a dependent client.

The Dependent Client: A Case Conceptualization

In the interview, you can expect the client with problems of dependency to treat you in a dependent fashion. Expect dependent clients to ask your opinion and advice, attempt to please you, be very demanding of your time, and when especially needy, appear on your doorstep asking for special help. Think about your own experience of dependent and needy people. What are your own thoughts and feelings toward this type of individual? Take a moment and write down some of these thoughts and feelings.

Dependent clients treat you as they were treated in their family of origin. Psychodynamic theory and Bowlby, in particular, suggest that clients repeat their developmental history again and again. When clients respond in a dependent, needy way in the interview, you can anticipate that somehow this behavior can be traced back to the past and their family of origin. How do you imagine dependent clients might have

	caring; suicidal gestures	tion; probable sexual abuse	may move rapidly between extreme closeness and distance	site of family; group/systems approaches are useful
Histrionic All could benefit at times with open access to emotions.	Seeks reassurance; seductive, concerned with appearance, too much affect; self-centered, vague conversation	Enmeshed, engulfing family, with little support for individuation; possible sexual abuse/seduction; little family expectation for accomplishment; aware of others not of self	Similar to the borderline without the externalized anger; actions directed inward rather than outward	Encourage individuation; use assertiveness, skills training, consciousness raising; examine history of problem; use cognitive-behavioral and systems interventions
Narcissistic A strong belief in ourselves is necessary for good mental health.	Grandiose, self-important, sees self as very unique; sense of entitlement; lacks empathy; oriented toward success and perfection	Received perfect mirroring for accomplishments rather than for self; engulfing family; child enacts family's wishes; anxious/ambivalent caregiver	Focuses on selfish needs, tends to engulf others with needs; is charming to get wishes met, Don Juan type; may pair with borderline	Interpret behavior; look to past; employ cognitive-behavioral, systems, sensitivity training in a group
Avoidant It is useful to deny or avoid some things.	Avoids people, shy, unwilling to become involved, distant; exaggerates risk	Either engulfing family or avoidant family; enacting what the family modeled	Not many friends; easily becomes dependent on them or therapist	Use many behavioral and cognitive techniques; assertiveness training and relaxation training useful
Dependent We all need to depend on others.	Dependency on therapist even outside of session; indecision; little sense of self	Engulfing, controlling family; not allowed to make decisions; rewarded for inaction; told what to do	Dependent on friends; drives people away with demands	Reward action; support efforts for self; use paradox, assertiveness techniques

Table 8.1 (continued)

Style and Positive Aspect	Behavior/Thoughts in Session	Possible Family History	Predicted Current Relationships	Possible Treatment Approach
Obsessive-compulsive				
Maintaining order and a system is necessary for job success.	Perfectionistic and inflexible; focuses on details, making lists; devoted to work; limited affect; money oriented; indecisive	Overattached family that wanted achievement; oriented to perfection, like narcissist, but keenly aware of others, with a limited sense of self	Controlling; limited affect; demands perfection from others; hard worker; cries at sad movies	Reflect and provoke feeling; orient to client's personal needs; support development of self-concept; orient to body awareness
Passive-aggressive				
All of us are entitled to procrastinate at times.	Procrastinates; seems to agree with therapist, then undercuts; seems to accept therapist, then challenges authority	Perhaps obsessive family; individual instead moves away from perfectionism and fights back; a more healthy defense needs to be developed	"Couch potato"; skilled at getting back at and at criticizing others; defends by doing nothing; resents suggestions; not pleasant on the job	Let client learn the consequences of behavior; do not do things for client, but confront and interpret and pay special attention to client reactions

SOURCE: A. Ivey, *Developmental Strategies for Helpers* (Pacific Grove, CA: Brooks/Cole, 1991). Used with permission.

adolescent or adult is particularly problematic for many in the helping field. Professional helpers are usually "nice" people and find it difficult to work with those who aren't nice. (Miller [1981] suggests one of the reasons for this is that counselors' own survival in their families of origin often required them to be nice.)

As noted earlier, conduct disorder children and antisocial personality clients tend to have serious histories of abuse, and therefore these clients will often treat you in some sort of an abusive fashion. *If you react to these clients as others in their history have, you can expect them to continue their behavior.* If you react differently—specifically, if you treat them differently than they were treated in the past—there is some possibility that they will develop a useful relationship with you, which can make a difference in their lives.

In short, to help clients you must react to client maltreatment of you with patience, firmness, a clear sense of boundaries, and evidence of caring, as displayed in the Rogerian relationship, but with a difference. It is your task to think quickly on your feet and not allow yourself to be taken in by the client's presentation. Simply seeing antisocial clients' world solely as they present it to you is likely to fail, since they can use your empathy and understanding to manipulate you.

Another important rule to remember is to *treat the dependent client differently.* With dependent clients you must offer a solid relationship. Do not run from dependent clients' demands, but remember to maintain your boundaries. In the beginning stages, allow some dependent behavior and then gradually lead clients toward more independence or interdependence. Encourage clients to share their feelings and thoughts toward you. Providing these clients with accurate nonjudgmental feedback on the nature of the relationship can be helpful.

These therapeutic efforts are designed to move dependent clients away from a hierarchical relationship. The dependent client has been at the low end of a relationship hierarchy for a long time, and moving them toward an egalitarian orientation in which plans for change are coconstructed can be extremely beneficial. Multicultural, feminist therapy, and developmental counseling and therapy all place special emphasis on the egalitarian relationship as basic to change processes.

From a psychodynamic frame of reference, the relationship you establish with the client is of key—perhaps of crucial—importance. Your understanding of your own developmental history plays a vital role. If you do not understand and accept your own relationship history, you are more likely to find yourself "triggered" by difficult clients and reacting to them ineffectively.

Following subsections discuss some specific techniques drawn from analytic theory that can be used in the therapeutic relationship to clarify how the past is repeating in the present.

Interpretation

Psychodynamic counseling approaches are interpretive. Interpretation is a sophisticated and complex skill in which intellectual knowledge of psychodynamic theory is integrated with clinical data of the client. In chapter 3, we defined the microskill of interpretation as the renaming of client experience from an alternative frame of reference or worldview. Applied specifically to psychodynamic approaches, the skill of interpretation comes from the worldview of psychoanalysis and seeks to identify wishes, needs, and patterns from the unconscious world of the client.

Some specific guidelines for interpretation may be suggested. First, the counselor needs to use attending skills carefully so the data for an interpretation are clear. Next, the interpretation should be stated and the client given time to react. The helper may "check out" the client by asking "How do you react to that?" or "Does that ring a bell?" or "Does that make sense?" The check-out encourages the client to think through and assimilate or reject the interpretation.

Intentional psychodynamic therapists produce clients who can make their own interpretations. When clients interpret their own story in new words, clients will realize an insight. Insight may be described as the ability to look at old information from new perspectives, and thus is directly related to intentionality and creative responding. The person who is able to interpret life experience in new ways through insight is able to generate new "sentences" to describe the world.

However, it is also important to note that these new descriptions are almost invariably verbal. A verbal insight, or new sentence, is most valuable if the client is able to take the new information out of the session and use it in daily life. A major criticism of some psychodynamic approaches is their constant emphasis on insight, which produces a client who is searching diligently in the past while continuing to have problems in coping with present-day living.

Interpretations have traditionally been made from an individualistic, ego psychology frame of reference that puts the locus of the problem and decision making in the individual. There is, however, an increased awareness of how the psychodynamic model can be extended through interpretations made from a family or multicultural frame of reference. Consider the following example with a client suffering from depression, as frequently occurs with the dependent personality style:

Client: I'm really depressed; it's been taking a long time for me to understand myself, but I can only be happy if I do something for others—but they always seem to want more. I feel I'm never liked for myself.

Individualistic interpretation: Your pattern seems to be to try to do things for others and pay little attention to yourself. That would seem to go back to the way you solved problems as a child. You didn't feel adequate, so you tried to please others. Here we see you continuing that behavior now.

Family interpretation: Your place in your family was as a placater. Everyone else was arguing, and you took on that role—and then they kept you in it and still do even today. You're very good at keeping your new family flowing smoothly.

Multicultural interpretation (gender-oriented): Women in North American culture are expected to take the caring role. We've learned to define ourselves through relationships with others. It's natural, but the question is What do you want?

Multicultural interpretation (ethnic/racially oriented): Puerto Rican women are expected to put the family interests ahead of their own—it's in our tradition of

Marianismo: How can we respect that tradition and find our place in this U.S. society?

Each of the interpretations above can be helpful. In fact, each approach can be useful with the same client at various points in the interview or treatment series.

Summary

Psychodynamic approaches are interpretive, but the assumptions on which these interpretations are based are often Eurocentric in origin. Ignoring family, gender, and multicultural issues and focusing solely on individualistic psychodynamic therapy can result in harm for minority clients (see Sue & Sue, 1990), women, and also North Americans of European origin. It is necessary to expand our conception of the psychodynamic approach to therapy to include the self-in-relation and to avoid placing the burden primarily on the individual.

Free Association

Just as the word *unconscious* can be used to summarize Freud's theory, so can the technique of free association be used to summarize psychodynamic methodology. At an elemental level, free association simply encourages the client and the counselor to say anything that comes to mind.

Freud developed free association in his early work with hysterics, encouraging these patients to search for underlying unconscious factors. He refined the technique in his own self-analysis, particularly in his work with dreams. It was out of dream analysis, in particular, that Freud discovered the "royal road to the unconscious." If one is allowed to say anything at all that comes to mind (no matter how seemingly irrelevant), there is a pattern that frequently emerges to explain the meaning of a behavior, a dream, or a seemingly random thought.

There are some practical, common questions that most therapists and counselors use at some point in the interviews. These questions relate to the concept of free association. When you ask a client "What comes to your mind?" "What do you think of next?" or even "What is the *last* thing that comes to mind?" you are using questions closely related to free association.

The exercise at the beginning of this chapter introduced you to this technique. Free association techniques can be used in the classic open way of psychoanalysis or in a more focused way to precisely encourage discussion of family and multicultural issues.

Free association is an invaluable technique, regardless of the theoretical technique you select. Because free association focuses on the client's construction of issues, it provides you with access to inner dialogues, thoughts, and feelings that you might miss from other frames of reference. Furthermore, free association gives you and the client access to often surprising and valuable information, sometimes even pointing out possible abusive history where other eliciting techniques failed to do so. Exhibit 8.1 lists a number of free association exercises and techniques.

Exhibit 8.1

 Free Association Exercises and Techniques

The purpose of these exercises is to illustrate some basic and practical aspects of psychodynamic functioning. The person who moves through each exercise carefully will have a more complete sense of the importance of free association and its potential implementations in the counseling interview. Yet these exercises are only a minor beginning to an incredibly complex theory.

1. *The symbols of everyday life.* Much of Freudian and psychodynamic thought is based on sexuality and sexual symbolism. A good way to understand symbols and their meanings is to go through a few basic free association/creativity exercises. Take a separate sheet of paper and brainstorm as many words as you can think of when you hear the word "penis." Make this list as long as you can. Now take the word "vagina" and make as extensive a list as you can.

Now having made the two lists, expand them further. What objects in everyday life remind you of the penis and the vagina? What about types of people, the universe, things in your own living room? Make that list as long and extensive as you can. It can be suggested that brainstorming and creativity are closely allied to the processes of free association. Having completed your list, you may find it helpful to turn to the tenth lecture in Freud's *A General Introduction to Psychoanalysis* (1920/1966), widely available in paperback form. You will find that many of the words and symbols you generated are listed in that chapter. It was in a similar, but less structured, fashion that Freud slowly constructed his entire theory of personality.

As time and interest permit, take the words *intercourse, death, love, hate, breast, masturbation, birth, body,* and other specific words of interest to you. In each case, brainstorming a list of words will reveal a general pattern of the symbols that represent that idea or concept in everyday life.

2. *The "Freudian slip."* Slips of the tongue are often small windows on the unconscious. A student once walked into our office and asked if we gave "objectionable" tests. It takes but a very quick free association to understand this student's unconscious feelings. Not all such slips are as easily understood. But if one allows oneself to free associate, it is often possible to find the meaning of the error in speech. Think back on your own speech errors or those of your friends, then free associate to their meanings.

The process of examining the psychology of errors may be studied in more detail in Freud's second, third, and fourth lectures (1920/1966). Errors also show in our forgetting appointments, dropping things at crucial times, behavior that seems to repeat itself unnecessarily, and in many other ways. Again, free association is a route toward understanding the meaning of these errors.

3. *Dream analysis.* Recall and write down a dream you have had. Then sit back, relax, and focus on one aspect of that dream. Letting your free associations lead you, open your mind to whatever comes. Then see if any patterns or new ideas emerge that help you understand the dream.

As an alternative, keep the whole dream in mind and relax. This time, free associate back to an early childhood experience. Then follow that experience and go back to an even earlier childhood experience. In some cases, a third experience association may be helpful. Return to your dream and determine if the dream related to your associations.

The preceding processes are similar to those employed in analysis of dreams. An examination of Freud's lectures five through fifteen will reveal that you have anticipated some of his constructs and ideas. It is possible, using free association techniques, to realize intuitively many of Freud's concepts before you read them. This direct experiencing of free association should help you to understand the intellective aspects of his theory more fully.

4. *Analysis of resistance.* Resistance is the name given to "everything in the words and actions of the . . . [client] that obstructs his gaining access to his unconscious" (Laplanche & Pontalis, 1973). Most likely, in one of the preceding exercises you "blocked" at some point and couldn't think of a word. Your free associations stopped for a moment. These blockages are miniexamples of resistance and illustrate the operation of the general defense mechanism of repression. To recover the lost association that was blocked, it is important that one first focus on the block itself. The following example may prove helpful. Let us assume you want to understand your feelings toward your parents or some other important person in your life in more depth. One route to this is free

associating a list of words that come to your mind in relation to this individual. For example, suppose that one free associates to one's lover the following: "warmth, love, that hike to Lake Supreme, bed, touching, sexuality, (block), tenderness, an argument over my looking at another person, anger, frustration, (block)." First, one can get a general picture of feelings and important thoughts via this free association exercise. It is next appropriate to turn to the block and to use one of the following techniques to understand the block (or resistance): (1) free associate, using the block as a starting point (a clue may come via this route); (2) sing a song, let it come to your mind as you relax, then free associate from that song; (3) draw a picture, and once again free associate; (4) go to the bookshelf and select a book, or go to a dictionary and select a word, and free associate from what you select (sometimes the answer will be there immediately).

This small set of exercises does not explain resistance in its full complexity. If you have entered into it fully and flexibly, you may have broken through one of your own blocks or resistances and developed a slightly better understanding of yourself. An examination of Freud's nineteenth lecture will amplify these concepts and perhaps suggest additional exercises for you.

5. *Analysis of transference.* We sometimes find people we immediately dislike. Psychodynamic theory suggests that we have transferred past feelings related to someone from our past onto this new individual. Select someone you have problems with and try some of the free association exercises already suggested. Later, examine Freud's twenty-seventh lecture and compare what you anticipated with what he said.

Free Association and Multicultural Images

Exhibit 8.2 presents an exercise in free association and imagery that includes gender-related, religious, or cultural symbols. This exercise, if presented well and timed carefully, can be highly useful in an interview situation. Most of us can recall key images from the past that can help us think about issues from new perspectives. If used sensitively, such imaging techniques, combined with free association, can be extremely helpful.

Dream Analysis

Dream analysis is another important technique of psychodynamic approaches. Dream analysis can be conducted at a surface level by examining the manifest or observed content of the dream. Underlying the conscious parts of the dream is the latent content containing deeper structures of meaning. Free association can be used by psychodynamic counselors in the analysis of dreams at both levels. It is also important to note that these techniques can be applied directly in work with children if used sensitively with concrete language.

When conducting a dream analysis for the first time, it is helpful to use the five-stage structure of the interview. Exhibit 8.3 provides an exercise in psychodynamic interviewing that focuses on a dream. The same structure provided in this exercise can be useful when working with a variety of other issues as well.

Adapting Techniques of Dream Analysis with Current Real Issues

Although dream analysis is often a good place to start practicing psychodynamic interviewing, a more effective approach is to use the five-stage structure with special emphasis on focused free association *with any important client topic*. We believe that although dreams may be "the royal road to the unconscious," free association is too useful a technique to be reserved only for dreams.

For example, you may be working with an adult child of an alcoholic (ACOA). Many ACOAs have split off and forgotten painful childhood experiences. Once you have developed a trusting relationship with the ACOA client, the focused free association techniques can be very useful in helping these clients recover their lost childhood experiences. In the following brief example, which has been abbreviated for clarity, note that the repetition of key words, as in Gestalt therapy, intensifies the experience for the client:

> *Client:* (a nondrinker going through a second divorce from a second alcoholic wife) Yes, I tried so hard to please Joanie, but she continued to drink no matter what I did. Everyone at the office says I'm good at getting along with people, but I simply could never please her.

Exhibit 8.2

Focused Free Association and Guided Imagery Using Gender, Religious, and Cultural Symbols

The following exercise is designed to help clients recognize and use strengths from their gender, religion, and/or cultural background. When employed carefully, using concrete language, the exercise also can be effective with children.

1. *Inform your client as to your process and intent.* Rather than surprise the client, tell her or him what is about to happen and why it is potentially helpful. Specifically, let the client know that all of us carry images that can be personally helpful and supportive in stressful situations.

2. *Generate an image.* Ask your client to relax and then to generate a positive image that can be used as a resource. Suggest that the image be related to gender, religion, or cultural background. It is possible that a single image may encompass all three dimensions. A Franco-American woman, for example, might focus on Joan of Arc. Alternatively, a Jewish-Canadian client might focus on the Star of David, a Navajo on a mountain or religious symbol, a Mexican-American on the Christian cross or the pyramids near Mexico City.

3. *Focus on the image.* Using developmental counseling and therapy techniques, ask your client to see the image in her or his mind. What does she or he see, hear, feel? Ask the client to locate the positive feelings in the body. Then identify that image and feeling as a positive resource always available to the client.

4. *Take the image to the problem.* Using relaxation and free association techniques, guide the client to the problem which has previously been discussed or to any problem the client chooses. Suggest to the client that he or she use the positive resource image to help work with the problem. It is important to stress to the client that the image may or may not solve the problem. If the problem seems too large the image should be used to work on a small part of the problem rather than to solve it.

Counselor: (Using nonverbal observation) I notice that when you said you "could never please her" that you seemed to almost cringe at that moment. Could you go back and visualize an image of Joanie and say "I could never please her."

Client: I can see her. "I could never please her."

Counselor: Again.

Exhibit 8.3

 An Exercise in Psychodynamic Interviewing

The purpose of this exercise is to illustrate how the skills and concepts explored in this text may be used to conduct a basic interview from a psychodynamic perspective. Analysis of a dream or a client's reaction to an authority figure works well in the following framework. Alternatively, you may have identified a repeating life pattern in which the client tends to have a certain style of response, thought, feeling, or behavior in several situations.

If you wish, you could go through the stages by yourself, thinking to yourself about one of your own dreams, your reactions to authority, or your own repeating patterns.

The framework presented here will provide you with an introduction to how psychodynamically oriented counseling and therapy may be conducted.

Stage 1: Rapport/Structuring

Develop rapport with the client in your own natural way. Inform the client that you will work through some basic psychodynamic understandings about a dream, a relationship with authority, or a life pattern. Decide the issue to be worked on mutually.

Stage 2: Data Gathering

Use the basic listening sequence (BLS) of questioning, encouraging, paraphrasing, and reflection of feeling to bring out the issue in detail. If a dream, be sure that you bring out the facts of the dream, the feelings in the dream,

and the client's organization of the dream. If you are working with an authority issue, draw out a concrete situation and obtain the facts, feelings, and organization of the issue. In the case of repeating patterns, draw out several concrete examples of the pattern. Once you have heard the issue presented thoroughly, summarize it using the client's main words and check it out to ensure that you have understood the client correctly.

At this point, it is often wise to stop for a moment and use the positive asset search. Specifically, use the BLS to draw out the facts, feelings, and organization of something positive in the client's life. This may or may not be related to the dream or authority figure. Clients tend to move and talk more freely from a base of security.

Stage 3: Determining Outcomes

Setting up a specific goal of understanding may be useful. A general goal may be to find earlier life experiences that relate to the dream, authority issue, or repeating life pattern. Use the BLS to specify what the client would like to gain from this interview.

Stage 4: Generating Alternative Solutions

Depending on your purpose and your relationship with this client, there are three major alternatives for analyzing the problem that may be useful.

Alternative 1: Summarize the dream,

authority issue, or pattern, and then summarize the desired outcome of the session. Ask your client "What comes to mind as a possible explanation?" If you have communicated the fact that you have been listening, you will often find that clients generate new ideas and interpretations on their own. The structure provided by the interview decisional model and listening is often sufficient to help clients analyze and understand their own problems.

Alternative 2: Summarize the issue and then reflect the central emotion you may have noted in the conflict or ask the client what one single emotion stands out from the first part of the interview. Ask the client to focus on that emotion and stay with that feeling. Through the use of the focused free association exercise, direct the client to concentrate on that emotion and then to free associate back to an earlier life experience—the earlier the better. (Free associations are more valuable if made from an emotional state rather than from a state of clear cognitive awareness.) Most clients' first association is with some experience in their teenage years, whereas others associate to a recent event. In either case, draw out the association using the basic listening sequence.

You now should have the facts, feelings, and organization of the dream, reaction to authority, or pattern and the facts, feelings, and organization of the first association. Based on a clear summary of these two, you and the client should be able to find some consistent pattern of meaning. The discovery and notation of these patterns are an example of a basic psychodynamic interpretation.

You will often find repeating key words in both the association and the original dream or problem. Deeper understandings may come from continuing the exercise as below.

Alternative 3: Continue as in 2 above, but ask your client to free associate to even earlier life experience. Again, use the focused free association technique. Draw out these earlier free associations with the BLS. You may assemble over time a group of recollections and you will find several patterns in the associations that repeat themselves in general daily life.

At this point, the client may make her or his own interpretations of meaning or you may add your own interpretations. Generally speaking, interpretations generated by the client are the more long lasting.

Stage 5: Generalization

Psychodynamic therapy is not typically oriented to transfer of learnings from the interview to daily life. However, it may be helpful to ask the client to summarize the interview. What did the client summarize as the main facts, feelings, and organization of the interview? As appropriate, you may want to add to the client's perspective and work toward some action.

Comment

It may be observed that the structure of the interview plus the microskills discussed earlier are most basic to structuring a successful psychodynamically oriented interview. However, cultural and individual empathy, client observation skills (both of verbal and nonverbal behavior, incongruities, pacing, and leading), and the positive asset search are all critical dimensions in a successful session. What psychodynamic theory adds to the process is a content, a specific direction and purpose for which to use the skills—the uncovering of life patterns and relating them back to earlier life experiences with specific theoretical interpretations.

Client: (more weakly) "I could never please her."

Counselor: Again.

Client: (almost inaudible and near tears). "I could never please her."

Counselor: What are you feeling in your body right now?

Client: My head aches. It hurts.

Counselor: Could you get with that feeling in your head? (pause) What comes to your mind as you think about your childhood in an alcoholic family? Can you get an image of yourself in your family?

Client: (pause) I see myself cringing in my bedroom. Mom is standing over me. She's drunk and she's going to hit me. I never could please her either.

A common pattern among children of alcoholics is to repeat the family structure they grew up with. In the example above, the client has played the peacemaking or placating role in the family of origin and repeats this pattern once again in relationships. The counselor in the case above noted that the client was trying to please the counselor again and again in the interview. As with the dependent personality presented earlier, ACOA clients will repeat with you in the interview how they themselves were treated in the past. The free association technique leads to an understanding of the parallels between the past and the future.

The Family Dream

Taub-Bynum (1980, 1992) found that dreams should also be related to the family structure, not just to the individual experience. He cites example dreams in a family context:

In one family, the following dream recurred often to a 15 year old female. She dreamed that she "escaped" from her parents' house and jumped into their car. As she drove away, the father would run toward her but would never manage quite to catch her. The closer he got, the faster the car went. Finally, the 15 year old female fully escaped only to run headlong into a telephone pole.

In this family's therapy session, the themes of autonomy and separation with a great deal of anxiety occurred repeatedly. This 15 year old fought continuously with her parents over her own intense involvement with a young man the family did not approve of. The girl felt dominated by and rebellious toward her parents, in particular her father. However, when she stayed away from home too long, she began to experience somatic problems and wanted to "lose" herself in other males.

The younger sibling dreamed that a large "awful" man ran around screaming at her mother, her oldest sister and herself. Finally the man stepped on all three, but did not kill them. The dream recurred several times.

The family that provided this dream series was composed of a father who had a manic/depressive illness, an extremely religious compulsive mother, and two adolescent siblings. All three females in the family had psychosomatic problems, i.e. stomach cramps, persistent gas pains, migraine and frequent depressive episodes. (1980, p. 228)

Taub-Bynum suggests that dreams are not just individual events but are also related to issues in the family. In the family presented above, we can see that the two daughters have shared images of the family gestalt. We also see that the dysfunctional family interaction resulted in somatic symptoms.

Treatment for such complex issues could follow a variety of paths. One possibility would be to take either of the daughters through the individualistic psychodynamic dream analysis shown in exhibit 8.3. Another course would be to work through the dreams using a similar procedure with the two young women or the family itself. The procedures and techniques of dream analysis remain essentially similar to those of free association shown in exhibit 8.1, but the focus of interpretations and felt body sense (particularly somatic symptoms) is interpreted in the context of the family unconscious as a whole.

Multicultural Approaches in Dreamwork

Dreams have different values among differing cultures. For instance, Australian Aboriginals consider the "dreamtime" more real than daily "reality" and use dreams as an important avenue to spiritual issues. Too often psychodynamic work is drawn from the traditional Freudian terminology, which often focuses on psychopathology rather than health.

Imagine that your Jewish client is facing a major difficulty in the family and dreams of Masada, an ancient fortress town in Israel where the Jews made a heroic stand against the Romans. A typical individualistic interpretation might be that the dream represents some sort of defense mechanism and the individual is defending against some underlying issue, possibly sexual in nature. A multicultural interpretation might be more simple. You could comment that the client is drawing on the natural bravery and selflessness of the culture. Further exploration may reveal that both the individual and the cultural interpretations provide deeper understanding of the dream and/or issue. The cultural metaphor may provide a clue to working with the underlying issue.

Many dream and life experiences can be interpreted from a religious or cultural perspective. Roman Catholic, Baptist, Mormon, Moslem, or Buddhist clients will tend to have dreams relating to their cultural tradition. We do not just incorporate individual interpretations of the world, we also make family, religious, and cultural experience part of our being.

The Senoi are a people of central Malaysia who believe that dreams provide the dreamer with positive ideas for more effective living (Stewart, 1951). The Senoi believe that dreams are real and are most helpful when viewed as providing clues the dreamer can use to help self or others. For example, a frightening dream of falling may be viewed by the Senoi as flying, and the dreamer may be told, "Next time you dream, imagine you are flying. Note the joyous feeling and see where you go." The dreamer often takes this positive suggestion and soon is in control of dreams.

Senoi dreamwork provides an important contrast to traditional psychotherapy. Instead of problems being "problems," they are reinterpreted as part of the "solution." This idea, of course, is similar to the theoretical points regarding dependency made earlier in this chapter—all behavior, thought, and feeling indeed has a purpose and is telling the client something about her- or himself.

Regression

Regression occurs when you facilitate clients returning to old traumatic experiences, particularly painful or difficult images, and encourage them to "relive" the trauma by describing to you what they saw, heard, and felt at that time. Regression theory holds that talking about a long-repressed difficulty in the safety of the therapeutic session can help the client "work through" the trauma.

Survivors of trauma, be it the experience of childhood in an alcoholic or abusive family, a rape survivor, or a Vietnam veteran, have all benefited from going back to the old trauma and talking about the issues with an understanding and supportive counselor. Clients can examine their experience at varying cognitive-developmental levels. The most powerful reexperiencing of trauma is at the sensorimotor level, particularly when the therapist uses images. Concrete description of specific events is also often powerful, but frequently less so. Formal operational and dialectic/systemic reflection on the experience helps put the situation in perspective.

Needless to say, regression work and the immediate experiencing possible at the sensorimotor or imaging level should be done with care. *It obviously would be unwise to encourage a rape survivor to go back and relive the experience if she was not ready to do so.* A basic rule of psychodynamic therapy is to not push the client further or faster than she or he wants to go. Regression techniques should only be used when the client is ready, for there is danger of pushing the client more deeply into depression or even a psychotic break.

Consider again the example of the ACOA client. Suppose the client is a trauma survivor and that free association techniques have uncovered the trauma. Through the use of imagery and here-and-now emphasis on "What are you seeing? Feeling? Hearing?" the ACOA can bring the old repressed memories and feelings to awareness at the sensorimotor level. Through discussing thoughts and feelings, the trauma can gradually be brought into focus and made part of conscious experience. However, before you decide to engage in regression and reliving, it is important to have a solid relationship and understand the issues the client faces.

Concrete Storytelling and Therapist Listening Skills

You perhaps have talked to people who have gone to the hospital for a major operation or been in a car accident. Have you noticed how important it is for them to tell you their story in considerable concrete detail, outline how they felt, and the meaning of the experience for them? You also may have found that they need to tell you their story several times. Perhaps you even started avoiding hearing about the incident because you had heard it so often.

People who have gone through traumas need to tell the concrete and specific details of their stories. If they are not allowed to tell their stories soon after they have happened, the memories can become repressed and "pop up" in later life through flashbacks, nightmares, or—more likely—behavior and thoughts in their relationships with significant others. For example, the ACOA client was repeating the past traumatic relationship with his mother with his wife. Psychodynamic theory holds that these *repetition compulsions* will repeat again and again until they are brought to consciousness and worked through.

With many clients who have experienced trauma, concrete discussion and formal reflection on the experience will be safer and wiser than direct and powerful age regression techniques. As understanding is developed, the client may later decide with you to explore the more powerful aspects of regression and reexperiencing.

The importance of empathy and the basic listening sequence of microskills should be apparent. You need to listen to the client's story carefully—perhaps several times over several interviews—before you encourage regression and reliving old experience. Regression is different from storytelling in that the story is not talked about—rather it is *relived*. But this reliving occurs in a new and safe context—the therapeutic interview.

Group Therapy

A regression alternative is for the ACOA, rape survivor, or Vietnam veteran client to talk about their experience in a supportive environment. This can be individual counseling, but often more effective than individual work is a group of individuals who have experienced a similar trauma.

In a supportive and understanding environment, the client can hear from and talk with others who have suffered similar traumas. The trauma and the client's reaction and behavior in the traumatic situation can be *normalized*. Many clients are troubled by their behavior in the traumatic situation. Incest survivors, for example, sometimes feel that they somehow "caused" the sexual trauma. A common reaction during rape is for the woman to depersonalize the situation by "floating out of the body." A Vietnam veteran may feel that he or she was "chicken" during a time of particularly bloody combat. Trauma survivors tend to feel that they are alone in their reactions. In the group, they find personal validation and validity in what they have done.

Out of such experiences, clients often discover systemic issues underlying their feelings around the trauma. Adult children of alcoholics and incest survivors may discover how their family system related to and now relates to their current issues. Women may find themselves working to change a culture that in many ways promotes rape. War veterans may work to help others suffering from similar issues. These adjuncts to traditional one-on-one therapy can be as important as, and even more important than, regression and therapy itself.

We use the word *survivor* rather than *victim* when discussing varying types of trauma in the hope that survivors will be empowered and encouraged to take action on their own behalf. A general rule of trauma work that will apply to discoveries you will make when you use regression techniques is that *whatever the client did or experienced was what they needed to do to survive.* This positive reframe of interpretation normalizes what the client often thinks was abnormal behavior.

Freud's Damaging Error

Freud originally discovered that many of his clients had been sexually, emotionally, or physically abused as children. His early writings even include the following statement: "Unfortunately, my own father was one of these perverts and is responsible for the hysteria of my brother" (Masson, 1985, pp. 230–31). Freud's early writings give considerable attention to the abusive experience of his clients. Needless to say, Freud's discoveries were not easily accepted in Victorian Vienna.

Shortly after the death of his father, Freud moved away from a consideration of child abuse and substituted his "fantasy theory" in its place. In the fantasy theory, which has been so highly influential in this century, the child is believed to have imagined the abuse. This idea of the child's fantasy remains predominant in much of today's psychoanalytic practice. Society somehow feels more comfortable blaming the child rather than facing up to the reality of child abuse and child assault.

It could be argued that Freud almost single-handedly set back the cause of children's rights at least a century when he abandoned his own early observations on the reality and dangers of child abuse. McGrath (1986) is one useful source for specifics of this important piece of psychodynamic history. Other important sources are Freud's letters to Fliess on this topic (Masson, 1985) and Malcolm's fascinating account *In the Freud Archives* (1985).

Miller (1981, 1984) also attacks basic psychoanalytic theory from another perspective, summarizing data indicating that many of Freud's interpretations were designed to avoid the truth rather than address realities that might confuse his basic theoretical points. For example, Miller points out that the famous story of the Wolf Man is discussed with no real attention to the sexual abuse the Wolf Man experienced as a child. Obholzer (1982) interviewed the Wolf Man, and one will easily conclude from her book that Freud distorted the truth and that treatment was a failure.

Fortunately, Miller, Bowlby, Taub-Bynum, and others have worked toward redressing Freud's error. Nonetheless, there are many practicing therapists who remain unaware of weaknesses in Freud's conceptions and still prefer to work within the fantasy theory.

Analysis of Resistance

Another important theoretical and methodological issue in psychodynamic approaches is analysis of resistance. Resistance includes everything in the words and behaviors of the client that prevents access to unconscious material. The temptation in many approaches to helping is to ignore resistance and find another, easier route toward client verbalization. The effective psychodynamic counselor or therapist, by contrast, often gives primary attention to areas of client resistance.

In the process of counseling, a client will sometimes fail to hear an important statement from the counselor. The client may say "What?" and a puzzled look may appear on her or his face. Alternatively, the client may hear the therapist but forget what was said within a minute or two. Other types of resistance occur when the client blocks on something he or she is trying to say, leaves out a key part of a dream, comes late to an interview, or refuses to free associate. Resistance shows up in many ways as the client unconsciously tries to sabotage the treatment process.

The "Freudian slip," in which the client substitutes one word for another or mixes two words together, often provides a clue as to underlying issues and resistance. For example, to develop a family history, a client brought out a tape recorder at a recent visit to interview his mother-in-law, saying, "I want to record you for mortality." Although often amusing, such slips of the tongue offer useful access to unconscious functioning.

The German word Freud used for resistance—*Widerstand*—is actually better translated as a rheostat that controls the amount of electricity available. Freud was telling us that resistance is the amount of unconscious psychic energy the client can allow out at a particular time. Unfortunately, *resistance,* the English translation, implies working against the therapist, a serious conceptual error in much of today's counseling and therapy practice. What many consider resistance is actually the client's best effort to communicate with you, not against you.

Resistance is an opportunity for a deeper understanding. The task of the psychodynamic counselor is to decide whether or not to confront client resistance immediately or at a later point. The resistance often represents a major incongruency or discrepancy in the client or in the relationship between the counselor and client. One approach to analysis of resistance is to label or interpret the resistance and then encourage the client to free associate to the facts and feelings associated with the resistance. The exercises in exhibit 8.1 provide some specifics for using client resistance in a more positive fashion.

Analysis of Transference and Countertransference

Transference refers to feelings and thoughts the client has toward the counselor. In transference analysis, we find the client does not have a clear picture of the nature of the helper owing to the neutrality and objectivity of the counselor. Therefore, the client is likely to project an imagined image on the therapist. The client has literally transferred feelings and thoughts he or she has toward other people onto the therapist. Transference provides the therapist with here-and-now information on the immediate life experience of the client.

The techniques of coping with a transference situation are similar to those of dealing with resistance. The transference is identified and labeled, and free association techniques are used to clarify meaning. Too premature and too direct examination of transference feelings can confuse and trouble the client, so this technique is primarily used in the middle or later stages of therapy. Virtually all counselors and therapists, regardless of their theoretical orientation, observe transference in their clients' comments. However, differing theories vary widely in their use of analysis of transference, and some ignore this concept completely.

A nontraditional, perhaps more multiculturally relevant, approach is to consider transference through family-of-origin work. Many of the examples in this chapter have focused on how clients literally transfer learnings from their families to their daily lives through personality style and/or defense mechanisms. Clients can much more easily talk about how they experienced life and learned modes of behavior in their families. Thus analysis of transference often works more smoothly if discussed from a family frame of reference (for example, Taub-Bynum, 1984; also see the later chapter on family issues).

Countertransference is the transference of often-unconscious counselor feelings and attitudes onto the client. Countertransference often results in counselor "blind spots" and can be destructive and disruptive to the interview process. The feelings that the counselor has toward the client must be identified, isolated, and worked through.

A major portion of training in psychoanalytic work is devoted to a form of therapy for the counselor in which the counselor shares feelings, attitudes, and fantasies held toward the client with a psychodynamic training supervisor. The supervisor also analyzes countertransference feelings through use of free association and concepts and methods of psychodynamic counseling similar to the typical counselor-client interview. Strong countertransference feelings and feelings of resistance may preclude counselors working with some clients until personal counseling or therapy is undertaken. Awareness of feelings toward the client and ability to cope with these feelings are essential to any therapist.

Analysis of Projective Identification

One of the most important and difficult psychodynamic concepts is that of projective identification (Klein, 1975; Segal, 1986). Projective identification carries the concepts of transference and countertransference to a new level of complexity and conceptual power. The formal definition of projective identification provided by Laplanche and Pontalis (1973) follows:

> Term introduced by Melanie Klein: a mechanism revealed in phantasies in which the subject inserts [the] self—in whole or in part—into the object in order to harm, possess or control it. . . .

> Projective identification may thus be considered as a mode of *projection* . . . the ejection into the outside world of something subject refuses in [her- or] himself—the projection of what is bad. (p. 356)

In our practical work in counseling and therapy, projective identification reminds us that we project our unconscious wishes for ourselves on others. We see in others parts of ourselves we want to deny or of which we are unaware. In a broad sense, we attribute qualities of ourselves to others. We identify in them parts of ourselves—thus the term *projective identification*.

The Family and Projective Identification

For example, you may be the child of an alcoholic or abusing parent. In your family of origin, you learned at an unconscious level that the way for you to survive was to watch out for danger, keep quiet, and, above all, be a peacemaker in the family. Other children of alcoholics may take different roles. For example, some act out, others become very passive and withdrawn, still others become psychically numbed and depressed. Varying patterns will exist in alcoholic families. Given that your experience of abuse led you to become a peacemaker, you are likely to enact that style in a variety of situations.

Children who grow up in other types of traumatized families may evidence reactions similar to those of the alcoholic family. For example, children of Vietnam veterans suffering from posttraumatic stress disorder, children who have grown up in religious cults, and children who may have lost a parent through death or even divorce may also take on a peacemaker role.

Undergirding the peacemaker role is unconscious rage, hurt, and frustration over never having been allowed to be one's real self as a child. The peacemaker role may be termed a false self. The angry, frustrated parts of the child are denied in the unconscious and split off from any type of awareness. Underneath, many "good children" contain considerable feelings of hurt.

Nonetheless, the peacemaker role "works" and helps the child in the traumatized family make it through high school and college and into the helping professions. In your relationships, as we have suggested throughout this chapter, you will continue the peacemaking function, but the underlying rage and hurt will still remain in your unconscious.

Projective Identification in Adult Life

Projective identification occurs in your relationships when you produce in others your own unacknowledged feelings. Through the best of intentions and behavior, you may have a spouse, lover, or child who enacts your feelings for you. You project your feelings onto others and they actually *embody* what is occurring inside you. It is well known in family systems theory that certain family members enact certain behaviors and feelings for the entire family. Projective identification as a concept is closely related to this systemic view.

Suppose that you, the peacemaker, become a therapist. Despite your desire to make peace and help your clients live and work in harmony, you find yourself working with very angry, hostile clients who are difficult for you to work with. But, having learned how to deal with such difficult people in your family of origin, you are very skilled in calming and managing these clients. Due to your success with these clients, you receive rewards from your profession and are acknowledged as a skilled therapist.

You enjoy this adulation, but at times worry because you are aware that some of your clients act out your own unconscious rage by abusing their spouses. You have had three completed suicides among your clients over the past ten years.

The Danger of Inflicting Your Past Life History on Your Client

The concept of projective identification reminds us that our unconscious desires can become the very life of our clients. We as therapists can remain "good" while our clients are "bad." Clients enact that split-off part of ourselves of which we are unaware.

To make the situation even more complex, you may encounter a borderline client whose own history of sexual abuse has made her particularly sensitive to others. Soon you find yourself attracted to this woman who flatters and admires you, and you think that you as a "good" therapist are really helping her. Then the client doesn't show up for sessions, and you learn that she has cut her wrists and is in a hospital. You feel "bad" and "guilty," since obviously you missed some blatant signs of her worsening condition.

The borderline client is particularly masterful at the art of projective identification—placing his or her feelings of love and rage in the counselor and therapeutic staff. These individuals are sometimes so effective that they can split the psychiatric staff into warring groups of "good" and "bad" team members. If you examine the developmental history of the borderline client, you will find that their skills of projective identification were learned as survival techniques in their developmental history. You and the staff never were really "good" or "bad," you simply were enacting the client's life history.

The Controversial Nature—and Therapeutic Usefulness— of Projective Identification

Klein's concept of projective identification is not always popular or accepted in the field. Esman (1985) presents a representative critique of Klein's thinking:

> Her theories of development and psychopathology are characterized by incredible complexity [and] idiosyncratic language. . . . Further, her work rests on certain basic assumptions, that to say the very least, are not fully shared by those who work outside her theoretical framework—which means virtually all other psychoanalytic and nonanalytic students of child development. (pp. 303–4)

When one encounters a critique of such vehemence, one senses that perhaps Klein has been able to project some of her own unconscious rage into the strong reactions of others—and without their awareness.

You and Projective Identification

Assuming that the concept of projective identification may have some meaning to you, what can you do about it and its obvious dangers? First and foremost is that you be aware of the concept and the potential that your desires and wishes for the client can become the client's wishes and behavior. Most of us do not consciously want clients acting out our own life scripts. Second, therapy or counseling may help you understand how your own life history relates to your work with clients. Third, supervision and consultation with understanding colleagues can help you understand your motivation and what is going on in the helping process, but you must be open to some surprises.

Finally, an extremely useful tool is to *notice what your body feels like or is doing* with certain clients. When a borderline or other problematic client seems difficult or you find yourself particularly entranced or attracted by a client, focus on your felt body sense. Where do you have a feeling? What are you feeling? Then free associate back to your own situation. Very likely there is something occurring in the interview that relates to something in you and your developmental past. This self-awareness can free you for more intentional therapeutic responding.

Summary

In this section on basic techniques of psychodynamic counseling, one central fact should stand out: *free association is the basis for all the techniques discussed.* Free association is the most direct route to reach unconscious experience. The techniques discussed (interpretation, focused free association, regression, dream analysis, analysis of resistance, analysis of transference and countertransference, interpretation, and analysis of projective identification) all rely on free association in some way.

To uncover unconscious material, the psychodynamic therapist must be skilled in creative free association and in inducing that same verbal skill in clients. To this basic skill, psychodynamic counselors will add intellectual discipline. Psychodynamic approaches are the most intellectually challenging and complex of all theories. At the same time, this may represent a major weakness of the approach, for discussion of underlying meaning can go on endlessly and act as an excuse for lack of behavior change.

Treating the Family and Multicultural Unconscious

All of the above constructs can be adapted and used with Taub-Bynum's ideas of the family unconscious. For example, instead of making interpretations from an individual basis, the therapist can interpret the client's behavior from a gender, family, or multicultural frame. Examples of different approaches with a dependent client follow:

Gender interpretation: (to European-American female client) Your dependency on others seems to make lots of sense. Perhaps we can start by valuing a woman's ability to care and be-in-relationship, and you have this ability. Now what would seem an appropriate balance of using your ability to care and be dependent in this relationship you're in now?

Family interpretation: (to male or female client from most cultural backgrounds) Dependent behavior is learned in the family of origin. Dependency there worked well for you to survive, but now it isn't working in these new relationships.

Multicultural interpretation: (to Japanese student in North America from abroad) As I listen to you, you say you find it lonely in the individualistic culture of Canada. It must be painful for you. Many Japanese find our society troublesome. It is indeed difficult for a person from a more interdependent culture to be comfortable here. There are some ways I can help you cope with this different type of culture.

Needless to say, each interpretation must be sensitively used and timed to the needs, interests, and background of the client. Notice that the microskill of focus is important in this type of interaction. Rather than focusing on the individual person, the attempt in gender, family, and multiculturally oriented responding is to help the client see her- or himself in context.

Similarly, dream analysis, transferential, and projective identification issues can be made more relevant to gender, family, and multicultural practice by adding the appropriate focus.

Limitations and Practical Implications of Applying Psychodynamic Approaches

Laplanche and Pontalis (1973) have made a careful study of the derivation and meaning of key psychoanalytic concepts, and they discuss the concept of wild analysis:

> Broadly understood, this expression refers to the procedure of amateur or inexperienced "analysts" who attempt to interpret symptoms, dreams, utterances, actions, etc. on the basis of psychoanalytic notions which they have as often as not misunderstood. In a more technical sense, an interpretation is deemed "wild" if a specific analytic situation is misapprehended in its current dynamics and its particularity, and especially if the repressed content is simply imparted to the client with no heed paid to the resistances and to the transference. (p. 480)

One of the major problems of the psychodynamic approach to counseling has been that amateurs who know just a little about the concepts apply them freely to friends and clients with no real understanding of their meaning and force. For example, the gender, family, and multicultural interpretations above could be helpful, or they could be wild analysis. As you move your psychodynamic practice past traditional individualistic approaches, there is danger that you may miss the unique individual before you.

Contrariwise, failing to consider such possible multicultural interpretations when they are appropriate may make you guilty of wild analysis. When we consider Freud's mishandling of the critical issue of child abuse, the question arises that perhaps it is the traditional Freudian interpretation still prominent in much of today's practice that truly represents wild analysis.

The concept that transference occurs in the therapeutic relationship represents one of the central contributions of psychodynamic theory to the field of professional helping. It is highly likely your clients will transfer their past history of interpersonal relationships into the interview. Before your eyes, you will find clients repeating with you their past relationships with significant others. If you are working with a client facing a divorce, you may find that client reacting to you personally in the here and now as he or she did with the spouse. Whether or not you choose to work on these issues, awareness of this transferential pattern is nonetheless essential, regardless of your theoretical orientation.

The repetition of your own life patterns in your relationship with the client and/or the client's transference to you is equally possible. This is countertransference. Certain clients "push a button" with us as therapists. These clients may represent, through their words and behaviors, issues in our own lives that we have not worked through. Dealing with the complex issues of transference and countertransference can be difficult, and it is here that supervision and consultation with colleagues and superiors may be most helpful to you and your clients. The best way to deal with your own countertransference toward the client is to openly acknowledge its possible existence.

The psychodynamic approach can be very useful for understanding clients and why they behave as they do. At the same time, the very real complexity of the client may mean that highly sophisticated psychodynamic therapists may spend so much time on endless analysis that the patient's behavior never changes. Thus, although psychodynamic theory can be considered a useful frame of reference for conceptualizing clients and for helping clients think about themselves in new and more positive ways, the approach may be most effective when used in concert with other theories, particularly cognitive-behavioral interventions, so that behavioral as well as intellectual change is actually ensured.

NOTE

1. Excessive dependency, of course, can be an issue in any culture. In Japan, which values dependency and interdependence, difficulty still can occur when a child who has an especially close relationship with the mother has to leave for school.

REFERENCES

ESMAN, A. (1985). Kleinian theory revisited. *Contemporary Psychology, 30,* 303–4.

FLAHERTY, M. (1989). *Perceived differences in early family relationship and parent/child relations between adults diagnosed as borderline personality or bipolar disorder.* Unpublished doctoral dissertation, School of Education, University of Massachusetts, Amherst.

FREUD, S. (1966). *A general introduction to psychoanalysis.* New York: Norton. (Original work published 1920)

IVEY, A. (1991). *Developmental strategies for helpers: Individual, family and network interventions.* Pacific Grove, CA: Brooks/Cole.

KLEIN, M. (1975). *Envy and gratitude and other works, 1946/1963.* London: Hogarth.

LAPLANCHE, J., & PONTALIS, J. (1973). *The language of psychoanalysis.* New York: Norton.

McGrath, W. (1986). *Freud's discovery of psychoanalysis: The politics of hysteria.* Ithaca, NY: Cornell University Press.

Malcolm, J. (1985). *In the Freud archives.* New York: Vintage.

Masson, J. (Ed.). (1985). *The complete letters of Sigmund Freud to Wilhelm Fliess: 1887–1904.* Cambridge, MA: Harvard University Press.

Miller, A. (1981). *The drama of the gifted child.* New York: Basic Books.

Miller, A. (1984). *Thou shalt not be aware.* New York: Signet.

Obholzer, K. (1982). *The wolf-man: Sixty years later: Conversations with Freud's controversial patient.* New York: Continuum.

Ponterotto, J., & Casas, M. (1991). *Handbook of racial/ethnic minority counseling research.* Springfield, IL: Thomas.

Rigazio-DiGilio, S., & Ivey, A. (1990). Developmental therapy and depressive disorders: Measuring cognitive levels through patient natural language. *Professional Psychology: Research and Practice, 21,* 470–75.

Segal, H. (1986). *The work of Hanna Segal: A Kleinian approach to clinical practice.* London: Free Association Books.

Stewart, K. (1951). Dream theory in Malaya. *Complex, 6,* 21–34.

Stiver, I. (1991). The meanings of "dependency" in female-male relationships. In J. Jordan, A. Kaplan, J. Baker Miller, I. Stiver, & J. Surry (Eds.), *Women's growth in connection* (pp. 143–61). New York: Guilford.

Sue, D., & Sue, D. (1990). *Counseling the culturally different* (2nd ed.). New York: Wiley.

Taub-Bynum, E. B. (1980). The use of dreams in family therapy. *Psychotherapy: Theory, Research, and Practice, 17,* 227–31.

Taub-Bynum, E. B. (1984). *The family unconscious.* Wheaton, IL: Quest.

Taub-Bynum, E. B. (1992). *Family dreams: The intimate web.* Ithaca, NY: Haworth Press.

Cognitive-Behavioral Counseling and Therapy: Behavioral Foundations

CHAPTER GOALS

Insight is not action. Understanding the underlying causes of individual problems does not necessarily change one's everyday life. Cognitive-behavioral therapy and counseling (CBT) is centrally concerned with concrete change and empowerment of clients—giving them control over their own actions and destiny.

This chapter seeks to:

1. Describe the evolving worldview of CBT, which has moved from an emphasis on observable behavior and action to include the inner world of cognitions.

2. Point out some multicultural implications of CBT and its practice.

3. Present central constructs of CBT, such as applied behavioral analysis, that are basic to both behavioral and cognitive interventions.

4. Present some key behavioral techniques, including relaxation training, systematic desensitization, and social skills training.

5. Examine assertiveness training, an especially useful cognitive-behavioral change method, through analysis of an interview transcript. Assertiveness training may be described as a core strategy in linking behavioral and cognitive systems.

6. Provide you with an opportunity to assemble these ideas in a model assertiveness training interview that will give you a practical introduction to behavioral counseling and therapy.

The Cognitive-Behavioral Frame of Reference

Historically, counseling and therapy texts have separated behavioral and cognitive theory and methods. During the past decade, however, those interested in behavioral change have developed a more cognitive orientation. Simultaneously, the more cognitive theorists have integrated behavioral techniques as part of a broader treatment series. The conceptions of the integrative cognitive-behavioral theorist Donald Meichenbaum will be discussed in this chapter; the more cognitively oriented theorists Albert Ellis and Aaron Beck will be featured in the following chapter. All three use many of the techniques and ideas discussed in both chapters. Finally, the multicultural critiques and analyses of Cheek (1976) and Kantrowitz and Ballou (1992) provide CBT with some important additional challenges.

The Power of Reinforcement: A Case Example

Historically, behavioral therapy is rooted in the work of the behaviorists John Watson, Ivan Pavlov, and B. F. Skinner. In Skinner's view, our behavior is determined by what happens to us as a result of our behavior. If we are reinforced for what we do, then likely we will continue to engage in that behavior. If we are ignored or punished, the behavior is likely to cease. In its most pure form, behavioral therapy seeks to help control the consequences of our behavior, thus leading us to change our actions.

Consider the following true scenario, as outlined in Ivey and Hinkle (1968), and its implications:

The cast: (a) A professor noted for the quality of his knowledge of subject matter. He understands that he will make a presentation and be video-recorded, but is unaware of the purpose of the session. (b) Six students trained in "attending behavior" and who know "how to pay attention" to the professor.

Outline of plot: The students are told to engage in "typical" classroom behavior for the first portion of the lecture. Then at a signal, they are to "attend" to the professor physically through eye contact and manifestations of physical interest. At another signal, they are to return to typical student nonattending behavior.

The question: What happens to the professor? And the students?

The play in synopsis form: The professor enters the room carrying his notes. He looks up at the T.V. camera peering into the room, then at his notes. He does not look at the assembled students. There is a 30-second pause and he begins. The lecture is heavily laden with references to "exciting" research and clearly shows extensive preparation. Occasionally, the professor looks up from his notes and observes the students engaging in typical classroom behavior of notetaking. He then returns to his paper and continues on. For ten minutes his hands remain motionless and do not rise above the seminar table.

The signal comes and the students are alerted. They are now focusing all attention on the professor. He, however, is deeply in his notes and does not look up for 30 seconds. When he does, it is only briefly, but he apparently notes a student attending and gazing at him. Shortly he looks up again briefly at the same student and is again reinforced. Again, he looks up for a longer time and sees the student following him closely. He next raises his head and looks around to the rest of the class. They too are attending to him. Immediately, he becomes animated, he gestures for the first time. His verbal rate increases, his physical involvement through gestures and other characteristics is obvious. The students raise a few questions and the professor continues his discussion without notes. The quality of his knowledge of the material is still apparent as the flow of content is constant, but with less reference to specific research. However, a new classroom scene emerges. He is involved and the students are involved.

At another signal, the students stop attending and return to their notepads. The professor continues his talk uninterrupted. He does not stop; but he noticeably slows down. He looks to the students for further support and reinforcement which is not forthcoming. His verbalization slows down further. Resignedly, he returns to his notes and continues through the rest of his lecture once again resting his presentation on others' knowledge instead of his own.

The students comment later that it was difficult to stop attending and return to typical student behavior as they had found the material most stimulating. The students state they had enjoyed his presentation while they had attended and felt they had deserted the professor who needed them as they needed and wanted him.

This is nothing but a simple exercise in what psychologists call the "Greenspoon Effect," after Dr. Joel Greenspoon of Temple Buell College. Psychology classes have for years reinforced their professors by alternately smiling and ignoring the professor. Typically, the students have used this as a game to get a professor to stand in a certain place in the classroom or perhaps get him walking back and forth in front of the class much like one of B. F. Skinner's pigeons. Students have not typically reinforced or rewarded a professor by attending to his presentation. (p. 4)

The power of such shaping techniques and positive reinforcement can never be forgotten. If you work *with* your clients, these concepts can be invaluable. Innumerable concepts and programs for modifying the behavior of children, prisoners, couples, athletes, overeaters, smokers, alcoholics, drug addicts, and many others have been based on the elementary ideas of positive reinforcement and reward.

Collaboration as Basic to Cognitive-Behavioral Therapy

The above description is *not* representative of cognitive-behavioral psychology today. After considerable theorizing, political struggle and infighting, research, and careful evaluation of clinical results, behavioral counseling and therapy now focus on personal choice and the value of collaboration. Furthermore, with the evolution of what is now termed *cognitive-behavioral therapy and counseling* (CBT), the role of cognition and thought (internal speech) has become important in the practice of most behavioral clinicians. Emotion has gained a new center stage, and CBT has become a major force in counseling and psychotherapy.

The Evolving Cognitive-Behavioral Worldview

Behavioral psychology is related to the concept of modernity, which is a philosophic approach that emphasizes the impact of science. Modernity and behavioral psychology are rooted in the ideal of progress—the faith that science can solve human problems—and in a devaluation of the past (Woolfolk & Richardson, 1984). The worldview of behaviorism may be described as antithetical to the psychodynamic approaches, which emphasize the idea that history drives and directs the present.

Behavioral psychology developed primarily in the United States and is very typically American in that it is scientific, forward-moving, optimistic, and concerned with "what works." The worldview presented by B. F. Skinner suggests that we humans can have the closest approximation to "freedom" through recognizing that we can control and shape behavior in our culture and our families if we choose. We can choose what behavior to reinforce. The question, of course, is Who decides?

An Evolving Behavioral Humanism

Albert Bandura, one of the most prominent behavioral psychologists, helped move the field to an evolving "behavioral humanism" and emphasizes that the client should be deeply involved in the choice and direction of treatment. Behavioral psychology now emphasizes individual rights and collaboration in the treatment process. Bandura's work on self-efficacy (1982, 1989), a concept very similar to intentionality, stresses that individuals grow best when they feel they are in control of their own destiny.

The Move Toward Cognition

In the classical Skinnerian view, internal mental processes and cognitions are given little attention; the focus has been instead on direct, observable behavior. Bandura's work was key in the shift to a more cognitive orientation. Cheek (1976) presents an important early statement of the cognitive-behavioral framework, and Meichenbaum (1991) is perhaps most prominent in solidifying what has become a major change in behavioral psychology.

Meichenbaum (1991) emphasizes person-environment interaction. He believes behavior to be reciprocally influenced by thoughts, feelings, physiological process, and the consequences of behavior. This approach may be contrasted with the behavioral tradition that placed the locus of control in the external environment. Clients assume a much more important role in this newer tradition.

> *CBT does not hold that there is "one reality,"* nor that the task for the therapist is to educate or correct clients' misperceptions (errors in thinking, irrational thoughts). Rather in the tradition of the Kurosawa movie, *Rashomon, CBT holds that there are "multiple realities."* The collaborative task for clients and CB therapists is to help clients appreciate how they create such realities (p. 4).

A Feminist Critique of CBT

Kantrowitz and Ballou (1992) applaud the shift of behavioral theory from a strict individual orientation to awareness of how the social context affects development. For example, if a woman has a behavioral difficulty, no longer can we find "fault" with the person. Therapists can more accurately see how environmental interactions affect behavior and internal thought.

However, Kantrowitz and Ballou point out that "individuals are expected to improve their adaptive capacities to meet the environmental conditions, which serve to reinforce the dominant (male) social standards" (p. 79). Assertiveness training is insufficient help for a woman suffering harassment in the workplace. Kantrowitz and Ballou state that action in the community and challenging standard social norms must be considered part of the therapeutic process.

CBT uses the word *cognitive* and as such gives primacy to thinking over feeling. How a person develops in the culture, particularly around issues of gender, are given relatively little attention in CBT theory. In short, despite its many positive qualities, Kantrowitz and Ballou maintain that CBT needs to be used with caution and sensitivity. Cheek's (1976) early work, discussed below, and Meichenbaum's new construction of CBT are important in addressing these issues.

The Multicultural Approach and Cognitive-Behavioral Issues

The origins of behavioral psychology obviously lie in concrete behavior, with minimal attention given to philosophic constructs. Thus behavioral counseling and therapy has presented somewhat of a puzzle to those committed to a multicultural approach. Behavioral techniques tend to be successful in producing change and, owing to their clarity of direction and purpose, are often understandable and acceptable to minority populations.

At the same time, the behavioral approach can run into problems in multicultural situations over the issue of *control.* Early ventures in behavioral psychology often gave the therapist, counselor, or teacher almost complete power, and decisions sometimes focused on controlling the client rather than helping the client control him- or herself. Behavioral psychology has been forced to overcome some of these early problems and the resultant fears among minority clients and their advocates.

Making CBT Culturally Relevant

Probably no one person has done more to make behavioral counseling and therapy multiculturally relevant than Donald Cheek, whose pioneering book *Assertive Black . . . Puzzled White* (1976) shows how to use assertiveness training in a culturally relevant way with African-American clients. In an imaginary introductory dialogue, Cheek speaks directly to some of the problems and issues underlying assertive behavior (comments from the authors in italics):

> Me [Cheek]:   . . . A Black person has got to know when to be assertive and when to kiss ass.
>
> [Knowing is a cognitive act. Cheek focused not just on assertive behavior, but also on the thinking, cognition, and emotion that guides that behavior. Cheek's 1976 book

can now be read as one of the clearest early presentations of cognitive-behavioral counseling.]

You: But so does everybody.

Me: I mean it in terms of survival baby—survival—I mean whether or not the man even lets you live. Ain't that many Whites who got to worry about being killed because they want to be assertive enough to vote. . . . You see the authors on assertiveness have not sufficiently considered the social conditions in which Blacks live—and have lived. That blind spot in many ways alters or changes the manner that assertiveness is applied. . . . Current assertive authors have a great approach—it's an approach which can really aid Black folks, in fact they need it—but at the time these authors are unable to translate assertiveness training into the examples, language and caution that fit the realities of a Black lifestyle. (pp. 10–11)

Cheek calls his approach to assertiveness and behavioral methods *didactic assertiveness training*. He points out that assertive behavior varies between African-American and White cultures and that both groups need to understand the frame of reference of the other. He also points out that the passive nonviolent stance of the Black freedom movement represented a particularly powerful type of Black assertiveness. Assertiveness is not aggression; rather, it is culturally relevant behavior and thinking in which people or groups stand up for their rights.

Meichenbaum (1985) also speaks to multicultural issues:

Given the marked variability of reactions to stressful events, stress training programs should take into consideration cultural differences in determining adaptive coping mechanisms. Attempting to train clients to cope in ways that may violate cultural norms could actually aggravate stress-related problems. In some cultures, people tend to cope with stressors passively, by trying to endure them rather than viewing them as challenges and problems to be solved. Stress management training must reflect these cultural preferences. (p. 17)

As early as 1976 Cheek said much the same thing. A culturally relevant cognitive-behavioral practice requires that you be able to work with the way your clients think as well as the way they behave. Both Cheek and Meichenbaum stress the importance of full collaboration with the client in the conduct of the interview and treatment series.

Central Constructs of Cognitive-Behavioral Therapy and Counseling

The following material focuses on constructs that are foundational to both behavioral and cognitive approaches of CBT. The next section elaborates on Meichenbaum's construction of CBT.

Applied Behavioral Analysis

Behavioral counseling rests on applied behavioral analysis, a systematic method of collaboratively examining the client and the client's environment and jointly developing specific interventions to alter the client's life conditions. Successful applied behavioral analysis rests on four foundations: (1) the relationship between the counselor and the client, (2) the definition of the problem through operationalization of behavior, (3) the understanding of the full context of the problem through functional analysis, and (4) the establishment of socially important goals for the client.

Client-Counselor Relationship

It was once thought that those who engaged in behavioral approaches were cold, distant, and mechanical. A classic research study in 1975 by Sloane and others forever changed this view. This research examined expert therapists from a variety of theoretical orientations and found that behavioral therapists exhibited higher levels of empathy, self-congruence, and interpersonal contact than other therapists, while levels of warmth and regard were approximately the same. Behavioral therapists may be expected to be as interested in rapport and human growth as those working from any other orientation. If one is to help clients develop, one must be a reinforcing person.

Behavioral therapists have very specific methodologies and goals. In addition to working toward rapport, behavioral therapists engage in careful structuring of the interview. They are willing and anxious to share their plans collaboratively with the client in the expectation that the client will share with them in the therapy process.

Relationship variables have differing meanings, according to individual and cultural background. It is important that eye contact, body language, vocal tone, and verbal following be culturally appropriate. Too many reflective listening skills can result in mistrust unless culturally appropriate sharing is included. A relationship can develop slowly or quickly.

For instance, working with urban Aboriginals in Australia or with the Inuit or Dene in the Arctic, the professional helper may take half an interview or more simply to become acquainted, learn the family system, share personal anecdotes, and so on before trying to find out what the client wants to talk about. At the other extreme, a relationship can develop quickly with many urban White professionals who can be fully intimate and open with a therapist immediately on entering the room.

If you have some skill in observation and listening, some beginning knowledge of multicultural differences in style, and a willingness to share at least part of yourself, you have the basics to establish yourself as a helper in multicultural settings.

Operationalization of Behavior

Clients often bring to the therapist clouded, confused, and abstract descriptions of their issues. You can help clients become much clearer if you focus on concreteness and specifics of behavior. The temptation for many formal operational counselors is to think and talk abstractly. Operationalization of behavior will help you and the client "get down to cases" and discover what is really happening.

An Example.   Let us assume that you have a client who is depressed and talks about feeling sad. In psychodynamic therapy, you might seek to discover the roots of the sadness, whereas in cognitive or humanistic therapies, you might want to help the client alter the way he or she thinks about the world. However, in behavioral therapy, particularly with applied behavioral analysis, the task is to determine what the patient does specifically and concretely when he or she feels depressed, as the following dialogue illustrates:

Counselor: You say you feel depressed. Could you tell me some of the specific things you do when you are depressed?

Client: Well, I cry a lot. Some days I can't get out of bed. I feel sad most of the time.

Counselor: How does your body feel?

[*Contrary to some stereotypes, behaviorally oriented therapists are very oriented to emotions and stress the importance of emotional issues. Many therapists would settle for "sad," but here special effort is taken to make the emotion more based in actual sensorimotor experience.*]

Client: It feels tense and drawn all over, almost like little hammers are beating me from inside. It gets so bad sometimes that I can't sleep.

The counselor's two questions have made the behaviors related to the general construct of depression far more obvious. Crying, failure to get out of bed, feelings of bodily tension, and inability to go to sleep are operational behaviors that can be seen, measured, and even counted. The feelings of sadness, however, are still somewhat vague, and further operationalization of the sentence "I feel sad most of the time" might result in the following, more specific, description of behaviors:

Counselor: A short time ago you said you feel sad much of the time. Could you elaborate a little more on that?

Client: Well, I cry a lot and I can hardly get moving. My wife says all I do is whine and complain.

Counselor: So sadness means crying and difficulty in getting moving . . . and you complain a lot. You also said you felt tense and drawn inside . . . hammers, I think you said.

Here the counselor ties in the vague feelings of sadness with the more concrete operational behaviors mentioned by the client and locates them more specifically in sensorimotor space.

Making the Behavior Concrete and Observable.   The objective of operationalization of behavior, then, is the concretizing of vague words into objective, observable actions. Virtually all behavioral counselors will seek this specificity at some point in the interview, believing it is more possible to work with objective behavior than with vague nonspecific concepts such as depression and sadness.

A simple but basic clue when engaging in operationalization of behavior is to ask "Can I see, feel, hear, or touch the words the client is using?" The client may speak of a desire for a "better relationship" with a partner. Since the behavioral therapist cannot see, feel, hear, or touch "better relationship," he or she would seek to have this concept operationalized in terms of touching, vocal tone, or certain verbal statements (for instance, "I wish my partner would touch me more and say more good things about me").

Again, it is important to note that making vague terms as specific as possible can be useful to you in other theoretical orientations. The clarity that comes with a careful behavioral analysis often provides a basic understanding for truly appreciating the client's worldview and environmental situation.

Functional Analysis

The A-B-Cs of Behavior.   An individual's behavior is directly related to events and stimuli in the environment. Another task of the behavioral therapist is to discover how client behaviors occur in the "natural environment." Behavioral counselors and behavioral therapists talk about the "A-B-Cs" of functional analysis—that is, the study of antecedent events, the resultant behavior, and the consequence(s) of that behavior. The behavioral counselor is interested in knowing what happened just prior to a specific behavior, what the specific behavior or event was, and what the result or consequence of that behavior was on the client and the environment. The next chapter, which will focus primarily on cognition, explores parallel "A-B-Cs" for inner thoughts and feelings.

In the following examination of functional cause-and-effect relationship, the counselor comes to understand the sequence of events underlying the overt behavior of a client. Out of such functional patterns, it is possible to design behavioral programs to change the pattern of events.

Counselor: So far, I've heard that you are generally depressed, that you get these feelings of tiredness and tension. Now could you give me a specific example of a situation when you felt this way? I want to know what happened just before the depression came upon you, what happened as you got those feelings and thoughts, and what resulted after. First, tell me about the last time you had these feelings.

Client: Well, it happened yesterday . . . (sigh) I came home from work and was feeling pretty good. But when I came in the house, Bonnie wasn't there, so I sat down and started to read . . .

Counselor: (interrupting) What was your reaction when your wife wasn't home?

Client: I was a little disappointed, but not much, I just sat down.

Counselor: Go ahead . . .

Client: After about half an hour, she came in and just walked by me. . . . I said hello, but she was angry at me still from last night when we had that argument. Funny, I always feel relieved and free after we have an argument . . . almost like I get it out of my system.

Counselor: Then what happened?

Client: Well . . . I tried to get her to talk, but she ignored me. After about ten minutes, I got really sad and depressed. I went to my room and lay down until supper. But just before supper, she came in and said she was sorry, but I just felt more depressed.

Counselor: Let's see if I can put that sequence of events together. You were feeling pretty good, but your wife wasn't home and then didn't respond to you because she was angry. You tried to get her to respond and she wouldn't [*antecedents*]. Then you got depressed and felt bad and went to your room and lay down [*resultant behavior*]. She ignored you for a while, but finally came to you and you ignored her [*consequences*]. The pattern seems to be similar to what you've told me about before: (1) you try something; (2) she doesn't respond; (3) you get discouraged, depressed feelings and tensions—sometimes even crying; and (4) she comes back to you and apologizes, but you reject her.

From a cognitive-developmental frame, the counselor summarized concrete cause-and-effect sequence through the A-B-C analysis. This awareness of sequence is characteristic of late concrete operations. Then, the counselor used the word *pattern,* thereby helping the client see that this one concrete example is representative of repeating behavior. If the client is not cognitively able to think in patterns (formal operations), it is preferable to stay with a single example and work on that specific situation.

Reinforcers and Reinforcement Patterns.   Important in performing functional analysis is being aware of how behavior develops and maintains itself through a system of rewards or reinforcers and punishments. At the simplest level, we can state that whatever follows a particular piece of behavior will influence the probability of that behavior happening again. In the above case, the husband gained no attention from his wife until he became depressed. At this point, and at this point only, she came to him. Therefore, the wife's behavior heavily influences the probability of his becoming depressed. On this subject, Skinner (1953) notes:

> Several important generalized reinforcers arise when behavior is reinforced by other people. A simple case is attention. The child who misbehaves "just to get attention" is familiar. The attention of people is reinforcing because it is a necessary condition for other reinforcements from them. In general, only people who are attending to us reinforce our behavior. . . . Attention is often not enough. Another person is likely to reinforce only that part of one's behavior of which he approves, and any sign of his approval becomes reinforcing in its own right. (p. 78)

Patterns of attention are particularly important in understanding human relationships. In the above case, the husband gets attention only when he becomes depressed, and his wife's attention at that time only reinforces further feelings of depression and hopelessness. If she were to attend to him when he initiated behavior, it is possible—even likely—that certain portions of his pattern of depression would be alleviated. However, neither does the husband attend to (reinforce) his wife's coming to him in the bedroom. He ignores her and thereby continues the pattern of mutual lack of reinforcement. Either individual could break the self-defeating pattern of antecedents, behavior, and consequences.

Any meaningful functional analysis must examine the reinforcement patterns maintaining the system of an individual or couple. The word *pattern* is formal, and with many clients, it will be necessary to work only with one single situation and examine in detail the concrete A-B-C sequence. Once several single situations have been mastered by the client, it may then be possible to examine formal patterns of behavior.

The social reinforcers of attention and approval are particularly potent and vital in human relationships. However, other reinforcers (money, grades, or other tangibles as well as social rewards such as smiles, affection, and recognition) must be considered in any functional analysis. In many cases, negative attention (punishment) is often pre-ferred to being ignored. Ignoring a human being can be a very painful punishment.

Establishing Behavior Change Goals

If a counselor is to help a client, the intended behavior change must be relevant to the client, as Sulzer-Azaroff and Mayer (1977) point out:

> Applied behavioral analysis programs assist clients to improve behaviors that will pro-mote their own personal and social development. Consequently, prior to its implemen-tation, a program must clearly communicate and justify how it will assist the client to function more effectively in society, both in the near and distant future. It also must show how any changes that accompany the behavior change of focus will not interfere with the client's or the community's short- and long-range goals. . . . It does not deal with bar pressing. . . . Nor should it serve individuals or agencies whose goals are to the detriment of either clients or their immediate and broader societies. (p. 7)

Making the Goals Concrete.   During the goal-setting phase of the interview, the counselor works with the client to find highly specific and relevant goals (Sulzer-Azaroff, 1985). Rather than setting a generalized goal such as "My goal is not to be depressed anymore," the behavioral counselor will work toward detailed specific plans. One early goal might be as basic as going to a movie or learning to dance. Later goals might be to join a community club, start jogging, and find a job. Applied behavioral analysis breaks the abstract idea of depression down into manageable be-havioral units and teaches clients how to live their lives more happily and effectively. One can do something about specifics; as concrete goals are achieved, the depression lifts.

Throughout applied behavioral analysis, there is an emphasis on concrete doing and action. The individual must do something that can be seen, heard, and felt. Thoughts are less important, but these become central in behavioral psychology's offshoot, cognitive-behavioral psychology (discussed in chapter 10). Interestingly, be-havioral psychotherapy often tends to be especially effective with depressed clients, as its emphasis on doing and acting rather than on self-reflection gets the client moving. The emphasis on movement, action, and doing, again, tends to be typically North American and pragmatic in orientation.

Behavioral psychology is concerned with *doing*. Functional analysis will have a more lasting meaning for you if you actually practice it. The exercises in exhibit 9.1 provide you an opportunity to do so.

=== **Exhibit 9.1** ===

Exercises in Applied Behavioral Analysis

The following exercises have been chosen as basic to successful behavioral and cognitive-behavioral practice.

Operationalization of Behavior

The following are vague statements a client might present in the interview:

"I'm depressed."
"I'm the best."
"I'm no good as a parent."
"He argues all the time."
"I'm unhappy."
"She doesn't love me anymore."
"The boss doesn't like me."
"The boss harassed me."

When clients give you vague statements such as the above, your task is to help them become more concrete and specific. For example, if the client said, "The boss harassed me," your task would be to obtain the concrete specifics of "harassment." You can obtain these concrete specifics by asking:

"Could you give me a specific example of what the boss did?"
"What do you mean, all the time?"
"What happened specifically?"
"What words does he use?"
"How loudly does he talk?"
"Where did he touch you?"
"What is the situational/environmental context?"
"Who holds the power?"
"What's the boss's behavior toward other men/women/minorities?"

Interview a friend or colleague. When you hear a vague statement such as those described above, ask open questions, using the above guidelines, until you get the concrete specifics of the behavior.

At times, you will want to concretize a sequence. In the example below, the focus is on making an argument specific. You can do this simply by asking:

"What happened in the argument?"
"What did she or he say?"
"What did you say?" (to concretize the event or behavior)
"What happened before?" (to obtain antecedents)
"What happened afterward?" (to obtain consequences)

To ensure that you have heard the client correctly, use the microskill of summarization to lay out the sequence of events. Also be aware of the social context of your analysis. You are seeking to help an individual, but your efforts will often be most effective if conducted with contextual awareness and action.

Again with your friend or colleague, using these ideas, draw out the sequence of events.

Functional Analysis

A functional analysis is a systematic and sequential operationalization of behavior. The questioning techniques above are basic to a functional analysis. In conducting a functional analysis, think about the A-B-Cs of behavior. In the following examples, note the importance of the word *do*, which focuses on action, so characteristic of behavioral counseling and therapy.

A—Antecedent events

You may examine antecedent events as well as feelings and emotions.

"What happened just before the argument?"

"What were you doing?"

"What were they doing?"

"Could you just step back and describe the event step-by-step—give me lots of details."

"What did you feel beforehand?"

"How did the other person seem to feel?"

It may also be useful to explore the environment.

"Where did this occur?"

"What else was going on?"

"Who else was there?"

You may think of the newspaper sequence of "who, what, when, where, why, and how" questions to enrich the background.

A critical question that should be asked at each segment of any careful functional analysis is *"Have we missed anything important?"* Summarize the antecedents to ensure that you have heard them correctly.

B—Behavior that occurred (resultant behavior)

Here you focus on the immediate argument and important sequence of events or interaction during the critical period. Use the questions suggested for functional analysis above and pay attention to feelings and emotions that accompanied the behavior.

Again summarize the behavior and check to see if you missed something important.

C—Consequences

The essential here is what specifically happened as a result of all the above.

Some possible helpful questions here include:

"What was the upshot of the whole event?"

"Could you explore what happened for you as a result and what happened for the other person?"

"How did you feel when it was over?"

"Are there situational, environmental checks on you or others that may have power and influence over the total situation?"

Again, summarize the behavior and check to see if you missed something important.

This completes the A-B-C analysis of behavior, which will give you a good conception of what occurred for the client or clients in many varying types of problem situations.

Establishing Behavior Change Goals

Once having completed a functional analysis, the task is to establish, with the client's participation, specific goals for behavioral change.

Many clients can participate very effectively in analyzing behavioral sequences, but when you ask them "What is your goal for change?" they often will return to vague, nonspecific concepts. Clients who have just been depressed, suffered sexual harassment, or experienced an argument may say "I want things to be better," which is too abstract for any real action. Your task as a therapist is once again to help them become more specific about their goals for change. Some helpful types of questions follow. This information provides you with data revealing that change can be sought in the areas of antecedents, the behavior itself, the consequences, or some combination of these three.

"Given that we have discussed your parental argument (your depression, the issue of harassment) and conflict in detail, what specifically would you like to change?"

"We could change how you behave before the argument occurs, how you talk and behave when one does occur, or what you do after an inevitable argument happens."

This example is likely to be too complex for most clients, and thus the following types of questions may be more useful.

"Ideally, what one single thing would you most like to change?"

"Let's explore that in more detail. What would you have to do differently?"

It is helpful to use a fantasy directive such as "Fantasize an ideal solution if everything were exactly like you'd wish it to be."

A situational question such as "What can we do to help change the system in which this happened?" will help add a multicultural focus.

Again, take a friend or colleague through the specifics of operationalizing behavior, defining the A-B-C sequence, and establish clear, measurable goals for behavioral change.

Regardless of whatever behavioral technique or strategy you chose to use from the several included in this chapter, your interventions will be most effective if they include a carefully constructed functional analysis and operationalization of behavior. Including situational/environmental issues in your functional analysis will help keep you aware of possible multicultural issues.

Meichenbaum's Construction of Cognitive-Behavioral Therapy

Donald Meichenbaum (1985, 1991) has been one of the primary forces in moving behavioral therapy to its present cognitive-behavioral orientation. In Meichenbaum's view, CBT is concerned with helping the client define problems cognitively as well as behaviorally and with promoting cognitive, emotional, and behavioral change and preventing relapse (see chapter 4).

Meichenbaum's conception of CBT summarizes many of the ideas of this book: Our task as therapists is to define the problem (and goals) with our clients; we then apply a wide variety of techniques to produce cognitive, emotional, and/or behavioral change. Finally, we must act if we are to ensure that behavioral change is to be maintained in the environment of the real world. Whether we commit ourselves to psychodynamic, behavioral, existential/humanistic, or some other orientation, meeting the criteria of this brief outline should be useful.

Meichenbaum's Central Constructs

Meichenbaum (1990, 1991) outlined ten central tenets of CBT. As you read the following, note how his modern view, based on traditions of behaviorism, expands our conception of the helping process. The following ten points are abstracted and paraphrased from Meichenbaum's presentation to the Evolution of Psychotherapy Conference in 1990 (published in 1991).

1. *Behavior is reciprocally determined by the "client's thoughts, feelings, physiological processes, and resultant consequences"* (p. 5). No one of these elements is necessarily most important. Thus the therapist can intervene in the interacting system by focusing on thoughts or feelings, using medication, or changing consequences. Meichenbaum points out that with clients suffering from depression, the amount of criticism coming from the spouse (resultant consequences in the environment) is the most important predictor of relapse.

2. *Cognitions do not cause emotional difficulties; rather, they are part of a complex interactive process.* A particularly important part of the cognitive process is "metacognitions" in which clients learn to comment internally on their own thinking patterns and thereby act as their own mentor or therapist. "Moreover, CB therapists insure that clients take credit (for) behavioral changes they implement" (p. 6).

The cognitive structures we use to organize experience are our *personal schemas.* We learned these constructions from past experience, and changing ineffective schemas is an important part of therapy (p. 7). For example, clients who are diagnosed with anxiety disorders have particular concerns about issues of loss of personal control and physical well-being. Depressed individuals are prone to be concerned about issues of loss, rejection, and abandonment. Individuals who are particularly concerned about the issues of equity, fairness, and justice are prone to have problems with anger.

Meichenbaum and Gilmore (1984) describe the case of a lawyer who was the only son of an immigrant father. The lawyer, who evidenced problems with controlling his anger and experienced accompanying hypertension, marital discord, and depression, reported that he would "never allow anyone to take advantage of [me] like people who took advantage of [my] father. Got that!" The lawyer carried with him a personal schema concerning the issues of fairness and equity that colored the way he appraised events. This personal schema not only contributed to his short fuse and anger problem, but it also played a role in his altruistic behavior as reflected in his being active in such movements as Amnesty International, a world agency for protecting human rights.

The cognitive-behavioral therapist helped this lawyer appreciate how he viewed the world and the impact of his personal schema (issues about fairness) on how he appraised events. Over the course of therapy, the client came to see the price he paid, the toll taken, both interpersonally and intrapersonally, for his particular way of viewing the world and himself. Collaboratively with the therapist, the lawyer came to better understand and alter his way of thinking and to cope with personal concerns.

3. *"A central task for the CB therapist is to help clients come to understand how they* construct and construe reality" (p. 7). In this statement Kelly's (1955) personal construct theory has been joined with the behavioral tradition. Meichen-

baum stresses that clients and counselors can work collaboratively to explore cognitions and desired changes.

4. *"CBT takes issue with those psychotherapeutic approaches that adopt a rationalist or objectivist position"* (p. 8). This is an important and radical position that challenges the concepts of Ellis (chapter 10). Meichenbaum's approach is more existential-humanistic in nature and is interested in how clients subjectively experience the world. He stresses the importance of reflecting key words and phrases of clients and of mirroring their feelings back to them "in an inquiring tone" (the microskills of encouraging and reflection of feeling). By mirroring, Meichenbaum seeks to help clients understand how they have constructed reality.

5. *"A critical feature of CBT is the emphasis on* collaboration *and on the* discovery *processes"* (p. 8). Meichenbaum talks about the importance of having clients make their own discoveries. He recommends using a variety of behavioral techniques, such as those presented in this chapter, to facilitate the discovery process.

6. *Relapse prevention is a central dimension of CBT.* Marlatt and Gordon's (1985) model (chapter 4) has become central to the thinking of many different approaches to counseling and therapy.

7. *"CBT holds that the* relationship *that develops between the client and the therapist is critical to the change process"* (p. 10). Empathy and listening skills (chapters 2 and 3) are critical as well as the important relationship dimensions stressed by Rogers (chapter 11).

8. *"Emotions play a critical role in CBT"* (p. 11). Much like psychodynamic theory, Meichenbaum's view of CBT suggests that clients bring into the therapy session the emotional experiences they have had with others. Past life experiences are seen as affecting how clients react with you in the session, and emotions are the route toward understanding the nature of the relationship.

9. *"CB therapists are now recognizing the benefits of conducting CBT with couples and families"* (p. 12). In this sense, CBT is moving toward the network treatment constructions of Attneave (see chapter 5).

10. *CBT can be extended beyond the clinic setting for both prevention and treatment.* Meichenbaum points out that CBT techniques have been used in probation offices, schools, hospitals, the military, and infant home visitations. It is becoming clearer that psychoeducational work is an important part of preventing drug and alcohol abuse and that it can be a useful part of any treatment program.

In summary, it can be seen that cognitive-behavioral therapy and counseling build on a behavioral foundation and provide an integrating framework for many differing and seemingly oppositional forms of therapy and counseling. Exhibit 9.2 presents an example of the application of cognitive-behavioral techniques in the treatment of agoraphobia.

Exhibit 9.2

Cognitive-Behavioral Assessment and Treatment of Agoraphobia

Behavioral and cognitive-behavioral techniques are by far the most extensively and carefully researched in the field of counseling and therapy. This exhibit focuses on one area of research—agoraphobia. Agoraphobia is described in DSM-III-R (American Psychiatric Association, 1987) as follows:

> A marked fear of being alone, or being in public places from which escape might be difficult or help not available in case of sudden incapacitation. Normal activities are increasingly constricted as the fears or avoidance behavior dominate the individual's life. The most common situations avoided involve being in crowds, such as on a busy street or in crowded stores, or being in tunnels, on bridges, on elevators, or on public transportation. Often these individuals insist that a family member or friend accompany them whenever they leave home. (p. 227)

The following comments illustrate how the cognitive-behavioral tradition has integrated epidemiological research, research on assessment, and research on treatment effectiveness. This comprehensive approach is common to research reviews on cognitive-behavioral methods and is probably one of the main reasons for its gradual gain in popularity in the field.

Incidence and Related Problems

Agoraphobia is an anxiety disorder and may occur with or without panic disor-

der. Females predominate over males by a ratio of four to one (Michelson, 1987; Dionne, 1990). It is important to look for related depression and panic attacks when agoraphobia appears, particularly so as up to 20 percent of those with panic attacks may have attempted suicide at some point in their lives (Dionne, 1990). Generally, the onset of the disorder is seen in the mid-twenties, but child school phobics are now being recognized as an early form of agoraphobia. In addition, there is some evidence of family transmission of the set of disorders, but not agreement on genetic versus environmental causation (Dionne, 1990).

Cognitive-Behavioral Assessment

Beyond DSM-III-R criteria, there are a number of standardized assessment instruments. One good example is the Standardized Behavioral Avoidance Course (S-BAC), which has the client walk through a standard course alone, beginning at the front door of the hospital and ending at a crowded shopping mall (Agras, Leitenberg, & Barlow, 1968). The actual measures on the S-BAC are distance traveled, psychophysiological monitoring (heart rate, breathing), and *in vivo* discussion of client cognitions and thoughts as they go through the process. (This example shows how applied behavioral analysis can be very systematically used.)

At a more general level, the A-B-C techniques of applied behavioral analysis presented earlier in this chapter can be used to determine more precisely what occurs before, during, and after an attack of agoraphobia (see Michelson, 1987, for a review of alternative clinical and research methods). In addition, CBT stresses the importance of assessing emotion and cognition.

Treatment

Graduated exposure has been found to be a highly useful strategy for the treatment of agoraphobia. Graduated exposure is similar to systematic desensitization described in this chapter except that clients are actually taken out into the field for graduated practice exercises. (For comprehensive treatment reviews, see Emmelkamp & Mersh, 1982; Michelson, 1987; Dionne, 1990). Another form of treatment is to have a family member or partner help the client work through graduated exposure. Deep muscle relaxation (as described later in this chapter) is helpful as part of a treatment program. Although controversial, the general feeling in the psychological field is that medication is not necessary for treatment.

The pinpointing of specific behaviors, positive reinforcement, and the concepts of charting are important skills for establishing a comprehensive treatment plan for agoraphobics. Social skills training and stress inoculation are obvious treatment adjuncts.

Cognitive techniques are described in more detail in chapter 10, but Michelson (1987) reviews cognitive studies in detail, and this type of work appears to be effective with agoraphobics. For example, Emmelkamp et al. (1986) compared *in vivo* graduated exposure with two types of cognitive therapy and found all three groups improved, with the greatest improvement in the graduated exposure groups. This study was further validated in a major study by the National Institute of Mental Health, which compared a cognitive intervention with psychophysiological and behavioral interventions. Clients in all approaches showed significant improvement (Michelson et al., 1985).

There is also some evidence that family treatment (chapter 13), problem-solving training (chapter 4), and other forms of helping can be useful. Logic suggests that a multidimensional treatment plan incorporating several of the methods discussed above may be useful. It is not which treatment is best, but which set of treatments is best. This latter interpretation allows us to think of comprehensive treatment plans in the hope that cognitive, behavioral, family systems, and other methods can be integrated more broadly than our "single-shot" interventions of the past. Family treatment may be a direction of the future owing to increasing evidence of intergenerational family issues (Dionne, 1990).

Cognitive-Behavioral
Treatment Techniques

Intentional CBT often starts with careful applied behavioral analysis. The central constructs and exercises presented earlier are essential assessment prerequisites for the treatment techniques discussed here. A critical task of the behavioral counselor is to select from among the many possibilities now existing the most appropriate behavioral change procedure for the individual client. Some key behavioral change procedures follow.

Pinpointing Behavior, Positive Reinforcement, and Charting

Pinpointing Behavior

Assume, for example, that you are working with a hyperactive child. A teacher or parent may complain about the child's overactivity and tell you that the child is "difficult to control." These are not directly observable behaviors. Your task is to pinpoint very precise behaviors, such as the number of times the child interrupts a classmate or teacher, the number of times the child leaves his or her seat during a specified time period, or the child's "time on task" (percentage of time the child is actually working on schoolwork).

Your skill in applied behavioral analysis is basic to pinpointing specific behavioral targets for change or reinforcement. As in operationalization of behavior, your goal is to pinpoint very specific behaviors associated with depression, arguments, or sexual harassment.

Positive Reinforcement

Perhaps the most direct behavioral technique is the provision of rewards for desired behavior. The systematic application of positive reinforcement to human beings began with an important experiment by Greenspoon (1955), who demonstrated that it was possible to condition people to "emit" more plural nouns whenever the "counselor" smiled or nodded his head. In the context of what appeared to be a normal interview, Greenspoon conducted a typical interview with the exception that whenever the client uttered a plural noun, the interviewer smiled and nodded. Very soon the client was providing him with many plural nouns.

Smiles, nods, and the attention of others are particularly reinforcing events. We all seek reinforcement and reward. Those who provide us with these rewards tend to be our friends; those who do not we tend to ignore or avoid. Money is another powerful positive reinforcer. It may be said that we work because we are rewarded or reinforced with money. In any applied behavioral analysis that is fully effective, the counselor will be able to note the positive reinforcers and rewards that maintain the behavior. The search for the A-B-Cs of behavioral sequences will often unravel seemingly complex and mystical behavior.

When learning theory concepts, such as extinction, shaping, and intermittent reinforcement, are joined together, extremely powerful and effective programs of human change can be developed. At the most sophisticated level, elaborate economies have been developed in prisons, psychiatric hospitals, schools, and other settings where tangible reinforcers in the form of tokens are given for desired acts immediately after they have been performed. At a later point the tokens may be exchanged for candy, cigarettes, or privileges. Important to the success of positive reinforcement and token economies is the clear identification, by the client, of the desired behavior with the reward. Too long a delay in reinforcement dulls its effectiveness in changing behavior.

Charting

One route toward identifying whether or not progress is being made with a behavioral change program is charting the changes made by a client. Charting is the specific recording of the number of occurrences of important behaviors before, during, and after treatment. For example, a teacher may be concerned with "out-of-seat behavior" of a hyperactive child. The goal of the behavioral program is to reduce this behavior using a modified token economy in which the child is rewarded for staying at the desk.

The chart in figure 9.1 illustrates the daily frequencies for out-of-seat behavior before the intervention was instituted, during the treatment, and after treatment was terminated. It is important to record behavior before the program is instituted so that the effectiveness of the behavioral program can be examined. Charting after program completion is important because when the intervention is removed, the behavior

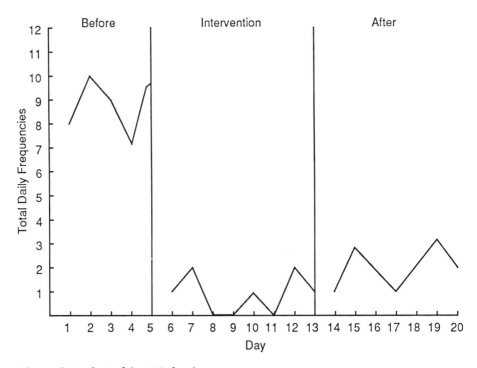

Figure 9.1   Out-of-Seat Behavior

sometimes returns to the previous level, indicating that the behavioral program was unsuccessful in maintaining desired outcomes. When charts indicate failure, another type of behavioral program (or even another type of counseling intervention, such as psychodynamic or humanistic) needs to be instituted. In such cases relapse prevention programs can be particularly useful.

Charting is often used in weight control programs, family communication skill training, aiding a child in keeping a room clean, stop-smoking programs, and in a wide variety of interpersonal or classroom situations. The very act of self-recording (charting) sometimes helps an individual modify her or his behavior without further instruction or counseling.

Many therapists, particularly those who work with children and adolescents, find that pinpointing behavior and conducting a thorough A-B-C analysis, as in exhibit 9.1, are vital if change is to occur. Once a change plan has been collaboratively agreed to with the client (and parents, if you are working with a child), charting is helpful for studying whether or not your intervention is effective and whether or not change is maintained after the intervention ceases.

Relaxation Training

Physical body tension is characteristic of many clients who enter counseling or therapy. This tension may show itself in a variety of ways, including statements of fear or tension in social situations; direct complaints of sore, constantly tense muscles; impotence and frigidity; difficulties with sleep; and high blood pressure. There is clinical evidence that borderline clients will reduce the number of suicidal gestures and "cutting" if they are supported with a relaxation training program. Most seriously depressed clients can benefit from relaxation training as part of their treatment regimen.

Surprisingly, simply teaching people the mechanics of systematic relaxation techniques has been sufficient to alleviate many seemingly complex problems. Rather than search for the reasons that a client is unable to sleep, for example, behavioral counselors have found it more effective in many cases to teach the client relaxation techniques. The simple procedure of training clients in relaxation can be an important way to bring totally new views of the world to them. Through finding that they can control their bodies, clients can move on to solve many complex personal difficulties.

For this reason, virtually all counselors and therapists today are becoming skilled at training clients in relaxation techniques similar to the exercises presented in exhibit 9.3. A client may learn the rudiments of relaxation training in a fifteen-minute session, but careful planning and training are needed if relaxation techniques are to become part of a client's life.

A variety of systematic relaxation tapes is now available commercially, making it possible for the busy behavioral counselor to delegate this training to the machine and to spend more time training the client how to use relaxation in specific situations. Relaxation may, for example, be an important part of assertiveness training. If a client describes physical tension in the stomach when talking with members of the

_____100   As I look at the examination I see a question or two which I really don't know and I absolutely panic. I leave the room.

The importance and value of this type of individualized, collaborative assessment cannot be overstressed. It is important that you personally take time to practice the construction of anxiety hierarchies. As relapse prevention reminds us, if we do not seek actively to transfer our learnings, the information will be lost.

Multicultural Implications

A special feature of anxiety hierarchies is that they concretize anxiety very specifically and in smaller units. If you worked with a woman or minority who suffers some type of harassment or discrimination in the workplace with which legal action was impossible, you could anticipate considerable stress. To help these clients understand and manage the stress, constructing an anxiety hierarchy can be helpful. Similarly, such hierarchies for eating problems, depression, phobias, and so on can be highly useful in clarifying diagnosis and helping plan more effective treatment.

Using the Hierarchy for Treatment

Following completion of the anxiety hierarchy, the client is asked to sit with eyes closed and visualize a variety of scenes close to the 0 point of anxiety. These scenes may be of school being over or of an enjoyable activity, such as a picnic or walking in the woods. The therapist asks the student to note the easy feelings of relaxation and then moves gradually up the hierarchy, having the client visualize each scene in the hierarchy. If tension is felt, the client may indicate this by a raised finger. For example, if tension was experienced as the student visualized the situation two days before the examination, the therapist and student would work to note the tense muscles and relax them while still thinking of the usually tension-producing scene.

Gradually, the client learns to visualize all the scenes in the anxiety hierarchy while relaxed. This type of training may take several interviews, but it has been demonstrated to be effective. When students find themselves in similar tension-producing situations, they are able to generate relaxation behaviors to counteract the feelings of tension.

Similar work with anxiety hierarchies has proven equally effective in many anxiety and phobic situations. Some of the most dramatic demonstrations of desensitization procedures have been with snake phobics who, as a final test, allowed a snake to crawl over them (Bandura, Blanchard, & Ritter, 1969).

Frigidity and impotency also have been successfully treated with this method. In these cases, couples construct anxiety hierarchies related to sexual experimentation and the sex act. Generally, it is found that the sex act is the most tension-producing experience of all. Couples are instructed in systematic relaxation and go through the anxiety hierarchy visualization, much as did the student with examination anxiety. When transferring the newly learned behavior to the bedroom, the couple is often instructed to stop further sexual experimentation until full relaxation is regained.

Modeling

Seeing is believing, it is said, and behavioral psychologists have found that watching films or videotapes of people engaging in successful behavior is sufficient for clients to learn new ways of coping with difficulties. For example, Bandura (1976) found that live modeling of snake handling was even more effective than systematic desensitization in teaching snake phobics to cope with their anxieties.

> After observing the therapist interacting closely with the snake, clients were aided through other induction procedures to perform progressively more frightening responses themselves. At each step the therapist . . . performed the activities fearlessly and gradually led the clients to touch, stroke, and hold the midsection of the snake's body with gloved and then bare hands for increasing periods. . . . As clients became more courageous, the therapist gradually reduced [the] level of participation and control over the snake until eventually clients were able to tolerate the squirming snake in their laps without assistance, to let the snake loose in the room and retrieve it, and to let it crawl freely over their bodies. (p. 256)

In a sense, modeling is one of the most simple and obvious ways to teach clients new behaviors. Seeing and hearing directly, either live or via film or tape, brings home a message much more clearly and directly than direct advice and description. Modeling can be combined with relaxation, assertiveness training, and other behavioral techniques in developing uniquely individualized programs for clients. Modeling is a key ingredient in social skills training.

Social Skills Training

An increasingly important part of cognitive-behavioral methods is that of skills training—teaching clients and others specific modes of responding. Skills training is the subject of three important books (Hargie, Saunders, & Dickson, 1987; Larson, 1984; Marshall, Kurtz, & Associates, 1982), which present a wide variety of systematic formulations for teaching communication skills, life skills for difficult/delinquent adolescents, marital skills, skills for psychiatric patients, among others. Skill training, in fact, is beginning to present itself as a theory of psychotherapy and change in its own right.

Most often, skill training involves the following cognitive-behavioral components:

1. *Rapport/structuring.* Clients/trainees are prepared cognitively and emotionally for the instruction.

2. *Cognitive presentation and cueing.* Usually, some form of explanation and rationale for the skill is presented. In stress inoculation, Meichenbaum, using Socratic-type questions, helps clients in a collaborative fashion better understand the nature of stress and why it is important to learn stress management.

3. *Modeling.* Role-plays, videotapes, audiotapes, and demonstrations are commonly used so that trainees can see and hear the behaviors of the skill in action. Cognitions from earlier stages are paired with specific observable behaviors.

4. *Practice.* One does not always learn a skill by cognitive understanding and watching. Most skill trainers require their clients/trainees to engage in the skill through role-played practice possibly supplemented by videotape and audiotape feedback. It is important that the skill be mastered to a high level or it is likely to be lost over time.

5. *Generalization.* All skill training emphasizes the decision to take the learning outside and beyond the immediate situation of the training session. In some cases, a full relapse prevention worksheet will be employed. The cognitive-behavioral therapist works with the client (or clients if the treatment is conducted on a group basis) to anticipate possible barriers or obstacles that might interfere with their employing coping skills. In this way, clients become their own therapists.

One cognitive-behavioral skill training program is that of the microskills framework of chapter 3 in which counseling and communication skills are taught. It has been found that teaching these skills is not only useful for training in counseling and therapy, but also for a wide variety of patient and client groups.

Social Skills Training with Psychiatric Inpatients

More specifically, Ivey (1971, 1991) videotaped depressed psychiatric patients talking about their issues with a therapist. The patients then viewed the videotape and observed and counted behaviors they themselves selected (for example, poor eye contact, slumped body posture). They then practiced the skills in role-plays with the therapist and counted and charted changes in pinpointed behaviors. This "media therapy" project proved effective in helping patients who had been in the hospital for up to four years move out of the hospital within from one to two months.

In addition to psychiatric patients, others have benefited from this form of training, including management interns, medical personnel, and hospice workers. Skill training itself is a major theoretical and practical form of treatment and is closely related to assertiveness training.

Assertiveness Training

Some individuals passively accept whatever fate hands them. You may know someone who acts as a "doormat" and allows friends and family to dominate him or her. This person may allow others to make decisions, let strangers cut in front while standing in line, or accept being ignored by a waiter for an hour. Individuals who may be overly passive in their behavior can benefit from assertiveness training and learn to stand up for their rights.

You may also know someone who is overly aggressive and dominating, who tells others what to do and what to think. This person may interrupt conversations rudely, cut in front of others in line, and yell at waiters. This aggressive individual can also benefit from assertiveness training.

Assertiveness training involves learning to stand up for your rights—but to simultaneously consider the thoughts and feelings of others. While emphasizing overt behavior, assertiveness training also focuses on client cognitions.

Alberti and Emmons (1970/1990) are recognized as the pioneers of assertiveness training. Bower (1990) and Bower and Bower (1985) have written highly useful statements on the framework. Bower (1976) and Phelps (1987) specifically apply the model to women. Cheek (1976) first discussed the multicultural implications of the framework and provided important linkage for more cognitively oriented assertiveness training.

The specifics of assertiveness training are outlined in exhibit 9.4. If you can conduct a basic applied behavioral analysis and can pinpoint behavior with some precision, you should be able to conduct assertiveness training with some understanding and skill.

Exhibit 9.4 is oriented toward behavioral assertiveness training with minimal attention to internal cognitive states. If your depressed, agoraphobic, or normal client does not have some attention paid to their internal states of thinking and feeling, change is much less likely to occur and be maintained. The cognitive dimensions of CBT stressed in chapter 10 are critical for producing enduring change.

Exhibit 9.4

An Exercise in Applied Behavioral Analysis and Assertiveness Training

The purpose of this exercise is to integrate the concepts of this chapter in a practical format that you can use to implement assertiveness training in your own counseling practice. With a role-played client who is willing to discuss a specific situation in which he or she may have been too passive or too aggressive, work carefully through the following interview:

1. *Rapport/structuring.* Remember that data indicate that behaviorally oriented counselors and therapists offer as much or more warmth than other orientations to helping. Establish rapport with your client in your own unique way and use attending behavior to "tune in" to the client and client observation skills to

note when you have established rapport.

Give special attention to structuring the interview and telling your client ahead of time what to expect. Behavioral counseling operates on a mutuality between counselor and client.

2. *Data gathering.* Your goal is to get a clear, behavioral definition of the problem. The basic listening sequence (BLS) will help you draw out the specific behavior. Identify a clear, specific instance in which the individual was not sufficiently assertive. Asking for concrete examples will facilitate operationalizing the present overly passive or overly aggressive behavior.

Use applied behavioral analysis to find out the antecedents of the behavior. What was the context, and what happened before the behavior occurred? Define the problem behavior even more precisely. Finally, what were the consequences after the behavior? In each case use questioning skills to describe the behavior.

A role-play is a particularly useful way to obtain further behavioral specifics. Once you have a clear picture of antecedent-behavior-consequence, have your client role-play the situation again with you acting as the other person(s). Make the role-play as real and accurate as you can.

Finally, draw out positive assets of the client and the situation. What strengths does the client have that will be useful in later problem solution? You may find it necessary to provide your client with positive feedback, as nonassertive clients often have trouble identifying any positives in themselves or the situation.

Again, one of the best ways to obtain behavioral data for assertiveness training is to assist your client in conducting a role-play with you in which the situation is recreated in behavioral specificity.

3. *Determining outcomes.* Develop clear, specific behavioral goals with your client. You will want to use listening skills and operationalization of behavior methods. Is the goal established by your client clear, specific, and attainable? Will it lead to change?

4. *Generating alternative solutions.*

At this point you have the goals of the client that can be contrasted with the problem as defined. In addition, you have some positive assets and strengths of the client.

With your client, review the goals and then practice in a role-play the new behaviors represented by those goals. Continue practicing with your client until the client demonstrates the ability to engage in the behavior.

You may find that relaxation training, charting, modeling, cognitive-behavioral therapy, and other behavioral techniques may be useful to supplement and enrich your behavioral program.

5. *Generalization.* It is easy for the successful therapist to stop at the fourth stage. Here it is critical that specific behavioral plans be made with your client for generalization of the behavior beyond the session. Use the relapse prevention form of chapter 4 with your client. Be clear and specific with your behavioral goals and anticipate the likely relapse potential. Behavior that is not reinforced after training is likely to be lost and then lamented two weeks later.

6. *Follow-up.* One week after the interview, follow up with your client and determine if behavior actually did change. Later follow-ups can be useful to both you and the client. As necessary, use the relapse form to analyze any difficulty with behavioral generalization.

Multicultural Dimensions

Imagine you are working with a woman or minority who is dealing with discrimination and the associated stress. One important dimension of being able to engage in assertiveness training is feeling good about oneself. Sometimes people who experience discrimination believe that the problems they suffer are "their fault" and that "if only" they behaved more effectively, their problems would resolve.

In addressing these attitudes, cognitive instruction, as discussed in chapter 10, can be a vital part of assertiveness training. Furthermore, the ideas of multicultural counseling and therapy (chapter 5) clearly show that the focus of your intervention must often be on changing the environment, not just the individual. In assertiveness training language, there is a need to help individuals change cognitions about themselves and their environments so that they can be more effective and assertive.

Cheek (1976), for example, talks of the importance of "a foundation for the Black perspective." Assertiveness training does not seek to have African-Americans behave or think like European-Americans nor to have women think like men. Assertiveness training seeks to recognize the perspective and worldview of different multicultural and gender groups. Cheek (1976) notes that the African-American cognitive perspective includes the following:

1. Familiarity and experience in both the African-American and European-American perspectives.
2. A frequent distrust of European-Americans, with accompanying emotions such as anger and rage.
3. An emphasis on race and its importance.
4. Internal conflict as to whether to talk in "White" or "Black." African-Americans are bidialectical.
5. An ability to "fake it" with European-Americans.

Cheatham (1990), Parham (1990), and White and Parham (1990) fifteen years later address many of the same issues, leading to the conclusions that behavioral change is insufficient and that cognitive work on societal issues must be part of any treatment program with minorities. Focusing on the individual solely will often be seen as "blaming the victim." Cheatham argues that techniques such as assertiveness training, although useful, beg the question of causation: Did the problem originate in the client or society? If the latter is the issue, Cheatham advocates action by the counselor in the community or society as the best route toward individual change. Given this, the non-African-American therapist or counselor must put behavioral treatment in context. Clearly, the techniques and ideas of this chapter have multicultural relevance, but they can only be accepted as part of the solution.

Similar issues of the meaning of assertiveness training with various groups can be raised. For example, assertiveness training for Latinas needs to be conducted with cultural sensitivity, for women from a Spanish-speaking tradition face different problems when they act assertively than do most European-American women. What is assertive for European-American cultures may be considered intrusive and aggressive by those from other cultural groups. This latter point is especially true for those who may come from more sensitive cultures.

European-American women usually find assertiveness training helpful, but it is most helpful if combined with issues around being a woman in society. Kantrowitz and Ballou (1992) give special attention to assertiveness training, stating that in a practical setting, assertiveness training should not be used to teach women a man's style of being. Cheek (1976) supports this point, noting that assertiveness training should be oriented to the African-American culture and not "make Blacks White."

Individual and societal issues have clearly become part of the assertiveness training movement.

Stress Inoculation and Stress Management

A useful technique is that of teaching clients how to deal effectively with stress (Meichenbaum, 1985). This training program involves three distinct phases: (1) helping clients develop a cognitive understanding of the role stress plays in their lives, (2) teaching specific coping skills so they can deal with stress effectively, and (3) working with thoughts and feelings about the stressful situation so they will be motivated to do something about stress. Meichenbaum makes the important point that cognitive awareness of stress is not enough to produce change, nor are learning skills. One must actually decide to do something.

An Example

A professional couple may be faced with difficulties in their lives and may very frequently argue with each other. Their problem could be defined as a "marital difficulty," or it could be defined as a problem in coping with stress. The couple both may work and have two children and be active in the community. There simply isn't time to "do it all" effectively, and this becomes a major stressor in itself. The first task in stress inoculation is to help the couple define the problem as one of stress. This itself can be useful, as the couple no longer has to "blame" each other for their difficulties and now can see the impact of their environment on the marriage.

Second, it is possible to teach stress reduction procedures, such as relaxation training and decision making (so that the couple does fewer things more systematically) and social skills (often via a form of assertiveness training), so that they might learn alternatives to constant work. These behavioral skills can lead to important changes and will likely involve techniques of modeling, role-play, and direct instruction.

Finally, knowing one has a problem with stress and having some skills are not enough. Will the couple decide for action? At the point of generalization, their emotional and cognitive world may again become stress engendering, and maladaptive thinking (and the accompanying dysfunctional emotions) will prevent them from a decision to act. The techniques of "cognitive-semantic therapy" or relapse prevention may be employed to ensure action. The therapist may follow up with this couple to ensure that they actually do implement the systematic plan of behavioral change that has been pinpointed.

Developing a Stress Management Program

Most therapists and counselors today find themselves required to do some sort of stress inoculation or stress management training. Stress management combines many of the behavioral techniques described in this chapter plus important cognitive techniques of the next chapter. Assertiveness training is often an important part of stress inoculation. A model group stress management program includes, but need not be restricted to, the following:

1. *Establishing rapport and program goals.* Usually, there is a special topic or need the group shares. For example, your group might be teenagers, adult children of alcoholics, women dealing with job stress, or an inpatient group diagnosed as borderline.

Your task at this stage is to establish rapport, share your program goals, and learn the individual needs of your members. Modify your program to meet their wishes and needs.

2. *Cognitive instruction.* Following the collaborative model, draw out from your group their ideas of the origins of stress and what it does. Help them organize their ideas and then provide additional information through handouts, lecture, or media, as appropriate.

3. *Stress management training.* Usually, this takes the form of relaxation training, sharing of coping mechanisms, and social skills and assertiveness training. Many workshops include training in listening skills such as those presented in chapter 3. Decision-making training such as that presented in chapter 4 is also important. Cognitive instruction following from the concepts in chapter 10 are also useful parts of the program.

You will want to tailor your stress management program to the special needs of your group.

4. *Homework.* Relapse prevention techniques, such as those summarized in chapter 4, are an important part of a stress management program. Unless your trainees are encouraged to "take home" what they have learned, the experience with you will likely be soon forgotten.

Extensions of Stress Management Training

The concepts of stress management and stress inoculation now have been expanded to include specific suggestions as to how to work with victims of trauma (rape, abuse, and even victims of terrorist attacks). These techniques are increasingly vital as a treatment framework in its own right. Meichenbaum (1985) presents his innovative ideas with many suggested clinical interventions.

A nine-session stress inoculation was used with rape survivors by Foa et al. (1991). The program was found to be more effective than supportive counseling, and long-term follow-up revealed significant improvement in post-traumatic stress disorder. The overall content of the sessions was similar to the general concepts presented in this chapter, although considerable emphasis was also given to cognitive variables as well as those described in the following chapter.

However, even more effective than stress management was systematic use of imagery, similar to that described in the psychodynamic chapters. Imagery and emotional reliving are becoming part of cognitive-behavioral procedures. Flowing from the network treatment procedures of multicultural counseling and therapy, it seems logical to conclude that a combination of supportive counseling, stress management, and imagery techniques might make a very powerful set of integrated treatments. Moreover, if family and support networks are involved, giving attention to gender, systemic, and cultural issues, the possibilities for change may be further increased.

Limitations and Practical Implications of Practicing Cognitive-Behavioral Therapy

Ineffective and careless counseling can endanger clients. In the preceding chapter, wild analysis provided an illustration of psychodynamic counseling at its worst. No matter how good the theory or the potential power of a counseling or treatment intervention is, the counselor has the professional and ethical responsibility to be aware of manifestations of false practice. The term *manipulative behavioral counseling* can be used to describe the therapy similar to wild analysis.

Manipulative behavioral counseling occurs when the counselor makes a decision for the client without client awareness or when the counselor has so much power in the client's life that the client has no choice but to go along with the behavioral program whether or not he or she agrees. For example, a focus of behavioral counselors has been to increase "time on task" (amount of time spent working at one's desk) in elementary classrooms. This can be a desirable educational goal, but sometimes these behavioral interventions have been implemented without child or parent awareness that anything was being changed.

It is as easy to use psychodynamic or humanistic counseling to the detriment of clients as it is to use behavioral techniques. Counseling theories and techniques are not at fault when abused; rather, the fault lies in the values of the manipulative and careless counselor.

Cognitive-behavioral techniques are often readily accepted by minority clients due to their clarity and effectiveness. At the same time, effectiveness does not equate with cultural appropriateness. As Cheek reminds us, cognitive-behavioral techniques need to be applied with the gender and culture of the client in mind.

The exercises of exhibits 9.1, 9.2, and 9.4 provide a solid beginning in cognitive-behavioral counseling and therapy, but it is important to remember that relapse prevention is an especially useful set of techniques to add to the final stages of the interview, regardless of what therapeutic technique or theory you are using. The fifth stage of the interview (generalization), follow-up with clients after the interview, and relapse prevention are critical elements for therapy.

Behavioral techniques "work," and clients often benefit from and enjoy the specificity of these techniques. At the same time, some clients will change their behavior but still feel that "something is missing." These clients may benefit from the addition of more cognitive methods (chapter 10) to your treatment plan, or some may want to examine the reasons their behavior developed as it did. In short, you may find that behavioral counseling benefits from association with other helping theories.

REFERENCES

AGRAS, S., LEITENBERG, H., & BARLOW, D. (1968). Social reinforcement in the modification of agoraphobia. *Archives of General Psychiatry, 19,* 423–27.

ALBERTI, R., & EMMONS, M. (1990). *Your perfect right* (6th ed.). San Luis Obispo, CA: Impact. (Original work published 1970)

AMERICAN PSYCHIATRIC ASSOCIATION. (1987). *DSM-III-R.* Washington, DC: Author.

BAILEY, B., GOOD, M., & MCGRADY, A. (1990). Clinical observations on behavioral treatment of a patient with insulin-dependent diabetes mellitus. *Biofeedback and Self Regulation, 15,* 7–13.

BANDURA, A. (1976). Effecting change through participant modeling. In J. Krumboltz & C. Thoresen (Eds.), *Counseling methods* (pp. 248–64). Troy, MO: Holt, Rinehart & Winston.

BANDURA, A. (1982). Self-efficacy: Mechanism in human agency. *American Psychologist, 37,* 122–47.

BANDURA, A. (1989). Human agency in social cognitive theory. *American Psychologist, 44,* 1175–85.

BANDURA, A., BLANCHARD, E., & RITTER, B. (1969). The relative efficacy of desensitization and modeling approaches. *Journal of Personality and Social Psychology, 13,* 173–99.

BOWER, S. (1976). Assertiveness training for women. In J. Krumboltz & C. Thoresen (Eds.), *Counseling methods* (pp. 467–74). Troy, MO: Holt, Rinehart & Winston.

BOWER, S. (1990). *Painless public speaking.* Northhamptonshire, U.K.: Thorsons.

BOWER, S., & BOWER, G. (1985). *Asserting yourself.* Reading, MA: Addison-Wesley.

CHEATHAM, H. (1990). Empowering Black families. In H. Cheatham & J. Stewart (Eds.), *Black families* (pp. 373–93). New Brunswick, NJ: Transaction.

CHEEK, D. (1976). *Assertive Black . . . puzzled White.* San Luis Obispo, CA: Impact.

DIONNE, H. (1990, October). *Parents with panic disorder: The impact on their children.* Unpublished comprehensive paper, University of Massachusetts, Amherst.

EMMELKAMP, P., BRILMAN, E., KUIPER, H., & MERSH, P. (1986). The treatment of agoraphobia. *Behavior Modification, 10,* 37–53.

EMMELKAMP, P., & MERSH, P. (1982). Cognition and exposure *in vivo* in the treatment of agoraphobia. *Cognitive Research and Therapy, 6,* 72–90.

FOA, E., ROTHBAUM, B., RIGGS, D., & MURDOCK, T. (1991). Treatment of post-traumatic stress disorder in rape victims: A comparison between cognitive-behavior procedures and counseling. *Journal of Clinical and Consulting Psychology, 99,* 715–23.

GRAZZI, L., LEONE, M., FREDIANI, F., & BUSSONE, G. (1990). A therapeutic alternative for tension headache in children: Treatment and one-year follow-up results. *Biofeedback and Self Regulation, 15,* 1–6.

GREENSPOON, J. (1955). The reinforcing effect of two spoken sounds on the frequency of two responses. *American Journal of Psychology, 68,* 409–16.

HARGIE, O., SAUNDERS, C., & DICKSON, D. (1987). *Social skills in interpersonal communication.* Cambridge, MA: Brookline.

HATCH, J., & SAITO, I. (1990). Growth and development of biofeedback: A bibliographic update. *Biofeedback and Self Regulation, 15,* 37–46.

HOOLEY, J., ORLEY, J., & TEASDALE, J. (1987). Levels of expressed emotion and relapse in depressed patients. *British Journal of Psychiatry, 7,* 643–47.

IVEY, A. (1971). Media therapy: Educational change planning for psychiatric patients. *Journal of Counseling Psychology, 20,* 338–43.

IVEY, A. (1991, September). *Developmental therapy and media therapy: An update.* Presentation to Veterans Administration Conference, Orlando, FLA.

IVEY, A., & HINKLE, J. (1968). Students, the major untapped resource in higher education. *Reach* (a publication of the Colorado State University *Collegian*), *6*, 1, 4.

KANTROWITZ, R., & BALLOU, M. (1992). A feminist critique of cognitive-behavioral therapy. In L. Brown & M. Ballou (Eds.), *Theories of personality and psychopathology: Feminist reappraisals* (pp. 70–87). New York: Guilford.

KELLY, G. (1955). *The psychology of personal constructs.* New York: W.W. Norton.

LARSON, D. (Ed.). (1984). *Teaching psychological skills.* Belmont, CA: Wadsworth.

LEARY, W. (1991, October 22). Black hypertension may reflect other ills. *New York Times,* p. C3.

MARLATT, G. (1980, March). *Relapse prevention: A self-control program for the treatment of addictive behaviors.* Invited address presented at the International Conference on Behavior Modification, Banff, Alberta.

MARLATT, G., & GORDON, J. (1985). Relapse prevention: Maintenance strategies in the treatment of addictive behaviors. New York: Guilford.

MARSHALL, E., KURTZ, P., & ASSOCIATES. (1982). *Interpersonal helping skills.* San Francisco: Jossey-Bass.

MEICHENBAUM, D. (1985). *Stress inoculation training.* New York: Pergamon Press.

MEICHENBAUM, D. (1990, December). *Evolution of cognitive behavior therapy: Origins, tenets and clinical examples.* Paper presented at the second conference on the Evolution of Psychotherapy, Anaheim, CA.

MEICHENBAUM, D. (1991). Evolution of cognitive behavior therapy. In J. Zeig (Ed.), *The evolution of psychotherapy, II.* New York: Brunner/Mazel.

MEICHENBAUM, D., & GILMORE, J. (1984). The unconscious reconsidered: A cognitive behavioral perspective. In K. Bowers & D. Meichenbaum (Eds.), *The unconscious reconsidered.* New York: Wiley.

MICHELSON, L. (1987). Cognitive-behavioral assessment and treatment of agoraphobia. In L. Michelson & L. Ascher (Eds.), *Anxiety and stress disorders* (pp. 213–70). New York: Guilford.

MICHELSON, L., MAVISSAKALIAN, M., & MARCHIONE, K. (1985). Cognitive-behavioral treatment of agoraphobia. *Journal of Consulting and Clinical Psychology, 53,* 913–25.

PARHAM, T. (1990). *Do the right thing: Racial discussion in counseling psychology.* Paper presented at the American Psychological Association Convention, Boston.

PHELPS, S. (1987). *The assertive woman.* San Luis Obispo, CA: Impact.

SKINNER, B. F. (1953). *Science and human behavior.* New York: Free Press.

SLOANE, R., STAPLES, F., CRISTOL, A., YORKSTON, N., & WHIPPLE, K. (1975). *Psychotherapy vs. behavior therapy.* Cambridge, MA: Harvard University Press.

SULZER-AZAROFF, B. (1985). Achieving educational success. Troy, MO: Holt, Rinehart & Winston.

SULZER-AZAROFF, B., & MAYER, G. (1977). Applying behavior-analysis procedures with children and youth. Troy, MO: Holt, Rinehart & Winston.

WHITE, J., & PARHAM, T. (1990). *The psychology of Blacks.* Englewood Cliffs, NJ: Prentice-Hall.

WOLPE, J., & LAZARUS, A. (1966). *Behavior therapy techniques.* Elmsford, NY: Pergamon Press.

WOOLFOLK, R., & RICHARDSON, F. (1984). Behavior therapy and the ideology of modernity. *American Psychologist, 39,* 777–86.

Cognitive-Behavioral Counseling and Therapy: Cognitive Approaches

CHAPTER GOALS

Integration of thought, action, and decision making is the task of cognitive-behavioral therapy and counseling (CBT). In this chapter, the focus is on the work of the therapists whose writing primarily emphasizes cognition. It is critical to recall that thought without accompanying action (cognition without accompanying behavior) is considered empty by Ellis, Beck, and Glasser.

This chapter has the following specific goals:

1. To present the worldview provided by the more cognitive portion of the cognitive-behavioral tradition.

2. To relate the cognitive orientation to multicultural counseling and therapy.

3. To describe the key ideas of three important cognitive-behavioral theorists— Ellis, Beck, and Glasser—and to illustrate some of their work with case examples.

4. To encourage you to test out the ideas of this theoretical orientation through practice exercises.

The Evolution to Cognition

Chapter 9 has shown the evolution of behavioral psychology to a more cognitive orientation. In different ways, three figures—Albert Ellis, Aaron Beck, and William Glasser—have been leaders in this direction. All three stress the importance of two goals in counseling and therapy: (1) to examine how clients think about themselves and their world and, if necessary, to help them change these cognitions; and (2) to ensure that clients act on those cognitions through behavior in their daily life—thus the term *cognitive-behavioral*.

Psychodynamic approaches have also influenced cognitive-behavioral theory. Both Ellis and Beck did their early work from a psychodynamic orientation but moved away as they found other methods more efficient. However, as in the psychodynamic orientation, cognitive-behavioral approaches to change stress the fact that insight (cognitive awareness) is important in maintaining change in behavior and thinking. Beck, in particular, often draws on past client history to understand present cognitions and behaviors.

Thus, in evolving cognitive-behavioral theory there are some useful elements to assist you in developing your own conceptualization (cognitions) about the therapeutic process and some techniques and actions (behaviors) that are useful in helping you decide the nature of your own work in the field.

The Cognitive Worldview and Its Relation to Cognitive-Behavioral Tradition

Most reviewers of the cognitive frame of reference trace the history of the movement to the stoic philosopher Epictetus, who noted that people "are disturbed not by events, but by the views they take of them." Changing how one thinks about the world, then, becomes a major goal of the cognitive-behavioral point of view.

A worldview in which thinking and ideas about the world are central can be traced beyond stoicism to Plato and also to the philosophies of idealism. The philosophies of idealism emphasize that the idea one has about the world is more important than what is "real." In fact, the concept of "reality" may be dismissed by the idealists as a mere "idea about things." More recent adaptations of the idealistic philosophic tradition are manifested in the work of Kant and Hegel. The work of Freud may be described as being in this tradition. Freud in some ways was a stoic, as he felt that little could be done about the human condition except to know it and understand it. Behavioral change may be helpful in this frame of reference but is still viewed as relatively limited in scope.

But what about "reality"? The British and American logical positivists and pragmatists (Bentham, Mill, James, Russell) have questioned that cognition and good thinking are meaningful or sufficient for living in the real world. Out of their philosophic work has arisen the optimistic scientific tradition of hypothesis testing and direct action on the world. Behavioral psychology, as represented by Skinner and the cognitive-behavioral work of Meichenbaum, is an obvious extension of this scientific, realistic orientation.

Existentialist philosophers such as Kierkegaard, Tillich, and Sartre question both idealistic and realistic philosophers and emphasize the act of individual choice and the process of intentionally choosing and deciding. Rogers and Perls clearly represent this orientation to helping.

The cognitive-behavioral worldview may be described as a beginning attempt to integrate the three major philosophic traditions of idealism, realism, and existentialism. Ellis, considered a pioneer of cognitive-behavioral theory, first maintained a psychodynamic practice. He then started work on his theory of rational-emotive therapy and was classified in the existential-humanistic tradition for many years. However, he continued to emphasize the importance of action in his practice, was noticed by behavioral psychology, and now primarily is considered a cognitive-behaviorist.

The worldview of cognitive-behavioral therapy, then, may be described as an evolving synthesis of the three major philosophic and psychological traditions of the Western world. The cognitive-behavioral theorist will ultimately be interested in knowing how the individual developed ideas or cognitions about reality, chooses and decides from the many possibilities, and acts and behaves in relationship to reality.

Multicultural Issues in Cognitive Therapy

The concept of worldview has been stressed throughout this book. A worldview is a way of organizing and construing our experience. You come to the study of counseling and therapy with a worldview that has been molded by your unique personal background, your family, and your cultural history. Kantrowitz and Ballou (1992) critique and challenge the cognitive-behavioral frame of reference:

> Challenging beliefs and thoughts may not fit well with many cultural and gender socialization patterns. Asians, for example, have been taught to create emotional harmony and avoid conflict in accord with their cultural norms. . . . Women's perceptions have been minimized and misunderstood. (p. 81)
>
> There is nothing in the theory which enhances sensitivity to gender, race, and class issues. . . . The lack of careful consideration of gender, class, race, and ethnic factors as well as contextual information, specific antecedents, and consequences of specific beliefs and behaviors is a problem in cognitive-behavioral conceptualizations of pathology. Also problematic is their attribution of responsibility, implied by their goal of changing the individual client. (pp. 82–83)

The last point is of particular importance. Multicultural counseling and therapy focuses on the importance of working with the client on issues of oppression and of seeking to change environmental context. One of the great cognitive shifts of this century has been the self-awareness movement of African-Americans, women, gay men and lesbians, the deaf, those who face physical issues, the aged, and others. It can be argued that the changes in consciousness brought about by the Black identity movement have done more for African-American mental health than all counseling theories combined.

Cheek and Integrative Theory

Although the consciousness-raising movement has resulted in the development of multicultural theories of helping, their relationship to cognitive theories discussed here and in the preceding chapter should be mentioned. Cheek (1976), in his pioneering work on assertiveness training (see the previous chapter), gave equal attention to the way African-American clients viewed themselves and their condition as he did to assertiveness training techniques themselves. Indeed, it could be argued that Cheek was the first cognitive-behavioral theorist. Moreover, he is very likely the first person in the CBT movement who included multicultural cognitive issues as an explicit part of the treatment process.

Cognitive Theory and the Multicultural Challenge

All three theorists discussed in this chapter—Albert Ellis, Aaron Beck, and William Glasser—have used their techniques successfully with culturally different clients. Part of what is involved in surmounting discrimination, prejudice, and unfairness is generating a new cognitive view of self and the ability to change situations. In the first case example in this chapter, Albert Ellis helps a young gay male come to terms with his affectational orientation.

In another example, a rational-emotive therapy group intervention program for African-American adolescents was developed by Piotrowski and Franklin (1990). The program identified problems the youth had in their daily lives and then analyzed these problems through the lens of RET method and theory. In this way the adolescents were able to use cognitive change techniques on themselves, balancing issues of personal responsibility with injustice in the environment. The program concluded with role-playing and assertiveness training exercises to help the youth generalize their cognitive learning to actual behavior outside the group.

It seems clear that cognitive techniques have potential and value in multicultural counseling. However, as Kantrowitz and Ballou (1992) comment, the emphasis in the approaches of Ellis, Beck, and Glasser is very much on individual change, with minimal attention given to consciousness raising of broader systemic issues.

Albert Ellis and Rational-Emotive Therapy

Albert Ellis's rational-emotive therapy (RET) originated in the mid-1950s as he became increasingly aware of the ineffectiveness of psychoanalysis to produce change in his patients. He found himself in an extremely successful private practice of psychoanalysis, yet was dissatisfied with the results he was obtaining. Gradually, he found himself taking a more active role in therapy, attacking the client's logic, and even prescribing behavioral activities for patients to follow after they left the therapy hour

(Ellis, 1983a). The result of this change has come to be known as rational-emotive therapy, a pioneering method of cognitive-behavioral therapy.

Role of Emotion.   Emotion is central in rational-emotive theory. Unless the "E" in RET is present, change is unlikely to occur. A rationalist position is not enough. Ellis, himself, is often seen personally as a highly rational and logical person. Yet, awareness of others' emotions and constructions of reality is central to his approach. For example, Weinrach (1990) provides a personal anecdote in which he describes his first observations of Ellis in action as he supervises a beginning helper:

> One of the students played a tape which reflected virtually no mastery of the RET concepts or techniques which had been exhaustively taught and demonstrated over the previous three days. . . . As the tape played, other group members and I expected Al to show some understandable frustration or exasperation. To the contrary, Al proved to be the ever-patient, tender, and gentle master teacher. He started at the very beginning and taught this student the basics of RET, step-by-step. That experience forced me to reconcile the discrepancy between Al's public and private personae. (p. 108)

Broad Basis.   Ellis's rational-emotive therapy, as with other cognitive-behavioral theories, is broad and eclectic. Ellis does not hesitate to use techniques from many differing theoretical orientations, according to the unique needs of the client. With a client having a sexual difficulty, Ellis may use his own cognitive strategies, but he will also use Masters and Johnson's (1970) sensate focusing techniques and the behavioral techniques of progressive relaxation and modeling (Ellis, 1983b).

Importance of Acceptance.   Ellis unconditionally accepts all manner of clients, just as does Rogers. And, like Perls, Ellis is searching for authenticity. Ellis encourages clients to think rationally and be in touch with their emotions. He may use bibliotherapy and ask clients to write journals to increase their understanding. He may use humor or sarcasm, as appropriate, with the client. He constantly stresses "homework" as important to the change process, seeking to have clients generalize ideas from the interview to their daily lives. It could be argued that his emphasis on what happens outside the interview was the precursor to relapse prevention described in chapter 4.

We will first consider Ellis's approach to therapy in action and then examine the constructs and systems underlying his interviewing style.

Case Presentation: Am I Gay?

Ellis's early work in sexuality and sexual counseling is particularly noteworthy (Ellis, 1958). He was one of the first to recognize that being a gay male or a lesbian may be an alternative life style rather than a "clinical problem." Ellis may or may not spend time developing rapport. He has a unique personal style and is known for starting the interview with a direct, rather confrontative challenge. Ellis is nonjudgmental about life-style issues. But he would urge that the individual make a decision based on personal preference rather than absolute musts and learn to live with that decision comfortably.

The following transcript[1] illustrates how Ellis (1971) rapidly moves into direct action with the client, with the goal of eventually helping the client decide how he wants to live with the idea of being gay. Ellis's work on this case is typical of much of his thinking. If the same client were treated today with rational-emotive therapy, we might anticipate that some attention would also be paid to the issue of discrimination against gay men and lesbians.

1. *Therapist:*   What's the main thing that's bothering you? [*Open question*]

2. *Client:*   I have a fear of that I'm gay—a *real* fear of it!

3. *Therapist:*   A fear of *becoming* a gay? [*Encourager*]

4. *Client:*   Yeah.

5. *Therapist:*   Because "*if* I were gay—," what? [*Open question, oriented to helping the client think in terms of logical consequences, a skill basic to RET work. Note that Ellis here focuses on thoughts or cognitions about being gay rather than on behavior. "It is not things, but how we view things" that is most important.*]

6. *Client:*   I don't know. It really gets me down. It gets me to a point where I'm doubting every day. I do doubt everything, anyway.

7. *Therapist:*   Yes. But let's get back to—answer the question: "If I were gay, what would that make me?" [*Directive, open question*]

8. *Client:*   (pause) I don't know.

9. *Therapist:*   Yes, you do! Now, I can give *you* the answer to the question. But let's see if you can get it. [*Opinion, directive*]

10. *Client:*   (pause) Less than a person?

11. *Therapist:*   Yes. Quite obviously, you're saying: "I'm *bad* enough. But if I were gay, that would make me a *total* shit!" [*Interpretation, logical consequences. Ellis often uses language to shock, and in this process, the client realizes that even if the "worst" is said, the client still survives and is respected by Ellis. Underneath the "tough" demanding exterior, Ellis demonstrates immense positive regard for the strengths within each individual.*

    This particular interpretation also focused on the logical consequences of the client's thinking. Note that A = the possible facts, B = the beliefs about the facts at A, and C = the emotional consequence. Ellis is particularly skilled at drawing out the cognitive thought patterns or sequences in client thinking and emotion.]

12. *Client:*   That's right.

13. *Therapist:*   Now, why did you just say you don't know? [*Open question*]

14. *Client:*   Just taking a guess at it, that's all. It's—it's just that the fear really gets me down! I don't know why.

15. *Therapist:*   (laughing) Well, you just gave the reason why! Suppose you were saying the same thing about—we'll just say—stealing. You hadn't stolen anything, but you thought of stealing something. And you said, "If I stole, I would be a thorough shit!" Just suppose that. Then, how much would you then start thinking about stealing? [*Expression of content—sharing information/instruction, closed question*]

16. *Client:*   (silence)

17. *Therapist:*   If you believed that: "If I stole it, I would be a thorough shit!" — would you think of it often? occasionally? [*Closed question*]

18. *Client:*   I'd think of it often.

19. *Therapist:*   That's right! As soon as you say, "If so-and-so happens, I would be a thorough shit!" you'll get obsessed with so-and-so. And the reason you're getting obsessed with being gay is this nutty belief, "If I were gay, I would be a total shit!" Now, look at that belief for a moment. And let's admit that if you were a gay, it would have real disadvantages. Let's assume that. But why would you be a thorough shit if you were gay? Let's suppose you gave up girls completely, and you just screwed guys. Now, why would you be a thorough shit? [*Encourager, interpretation, directive, open question. Here we see the more inclusive microskill of logical consequences, as discussed in chapter 3, used in its fullest sense.*]

20. *Client:*   (mumbles incoherently; is obviously having trouble finding an answer)

21. *Therapist:*   Think about it for a moment. (pp. 102–3) [*Directive*]

In later stages of the interview, Ellis seeks to have the client decide what he wants to do for logical reasons that are satisfactory emotionally — thus the term *rational-emotive.* The individual must think and feel a decision is correct. This interviewing style may be most appropriate for Ellis, as it is congruent with his personality. It is not wise that you be as forceful and direct if this style is not personally authentic for you. Some confuse Ellis's personal style with his theory. It is possible to use the theory of rational-emotive therapy in a fashion that is authentic to you.

Integrating Theory and Action.   The goal of the client and therapist in this session was to change cognitions about the idea of being gay (cognitive), to make decisions about how one wants to live (cognitive-existential), and to then act/behave according to those decisions (behavioral). This preceding sentence reflects the integration of the three basic philosophic traditions of idealism, existentialism, and realism.

When encouraging the client to act on his cognitions, Ellis is likely to use role-plays similar to those of social learning theory (modeling) or Kelly's (1955) fixed-role therapy. He almost certainly would recommend "homework" in the final stages of the interview to ensure that the client does something different as a result of the session. In the follow-up interview, Ellis would likely check carefully on whether or not the client had done anything differently in the time between sessions.

Current therapeutic work with clients debating sexual orientation would possibly include homework assignments to help build awareness of the gay pride movement and examine the role of media in stereotyping, and bibliotherapy. Ellis has a long history of tolerance for difference. He would support a gay male or lesbian client in activities oriented toward helping the community become more aware of the group's special needs. While working with a client, Ellis would continue to challenge the basic assumptions and logical structure of the client's thinking. He would never hesitate to challenge any client whose thought and emotional patterns are self- or socially defeating.

Central Theoretical Constructs and Techniques of RET

Ellis and the RET approach focus more on dysfunctional thoughts than do other therapies, although the importance of emotional foundations is also stressed. The RET view is that people often make themselves emotional victims by their own distorted, unrealistic, and irrational thinking patterns. Ellis takes an essentially optimistic view of people, but criticizes some humanistic approaches as being too soft at times and failing to address the fact that people can virtually "self-destruct" through irrational and muddled thinking. The task of the RET therapist is to correct clients' thought patterns and minimize irrational ideas, while simultaneously helping them change their dysfunctional feelings and behaviors.

However, one cannot change irrational and ineffective thinking unless one first can identify such statements in the interview. Let us look at this most basic skill.

Identifying Irrational Statements

In the interview, clients will frequently use such irrational statements as "If I don't pass this course, it is the end of the world," "Because my parents have been cruel to me as a child, there is nothing I can do now to help myself," "As the economy is lacking jobs, there is no meaning to my life," "If I can't get that scholarship, all is ended," and "The reason I have nothing is that the rich have taken it all." All of these statements at one level are true, but all of them represent "helpless" thinking, a common end result of irrational thought.

For example, the gay client presented in the foregoing transcript began with an irrational statement that Ellis helped extend and clarify. For example, "Therapist 11: Yes. Quite obviously you're saying: 'I'm *bad* enough. But if I were gay, that would make me a *total* shit.' " Here Ellis identifies a key irrational statement that will be the focus of the ensuing interview and treatment series.

There are many irrational or dysfunctional ideas. Following are five particularly common ones identified by Ellis (1967). In these statements you will also find an underlying demand for perfection accompanied by a denial of the impossibility of that perfectionistic demand. Read these examples carefully and think about those that might apply to you:

1. It is a *necessity* to be loved and approved of by *all* important people around us. "If he (or she) doesn't love me, it is awful."
2. It is *required* that one be *thoroughly* competent, adequate, and achieving if one is to be worthwhile. "If I don't make the goal, it's all my fault."
3. Some people are bad and *should* be punished for it. "He (or she) did that to me and I'm going to get even."
4. It is better to *avoid* difficulties and responsibilities. "It won't make any difference if I don't do that. People won't care."
5. It is *awful* or *catastrophic* if things are not the way they are supposed to be. "Isn't it terrible that the house isn't picked up?" (p. 84)

This list can be amplified, but more at issue is your ability to recognize irrational thinking in whatever form it takes. Listen carefully to those around you, and you'll discover that the world is full of irrational ideas and thoughts. Particularly, search the above statements for "all-or-none" thinking — irrational thinking that helps the client avoid the complexity of life. The words *should, ought,* and *must* are useful indicators of irrational thinking.

The basic therapeutic maneuver is always to be on the alert for irrational thinking and when it is observed, to work on it directly, concretely, and immediately. RET counselors vary in their use of microskills, but Ellis uses a large number of open and closed questions, directives, interpretation, and advice and opinion. The listening skills of paraphrasing and reflection of feeling play a less prominent role in his therapy.

An abbreviated RET self-help form is presented in exhibit 10.1. This form may be helpful in aiding you to identify your own and your clients' faulty thought patterns. In addition, this exhibit summarizes the A-B-C/D-E-F patterns discussed in the following subsection.

The A-B-Cs of Cognition

Perhaps Ellis's most important contribution is his A-B-C theory of personality,[2] which can be summarized as follows:

A — the "objective" facts, events, behaviors that an individual encounters.

B — the person's beliefs about A.

C — the emotional consequences, or how a person feels and acts about A.

People tend to consider that A causes C, or that facts cause consequences. Ellis challenges this equation as naive, pointing out that it is what people think about an event that determines how they feel. Applying the A-B-C framework to the preceding interview with the gay client, we see that:

A — The "objective fact" is the possibility of being gay.

B — The client believes being gay is bad and self-denigrating.

C — Therefore, as an emotional consequence, the client experiences guilt, fear, and negative self-thoughts.

In this case the client has short-circuited B, concluding that "if I am a gay, I am bad. Thus . . ." Ellis's goal is to attack this belief system. What the client thinks about being gay is causing his anxiety and difficulties, not the objective facts of the situation. There are obviously numerous people, gay, lesbian, and heterosexual, who believe that alternative life styles are valid and who do not come to the same conclusion at C that this client does.

Ellis's approach in this case, then, was to challenge the client's logic: "If I were gay, I would be a total shit." He points out the A-causes-C conclusion and challenges the irrationality of this "logic." Again, it can be seen that it is not the specific beliefs that are challenged, but rather the unfoundedness of those beliefs, which leads to illogical conclusions.

Ellis does not challenge the client's goals and values (that he doesn't *want* to be gay) but instead attacks his *absolute demands* about achieving these values (that

===== **Exhibit 10.1** =====

 Rational-Emotive Therapy Self-Help Form

This form can be used for examining yourself. It also can be used with equal effectiveness in the interview with your clients and/or as a homework assignment for them.

A. *Objective fact, event, or behavior.* List and describe the activating events, thoughts, or feelings that happened just before you felt emotionally disturbed or acted in some self-defeating way.

B. *Identify the irrational beliefs.* Look at the description of events, thoughts, or feelings above and examine them for irrational thinking.

C. *Emotional consequences.* How did you feel after the fact, event, or behavior? What did you do to produce it? How would you like to change?

Write A and C on a separate piece of paper.

B. *Irrational Beliefs* Circle all those that apply or add additional beliefs.	D. *Disputes* Look at the irrational belief and then challenge it. Examples: "Why MUST I do so very well?" "Where is it written that I am a BAD PERSON?" "Where is the evidence that I MUST be approved or accepted?"	E. *Effective Rational Beliefs* These can replace irrational beliefs. Examples: "I would prefer to do well, but I don't HAVE TO BE that perfect." "I am a person who acted badly, but not a BAD PERSON." "There is no evidence that I HAVE TO BE approved, although I would like to be."
1. I MUST do well or very well.		
2. I am a BAD or WORTHLESS PERSON when I act weakly or stupidly.		
3. I MUST be approved or accepted by people whom I find important.		
4. I NEED IMMEDIATE GRATIFICATION for my needs.		

5. Other people MUST live up to my expectations or it is TERRIBLE.		
6. It's AWFUL or HORRIBLE when major things don't go my way.		
7. I CAN'T STAND IT when life is really unfair.		
8. Additional irrational beliefs		

F. More positive and rational feelings and behaviors. Finally, place here the feelings, behaviors, and thoughts you are experiencing after challenging and working on your irrational beliefs.

Can you make the following commitment? "I will work hard to repeat my effective rational beliefs forcefully to myself on many occasions so that I can make myself less disturbed now and act less self-defeatingly in the future."

SOURCE: This form is summarized from a longer form authored by Joyce Sichel and Albert Ellis (1984) copyrighted by and available from the Institute for Rational-Emotive Therapy, 45 East 65th Street, New York, N.Y. 10021. It is used here by their permission.

under *no* conditions *must* he be gay; that he would be a worthless "shit" if he were gay). The emphasis of the therapy is on changing the way the client thinks about the behavior, rather than on changing the behavior itself. Recall Epictetus—it is not events but our view of events that is critical.

The A-B-C framework is really the nugget of Ellis's theory. It is not the event that really troubles us, but instead the way we think about the event. Ellis's theory is closely akin to humanistic therapies that focus on meaning and the importance of how a person interprets the world. Frankl (chapter 12), for example, survived the horrors of a Nazi concentration camp. He comments on how his survival depended on his ability to believe certain things about the events around him and to find something positive on which to depend. Beliefs were more important to survival than objective facts.

The D-E-Fs of Promoting and Maintaining Change

"D" stands for disputing irrational beliefs and thinking. It is at this point that Ellis's work first became controversial. When the logic of the client's A-B-C thought patterns is ineffective, Ellis becomes directly challenging and confrontative: "But why would you be a thorough shit if you were a gay? Let's suppose you gave up girls completely, and you just screwed guys. Now, why would you be a thorough shit?" This language and style offended many people in the 1950s and 1960s, a time when Rogerian listening and respect were at their greatest influence. Furthermore, Ellis's tolerance and openness to cultural difference were ahead of his time.

It is now widely recognized that disputing and challenging clients' logical systems is an effective mode of intervention and that rational disputation is an important therapeutic strategy. In the later sections of this chapter, you will see that Beck and Glasser both use disputation, but in a more gentle manner than that associated with Ellis.

"E" is the effect that disputation (or other interventions) have on the client. At this point, the client generates a more effective belief system or philosophy about the situation. In the above example, the fact of being gay has not been changed, but the client generates a new way of thinking about himself: "It's OK to come out of the closet and be a gay man—if I wish to take that direction."

"F" stands for new feelings. The client has new emotions associated with the situation: "I'm gay and I'm proud and I feel good about myself." RET emphasizes emotional change as foundational. Although much of RET work focuses on logical thinking, unless logic is ultimately integrated with emotion, change will be unlikely to last. Emotional change is basic if we are to prevent relapse into old ways of thinking and feeling.

Ellis and Multicultural Issues

Ellis's general attitude toward multicultural issues is one of respect for clients' particular values. He does not seek to change these values unless they are self-defeating and overly rigid. Ellis (1991) presents a case example that illustrates this approach:

> I am seeing a woman right now who is a Mormon, semidevout, but she is also pregnant and has a lover who is an Orthodox Jew whom she might well decide not to marry. So her problem is whether to get an abortion, because if she does, her church and her Mormon family will probably excommunicate her. So I deal with her differently than I would with somebody who comes from a less rigid family and religion. I know that she is going to have a hard time with her cultural group if she does get an abortion, and therefore, in her particular case, it might even be better to have the child and see another man who might want to marry her and become a Mormon.
>
> So when people have strong religious and cultural values, I accept their values but also show them how they may be defeating themselves in terms of their own standards. They can, using RET, choose to stick with their cultural values or decide to change them without damning themselves. Thus, if my Mormon client did decide to go through with an abortion, I would help her to accept herself, in spite of her "wrong" act, and then to plan on becoming pregnant again after she marries. So there are some "samenesses" about RET theory and practice for most people and most cultures. But clients can also keep their cultural values and then not needlessly upset themselves when they lead to frustration and/or are not perfectly followed. (p. 16)

Extending RET

At times, Ellis moves to what could best be considered an instructional model in which he actively teaches clients how to think. This instructional model is supplemented by homework assignments in which clients are encouraged to try out newly learned behaviors and to report back on their success. Ellis often has his clients take audiotape recordings of the interview home with them so that they can review the session during the week.

If the task of the RET counselor is to free the client from irrational thinking, a parallel and more positive goal is to equip the client with beliefs that are satisfactory and functional for everyday life. For example, it is not enough to help free the gay client from irrational thoughts and fears about being gay. It is also necessary to provide an opportunity for this client to explore a new set of beliefs and actions and to test their rationality and workability.

Summary

The following puts the basic tenets of RET into brief list form:

1. Expect your clients (and yourself, your family, and your friends) frequently to make impossible, perfectionistic statements about themselves and others.

2. The basic treatment rule is to dispute the rationality of the perfectionistic cognition and to teach clients how to do their own realistic, open-minded disputation.

3. In therapy, it may be useful to work through several irrational statements in a step-by-step A-B-C process and search for repeating patterns of thought and emotion.

4. Agreed-on homework can help your clients take their new knowledge into the real world.

5. Do not hesitate to add Gestalt, behavioral, or other techniques to the RET structure if you feel it helps you and your client reach your joint goals.

Rational Recovery: RET's Approach to Alcoholism

Theories of psychotherapy have given insufficient attention to treatment issues around alcoholism. It is important to remember that at least half of the clients that come to counseling and therapy are affected in some significant way by alcohol or drugs. Clients may be addicted themselves, be in a relationship with a substance abuser, or be the child or grandchild of an alcoholic. Alcohol can be described as an unseen dimension in much of psychotherapy and counseling.

There are now over three hundred groups using RET as a system of treating alcoholism, and Rational Recovery (RR) is becoming a major alternative to Alcoholics

Anonymous. Founded in 1986 by a licensed social worker, Jack Trimpey, Rational Recovery recognizes that substance abuse may have many biological foundations (Trimpey, 1989). Nonetheless, treatment can be facilitated by an RET approach. Ellis (1992) comments:

> Many (not all) problem drinkers first tend to bring out dysfunctional Consequences (C's), such as anxiety and depression, when unfortunate Activating Events or Adversities (A's) occur in their lives, mainly by constructing irrational or self-defeating Belief's (B's). Second, they then tend to construct more irrational beliefs (B's) about their feelings of depression and anxiety—especially, "I must not be anxious! I can't stand this anxiety!"—and consequently (C) take to drinking in order to allay their pain. Third, problem drinkers often take their secondary Consequence, "alcoholism," and create more irrational Beliefs about that—such as, "I must not be an alcoholic. What a worm I am for drinking too much." This creates a tertiary Consequence (C), self-damnation, that frequently drives them to drink even more. (p. 5)

Treatment involves analysis and disputation, usually done in groups with the support of professionals. RR diverges from AA in its attempt to bring professionals more directly into the treatment process, although RR members pay no fees. Although both AA and RR emphasize an educational approach, RR differs from AA in that spiritual concepts such as a "Higher Power" are not emphasized. Ellis (1992) comments that many clients are nonreligious and thus seek help in groups such as RR, Secular Organizations for Sobriety (SOS), and Men and Women for Sobriety (MFS and WFS).

As a counselor and therapist, it is vital that you bring an understanding of the many effects of alcohol and substance abuse into the therapeutic hour. If you have an understanding and appreciation of the value of the Alcoholics Anonymous twelve-step program, Rational Recovery, and other treatment programs, you can conduct counseling and therapy as part of an overall treatment program that includes and does not deny the issues of substance abuse in this society.

Aaron Beck and Cognitive Therapy

Aaron Beck, a leading cognitive-behavioral therapist, first became known for his success in treating depression. The personal strength and warmth of Beck are perhaps best illustrated by a case from his well-known book *Cognitive Therapy and the Emotional Disorders* (1976). He describes a depressed patient who had failed to leave his bedside for a considerable period of time. Beck asked him if he could walk to the door of his room. The man said he would collapse. Beck said, "I'll catch you." Through successive steps and longer walks, the man was shortly able to walk all over the hospital and in one month was discharged.

Relationship as Central to Change.   How are such "miracles" accomplished? First, Beck is a powerful and caring individual who himself believes that change is possible. He is willing to provide himself as a support agent for the client and has specific goals and behaviors in mind for the client. In this case, he sought to change the way the depressed person thought about himself. Through slow, successive approximations, from shorter to longer walks with Beck's help, the client was able to change his behavior.

This case illustrates the importance of relationship and behavior as well as cognitive change. In Beck's framework, we would call the basic cognitive change a move from "I can't" to "I can." Basic to much of behavioral work is to take small steps toward success. Somewhere along the continuum of change, clients will likely realize that they *can* do something to help themselves. It is this attitude of "I can" that is basic to generalizing learned behavior and ways of thinking from the therapy hour to real life.

Clearly, someone who facilitates this type of change for clients has something special, a charisma as full of impact in its way as that of Ellis. Beck's approach is compared, using meta-analysis, with Ellis's in exhibit 10.2.

Exhibit 10.2

 ## Meta-Analyses of Ellis's RET and Beck's Cognitive Therapy

---

Two major reviews of research studies on these two important techniques have recently been completed. The findings on both RET and cognitive therapy are encouraging. There are fewer studies on Beck's more recent cognitive therapy.

Rational-Emotive Therapy

Lyons and Woods (1992) have reviewed seventy outcome studies involving RET and conducted a meta-analysis. General results indicate that clients who receive RET benefit from the process. Of special interest is the fact that experienced therapists were more impactful than beginners. Those clients who experienced short-term treatment of one or two interviews did not change as much as clients who experienced RET for a longer time period.

Of special interest in the above study

is that cognitive-behavioral and behavioral therapy methods were equally effective in RET. The authors of the study comment, "RET was shown to be an effective form of therapy. Perhaps it is time to stop the needless and inefficient discussion of the efficacy of this therapy. Rather a better focus of investigations and reviews would be to determine which factors, or combinations thereof, contribute most to the effectiveness of RET" (pp. 20–21). In effect, perhaps the answer is not which therapeutic method is best or most effective but which combination of therapies will be most helpful to our clients.

Cognitive Therapy

Twenty-eight studies of Beck's cognitive therapy for depression were examined through meta-analysis (Dobson, 1989).

There were clear indications that cognitive therapy was more effective than a waiting list or no-treatment control groups, pharmacotherapy, behavioral therapy, or other psychotherapies. Of particular importance, Dobson found eight studies comparing cognitive therapy with medication. "Cognitive therapy clients, on average, did better than 70 percent of drug therapy patients" (p. 415).

Beck's cognitive therapy was built on clinical work and theorizing around depression. The research evidence is that the therapy works. Beck (1991) himself provides a thirty-year perspective on theory and research in cognitive therapy. Five studies indicate that cognitive therapy prevents relapse better than do antidepressant drugs (Hollan & Najavits, 1988).

Similarly, the important National Institute of Mental Health study of depression found cognitive therapy superior to antidepressant drugs and interpersonal therapy in terms of recurrence of depression during follow-up (Shea et al., 1990).

Beck summarizes additional studies showing that cognitive therapy is particularly effective with clients suffering panic attacks and generalized anxiety disorder. There is promising evidence that the system is effective with clients experiencing eating disorders, heroin addiction, couple's problems, and schizophrenia. The data seem clear that cognitive therapy and cognitive-behavior modification have both immediate and lasting value for clients.

Beck has outlined important principles for working with many types of patients. Since his early work with depression, he has demonstrated that his concepts are equally effective with anxiety disorders (Freeman & Simon, 1989), personality disorders (Beck, Freeman, & Associates, 1990), and many other issues. The following transcript reveals some of the characteristics of Beck's interviewing style.

Case Presentation: Depression

In the following session, Beck uses a relatively direct interviewing style. When the client says "Now I'm all alone!" Beck probes this statement for underlying meaning and logic. In this search for meaning, there are clear parallels to the approach of Frankl. By implicitly questioning the logic underlying the client's overgeneralization or automatic thought, Beck attempts to produce change in cognitive processes similar to Ellis's attack of irrational thought patterns.

In theory and practice, Beck focuses on identifying automatic thoughts, internal self-statements that help clients organize their thinking patterns. This is a critical difference from the approach of Ellis. Beck does not focus on unconscious motivation; nonetheless, his psychodynamic roots still influence his work to some extent. For example, he considers automatic thoughts to be rooted in early parent-child interactions and to repeat in adulthood.

In the following vignette (Diffily, 1984), Beck uses many questions to encourage clients to explore themselves and their situations.[3]

Strain grips the face of the young woman on the television monitor. Hers would be a pretty face were it not for the puffy, reddened eyes, and the glistening tear-tracks splotched on her cheeks.

"My husband wants to leave me," Linda is saying to someone out of camera range. "He wants to go for an unspecified length of time. Then maybe he'll come back. He says it's non-negotiable; he wants no more commitment." She has difficulty controlling her voice; breathy sobs punctuate her recitation.

"I've gotten more and more depressed," Linda continues. "It felt like I had a guillotine over me, or like I had cancer. I told him maybe he'd better leave. And now—" (she begins sobbing in earnest) "—now I'm all alone!"

The camera draws back, bringing into view a man seated at the table with Linda. His most striking feature is a thatch of thick white hair smoothed back from his face. Behind his glasses the psychiatrist's eyes are at once gentle and probing. He regards Linda calmly.

"What do you mean, all alone?" asks Beck.

[*This is the first step toward searching for automatic thoughts. By asking "What do you mean, all alone?" Beck is moving beneath the surface structure sentence to find the underlying thinking patterns.*]

"I don't have Richard!" she gasps, mopping at her eyes with a tissue from the box on the table. "Life wouldn't mean anything without him. I love him so much."

[*Here we see A—the objective facts, "I don't have Richard"—and C—the emotional consequence, a classic Ellis irrational thought pattern. Beck, however, is searching for the automatic thought patterns underlying the depression.*]

"What do you love about him?" Beck asks.

"I don't know," Linda says, shaking her head, confused. "I guess I live for him. He's so rotten. But I remember the good stuff."

[*In this exchange, the client begins to examine her own faulty automatic thoughts.*]

CLICK. In the darkened viewing room, Beck pushes a switch and freezes the images of Linda and himself on the monitor. He turns to a visitor and explains his strategy for this emergency therapy session. "First, you always summarize the patient's thoughts to her. This gives clarity and reassures her that you understand. Second, you have to figure out where you're going to move in. It's very difficult in a crisis situation. You have to think on your feet." Beck explains that according to his theory of depression, the patient will underestimate herself and exaggerate her degree of loss and a negative view of the future. "You have to explore these channels and work it through."

CLICK. The video images move and talk. On the screen, Beck summarizes for Linda his first therapy session with her six weeks earlier, reminding her that Richard had made certain promises and commitments regarding their marriage. "What happened between then and now?"

[*Highly characteristic of the cognitive-behavioral approach is the search for sequence. Much like the antecedents, behaviors, and consequences of functional analysis explored in chapter 9, CBT is concerned with ordering of events but gives much more stress to internalized thoughts and feelings than do behavioral methods.*]

"I don't know. I really think he lied to me." She begins to sob again. "This is like a bad dream."

"Richard deceived you?"

"He did. I feel like a fool," Linda cries, "for believing him."

CLICK. To his visitor, Beck says, "This is aggravating the problem; she is feeling deceived, feeling foolish. Which angle am I going to explore—her actual loss, or the hurt to her pride? You have to make a split-second decision."

CLICK. On the screen, Beck is talking quietly to Linda. "What have you lost?" He is going for the loss angle first.

"I lost my best friend, someone to talk to." She pauses and adds ruefully, "Even though he didn't want to listen to me." What else? "I've lost the father of my children. Financial support, security."

[Note the "all-or-none" thinking on the part of the client. The CBT therapist will recognize the very real hurt, but will not accept that all is lost. Common to irrational ideas and automatic thoughts is overgeneralization of negatives and deletion of possible positives.]

"What hurts you most?" Beck wonders. "The money?"

"No—losing him. I've lost all my hopes." What hopes? "That things would work out for us." Aren't there other hopes? Beck asks. Linda looks doubtful. "I guess I'm not letting them come in. But who would want me? He rejected me. I'm not lovable."

[The above is a good example of rational disputation in which the client's faulty thinking patterns are challenged by the therapist. Note below how humor can be used to challenge patterns of thinking.]

"Do you really believe that? Is Richard the supreme arbiter of that?" Beck says. "Should we trust his judgment?" Laughter. Linda, incredibly, is laughing. "Don't make me laugh when I'm crying!" she is saying through a mixture of giggles and sobs.

A brief smile plays across Beck's face; he continues pressing his point. "Richard broke promises to you on and off for months. And you feel terrible that a guy like that doesn't love you? Why should his problem be reflected in your self-image?"

Beck asks Linda to list her husband's good and bad qualities. He records them on a long sheet of lined paper divided into two columns. When Linda finishes her list, the "bad" column is twice as long as the "good" column.

[This may be recognized as a variation of the decisional balance sheet of chapter 4. Problem-solving techniques are often used in CBT.]

"Is this the kind of man you'd want for a mate?" the psychiatrist asks.

"It really sounds dumb when you write it out," she admits.

Eventually Beck elicits another admission from Linda: Even though she is suffering from dire emotional stress and pain, she can endure it and even adopt a more positive view of her future. "I guess I've been standing it so far," Linda says, "so I can stand it now."

[The faulty automatic thoughts about her husband have been adequately challenged, and Linda can now revise her personal constructions of herself, her ex-mate, and her situation.]

CLICK. Beck's visitor, moved by the emotions and the glimpse of hope she has viewed on videotape, has a question for him.

"Didn't you want to hug Linda, to comfort her, instead of just asking questions?"

"Empathy and understanding," the psychiatrist answers, "are not enough in therapy. As in any branch of medicine, you tend to empathize with the patient. But most reassuring to the patient is your understanding of her problem, and your ability to give her a mastery of the situation." In no way, Beck emphasizes, was Linda's depression "cured" by this one session; she had to come back for therapy on a regular basis for a while. But using his therapeutic approach—one that has inspired considerable interest and excitement among mental health professionals worldwide—a therapist can "snap people out of a severe depression very quickly" and help them start coping with their problems in a constructive, rewarding way. (pp. 39–46).

Beck's Central Theoretical Constructs and Techniques

Beck gives central attention to the cognitive process. He points out that there is a constant stream of thoughts going through our minds, not all of which we listen to. These thoughts move so rapidly that Beck calls them "automatic thoughts" and points out that it is difficult to stop them. In the case of the woman described in the transcript, she automatically thought her life would be "over" and she would be "alone" without her husband. Beck is concerned with stopping such harmful automatic thoughts and having the person examine his or her mode of thinking and eventually develop new forms of cognition.

Changing Faulty Thought Patterns

In Beck's model, the therapist seeks to change the clients' thinking patterns and way of constructing their worldviews. This requires the following steps, all of which may be identified in the case example above:

1. *Recognizing maladaptive thinking and ideation.* The woman in the case example above felt that "all was lost" because of her husband leaving.

2. *Noting repeating patterns of ideation that tend to be ineffective.* Beck terms such repeating patterns *automatic thoughts.* You may, for example, have been frightened by a dog and now all dogs are scary for you. You "automatically" think all dogs are dangerous. The therapeutic task is to break down the illogical thinking patterns to help you realize the distinctions between safe and unsafe dogs. With the depressed woman, the task becomes to help her recognize that her present difficulties do not mean that she needs to be totally depressed.

3. *Distancing and decentering help clients remove themselves from the immediate fear, thought, or problem so they can think about it from a distance.* This results in obsessive thinking becoming less of a "center" in the person's life. When Beck asked, "Do you really believe that? Is Richard the supreme arbiter of that?" and the client laughed, she was clearly decentering her thoughts about the issue.

4. *Changing the rules.* This is important in working with faulty thinking and automatic thoughts. The therapist talks with the client about the logic of the situation. For example, you may rethink your dog phobia through realizing that the chances of being bitten by a dog are at best one in a thousand. When Beck had his client fill out an elementary problem-solving balance sheet of the pros and cons of her husband, he helped her change the rules of her thinking.

Beck's system has proven particularly effective with depressed clients whose worldview is full of pessimistic automatic thoughts that forcefully affect their behavior. Beck (1972) has a list of "faulty reasonings" that in many ways is similar to Ellis's conceptualizations of irrational ideas. Beck's list includes such concepts as dichotomous reasoning (assuming things are either all good or all bad — "I'm either perfect or I'm no good"), overgeneralization ("If my husband leaves me, I'm totally alone"), magnification (Ellis terms this *catastrophizing*), and flaws in inference or logic.

Clients will manifest a multitude of variations on perfectionism. Automatic thoughts and irrational ideas tend to be obsessive in nature, as they are repeated over and over again. An underlying structure of obsessive behavior and thought is often perfectionism. However, what makes ideas irrational are their unattainability, overgeneralization (one *must* reach 100 percent of everything), or significant distortion of occurrences.

Beck's cognitive therapy assumes that clients can examine themselves. Many patients, particularly the depressed, are embedded in their own construction of the world. Beck recognizes that their particularly self-centered worldview may indeed be accurate, but if one thinks about alternatives, these alternatives may be even more useful and certainly more growth producing. In this area, important parallels to Kelly's (1955) personal construct theory should be noted. The depressed individual has a set of ineffective personal constructs, which are hypotheses this person uses to frame the world. The task of the therapist is to change the client's constructs in the expectation that if the way one views the world is changed, the way one acts in the world will also change. Exhibit 10.3 provides an exercise for taking the cognitive-behavioral approach into practice.

The Daily Record of Automatic Thoughts

As indicated in the case example above, negative automatic thoughts often take time to alleviate and change. One technique Beck recommends is the use of the daily record of automatic thoughts. Table 10.1 depicts a portion of the record of the automatic thoughts of a male who was diagnosed as having an obsessive-compulsive personality disorder. Using the daily record method can help the client learn how to identify thinking patterns using one or more of the four steps indicated above.

Experience has shown that automatic thoughts often reappear unless closely monitored for a period of time outside of the interview. The client is instructed to mark on the daily record each time an automatic thought intrudes and the client feels uncomfortable. Just the act of recording by itself reinforces and promotes change.

It is crucial that the therapist monitor this form and encourage clients to continue using the form for a sufficient time period to ensure that automatic thoughts do not relapse. If the daily record is discontinued too soon, the client will likely relapse into old patterns of automatic thoughts. Table 10.1 reveals that the obsessive-compulsive client was able to monitor emotions and thoughts in two situations and change the outcome to a more positive one. For example, his record notes he was in tears at the movie. Many obsessive-compulsive types, contrary to popular stereotype, cry easily yet feel uncomfortable about it. The data gained from the daily record provide the counselor with new information for further cognitive-behavioral treatment. At this point, the cognitive therapist can focus on a variety of techniques to understand the meaning of the tears, such as the use of images at the sensorimotor level.

Exhibit 10.3

An Exercise in Cognitive-Behavioral Therapy

The diverse content of cognitive-behavioral theory can be organized into a systematic interview using the following structure. It is suggested that you find a volunteer client who is willing to work through the several stages. A suggested topic for the session is some form of irrational idea, faulty thinking, or private rule. Perhaps the most common and useful topic for this session is the frequent desire many of us have for being "perfect."

1. *Rapport/structuring.* As before, develop rapport in your own way and inform your client that you would like to work on some aspect of his or her desire for perfection.
2. *Data gathering.* Using the basic listening sequence, draw out the facts, feelings, and organization of the client's desire for perfection. Try to enter the client's meaning system and reflect the underlying meaning you observe. Point out something positive in the client's meaning system as part of the exploration. Search for irrational ideas or faulty reasoning.
3. *Determining outcomes.* Pinpoint very specific goals for your client. They should be cognitively and behaviorally specific and measurable. As one rule, can you and the client "see, hear, and feel" concrete change? The concept of concreteness involves

specifics, not vague generalizations ("Could you give me a specific example of a better resolution of your drive for perfection?"). Here you may find your client resisting and retreating once again to faulty, irrational thinking in defining goals.
4. *Generating alternative solutions.* Here the world is literally open for you, and *you* will have to decide your route toward action. You may wish to attack the faulty, irrational thinking using the Beck or Ellis model, or you may wish to recreate the original situation using some of the free association methods of chapter 8. Or, you may decide stress inoculation, skills training, or assertiveness training may be called for. Aspects of other theories may occur to you at this point as more appropriate.
5. *Generalization.* Cognitive-behavioral approaches emphasize the importance of taking behavior back home. Several alternatives for ensuring generalization have been made throughout this text. You may wish to have your client fill out a relapse prevention form or you may simply assign "homework" and follow up during the week with a phone call to see if cognitive and behavioral change is indeed occurring.

Table 10.1   An Obsessive-Compulsive Personality's Daily Record of Automatic Thoughts

Date	Situation (describe briefly)	Emotions	Automatic Thoughts	Rational Response	Outcome
5/12	Office	Anxiety, fear	If I don't do the report perfectly, I'll get fired.	Do the best you can. Nobody's perfect.	Felt better. Boss liked report.
	Dinner	Anger	Why doesn't my wife have things ready on time?	I'm lucky she cooks at all. I need to help her more.	I helped with meal.
	Movie	Tears, sadness	Why am I doing this? It always happens in sad places.	Just enjoy the movie. It's OK to cry.	More tears? Why?

The daily record can also provide the counselor or therapist specifics of client behavior and thinking for further diagnosis and assessment. This is an important technique and one highly useful in counseling and therapy from many theoretical orientations. It is recommended that you use this format in several practice exercises so that you can master this important part of cognitive theory.

Adding Family/Multicultural Dimensions. The chart of automatic thoughts tends to put the responsibility for most change within the client. As such, multicultural theory would point out that this method fails to consider contextual issues. Gender and multicultural dimensions can be added to the automatic thoughts chart by adding a column focusing on context. In the above example, the obsessive-compulsive male could review the entire record as an example of sex-role stereotyping learned in the family of origin. In this case, cognitive consciousness raising about the oppressiveness of male roles may be beneficial.

For many individuals, reviewing automatic thought patterns from a gender, family, or multicultural perspective can be very helpful. Women and minorities, for example, may sometimes blame themselves for lack of job advancement. If the record of automatic thoughts is reviewed for examples of sexism or racism, this may change the meaning and the cognitions of the client. At the same time, it is important to balance internal and external responsibility for change. Information gained from such analysis may require you as counselor or therapist to take action in the environment. We must never forget that many, perhaps most, of our clients are in some way harmed by context. To place internal responsibility for change on one person is sometimes highly naive.

The Use of Images

Our clients have basic images of themselves and situations and are often unaware of these images. These images are usually the basis for automatic thoughts. The importance of visual images in developmental counseling and therapy and in psychodynamic therapy was stressed in chapter 8. Beck often searches for client images as he seeks to understand automatic thoughts and behavioral patterns.

In the case of the obsessive-compulsive client's tears, Beck might ask the client to imagine the movie first and then free associate to earlier childhood experiences. Interpretation would be minimized, and the major focus would be on adaptive behavior and thought. Shedding tears at movies could also be reframed as a very adaptive behavior for males that could be beneficial in other situations. What might be termed pathological from a male stereotypical frame of reference could in another view be a positive outlet, a release from the tight constructs of the obsessive-compulsive personality.

Many of your clients' automatic thoughts are images that can be accessed for better understanding, as with the following client with an avoidant history discussed by Beck, Freeman, and Associates (1990):

> During the first few sessions with the therapist, she received the standard cognitive therapy for personality problems. In one visit, after she had been given a homework assignment that she failed to follow through with, she told her therapist that she was feeling particularly upset over not having done the homework. The therapist asked her where the feeling was localized. The patient responded that she felt it somewhere in her "stomach." The therapist then asked her whether she had an image in reference to what was upsetting her. She then said the following, "I see myself coming into the session. You are larger than life; you are critical and demeaning; you are like a big authority."
>
> The therapist then asked when this had occurred previously. The patient responded that she had experienced this many times during childhood when she had unpleasant encounters with her mother. Her mother drank a good deal and was frequently irritable toward the child when she had been drinking. One day the child came home from school early, and the mother "blasted her" for waking her up. (pp. 92–93)

This example reveals psychodynamic thought and Beck's system, although Beck tends not to use psychodynamic labels or explanations. In her past, the client learned to avoid authority figures because they were painful. This past experience was the origin of automatic thoughts such as "I am a bad person" and "I am wrong because I upset my mother." This learned pattern of automatic thoughts was transferred to the interview with the therapist. Clients' automatic thoughts will appear with you as well as with others. Again, this can be thought of not so much as transference but as learned cognitions and behaviors.

Children also find images helpful. Ivey and Ivey (1990) describe work with an eight-year-old child who was experiencing serious child abuse. Through the use of images in a manner similar to that described above, the child was able to recount previously forgotten experiences that had led to behavioral problems at school. In working with children, therapists can benefit from adapting Beck's cognitive techniques and conceptualizations.

Reliving Childhood or Other Traumatic Experiences

In what is termed *regression* in psychodynamic therapy, the client returns to painful, often traumatic scenes via images and "relives" them again in the safety of the therapeutic hour. The avoidant client above was encouraged by the therapist to relive the past situation with her possibly alcoholic mother. Through the use of images, role-plays, and even the Gestalt empty chair technique ("talk to your mother as if she were sitting there"), clients are able to reexperience old, often forgotten and repressed events.

Reliving old situations can be highly dramatic and emotionally draining. In a situation of trust and safety, the client can release emotional energy and "work through" the trauma more completely. Psychodynamic theory talks of removing the repressed event, whereas cognitive theory focuses on completing the learning involved in the event. For example, the automatic thoughts of a child of an alcoholic parent often involve varying forms of unrealistic perfectionism. Through the use of images and by working through old events, the client is often able to develop more rational and effective ways of behaving, and automatic thought patterns can be changed.

Beck points out that depressed clients first need to have their depression removed before they can encounter the challenge of reworking issues through extensive use of images. He recommends using images and reliving old events particularly for clients with personality disorders. The techniques discussed in these sections are powerful and should be used only by those with considerable experience or those who are under clinical supervision.

Other Techniques and the Issues of Trauma and Substance Abuse

Much like rational-emotive therapy, Beck's cognitive therapy does not hesitate to draw on techniques and concepts from other theories. Problem-solving techniques, relaxation training, role-plays, and skills training are all part of the cognitive therapist's potential repertoire.

Many of your depressed clients will likely have serious histories of abuse, neglect, and trauma. For example, Rigazio-DiGilio (1989) found that seventeen of twenty inpatient depressives had serious instances of family trauma. Given Miller's (1981) observations on the incidence of child abuse and Brassard, Germain, and Hart's (1987) convincing summary of child and adolescent maltreatment literature, it is likely that use of images and reliving of old traumatic events will play an increasingly important part in your practice.

Past traumatic issues that clients bring to therapy are complicated by the fact that 50 percent of psychiatrically diagnosed clients have some serious alcohol or drug problems—that is, they have a dual diagnosis (Evans & Sullivan, 1990). It is critical that you have some form of substance abuse treatment options available to you as well as the more traditional counseling theories. Cognitive-behavioral, developmental, and family systems concepts (chapter 13) are useful in generating treatment programs for dual diagnosis clients and those who have drug and alcohol problems, including a family history of substance abuse.

William Glasser and Reality Therapy

If Albert Ellis's rational-emotive therapy could be summarized as "Be rational and think about things logically," William Glasser's reality therapy could be summarized by saying, "Take responsibility and control of your own life and face the consequences of your actions." Although research on reality therapy is limited, it is a frequent treatment of choice if one works with difficult clients, particularly acting-out or delinquent youth or adults.

Especially in the early stages of therapy, some younger clients, particularly those who are acting out or delinquent, will not "stand still" for the approaches of Ellis and Beck. However, after you establish a working alliance with such clients, perhaps through reality therapy, you can return successfully to cognitive-behavioral techniques.

Glasser's reality therapy can be considered a cognitive-beahvioral therapy, but one that focuses very much on realism and how to treat difficult clients. We will first examine a case study and then return to theoretical constructs.

Case Presentation: Probation Client

Counseling sessions within reality therapy can range from a regularly scheduled fifty-minute hour to brief personal encounters in the dining room, classroom, or other setting. Many clients do not want to come to the office for the highly verbal and sophisticated treatments we as therapists might prefer to offer. Reality therapy offers a viable alternative that you can use as a basis for working with difficult clients, and later incorporate other forms of helping within it.

The following interview shows the second phase of reality therapy. The client is an eighteen-year-old young man on probation for repeated offenses of a minor nature, including selling alcohol to minors, assault, and petty theft. The counselor in this case is a county probation officer, and the meeting occurs in the community half-way house. They are just finishing a game of Ping-Pong.

1. *Counselor:* Got ya! 21 to 18. Took me three games, but I finally got one.
2. *Client:* Yeah, you pulled it off finally. Man, I'm pooped. (They sit down and have a cup of coffee.)
3. *Counselor:* So, how have things been going? [*Open question*]
4. *Client:* Well, I looked for jobs hard last week. But nothing looked any good. The bastards seem to know I'm coming and pull the help wanted sign down just as I come walking in.

5. *Counselor:*   So, you've been looking hard. How many places did you visit? [*Paraphrase, closed question; note search for concrete behavior*]

6. *Client:*   Oh lots. Nobody will give me a chance.

7. *Counselor:*   Maybe I can help. Tell me some of the places you've been. [*Directive, with continued emphasis on concreteness. Where Beck and Ellis often move clients to formal operational thought, the Glasser approach focuses on specifics—one of its values for the many concrete operational clients you will encounter.*]

8. *Client:*   I tried the gas station down the street. They gave me a bad time. Nobody wants me. It's really tough.

9. *Counselor:*   Where else did you go? [*Closed question*]

10. *Client:*   I tried a couple other stations too. Nobody wants to look at me. They don't pay too good anyway. Nuts to them!

11. *Counselor:*   So you haven't really done too much looking. Sounds like you want it served on a silver plate, Joe. Do you think looking at a couple of gas stations is really going to get you a job? [*Paraphrase, interpretation, logical consequences. Here we see a lead, particularly typical of reality therapy, that places considerable emphasis on the consequences of actions. The point is similar to applied behavioral analysis, but the way of reaching consequences is quite different.*]

12. *Client:*   I suppose not. Nobody wants to hire me anyway.

13. *Counselor:*   Let's take another look at that. The economy is pretty rocky right now. Everyone is having trouble getting work. You seem to think "they" are after you. Yet, I've got a friend about your age who had to go to thirty-five places before he got a job. How does that square with you looking at three places and then giving up? Who's responsible—you, the service station owners, or the economy? [*Directive, information giving, open question; note confrontation and emphasis on the word* responsible. *Responsible action is the formal operational concept toward which most of reality therapy aspires.*]

14. *Client:*   Yeh, but, there's not much I can do about it. I tried . . .

15. *Counselor:*   Yeh, at three places. Who's responsible for you not getting a job when you only go to three places? At a time like this you've really got to scramble. Come on, Joe! [*Interpretation plus logical consequences*]

The interview continues to explore Joe's lack of action, with an emphasis on responsibility. At points where a Rogerian counselor might have paraphrased or reflected feelings and attitudes (such as at Client: 4, 8, and 10), the reality therapist opted for more behavioral specifics through questions and interpretation. The process of examining Joe's behavior is closely akin to that of the behavioral counselor using applied behavioral analysis. However, the use of the behavioral data is quite different in reality therapy. Instead of seeking to change behavior, the reality therapist works on changing awareness of responsibility. Once the focus of responsibility has been acknowledged and owned by the client, it is possible to start planning a more effective job search. Later in the interview, the process of planning evolves.

51. *Counselor:*   So, Joe, sounds like you feel you made a decision this past week not to really look for a job . . . almost as if you took responsibility for not getting work. [*Reflection of meaning, interpretation. Note that placing the locus of decision in the client can be a helpful strategy in any approach to helping. It is here that reality therapy truly becomes cognitive-behavioral. At the same time, this is a clear example of moving away from a societal, contextual focus.*]

52. *Client:*   Yeh, I don't like to look at it that way, but I guess I did decide not to do too much.

53. *Counselor:*   And what about next week?

54. *Client:*   I suppose I ought to look again, but I really don't like it.

The reality therapist at this point moved to a realistic analysis of what the client might expect during the coming week on the job market, constantly emphasizing the importance of the client, Joe, taking action and responsibility for his life. A practice role-played job interview was held, and several alternatives for generating a more effective job search were considered. Joe tried to escape responsibility at several points ("I couldn't do that"), but the counselor confronted him and allowed no excuses or ambivalence.

A reality therapist will use skills and ideas of other theoretical orientations when they serve the purpose of assisting the client to confront reality more effectively. More likely, the reality therapist will be her or his natural self and use humor, sarcasm, and confrontation in very personal ways to assist the client in understanding behavioral patterns and developing new action approaches. Role-playing, systematic planning, and instruction in intentional living are important tools in reality therapy.

Although many who practice reality therapy approaches may be in power situations (guards, principals, rehabilitation counselors), they still tend to be themselves and to use reality therapy as an extension of themselves; this adds a tone of genuineness and authenticity to the process at a more significant level than would be possible with other approaches. For example, a prison guard trained in reality therapy can simply state his position realistically as one of power and control. Then, with the role relationships clearly established, the process of involvement, teaching of responsibility, and relearning can occur.

Central Theoretical Constructs of Reality Therapy

In describing the basic tenets of reality therapy, Glasser (1965) states that all clients have been unsuccessful in meeting their needs and that in attempts to meet their needs, they often tend to select ineffective behaviors that virtually assure their failure. Further,

All patients have a common characteristic: they all deny the reality of the world around them. Some break the law, denying the rules of society; some claim their neighbors are plotting against them, denying the improbability of such behavior. Some are afraid of crowded places, close quarters, airplanes, or elevators, yet they freely admit the irration-ality of their fears. Millions drink to blot out the inadequacy they feel but that need not exist if they could learn to be different; and far too many people choose suicide rather than face the reality that they could solve their problems by more responsible behavior. Whether it is a partial denial or the total blotting out of all reality of the chronic back-ward patient in the state hospital, the denial of some or all of reality is common to all patients. Therapy will be successful when they are able to give up denying the world and recognize that reality not only exists but that they must fulfill their needs within its framework.

A therapy that leads all patients toward reality, toward grappling successfully with the tangible and intangible aspects of the real world, might accurately be called a therapy toward reality, or simply Reality Therapy. (p. 6)

Reality therapy can best be described as a commonsense approach to counseling. What Glasser advocates is finding out what people want and need, examining their failures and their present assets, and considering factors in the environment that must be met if the needs are to be satisfied. One cannot meet needs except in a real world; people must face a world that is imperfect and not built to their specifications and must act positively in this world. The worldview of reality therapy is that people can do something about their fate if they will consider themselves and their environment realistically. In this sense, reality therapy has much in common with decisional coun-seling. (Variations of decisional counseling are often used in work in correctional facil-ities.)

The Importance of Responsibility

As might be anticipated, reality therapy focuses on conscious, planned behavior and gives relatively little attention to underlying dimensions of transference, unconscious thought process, and the like. The goal is to consider the past as being past and done with; the present and the future are what are important. Yet reality therapy does not emphasize applied behavioral analysis or the detailed plans of assertiveness training or systematic desensitization. Rather, almost like rational-emotive therapy, reality therapy focuses on responsibility and choice. What is central is that clients examine their lives to see how specific behavior is destructive. The more important step, how-ever, is to take responsibility, which Glasser (1965) defines as "the ability to fulfill one's needs and to do so in a way that does not deprive others of the ability to fulfill their needs" (p. 13). Learning responsibility is a lifelong process.

Given the population that reality therapy often serves (clients of street clinics, prison inmates, school children, and others in institutional settings), it is clear that relationship and trust are particularly important. The institutions with which chil-dren and prisoners cope do not easily build the almost automatic trust relationship that seems to be a given in a traditional client-therapist setting. The *personhood* of the reality therapist becomes especially important. The qualities of warmth, respect and caring for others, positive regard, and interpersonal openness are crucial.

Reality therapy is much more likely to be practiced in settings other than the coun-seling office, although this method is also used in the standard clinical setting. The individual practicing reality therapy likely may be out on the playground, in a delinquent detention center, may be a classroom teacher, or perhaps work as a prison guard. The possible multiplicity of relationships requires a special type of person to maintain consistency. This challenge provides an opportunity for the reality therapist to serve as a continuing model of personal responsibility to the client outside the counseling environment.

Recent Cognitive Trends in Reality Therapy

A critical part of reality therapy is client awareness of consequences of actions: "If you do X, then what is the consequence?" Reality therapy, in a highly nonjudgmental fashion, attempts to help individuals learn what they can expect when they act in certain ways. In this sense, you may again note a similarity and a difference from rational-emotive therapy. In RET, the consequences are those inside the person (feeling depressed, and so forth), whereas in reality therapy, the consequences may indeed be inside, but the emphasis is on what happens in the outside world when the client fails to face reality and be responsible.

Glasser has continually expanded his thinking but has remained true to the basic constructs of the method and theory described above. In his 1981 book, *Stations of the Mind,* he builds a comprehensive picture of the workings of the "internal world" of the mind. Glasser notes that the "internal reality" of the mind (cognitions) must be able to understand how the individual relates to external reality.

Control Theory

Control is an increasingly important aspect of Glasser's current thinking. "We Always Have Control Over What We Do" is a chapter heading in Glasser's book for the popular market, *Take Effective Control of Your Life* (1984). At issue is how the individual exercises that control. One can choose misery as a way of life because it is an excuse from trying harder and may win help or pity from others, and so on. Psychosomatic illness is considered a specific type of internal control to help individuals avoid reality. A "headaching" person may benefit because this is the only time he or she is able to lie down and rest. Drugs and alcohol are still other ways people exert control to avoid facing reality.

Careful analysis of Glasser's recent work suggests that he is moving closer to the position of Ellis and the cognitive-behavioralists in that he gives increased attention to the way people think about things. However, he still uses the basic structure of reality therapy to produce change. His theory of control provides an important additional tool to the therapist working with an individual client. The therapist insists that the client "own" thoughts, behavior, and feelings and be responsible for them. The logic is that if one can exert control toward seemingly unsatisfactory ends such as drugs, headaches, stealing, and interpersonal conflict, then one can reframe control more positively.

Glasser talks about "positive addictions," which range from spending time with friends to jogging to movies to meditation—anything through which an individual can obtain a "high" in a more satisfactory and healthy way. The world offers us the opportunity for negative addiction or for positive addiction. We choose our addictions and our fate. We can choose headaches or we can choose joy. The choice is ours. We are in control.

Glasser's new emphasis on control indicates that he is moving toward a more immediate, confrontational, and cognitive point of view. With certain clients, we may expect direct and forceful confrontations of thought patterns, active teaching of alternative perceptions of reality, and an emphasis that focuses more on internal states and thoughts. Needless to say, the client must be ready for this new challenge. The "how" of control theory has not really been addressed, except by implication. At the moment, traditional reality therapy and the new dimensions of control theory seem somewhat at odds. We may anticipate for the future, however, a more complete integration of Glasser's thinking with illustrations of how a new theory of reality therapy may be used in more practical ways. In the past, Glasser seemed to stress the importance of the client adapting to the world as it is. He now appears to be adding the dimension of internal cognitive states to his basic view.

Limitations and Practical Implications of Cognitive-Behavioral Counseling and Therapy

In general, the same limitations of the cognitive-behavioral tradition cited in chapter 9 and discussed in other chapters hold true here. Specifically, a charismatic "high-powered" therapist may dazzle and harm an unsuspecting client. Similarly, a warm and gentle therapist also can emotionally "seduce" clients and manipulate them, either consciously or unconsciously. Some would like to think that therapists do no harm. However, advertent or inadvertent harm occurs again and again in all forms of therapy.

Ellis's personal style is considered by some to be abrasive, and thus some people have discounted his important and seminal work. Ellis's personal style is not his theory; his style is authentic to him. Just as with Rogerian therapy, it is important that you find your own personal way of integrating Ellis's work into your array of skills and theories.

The constructs of RET have been vastly influential. Ellis's three major tenets are critical additions to the skills and understandings of any professional helper, regardless of theoretical orientation: (1) RET points out to us that it is possible to change the ways we think about things and that cognitive change is often sufficient for significant improvement; (2) the A-B-C and D-E-F frameworks for analyzing client irrational cognitions have become a standard of the field; and (3) Ellis has provided significant leadership in generating a more culturally equitable approach to helping.

Beck developed his cognitive framework independently from Ellis, and Beck's work currently appears to be increasingly influential and to be gradually developing a significant research base. Beck's concept of automatic thoughts is a significant extension of Ellis's framework. Whereas Ellis appears to deny the importance of developmental history and psychodynamic formulations, Beck seems able to integrate these ideas comfortably. Beck points out to us clearly that early client history can often influence cognitive patterns, and his use of imagery in accessing both thoughts and past experiences is important. However, Beck, Ellis, Meichenbaum, and Glasser would all agree that it is not always essential to delve into past history.

For some, including Glasser's reality therapy as a cognitive-behavioral technique may seem unusual, as Glasser tends to work outside the therapeutic mainstream. Glasser tends to discount early childhood experience and focus practically on what needs to be done now. With its clear emphasis on logical consequences of personal actions and the importance of personal control, Glasser's reality therapy will remain appropriate in work with difficult clients or in institutional settings in which regular interviews and careful treatment plans are not always feasible.

All three of the cognitive-behavioral approaches discussed in this chapter tend to put the problem "in the client." This, of course, is true for most individualistically oriented helping theories. Reality therapy, for example, stresses the need for the client to adapt to necessary environmental contingencies. Sometimes clients come from oppressive family, neighborhood, and cultural histories. Although it is important that the client adapt to reality, such adaptation can result in clients returning to oppressive systems with the idea that the "fault" is in them rather than in the environment. RET and Beck's cognitive approach also can fall prey to what some call "blaming the victim" and to a focus on curing the "ills" of the client, when family and society are also responsible.

Nonetheless, each of these therapeutic systems is open to cultural and family perspectives and cultural difference. Guidelines for using cognitive-behavioral methods in multicultural settings are not extensive, however. When practicing cognitive-behavioral counseling and therapy, it is incumbent on you as the therapist to be culturally aware. In this sense, a review of Cheek's early work on assertiveness training with African-American clients described in the previous chapter can be particularly helpful. His work provides a model for balancing individual and cultural issues in the therapy and counseling situation.

The major focus of work in cognitive approaches is at the concrete and formal operational levels of cognition. Relatively little attention is given to systemic, gender, and multicultural issues that affect client cognitions. For the most part, responsibility for change is placed in the individual.

NOTES

1. This transcript was edited for clarity. The italics are Ellis's.
2. In the preceding chapter, we spoke of the A-B-Cs of behavior—the antecedents, behaviors, and consequences. You will find it helpful to be skilled in both types of A-B-C analysis. At times, the more behaviorally focused analysis can be used to clarify the cognitive thought processes. Similarly, if you can understand the client's cognitive patterns, you will have some ability to predict what actually happens behaviorally.
3. Cited in A. Diffily (1984). Reprinted with permission of the *Brown Alumni Monthly*.

REFERENCES

BECK, A. (1972). *Depression: Causes and treatment.* Philadelphia: University of Pennsylvania Press.

BECK, A. (1976). *Cognitive therapy and the emotional disorders.* New York: International Universities Press.

BECK, A. (1991). Cognitive therapy: A 30-year retrospective. *American Psychologist, 46,* 368–75.

BECK, A., FREEMAN, A., & ASSOCIATES. (1990). *Cognitive therapy of personality disorders.* New York: Guilford.

BRASSARD, M., GERMAIN, R., & HART, S. (1987). *Psychological maltreatment of children and youth.* New York: Pergamon Press.

CHEEK, D. (1976). *Assertive Black . . . puzzled White.* San Luis Obispo, CA: Impact.

DIFFILY, A. (1984). Aaron Beck: A profile. *Brown Alumni Monthly.* Providence, RI, pp. 39–46.

DOBSON, K. (1989). A meta-analysis of the efficacy of cognitive therapy for depression. *Journal of Consulting and Clinical Psychology, 57,* 414–19.

ELLIS, A. (1958). *Sex without guilt.* Secaucus, NJ: Lyle Stuart.

ELLIS, A. (1967). Rational-emotive psychotherapy. In D. Arbuckel (Ed.), *Counseling and Psychotherapy.* New York: McGraw-Hill.

ELLIS, A. (1971). *Growth through reason.* Palo Alto, CA: Science and Behavior Books.

ELLIS, A. (1983a). The origins of rational-emotive therapy (RET). *Voices, 18,* 29–33.

ELLIS, A. (1983b). The use of rational-emotive therapy (RET) in working for a sexually sane society. In G. Albee, S. Gordon, & H. Leitenberg, (Eds.), *Promoting sexual responsibility and preventing sexual problems.* Hanover, VT: University Press of New England.

ELLIS, A. (1991). Using RET effectively: Reflections and interview. In M. Bernard (Ed.), *Using rational-emotive therapy effectively* (pp. 1–33). New York: Plenum.

ELLIS, A. (1992). *Rational recovery systems: An alternative to Alcoholics Anonymous.* Unpublished manuscript, Institute of Rational-Emotive Therapy, New York.

EVANS, K., & SULLIVAN, M. (1990). *Dual diagnosis: Counseling the mentally ill substance abuser.* New York: Guilford.

FREEMAN, A., & SIMON, K. (1989). Cognitive therapy of anxiety. In A. Freeman, K. Simon, L. Beutler, & H. Arkowitz (Eds.), *Comprehensive handbook of cognitive therapy* (pp. 346–66). New York: Plenum.

GLASSER, W. (1965). *Reality therapy.* New York: HarperCollins.

GLASSER, W. (1981). *Stations of the mind.* New York: HarperCollins.

GLASSER, W. (1984). Take effective control of your life. New York: HarperCollins.

HOLLAN, S., & NAJAVITS, L. (1988). Review of empirical studies of cognitive therapy. In A. Frances & R. Hales (Eds.), *American Psychiatric Press Review of Psychiatry* (Vol. 7, pp. 643–66). Washington, DC: American Psychiatric Press.

IVEY, A., & IVEY, M. (1990). Assessing and facilitating children's cognitive development: Developmental counseling and therapy in a case of child abuse. *Journal of Counseling and Development, 68,* 299–305.

KANTROWITZ, R., & BALLOU, M. (1992). A feminist critique of cognitive-behavioral theory. In L. Brown & M. Ballou (Eds.), *Personality and psychopathology: Feminist reappraisals.* New York: Guilford.

KELLY, G. (1955). *The Psychology of personal constructs* (Vols. 1 and 2). New York: W.W. Norton.

LYONS, L., & WOODS, P. (1992). The efficacy of rational-emotive therapy: A quantitative review of the outcome literature. *Clinical Psychology Review,* in press.

MASTERS, W., & JOHNSON, V. (1970). *Human sexual inadequacy.* Boston: Little, Brown.

MILLER, A. (1981). *The drama of the gifted child.* New York: Basic Books.

PIOTROWSKI, C., & FRANKLIN, G. (1990). A rational-emotive approach to problems of Black adolescents. *Journal of Training and Practice in Professional Psychology, 4,* 44–51.

RIGAZIO-DIGILIO, S. (1989). *Developmental theory and therapy: A preliminary investigation of reliability and predictive validity using an inpatient depressive population sample.* Unpublished doctoral dissertation, University of Massachusetts, Amherst.

SHEA, M., ELKIN, I., IMBER, S., STOSKY, S., WATKINS, J., COLLINS, J., PILKONIS, P., LEBER, W., KRUPNICK, J., DONAN, R., & PARLOFF, M. (1990). *Course of depressive symptoms over follow-up: Findings from the National Institute of Mental Health Treatment of Depression Collaborative Research Program.* Manuscript submitted for publication cited in A. Beck, Cognitive therapy: A 30-year retrospective. *American Psychologist,* 1991, *46,* 368–75.

TRIMPEY, J. (1989). *Rational recovery from addiction: The small book.* Lotus, CA: Author.

WEINRACH, S. (1990). Anecdotes. In D. DiMattia & L. Lega (Eds.), *Will the real Albert Ellis please stand up?* (pp. 42–43, 108–9, 124–25). New York: Institute for Rational Emotive Therapy.

The Existential-Humanistic Tradition: Existential-Humanistic Theory and Person-Centered Theory

CHAPTER GOALS

The goals of this chapter are to:

1. Describe the general worldview of existential-humanistic theory. The worldview of this orientation greatly influences the practice of counseling and therapy, even though the practitioner may follow another theoretical direction.

2. To examine person-centered theory and its possible relevance for work with multicultural populations.

3. Present central theoretical and practical constructs from the work of Rogers over three main periods of his development.

4. Provide you with an opportunity to practice person-centered therapeutic techniques.

The Existential-Humanistic Frame of Reference

The existential-humanistic view focuses on men and women as people who are empowered to act on the world and determine their own destiny. The locus of control and decision lies within the individual, rather than in past history or in environmental determinants. At the same time, the humanistic aspect of this tradition focuses on *people-in-relationship* one to another. It is this combination of individual respect and the importance of relationship that gives this framework its long-lasting strength.

Although the roots of the existential-humanistic tradition lie in philosophy, Rogers and his person-centered counseling have been most influential in popularizing the existential-humanistic point of view and making it accessible and relevant to clinical and counseling practice. Rogers's techniques are designed to help you enter the worldview of the client and then to facilitate the client finding his or her own new direction and frame of thinking.

The existential-humanistic tradition does not have all the answers for helping victims and survivors, but its deep tradition of caring and of individual free choice is an important part of any treatment you may engage in. The philosophic aspects of this theoretical approach are well received in virtually all cultures, and its major theorists have had wide impact and acceptance throughout the world.

The Existential-Humanistic Worldview

Existentialism's roots may be traced to the Danish philosopher Kierkegaard, but the movement came into full bloom following World War II with the writings of Sartre (1946, 1956) and Camus (1942, 1958). Heidegger (1962), Laing (1967), Husserl (1931), and Tillich (1961) loom large among the many existential philosophers, psychologists, and theologians that influenced this approach. May (1969, 1958, 1961) has been particularly important in bringing existential thought to the awareness of counselors and psychologists in the United States.

However, Binswanger (1958, 1963) and Boss (1958, 1963) have been particularly relevant in organizing the many threads of existentialism for the practice of counseling and therapy. *Being-in-the-world* has been defined as the most fundamental concept of existentialism. We are in the world and acting on that world while it simultaneously acts on us. Any attempt to separate ourselves from the world alienates us and establishes a false and arbitrary distinction. Alienation results either from separateness from others and the world or from our inability to choose and act in relationship. The central task of therapy and counseling, then, is to enable the alienated client to see him- or herself in relationship to the world and to choose and act in accordance with what he or she sees. Racism, sexism, homophobia, and the failure to understand difference lead to alienation by producing separation from others, a main cause of existential anxiety and aloneness.

Being-in-the-World

To facilitate analysis, existentialists often think of the individual in terms of the *eigenwelt* (the person and her or his body), the *mitwelt* (other people in the world), and the *umwelt* (the biological and physical world). Alienation can be experienced in one or more areas — that is, the person may be alienated from her or his own self and body, from others, or from the world. A general process of existential analysis is to enable the person to study what the world (both *mitwelt* and *umwelt*) and her or his relationship to that world are like. Then, having examined the world, the person is assumed free to act, rather than only to be acted upon.

The issue of action, however, brings with it the possibility of existential anxiety. Although existential anxiety may result from alienation, it may also result from failure to make decisions and to act in the world. Choices and decisions are often difficult; any time we choose, we must accept the fact that by choosing we deny other alternatives and possibilities. Although choice may be painful, it is likely to be less so than the anxiety created by not choosing.

Existential Commitment, Intentionality, and the I-Thou Relationship

Existential commitment is the decision to choose and to act; such action can be expected to alleviate anxiety. Yet because of our being-in-the-world we must constantly make choices, which reactivates anxiety. This circle of choice and anxiety causes some existentialists (such as Sartre and Kierkegaard) to become pessimistic and dubious. Others (such as Buber and Tillich) regard the issue of choice as opportunity rather than as problematic.

As used throughout this book, intentionality is a key existential construct that holds that people can be forward moving and act on their world, yet must remain keenly aware that the world acts on them as well. Intentionality provides a bridge to humanism, a worldview that finds its full bloom in Carl Rogers and Martin Buber. As Abbagnano (1967) puts it: "Humanism is . . . any philosophy which recognizes the value and dignity of [the person] and makes [her or] him the measure of all things" (p. 69). The existential-humanistic tradition recognizes the infinite variety of life experience and being-in-the-world as an opportunity rather than as a problem. Basic to this philosophy is assuming responsibility for choice and acting intentionally in the world.

The person who adopts the existential-humanistic position has made an intentional commitment toward what is positive and possible in human relations. Buber (1970) talks of the importance of "I-Thou" relations between people — that is, a relationship in which others are seen as people rather than as objects:

> Whoever says [Thou] does not have something for his [or her] object. For wherever there is something, there is also another something; every It borders on other Its; It is only by virtue of bordering on others. But where [Thou] is said, there is no something. [Thou] has no borders. (p. 55)

The intentional individual seeks I-Thou relationships as opposed to it-it relationships, in which people are seen as things. Buber's concept of I-Thou relationships speaks directly to multicultural concerns: How can we learn to stand in relationship to those different from ourselves?

Summary

The existential-humanistic point of view is an attitude toward the counseling interview and the meaning of life. The main points of this mode of counseling can be summarized as follows:

1. We are in the world; our task is to understand what this means. It is clear that the meanings we generate vary from culture to culture.

2. We know ourselves through our relationship with the world, and in particular through our relationships with other people.

3. Anxiety can result from lack of relationship (with ourselves, with others, or with the world at large) or from a failure to act and choose.

4. We are responsible for our own construction of the world. Even though we know the world only as it interacts on us, it is we who decide what the world means and who must provide organization for that world.

5. The task of the existential-humanistic therapist or counselor is to understand the client's world as fully as possible and ultimately to encourage her or him to be responsible for making decisions. However, existential counselors will also share themselves and their worldviews with clients as is appropriate.

6. A special problem is that the world is not necessarily meaningful. Existentialists such as Sartre and Kierkegaard often develop a negative and hopeless view of what they observe to be the absurdity and cruelty of life. However, humanistic existentialists such as Buber and May suggest that the very confusion and disorder in the world are an opportunity for growth and beauty.

7. The distinction between existential and existential-humanistic positions can be defined as one of philosophy or faith. If a person sees the many possibilities in the world as a problem, he or she has a problem. If a person sees the array of possibilities as infinite opportunity, she or he will choose to act.

Multicultural Issues and the Existential-Humanistic Tradition

Lerner (1992) notes that the positive view of human nature and the desire for an egalitarian approach make existential-humanistic theory and practice appealing to women and other multicultural groups. At the same time, a multicultural approach raises some issues about the existential-humanistic tradition. Moreover, the intense preoccupation with the individual and free choice is at times incompatible with a more environmentally oriented approach.

For example, the work of Rogers and Frankl has been immensely popular in Japan. At the same time, Japanese culture places more importance with the group and the individual-in-relation than do these European-North American theories. Techniques of listening and focusing on individual decisions may at times be inappropriate with

African-American, Native American, and Latina/o cultures, which focus on the person-in-relationship.

Ballou and Gabalac (1985) note that women and other oppressed groups "are denied inclusion in the rewards and necessary conditions for growth. The third force neglect of these dynamics is a tragic flaw, one which not only does not account for external forces in its conception, but which incorrectly places the total responsibility and obligation on the individual for her growth and development" (p. 74).

The authors comment that person-centered theory and other humanistic approaches often submerge the *umwelt* and *eigenwelt* of existential theory into an individualistic "I-centered" theory. When this happens, Buber's elegant statement of "I and Thou" is lost, as is the awareness of our connectedness to the world at large—the *umwelt*.

Lerner (1992) criticizes Rogers's view as particularly limited in terms of placing responsibility for development, growth, and change almost totally with the individual. Rogers "pays almost no attention to the so-called 'real world' or 'reality' " (p. 11). For women and other groups, Lerner maintains that Rogers's and other humanistic practices are potentially harmful: "No person constructs their own reality without external influences. The theories did not take into account exactly how influential external forces really are" (p. 13).

Let us consider this criticism as we explore the work of the most influential of the existential-humanistic therapists, Carl Rogers.

The Rogerian Revolution

The word *self-actualization* is now a basic part of North American culture and can be traced to Rogers's influence, as can be seen in the following comments of Rogers and Wallen (1946):

> Counseling . . . [is] a way of helping the individual help [the] self. The function of the counselor is to make it possible for the client to gain emotional release in relation to . . . problems and, as a consequence, to think more clearly and more deeply about . . . self and . . . situation. It is the counselor's function to provide an atmosphere in which the client, through . . . exploration of the situation, comes to see . . . self and . . . reactions more clearly and to accept (personal) attitudes more fully. On the basis of this insight [the client] is able to meet . . . life problems more adequately, more independently, more responsibly than before. (pp. 5–6)

This worldview, now commonplace in counseling and therapy and in Western society as a whole, represented a radical departure following World War II. Whereas psychodynamic and behavioral counseling and therapy viewed humankind as the often unknowing pawn of unconscious forces and environmental contingencies, existential-humanistic psychology, particularly as interpreted by Rogers, stressed that the individual could "take charge" of life, make decisions, and act on the world.

Undergirding this worldview is a faith that people are positive, forward moving, basically good, and ultimately self-actualizing. Self-actualization, or mental and emotional health, may ultimately be defined as experiencing one's fullest humanity.

Self-actualizing people enjoy life thoroughly in all its aspects, not only in occasional moments of triumph. The task of the counselor is to assist the person in attaining the intentionality and the health that are natural to each individual. When a person becomes truly in touch with the inner self, that individual will move to positive action and fulfillment.

Adding Multicultural Dimensions to Self-Actualization Theory

The concept of self-actualization as described above has been criticized from a multicultural frame of reference (see Rigney, 1981; Lerner, 1992). If carried too far, self-actualization can become self-centeredness. In North America, the stress on self-actualization at times obscures the idea of the person-in-relationship to others.

Different cultures and social classes place different emphasis on *eigenwelt* (the person and her or his body), *mitwelt* (other people in the world), and *umwelt* (the biological and physical world). Some upper- and middle-class clients have learned to believe that the *eigenwelt* is perhaps the only desirable mode of being. This focus has led to some alienation of women and others from counseling and therapy.

The microskill of focus is a simple, but effective, way to balance *eigenwelt*, *mitwelt*, and *umwelt*. Assume the following lesbian client is oriented to relationship as well as self-actualization. Note the variation in responses as the therapist focuses on different dimensions.

Client: The professor just doesn't understand. He keeps talking about self-actualization and finding one's own way. I can't find my own way. My lover, Jenny, and I are very close. I don't want to be separate from her—we are as one. Right now she's sick and how can I find my own way if she's not OK? I don't even feel able to go out and work right now.

Therapist: (focusing on *eigenwelt*) *You're* feeling overwhelmed, and *you* don't quite know what to do. What can *you* do to work through *your* present difficulties?

[*The italics highlight* you *as representative of a possible* eigenwelt *response that may lead the client to self-actualization.*]

Therapist: (focusing on *eigenwelt* and *umwelt*) *Jenny's* terribly important to *you*. The *relationship* sounds like the most important thing in *your* life right now. The question is how the *two of you* can survive this difficult time. *You're both* worried and upset and feel lost.

Therapist: (focusing on *umwelt*) The possibility of losing your *job* sounds very worrisome. You are wondering if issues of discrimination aren't part of the picture as well. Tell me some more about what's going on *at work*.

Each of the above listening responses can be useful and can be used in the Rogerian existential approach. Rogers constantly sought to help people work together. In some ways, the very terms *person-centered* and *client-centered*, attractive though they may be, can obscure the theoretical and practical value of Rogerian theory for non-middle-class and non-European-North American clients.

Fusion and Boundaries in Relationships

The foregoing example focused on an issue in relationship — namely, fusion — that has controversial interpretations in the field. Fusion is an important concept in counseling and therapy with lesbian clients (Mencher, 1990) as well as heterosexual couples. Fusion represents deep closeness between individuals so that at times the two individuals feel as one. This is seen by Mencher as a strength of lesbian relationships. This closeness is very reassuring, giving each individual a sense of being-in-relationship. However, much of traditional theory holds that fusion is pathological and something to be avoided and that what is important is maintaining firm interpersonal boundaries.

Fusion operates in many, perhaps most, heterosexual relationships as well. The best human relationships include some dimension of fusion. However, just as with all dimensions of human experience, one can experience "overfusion" and lose a sense of self. What is desirable is a balance. Moreover, what in some cultures is considered fusion may be normal closeness of relationship in another. For instance, the well-defined boundaries of a New England Yankee or a German-American may be seen as "overly distanced" from another cultural standpoint.

If, as a therapist, you focus totally on the primarily North American male values of individuation, self-actualization, and autonomy, you will view things in terms of boundary and distancing issues and may miss important relational issues of interpersonal closeness. Rogers would likely now argue that a balance of self-actualization (*eigenwelt*) and relationship (*mitwelt*) is required. His theory was one that continued to grow and develop continually until his death. There is no reason to stop the growth of his orientation despite his absence.

Rogerian therapy is a highly verbal approach and may require complex cognitive skills on the part of the client. As such, the theory tends to be less effective in actual practice with children, adolescents, and less verbal clients. The economically disadvantaged often find most immediate benefit from a direct action approach, rather than a self-reflective one. Behavioral, family systems, consciousness-raising, community organization, and developmental methods and techniques therefore are often the treatment of choice for these groups.

The Influence of Rogers

Despite the above-mentioned difficulties, the humanistic philosophy remains important in all counseling and therapy and has been supported by research over the years (see exhibit 11.1). Most practitioners who have adopted other theories or taken an eclectic or metatheoretical approach still employ Rogers's interviewing skills and humanistic attitudes.

It should be noted that Rogers was never content with the status quo. He constantly changed, shaped, and adapted his ideas over the years, increasingly emphasizing in his later years the importance of awareness and action on issues. This chapter presents three views of Rogers: nondirective, client-centered, and person-centered. Although his methods changed at each stage of his development, his underlying faith in humanity and the individual-in-relationship remains constant.

Exhibit 11.1

Research on Person-Centered Theory

Because Rogers's methods have deeply influenced other approaches to helping, detailed attention will be given to research on his framework.

Landmark Research

A landmark series of studies by Fiedler (1950a, 1950b, 1951) sought to define the ideal therapeutic relationship and studied therapists of psychoanalytic, Rogerian, and Adlerian persuasion. Fiedler found that expert therapists of these various persuasions appeared more similar to each other than they did to inexperienced therapists within the same theoretical orientation. An equally important study was conducted by Barrett-Lennard (1962), who found higher levels of facilitative conditions among experienced therapists.

Relationship as Central in Many Theories

The above-mentioned studies prompted an avalanche of studies of the Rogerian qualitative dimensions during the ensuing years. Useful reviews of this research may be found in Anthony and Carkhuff (1977), Auerbach and Johnson (1977), and Garfield and Bergin (1986).

The influential study by Sloane et al. (1975) found that behavioral therapists exhibited higher levels of empathy, self-congruence, and interpersonal contact than did psychotherapists, whereas levels of warmth and regard were approximately the same. There was no relationship, however, between these measures and eventual effectiveness of the therapy.

Therapist Warmth

It is interesting to note that behavioral therapists, often thought of as cold and distant, proved warmer than did psychotherapists. Sloane and Staples reviewed this landmark study in 1984 and made this critical summarization: "Successful patients in both therapies rated their personal interaction with the therapist as the single most important part of treatment" (p. 225). It is difficult to deny or disregard such a powerful statement by clients.

Research Findings

In a comprehensive review of psychotherapy research, Strupp (1989) comments: "The first and foremost task for the therapist is to create an accepting and empathic context" (p. 718). The Psychotherapy Research Project of the Menninger Foundation, which compared different types of therapy, finds that "supportive mechanisms infiltrated all therapies, psychoanalysis included, and accounted for more of the achieved outcomes (including structural changes) than anticipated" (Wallerstein, 1989, p. 195). Coming nearly forty years after the Fiedler studies, the consistency of research on the Rogerian model is notable.

A Different View

However, Mitchell, Bozarth, and Krauft (1977) read the literature on Rogerian theory quite differently, concluding: "The recent evidence, although equivocal, does seem to suggest that empathy, warmth, and genuineness are related in some way to client change, but that their potency and generalizability are not as great as was once thought" (p. 483). Work by Lambert, DeJulio, and Stein (1978) severely criticizes empathy research, suggesting that methods have not always been adequate. A major study using person-centered methods with schizophrenics (Rogers et al., 1967) was not truly successful.

Matching Therapeutic Style to Client Needs

Rogers pointed out in 1975 that many therapists fall short of offering empathic conditions and that therapy and counseling can be for better or worse. Strupp

and Hadley (1976) and Strupp (1989) have illustrated this point. They reviewed a large number of studies indicating possible deterioration as an effect of the psychotherapeutic process and point out the importance of a solid relationship appropriate to the need level of the client. Strupp (1977) catches the essence of his argument, saying that "the art of psychotherapy may largely consist of judicious and sensitive applications of a given technique, delicate decisions of when to press a point or when to be patient, when to be warm and understanding, and when to be remote" (p. 11). Strupp suggests that simple application of a few empathic qualities is not enough. These qualities also must be in synchrony with the client, at the moment, in the interviewing process (see especially, Strupp, 1989).

Case Examples from Three Periods of Rogers's Work

Rogers believed in and acted on his theories. His life was a personal demonstration of intentionality and self-actualization, as he constantly changed and grew. Three main stages[1] of his process have been identified, as follows:

1. *Stage 1: Nondirective (1940–50).* This stage emphasized the acceptance of the client, the establishment of a positive nonjudgmental climate, trust in the client's wisdom, and permissiveness. It uses clarification of the client's world as the main technique. Rogers's writings give a central emphasis to skills in the counseling process.

2. *Stage 2: Client-centered (1950–61).* This stage centers on reflecting the feelings of the client, incorporates resolving incongruities between the ideal self and real self, avoids personally threatening situations for the client, and uses reflection as the main technique. Skills are not emphasized; rather, a major emphasis on the counselor as a person is evolving.

3. *Stage 3: Person-centered (1961–87).* This stage is characterized by increased personal involvement, with more stress on relational issues. While maintaining

consistency with all past work, Rogers moved increasingly to emphasizing present-tense experience, a more active and self-disclosing role for the counselor, group as well as individual counseling, and consideration of broader issues in society such as cultural differences and the use of power. The emphasis on skills has remained minimal, with an emphasis instead on counselor attitudes. Coupled with this is an extensive emphasis on experiencing oneself as a person-in-relation to others. A review of Rogers's transcripts, however, reveals a more interpretative helping style.

In the following pages, brief examples of each of the three major phases of Rogers's growth and development will be explored through the presentation and analysis of brief excerpts from interview sessions typical of each period.

The Nondirective Period

A special gift made by Rogers to the counseling profession was a new openness to what was happening in the interview process. Through detailed notes and discussion and through the new medium of audiorecording, Rogers shared in great detail what he actually did in the counseling interview. Up to that time, the primary mode of training counselors and therapists had been in formal classrooms and one-to-one discussion of what the therapist remembered from an interview.

A classic research study by Blocksma and Porter (1947) revealed that what therapists say they do in an interview and what they actually do are two different things. Rogers's ability to share what he was doing, coupled with the work of Blocksma and Porter, has forever changed the nature of counseling and therapy training. There remains, however, strong resistance to this openness, particularly among some psychoanalytic therapists, who often prefer more abstract discussions of underlying unconscious conflicts to what actually happens in the session.

Interview Example

The following typescript is taken from Rogers's nondirective phase when he was trying explicitly to draw out the client and impose as little of the counselor's orientation as possible (Rogers & Wallen, 1946). His belief was that interference from the counselor would only slow natural client growth. The microskills used in this interview are all attending skills and are extremely apparent. As a useful practice exercise, fill in the blank space to the left of the counselor response with the microskill(s) being used. (A listing of the microskills used can be found at the end of the chapter.)

    1. *Client:*   I wish I knew how to pray.

____2. *Counselor:*   Do you want to tell me some more about that?

    3. *Client:*   I'm all in a mess. I can't sleep. Last night I walked the streets most of the night in a pouring rain. I haven't been able to sleep all the time I've been on leave. I was home for awhile, and I couldn't even talk to my folks there. You see, my buddy was killed, and I just can't get over it.

____4. *Counselor:*   That's been a pretty upsetting blow to you.

5. *Client:*   Well it has. You see, my buddy was my only real friend—I don't make friends easily, never have had very many—and he and I always stuck together. [Tells how they met and some of the things they had been through.] We worked on the same gun crew, and we knew each other so well we never had to tell each other what to do. We could just signal by the way we looked. In this particular scrap the enemy planes were coming over plenty. It was pretty hot. The ammunition box was getting empty, and I just glanced at my buddy. He knew what I meant, and he went to get another box. While he was doing that a shell exploded right near him and killed him. (pause) I just can't get over it. I feel—I feel as though I caused his death.

___6. *Counselor:*   You feel that somehow you are to blame for the fact that he was killed.

7. *Client:*   Yes I do. I don't see why. Well, there's one thing I haven't mentioned. Maybe that has something to do with it. My buddy and I, we got along swell. We hardly ever quarreled, but just the day before this all happened we had quite an argument. [He relates the details of the argument.] We really got sore at each other. I wouldn't even speak to him for several hours afterwards. You know, I think that does have something to do with it. I guess that quarrel makes me feel that I am to blame for what happened.

___8. *Counselor:*   You feel that your being angry at him in some way was responsible for killing him.

9. *Client:*   You know, I think that's it. I haven't thought that through before. Maybe I was scared to think it through. Somehow it helps to talk about things like this. You see, I didn't usually quarrel with my buddy, and I guess it hit me hard to think that we had an argument just the day before he was killed. It doesn't seem so bad when you tell about it. He was really a great guy. [He goes on to tell at some length about his buddy and his buddy's accomplishments and the good relationship they had together. The conversation then turns into other channels, and he talks about his own family and again mentions the fact that he had been very upset while home on leave.] I don't know what you've done sir, but this has sure helped me a lot. I don't see why I felt so much to blame as I did.

___10. *Counselor:*   It seems to have helped to get it off your chest. Is that it?

11. *Client:*   It sure has. I wonder, sir, if it would be too much if I could write to you if I ever feel this way again. I'm probably shipping out pretty quick so I don't think I'll have a chance to see you again, but maybe I could write you a letter.

___12. *Counselor:*   I'd be delighted to get a letter from you even if you're not feeling upset. I hope you will write to me.

13. *Client:*   Well, thanks a lot for talking with me. I've got to go now but you may be hearing from me. (pp. 120–21)

Rogers provides an interesting personal analysis of this interview in which he points out that the counselor does not direct the depth of the interview, but rather attempts to establish conditions so that the client can determine how far or deep to go. Whereas many counselors might have wanted more concreteness and specifics about the situation, the worker in this case accepts the sailor's definition of what happened however he wants to talk about it. A psychodynamic counselor might object to the failure to consider unconscious thought processes underlying the relatively simple surface structure sentences of the sailor; other theorists might have different objections.

Rogers's Response to Critics

Rogers tended to reply in a particularly disarming fashion to those who criticized his work. He suggested that each therapist must find her or his own way of being authentic with another person, and that those whose views differed from his would select counseling theories that worked best for them. Thus Rogers exhibited unusual congruence within himself. Not only did he emphasize and respect clients' right to determine what was right for themselves, but he also respected his critics' ability to determine what was right for themselves.

Missing from the above transcript is Carl Rogers, the person. Rogers had an unusual ability to communicate warmth and authenticity nonverbally. Those who adopt the client-centered approach would stress that your personhood and ability to be with the client in the session are as important as, perhaps even more important than, the specific words you say. It is this philosophic and humane dimension of the theory that has perhaps had the most effect on the practice of all counseling and therapy.

Nondirective Listening

Rogers's nondirective style has continuing relevance. When clients are truly into their own experience, it is important to focus totally on them. Clients need to be heard, and we as counselors and therapists need to learn their construction of the world. Through empathy and by using the listening skills, we provide clients with a chance to learn what they themselves think.

The importance of listening is illustrated dramatically in studies by Inbar et al. (1989) of soldiers who experience combat stress. These researchers found that combat stressed soldiers benefited from talking about their difficulties with supportive staff personnel. Having combat stress treated as a normal response to an abnormal situation enabled the soldiers to return to their posts with minimum long-term effects. If combat difficulties are ignored as they were in the Vietnam War, there is evidence that they will reappear later as posttraumatic stress disorder.

A pure listening approach as represented in the foregoing transcript is not always appropriate. At times, the nondirective style can bring about difficulties in multicultural counseling. For example, African-American clients working with a European-American therapist sometimes mistrust the Rogerian mirroring response. They might want to know who you are as a person, and they might reject a helping approach that is solely focused on mirroring back what is said. Sue and Sue (1990) found that some traditional Asian-American clients often prefer a more directive approach and will not respect a counselor who cannot and will not give advice and direction.

Thus, although listening is considered a central skill in counseling and therapy, it is one of many techniques that form the total strategy of professional helping. During the client-centered period, Rogers was increasingly willing to interpret and influence clients.

The Client-Centered Period

Most excerpts from Rogers's work from this period are highly verbal and would require a client deeply interested in introspection. Thus there may be less of value in this period for multicultural counseling than in his other periods. The client-centered style of helping is currently used relatively infrequently.

Interview Example

The following interview segment illustrates the work of the second period of Rogers (1961, pp. 84–85). The client, Mrs. Oak, talks about how hard it is for her to accept any help or positive reactions from others. The complexity of the counselor's sentences has greatly increased compared with those in the nondirective period interview. Although the emphasis is still very much on the client and the client's perceptions, there is also an interpretive dimension in that the counselor seems to lead the client at times.

> *Client:*   I have a feeling . . . that you have to do it pretty much yourself, but that somehow you ought to be able to do that with other people. [She mentions that there have been "countless" times when she might have accepted personal warmth and kindliness from others.] I get the feeling that I just was afraid I would be devastated. [She returns to talking about the counseling itself and her feeling toward it.] I mean there's been this tearing through the thing myself. Almost to—I mean, I felt it—I mean I tried to verbalize it on occasion—a kind of—at times almost not wanting you to restate, not wanting you to reflect, the thing is mine. Course all right, I can say it's resistance. But that doesn't mean a damn thing to me now . . . The—I think in—in relationship to this particular thing, I mean, the—probably at times, the strongest feeling was, it's mine, it's mine. I've got to cut it down myself. See?
>
> *Counselor:*   It's an experience that's awfully hard to put down accurately into words, and yet I get a sense of difference here in this relationship, that from the feeling that "this is mine," "I've got to do it," "I am doing it," and so on, to a somewhat different feeling that "I could let you in."
>
> [*The counselor's reflection of meaning catches the main points of Mrs. Oak's statement in brief form, thus feeding back to her what her inner world is truly like. In addition, the basic incongruity between real and ideal self is reflected back to the client. Mrs. Oak's statement has a vagueness that would prompt many other counselors to search for more concreteness and to ask for specifics. A psychodynamic therapist might observe the sexual symbolism in the words "I've got to cut it down myself" and the therapist's response "I could let you in."*]
>
> *Client:*   Yeah. Now I mean, that's—that it's—well, it's sort of, shall we say, volume two. It's—it's a—well, sort of, well, I'm still in the thing alone, but I'm not—see—I'm—
>
> *Counselor:*   M-hm. Yes, that paradox sort of sums it up, doesn't it.
>
> *Client:*   Yeah.
>
> *Counselor:*   In all of this, there is a feeling, it's still—every aspect of my experience is mine and that's kind of inevitable and necessary and so on. And yet that isn't the whole picture either. Somehow it can be shared or another's interest can come in and in some ways it is new.
>
> [*There is an interpretive flavor to the last two therapist statements as new meanings are put on old experience. Yet as they very much come from the client's worldview, these leads are a reflection of meaning but close to a paraphrase. The increased involvement of the therapist since Rogers's first period is apparent. Note also that the therapist goes so*]

far as to use "I" when talking about the client rather than "you"; this could be considered a sign of strong empathy in that the counselor can see the world through the client's eyes.]

Client: Yeah. And it's—it's as though, that's how it should be. I mean, that's how it—has to be. There's a—there's a feeling, "and this is good." I mean, it expresses, it clarifies it for me. There's a feeling—in this caring, as though—you were sort of standing back—standing off, and if I want to sort of cut through to the thing, it's a—a slashing of—oh, tall weeds, that I can do it, and you can—I mean you're not going to be disturbed by having to walk through it, too. I don't know. And it doesn't make sense. I mean—

Counselor: Except there's a very real sense of rightness about this feeling that you have, hm?

Client: M-hm. (pp. 84–85)

[*It is particularly important to note the emphasis in the paraphrase. The therapist has selectively attended to the positive aspects of the client's message ("this is good") and simultaneously ignored negative aspects ("it doesn't make sense"). Behavioral counselors have often pointed out that Rogerian counseling involves selective attention and that as complete a verbal "shaping" process occurs in this mode of counseling as in more systematic behavioral approaches. Regardless of whether this view is accepted or not, the selective attention to positive, forward-moving aspects of the client is an example of the positive emphasis of this theory.*]

Rogers goes on to comment that this was a turning point for Mrs. Oak, who learned that it was all right to accept others and to discover positive things in herself. This acceptance is, of course, crucial in the development of a positive self-actualizing personality.

A Multicultural Critique of the Client-Centered Period

The focus in the foregoing interview is still very much on the individual and her construction of events. Very little attention is paid to how others might view the same events. The goal of the interchange seems to focus on Mrs. Oak finding her own "space." Rogerian theory holds that after Mrs. Oak has found herself, she will be better able to relate with others. A feminist or multicultural critique might be that Mrs. Oak could find herself even more rapidly given a more immediate focus on relationships and the role of women in society, with a secondary focus on her own perceptions.

The emphasis in the first two periods of Rogers's work was on individual counseling and therapy. LaFromboise and Low (1989) comment that a broader approach than just individual problem solving may be necessary with Native Americans:

Traditionally, Indian people live in relational networks that serve to support and nurture strong bonds of mutual assistance and affection. Many tribes still engage in a traditional system of collective interdependence, with family members responsible not only to one another but also the clan and tribe to which they belong. The Lakota Sioux use the term *tiospaye* to describe a traditional community way of life in which an individual's well-being remains the responsibility of the extended family. . . . When problems arise among Indian youth, they become problems of the community as well. The family, kin, and friends join together to observe the youth's behavior, draw the youth out of isolation, and integrate that person back into the activities of the group. (p. 121)

If Mrs. Oak was a Lakota Sioux, the individual-focused approach of the interview likely would be inappropriate. Although it would be important to listen to her individual constructions (as in the nondirective period), the focus of counseling interventions would probably emphasize the *mitwelt,* the family, extended family, and community. For a Lakota Sioux, an individual issue remains unsolved until it is considered in the broader network of relationships. In addition, it would be important for you as therapist to present yourself in the interview as a real person with real thoughts and feelings. In multicultural settings, the boundaries between therapist and counselor change, which presents a very real challenge to the practice of traditional counseling and therapy.

Rogers moved toward multicultural emphasis and understanding in his final, person-centered period.

The Person-Centered Period

Stage 3 of Rogers's development reflects a vastly increased involvement and activity on the part of the counselor. Rogers became interested in encounter groups and broadened his view of helping. To the traditional skills of reflection of feeling and paraphrasing, he added new skills of self-disclosure, feedback, and questions.

Interview Example

In the following interview, Rogers (1970) acts as facilitator for an encounter group:

Art: When the shell's on it's, uh . . .

Lois: It's on!

Art: Yeah, it's on tight.

Susan: Are you always so closed in when you're in your shell?

Art: No, I'm so darn used to living with the shell, it doesn't even bother me. I don't even know the real me. I think I've, well, I've pushed the shell away more here. When I'm out of my shell—only twice—once just a few minutes ago—I'm really me, I guess. But then I just sort of pull in a cord after me when I'm in my shell, and that's almost all the time. And I leave the front standing outside when I'm back in the shell.

Facilitator: And nobody's back in there with you?

[Art is the focus of group interaction at the moment. He describes his feelings of being shut off from people in a vivid metaphor of life in a shell. Art as a group member is using effective self-disclosure skills. Lois and Susan, through completion of Art's sentence and the focused closed questions, show that more people than group leaders and counselors can be helpful. The facilitator's interpretation is critical because it brings past and present experience together in one existential moment. Art is experiencing being alone in the shell at this moment as he has in the past in other situations. Yet, paradoxically, he is alone with a supportive facilitator and group. This integration of past and

present experience in "moments of truth" appears in most theories of helping and is particularly important.]

Art: (crying) Nobody else is in there with me, just me. I just pull everything into the shell and roll the shell up and shove it in my pocket. I take the shell, and the real me, and put it in my pocket where it's safe. I guess that's really the way I do it—I go into my shell and turn off the real world. And here—that's what I want to do here in this group, y'know—come out of my shell and actually throw it away.

Lois: You're making progress already. At least you can talk about it.

Facilitator: Yeah. The thing that's going to be the hardest is to stay out of the shell.

Art: (still crying) Well, yeah, if I can keep talking about it I can come out and stay out, but I'm going to have to, y'know, protect me. It hurts. It's actually hurting to talk about it. (p. 26)

[*Lois provides a good example of a feedback statement, and the facilitator expresses his opinion and reaction. Together the two support Art in the immediate moment and help him clarify his own experience.*]

Rogers was personally deeply affected by his learnings in group work, and during this period, he also developed an interest in couples counseling (1972), personal power (1977), the learning process (1969), and world peace (Gendlin, 1988). Despite these diverse interests, which continued to grow and expand until his death at the age of 85 in 1987, Rogers maintained his consistent respect for the individual, stressed the importance of research, and constantly emphasized the ability of the person to find his or her own direction, but always in relationship to another human being.

Central Theoretical Constructs and Techniques

The central issue in Rogerian and existential-humanistic counseling lies in how the individual perceives the world. "Experience is reality" is a statement that implies both explicitly and implicitly that what one thinks is happening in the world is indeed happening. There are an infinite number of ways in which we might view the world, an infinite number of ways of interpreting that world, and an infinite number of ways of acting on that world.

A Person-Centered Theory

Rogers's best-known book is entitled *On Becoming a Person* (1961), and that title is a reflection of the theory and the man. In the Rogerian view, there seems to be no definable end to counseling work; this emphasis on process toward possible futures is particularly illustrative of the existential-humanistic orientation, which stresses individual choice.

At the same time, there is a potential problem in the term *person-centered* in that counselors and therapists have sometimes limited the scope of what Rogers meant by the concepts of *eigenwelt, mitwelt,* and *umwelt.* Although Rogers did not use the language of German existentialism, he was very concerned that persons extend their view beyond themselves to others and to the world at large. Rogers would endorse expanding his and others' humanistic concepts to issues beyond the individual.

Exhibit 11.2 provides you an opportunity to construct, using only listening skills, an interview in Rogers's person-centered mode. You may be surprised to find that you can conduct a complete and effective session using only the skills of the basic listening sequence. This exercise does not introduce you to the full range of Rogerian response possibilities, but it does illustrate what is possible if one is willing to enter the world of the client and truly attempt to see the world as the other perceives it.

Exhibit 11.2

 An Exercise in Person-Centered Counseling

A person-centered theorist might argue that our world is too full of advice giving and people telling other people what to do. Your goal in this exercise is to enter the frame of reference of the client and use only listening skills represented by the basic listening sequence and perhaps reflection of meaning. *No advice, suggestions, or interpretation is allowed!* To make the task somewhat easier, you may use questions, but aim each question toward the frame of reference of the client. A good topic for your real or role-played "client" may be the act of procrastination, putting off something until later. However, any of a variety of topics may be used for the practice session.

Rapport/Structuring

Begin the interview by establishing rapport until you and the client are comfortable. Remember that rapport is particularly important throughout the session. Structure the interview honestly by saying that you want to understand and listen and not give advice. You

might initiate the session by saying, "You want to talk about . . ."

Data Gathering

Use primarily the reflective listening skills of encouraging, paraphrasing, and reflection of feeling. Periodically summarize what the "client" says so the session has a continuous structure. After you have heard the problem fairly clearly, you may wish to paraphrase or reflect positive meanings or actions inherent in what the client has been saying. This is a specific way to manifest positive regard and demonstrate the positive asset search.

Determining Outcomes

Your client very likely has implied how he or she would like things to be. As you begin to understand the client's problem, paraphrase or summarize how the client would like things to be. Here, you will likely find it necessary to ask a question related in some form to the following: "How would you like things to be?" You have heard the "real self" and the real problem during data gathering, and this is the opportunity to draw out the "ideal self" or the ideal solution.

Generating Alternative Solutions

Important in person-centered theory is the distinction between the real and ideal. Summarize this incongruency of real and ideal with the confrontation statement "On one hand, your problem is . . . , but on the other hand your ideal solution is . . . Now what comes to your mind as a possible resolution?" Alternatively, you may wish to talk about how the person views him- or herself and how he or she would like to view him- or herself. Again, the question may not be necessary as the clear summary of the real and ideal often enables clients to start generating their own solutions out of their own personal constructs.

Use the basic listening sequence and reflection of meaning to understand and listen to what the client generates. This may be considered the action phase of the interview in which the client generates a new view on the problem from his or her own internal frame of reference.

Generalization

Person-centered theory has not traditionally given much attention to generalization and perhaps that is why research as to its effectiveness has not been as promising as once was hoped. You may wish to summarize what the client has generated as alternative solutions and see if the client is interested in actually doing something about her or his situation. As Rogerian theory does not emphasize this phase of helping, you may find it worthwhile to consider generalization techniques from relapse prevention or you may simply ask the client "What one thing will you do or think differently this coming day because of our discussion?"

Simply being heard accurately frees many people for creative, intentional responding. This exercise is taken from the nondirective period of Rogerian theory, but may be adapted to include other skills (self-disclosure, feedback) added in later Rogerian periods. If you have mastered the constructs presented in preceding chapters, you can rather rapidly enter into a relatively effective person-centered interview.

Gendlin's Interpretation of Rogers's Influence

Gendlin (1970) summarizes in a few brief words the change process of person-centred therapy throughout its periods and changing styles:

> By saying what the client said, something new will occur, the client will soon say something new, and then we can respond to that. By featuring responsivity at every small, specific momentary step, . . . the therapist carries forward not only what the client verbally stated, but also the client's experiential process. . . . This responsivity to specific felt meaning at each step engenders, carries forward, and changes the individual's ongoing experiential process. This is the underlying principle that is implicit in client-centered therapy and its early quaint rules for therapist responding. (pp. 32–33)

In effect, Gendlin suggests that when the client shares her or his experience with the counselor, and the counselor responds with accurate listening, the client is moved forward by the interaction. Even if the counselor just directly repeats what the client says, the client's world will have been changed by the very act of being heard. Being heard by another person can thus be considered an action on the world.

Many, perhaps most, clients do not feel they have power and influence on others or their surroundings. By the giving of themselves to their clients through empathic attending skills, counselors empower their clients. Clients speak; therapists listen carefully and attempt to understand clients' perceptions of the world. Having been heard and understood, clients can move forward.

Gendlin's description of the key aspects of Rogers's work can be extended to the larger framework of group work and to issues of conflict resolution. One of the most powerful things we can do in groups and in complex negotiations is to hear the other person and how they construct the world. In an interview with eighty-two-year-old Rogers (Rogers calls peace . . . , 1984), the *APA Monitor* reported:

> His work over one weekend with Irish Protestants and Catholics joined by a representative of the British government achieved what he called "surprising results" and led to a film that the participants hoped to take to schools, churches, and similar neutral settings. The proof of its success, he added, came when paramilitary groups on both sides, who were opposed to his attempt to overcome centuries of hostility, destroyed four copies of the film before it could be shown.
>
> This summer he attended a conference in Hungary in which 300 persons from 27 countries—Western democracies as well as Eastern-bloc communist countries—grappled with the issues that divided their nations. Although participants were often more revealing in private conversations than in public sessions, Rogers said the conference was extremely successful in teaching individuals to *listen to the view of others*. (p. 15) (Emphasis added)

In these workshops, Rogers (1) encouraged participants to explore their hostile attitudes and feelings, which the facilitator had accepted, thus helping remove irrational aspects of their thinking; (2) focused on persons and attitudes, thereby forging an important beginning once the underlying rage was accepted and understood; and (3) fostered "direct confrontation of opponents in a confined area." Rogers found in the holding environment of a group that listened and sought to understand, combatants could learn to accept one another and work toward mutual goals.

The theoretical movement of Rogers seems to have begun and ended with careful listening. Rogers fostered the awareness that listening could serve as a foundation of challenging sharing and feedback, interpretations, and even direct hostile confrontation. Rogers and Gendlin are telling us that the first step toward mutual understanding is listening and learning how the other person construes events. Until we really hear the other person and understand their mode of being-in-the-world, very little will happen in any relationship.

Seeing the World from the Client's Perspective

Given the infinite possibilities in life, each person's experience and perceptions will be at least somewhat different from anyone else's. A central task of the counselor is to understand and empathize with the unique experiential world of the client.

Perhaps more than anyone else, Rogers was able to listen empathically and carefully to other human beings. As he understood them and their perceptions, he consistently found positive, self-actualizing forces in them. Those committed to the humanistic counseling approach are almost always able to find positive elements in even the most troubled individual.

The following story provides a beginning point for exploring the complexity of human interactions and the Rogerian positive approach:

> A small child attempts to string beads onto a shoelace. The plastic end of the lace has been torn off, and the tip is frayed badly. The child sits quietly and determinedly for fifteen minutes, attempting an impossible task. Then, with a sudden shout of frustration, the beads and the lace are thrown about the room. At that moment the child's father comes over and strikes the child for "lack of patience."

In this case, the child is obviously forward-moving and purposeful. But the perception of reality is unrealistic, in that the task is impossible, given the frayed string and the age of the child. Viewing the child from an objective perspective, it is easy to see that the child's expression of anger is a normal reaction to growing frustration. *But what about the father's reaction?*

The father's behavior appears reprehensible and irrational. Such behavior cannot represent forward-moving self-actualized personhood. In such a real-life case, the counselor would first consider the situation for possible danger to the child and would take specific action to ensure that the child was safe from abuse.

Assuming that abuse is not an ongoing issue, how would the Rogerian therapist deal with this situation? In counseling the father would be encouraged to talk about the situation in considerable detail. There would be an emphasis on the emotional underpinnings of the incident, and quite likely, the father would share other incidents in which he lost his temper.

This example illustrates an important point: *Human interactions are often more complex than they seem at a surface level.* As the complex father/child interaction is explored in depth over a series of sessions, the counselor might uncover the fact that the father has tried very hard to find work but has been unsuccessful, that the father is a single parent, and that he himself was abused as a child. The person-centered counselor would tend to focus more on the experience and emotion of the father and pay relatively less attention to the facts of the incident. The counselor would reflect the positive elements of the father's behavior (trying to make it, to do the "right thing") and understand and accept the negative behavior. The counselor's strong positive regard would come through, and the father's striking of the child could be viewed as a natural reaction to frustration similar to the child's natural reaction to frustration.

The above interpretation, however, would not be made explicit. Rather, the counselor would communicate her or his faith that the father could become more intentional and self-actualized if he so chose.[2] At issue here, however, is that children and those who experience abuse may not have time to wait for the perpetrator to heal. Abuse and assault must not be allowed to happen again. In such situations it is important to use a balanced approach: the counselor acts to stop the abusive situations and then applies Rogerian concepts as part of a broader treatment plan.

The Real Self and the Ideal Self:
Multicultural Implications

A critical issue in Rogerian counseling (presently the most popular existential-humanistic view) is the discrepancy that often occurs between the real self and the ideal self. An individual needs to see her- or himself as worthy. Often an individual loses sight of what he or she really is in an effort to attain an idealized image. This discrepancy between thought and reality, between self-perception and others' perceptions, or between self and experience leads to incongruities. These incongruities in turn result in areas in which the person is not truly her- or himself. The father who strikes the child lacks congruence. The objective of therapy with this client is to resolve the discrepancies between ideal and real self, thus eliminating the tension and substituting forward-moving self-actualization.

From a multicultural frame of reference, the emphasis in Rogerian theory on ideal self and real self tends to obscure relational and broader environmental issues. As such, you may find it helpful to add a broader focus when working with many clients. For example, it would be within the Rogerian tradition to help clients focus on *real relationships* and *ideal relationships*. Such a focus would help individuals think of themselves as persons-in-relation to significant others. This focus would entail a change in the style of counseling and therapy usually associated with Rogers. But when one considers Rogers's life development, one would suspect that these concepts are not too distant from where he was heading at the end of his life. Clearly, Rogers was focusing on a more *ideal world* as contrasted with the *real world (umwelt)*.

Furthermore, theorists of a more psychodynamic orientation have argued that Rogers's emphasis on the self as a central construct goes back to his own roots in a strict German family. His self-psychology from this frame of reference represents an unconscious rebellion against and an attempt to cope with family and cultural controls. Rogers, who once studied for the ministry, constantly stressed the importance of a natural relationship among human beings. He rejected the concepts of psychoanalytic transference and countertransference as unnecessary. Exhibit 11.3, however, presents data supporting the idea that Rogers was not as free of past developmental history as he stated in his theories.

Limitations and Practical Implications of
the Existential-Humanistic Tradition

The beauty and strength of the existential-humanistic tradition lie in its strong faith in humankind, opportunity for personal growth, and the infinite possibility of experience. However, some naive therapists and counselors have taken only the concept of "infinite possibility" and have led clients into destructive, closed circles of existence.

As with psychodynamic theory, the existential-humanistic approach tends to be highly verbal. Concerned with the meaning of life and individual satisfaction, the therapy can be verbose. As such, it appeals mainly to middle- and upper-class individuals. The positive philosophy of Rogers appears to be particularly applauded by those of a multicultural orientation, but Rogerian methods of slow reflection, lack of

Exhibit 11.3

A Current Controversy in the Field: Does Transference Exist in Rogerian Therapy?

Rogers emphasized the importance of here-and-now interactions between client and counselor and felt that transferential concepts and discussion of the past were not useful dimensions of the counseling process.

In the film *Three Approaches to Psychotherapy* (Shostrum, 1965), the client, Gloria, is interviewed by Carl Rogers, Fritz Perls, and Albert Ellis. The film has had an immense influence on the acceptance of Rogers's work. In the film, he appears warm and accepting toward Gloria, who indicates that she enjoyed his work with her above the others.

Rogers commented in some detail that the film is evidence that transferential concepts are not needed and used the film to stress the importance of focusing on the person. This film and Rogers's negation of transference have influenced many counseling and therapy training programs, which prefer to ignore psychodynamic concepts.

Weinrach (1990) discovered that a final extra 249 words were deleted from this famous film. Just prior to the deleted words, Gloria comments, "Gee, how nice I can talk to you and I want you to approve of me and I respect you, but I miss that my father couldn't talk to me like that. I mean I'd like to say, 'Gee, I'd like you for my father.' " Rogers comments that Gloria would make a "pretty nice daughter." The film concludes as they discuss Gloria's father's inability to accept her as she is. At this point, Rogers makes his points against a transferential interpretation.

Weinrach presents the full text that continues the father-daughter issue. The following interpretation missing from the published film is an example of a psychodynamically oriented statement that one would not expect of Rogers: "Rogers: The phrase that comes to my mind—I don't know if it is appropriate or not—you're slapping your father in the face, aren't you?" [*Interpretation; the focus is on Gloria transferring unconscious feelings toward her father to her present behavior.*]

Weinrach points out that transferential relationships can complicate our interventions unless we are aware of them and their implications. He also points out that Rogers himself may be seen as involved in a complex countertransferential relationship with Gloria. Weinrach comments that if the full film had been shown, Rogers might have been seen less as a role model and more as a "mortal therapist who missed or unintentionally ignored an important clinical issue."

Bohart (1991) takes issue with Weinrach, commenting that transferential concepts are highly intellectualized and miss the essence of the Rogerian relational approach. He describes the above missing segment of the interview as more evidence of Rogers's caring and empathy.

Beaver (1991) adds additional comments on the failure of Rogers to consider Gloria as a woman in a society dominated by men. Rogers's focus was on a single person in front of him, and he did not consider any contextual issues except as Gloria constructed them. Clearly, Gloria faced many multicultural issues in terms of male-female relationships, societal expectations, and father-daughter relationships. These matters must be considered in understanding how a woman's *self-in-relation* is established.

This is the type of controversy you as a professional helper will encounter again and again. Given the discussion in this chapter, do you endorse Weinrach's, Beaver's, or Bohart's interpretation of the data? Recall that more than one perspective may be "correct" and that the meaning of "correctness" depends on the constructed worldview of the observer. On this last point, we might expect Rogers to concur.

action, and failure to consider immediate problem solving seem inappropriate for these groups. The tendency for existential-humanistic counseling to ignore person-environment transactions in daily practice is a major limitation with some clients. The intense preoccupation with the individual and free choice is at times incompatible with a more environmentally oriented and contextually aware approach.

However, the existential-humanistic philosophic tradition does speak to multicultural concerns in that it, perhaps more than any other set of theories, focuses on *human relationship.* If we supplement the basic ideas of Rogers with more focused emphasis on the *mitwelt* and *umwelt,* perhaps we are doing as he would wish.

Given its problems and drawbacks, what does the existential-humanistic movement offer the beginning counselor or therapist that is immediately useful? Perhaps the major contribution of Rogers has been his emphasis on empathic and accurate listening and his willingness to open the interview to inspection and research through audiotape and films. The attending skills explored in chapter 3 rest heavily on Rogers's classifications and discussion in his early work. The qualitative conditions of warmth, respect, and concreteness (chapter 2) are derived from his seminal thinking. The methodological message that Rogers has given us is that we, as prospective and active counselors and therapists, must listen to the client and open the interview and ourselves to scrutiny. Only in this way can we grow and learn about our own possibilities to enrich the lives of others.

NOTES

1. Although three main periods have been identified in Rogers's development, his early major work, *Counseling and Psychotherapy* (1942), first presented typescripts of his work and commentary on counseling theory. He talks about nondirective therapy in this book, and gives considerable attention to insight and practical matters of the counseling interview. Further, at that time, Rogers used more questions and interpretations than he did later in his nondirective period.

2. By way of contrast, it is important to note that other orientations to helping (behavioral, feminist, cognitive-behavioral, developmental) might concentrate more directly on the specific problem. Although they would hope to keep Rogerian respect for the perpetrator central, these counselors would tend to act more directly and immediately to stop damaging behavior and promote change.

REFERENCES

ABBAGNANO, N. (1967). Humanism. In P. Edwards (Ed.), *The encyclopedia of philosophy* (Vol. 3, pp. 69–72). New York: Macmillan.

ANTHONY, W., & CARKHUFF, R. (1977). The functional professional therapeutic agent. In A. Gurman & A. Razin (Eds.), *Effective psychotherapy* (pp. 103–19). Elmsford, NY: Pergamon Press.

AUERBACH, A., & JOHNSON, M. (1977). Research on the therapist's level of experience. In A. Gurman & A. Razin (Eds.), *Effective psychotherapy* (pp. 84–102). Elmsford, NY: Pergamon Press.

BALLOU, M., & GABALAC, N. (1985). *A feminist position on mental health.* Springfield, IL: Thomas.

BARRETT-LENNARD, G. (1962). Dimensions of therapist response as causal factors in therapeutic change. *Psychological Monographs, 76,* 43. (Ms. No. 562)

BEAVER, A. (1991, September). *Some potential issues of unconscious sexist behavior in counseling and therapy.* Paper presented at the University of Massachusetts, Amherst.

BINSWANGER, L. (1958). The existential analysis school of thought. In R. May, E. Angel, & H. Ellenberger (Eds.), *Existence* (pp. 191–213). New York: Basic Books.

BINSWANGER, L. (1963). *Being-in-the-world: Selected papers of Ludwig Binswanger.* New York: Basic Books.

BLOCKSMA, D., & PORTER, E. (1947). A short-term training program in client-centered counseling. *Journal of Consulting Psychology, 11,* 55–60.

BOHART, A. (1991). The missing 249 words: In search of objectivity. *Psychotherapy, 28,* 497–503.

BOSS, M. (1958). *The analysis of dreams.* New York: Philosophical Library.

BOSS, M. (1963). *Psychoanalysis and daseinanalysis.* New York: Basic Books.

BUBER, M. (1970). *I and thou.* New York: Scribner's.

Camus, A. (1942). *The stranger.* New York: Random House.

CAMUS, A. (1958). *The myth of Sisyphus.* New York: Knopf.

FIEDLER, F. (1950a). A comparison of therapeutic relationships in psychoanalytic, nondirective, and Adlerian therapy. *Journal of Consulting Psychology, 14,* 435–36.

FIEDLER, F. (1950b). The concept of an ideal therapeutic relationship. *Journal of Consulting Psychology, 14,* 239–45.

FIEDLER, F. (1951). Factor analysis of psychoanalytic, nondirective, and Adlerian therapeutic relationships. *Journal of Consulting Psychology, 15,* 32–38.

GARFIELD, A., & BERGIN, A. (1986). *Handbook of psychotherapy and behavior change.* New York: Wiley.

GENDLIN, E. (1970). A short summary and some long predictions. In J. Hart & T. Tomlinson (Eds.), *New directions in client-centered therapy.* Boston: Houghton-Mifflin.

GENDLIN, E. (1988). Carl Rogers. *American Psychologist, 43,* 127–28.

HEIDEGGER, M. (1962). *Being and time.* New York: HarperCollins.

HUSSERL, E. (1931). *Ideas: General introduction to pure phenomenology.* London: Allen & Unwin.

INBAR, D., AVIRAM, U., SPIRO, S., & KOTLER, M. (1989). Officers' attitude toward combat stress reaction: Responsibility, treatment, return to unit, and personal distance. *Military Medicine, 154,* 480–89.

LAFROMBOISE, T., & LOW, K. (1989). American Indian adolescents. In J. Gibbs & L. Hwang (Eds.), *Children of color* (pp. 114–47). San Francisco: Jossey-Bass.

LAING, R. (1967). *The politics of experience.* New York: Ballantine.

LAMBERT, M., DEJULIO, S., & STEIN, D. (1978). Therapist interpersonal skills. *Psychological Bulletin, 85,* 467–89.

LERNER, H. (1992). The limits of phenomenology: A feminist critique of the humanistic personality theories. In L. Brown & M. Ballou (Eds.), *Theories of personality and psychopathology* (pp. 8–19). New York: Guilford.

MAY, R. (1958). The origins and significance of the existential movement in psychology. In R. May, E. Angel, & H. Ellenberger (Eds.), *Existence* (pp. 3–36). New York: Basic Books.

MAY, R. (Ed.). (1961). *Existential psychology.* New York: Random House.

MAY, R. (1969). *Love and will.* New York: W. W. Norton.

MENCHER, J. (1990). Intimacy in lesbian relationships: A critical reexamination of fusion. *Work in Progress.* Stone Center Series No. 42. Wellesley College, Wellesley, MA.

MITCHELL, K., BOZARTH, J., & KRAUFT, C. (1977). A reappraisal of the therapeutic effectiveness of accurate empathy, nonpossessive warmth and genuineness. In A. Gurman & A. Razin (Eds.), *Effective psychotherapy* (pp. 482–502). Elmsford, NY: Pergamon Press.

RIGNEY, M. (1981, April). *A critique of Maslow's self-actualization theory: The "highest good" for the aboriginal is relationship* [Videotape]. Adelaide, Australia: Aboriginal Open College.

ROGERS, C. (1942). *Counseling and psychotherapy.* Boston: Houghton-Mifflin.

ROGERS, C. (1961). *On becoming a person.* Boston: Houghton-Mifflin.

ROGERS, C. (1969). *Freedom to learn.* Columbus, OH: Merrill.

ROGERS, C. (1970). *On encounter groups.* New York: HarperCollins.

ROGERS, C. (1972). *Becoming partners.* New York: Delta.

ROGERS, C. (1977). *On personal power.* New York: Delacourt.

ROGERS, C., GENDLIN, G., KIESLER, D., & TRUAX, C. (1967). *The therapeutic relationship and its impact: A study of psychotherapy with schizophrenics.* Madison: University of Wisconsin Press.

ROGERS, C., & WALLEN, J. (1946). *Counseling with returned servicemen.* New York: McGraw-Hill.

Rogers calls peace results "surprising." (1984, November). *APA Monitor,* p. 15.

SARTRE, J. (1946). *No exit.* New York: Knopf.

SARTRE, J. (1956). *Being and nothingness.* London: Methuen.

SHOSTRUM, E. (Prod.). (1965). *Three approaches to psychotherapy* [Film]. Santa Ana, CA: Psychological Films.

SLOANE, R., & STAPLES, F. (1984). Psychotherapy versus behavior therapy: Implications for future psychotherapy research. In J. Williams & R. Spitzer (Eds.), *Psychotherapy research: Where are we and where should we go?* (pp. 203–15). New York: Guilford.

SLOANE, R., STAPLES, F., CRISTOL, A., YORKSTON, N., & WHIPPLE, K. (1975). *Psychotherapy versus behavior therapy.* Cambridge, MA: Harvard University Press.

STRUPP, H. (1977). A reformulation of the dynamics of the therapist's contribution. In A. Gurman & A. Razin (Eds.), *Effective psychotherapy* (pp. 1–22). Elmsford, NY: Pergamon Press.

STRUPP, H. (1989). Psychotherapy: Can the practitioner learn from the researcher? *American Psychologist, 44,* 717–24.

STRUPP, H., & HADLEY, S. (1976). Contemporary view on negative effects in psychotherapy. *Archives of General Psychiatry, 33,* 1291–1302.

TILLICH, P. (1961). Existentialism and psychotherapy. *Review of Existential Psychology and Psychiatry, 1,* 8–16.

WALLERSTEIN, R. (1989). The psychotherapy research project of the Menninger Foundation: An overview. *Journal of Consulting and Clinical Psychology, 57,* 195–205.

WEINRACH, S. (1990). Rogers and Gloria: The controversial film and the enduring relationship. *Psychotherapy, 27,* 282–90.

WEINRACH, S. (1991). Rogers' encounter with Gloria: What did Rogers know and when? *Psychotherapy, 28,* 504–6.

SKILL CLASSIFICATION OF NONDIRECTIVE SESSION
(pp. 293–94)

2. Closed question
4. Reflection of feeling
6. Paraphrase
8. Paraphrase
10. Reflection of feeling/paraphrase. Note check-out, "Is that it?"
12. Expression of content and feeling—self-disclosure

The Existential-Humanistic Tradition: Logotherapy and Gestalt Therapy

CHAPTER GOALS

This chapter has the following specific goals.

1. To present Frankl's logotherapy — its central constructs, example techniques, and a brief multicultural examination.

2. To present some of the central techniques of Perls's Gestalt therapy and a brief multicultural examination.

3. To summarize some limitations and issues for the future of the existential-humanistic tradition.

Implementing the Existential-Humanistic Tradition

As a counselor or therapist, you will likely work with individuals who have suffered severe life difficulties and trauma. You may conduct counseling and therapy with survivors of physical, sexual, and emotional child abuse, rape, or extreme racism or discrimination. One of the most difficult situations you may face will be working with individuals who find that they carry the HIV virus or actually have AIDS. Each of these clients has suffered major personal assaults. How can you then make any sense of what has happened?

Logotherapy is Viktor Frankl's personal answer to the major life crisis he faced. You may find his courageous answer to the most complex issues of life beneficial not only to your clients, but also to you. When concrete actions fail and life seems to have no positive meaning, Frankl's logotherapy can be invaluable.

Fritz Perls takes a very different direction from Rogers and Frankl and also offers an important humanistic view of the individual. You will find that his techniques are extremely directive. Whereas Rogers would listen, Perls would be active and on the spot in directing the change process.

Frankl provides a balancing force between Rogers and Perls. Rogers might be described as an attending or listening therapist and Perls as an influencing therapist. Frankl appears to use both attending and listening skills according to the varied needs of the client. All three individuals offer much of practical value to the practice of counseling and therapy.

Viktor Frankl and Logotherapy

Logotherapy holds that the critical issue for humankind is not what happens, but how one views or thinks about what happens. Thus Frankl stresses the importance of cognitive change. But logotherapy is also concerned with action; it emphasizes changing behavior in the real world. Frankl was a forerunner to the cognitive-behavioral movement (Mahoney & Freeman, 1985; Frankl, 1985a), and his position provides an important bridge between existential-humanistic and cognitive-behavioral theories.

Frankl is a cognitive theorist with an existential-humanistic message of faith and hope. His logotherapy is concerned with the search for meaning in life. Frankl was able to reframe his life situation in the concentration camp and find positive reasons for living in the midst of negatives. He faced the existential dilemma of the meaning of life under the most extreme conditions. Through finding positive meaning in suffering, Frankl has given us all new hope.

Given how Frankl learned to live effectively with dehumanization and ultimate anti-Semitism, his philosophy has profound implications for multicultural counseling and therapy and for those who have suffered trauma. Any number of people have benefited from reading Frankl's *Man's Search for Meaning* (1946/1959), available in over twenty languages. Many of your clients will gain significantly if you refer them to this powerful little paperback book. *Simply reading Frankl can be therapeutic for many clients.*

Rather than presenting a clinical case study, we offer some quotations from Frankl's writings in the hope that you will be encouraged to read further on your own.

Case Example: Frankl's Search for Meaning

Frankl's positive view of the human condition reflects a lifetime of struggle to find the positives in humankind. Frankl is best known through his compelling and important book *Man's Search for Meaning* (1946/1959). In this small but highly affecting volume, Frankl relates his experiences in German concentration camps during World War II. Although Frankl describes the horrors of the concentration camp, the book is more a testimony to the power of the human spirit and its capability of survival under the most inhuman of conditions.

Following are some quotations from Frankl's book. Despite the dehumanizing environment, Frankl finds something meaningful that enables him and others to survive. In the quotes below, we have highlighted the positives in the negative situation by using italics. In many cases Frankl focused his attention away from the immediate situation and toward positive relationships with the world—an action that helped him survive.

> We stumbled on in the darkness, over big stones and through large puddles, along the one road leading from the camp. The accompanying guards kept shouting at us and driving us with the butts of their rifles. Anyone with very sore feet supported himself on his neighbor's arm. Hardly a word was spoken; the icy wind did not encourage talk. Hiding his mouth behind his upturned collar, the man marching next to me whispered suddenly: "If our wives could see us now! I do hope they are better off in their camps and don't know what is happening to us."
>
> *That brought thoughts of my own wife to mind.* And as we stumbled on for miles, slipping on icy spots, supporting each other time and again, dragging one another up and onward, nothing was said, but we both knew: *each of us was thinking of his wife.* Occasionally I looked at the sky, where the stars were fading and the pink light of the morning was beginning to spread behind a dark bank of clouds. *But my mind clung to my wife's image, imagining it with an uncanny acuteness. I heard her answering me, saw her smile, her frank and encouraging look. Real or not, her look was then more luminous than the sun which was beginning to rise.*
>
> *A thought transfixed me: for the first time in my life I saw the truth as it is set into song by so many poets, proclaimed as the final wisdom by so many thinkers. The truth—that love is the ultimate and the highest goal to which man can aspire. Then I grasped the meaning of the greatest secret that human poetry and human thought and belief have to impart: The salvation of man is through love and in love. I understood how a man who has nothing left in this world still may know bliss, be it only for a brief moment, in the contemplation of his beloved.* In a position of utter desolation, when man cannot express himself in positive action, when his only achievement may consist in enduring his sufferings in the right way—an honorable way—in such a position man can, through loving contemplation of the image he carries of his beloved, achieve fulfillment. For the first time in my life I was able to understand the meaning of the words, "The angels are lost in perpetual contemplation of an infinite glory."
>
> In front of me a man stumbled and those following him fell on top of him. The guard rushed over and used his whip on them all. Thus my thoughts were interrupted for a few

minutes. *But soon my soul found its way back from the prisoner's existence to another world, and I resumed talk with my loved one: I asked her questions and she answered; she questioned me in return, and I answered.* (pp. 58–60)

In the winter and spring of 1945 there was an outbreak of typhus which infected nearly all the prisoners. The mortality was great among the weak, who had to keep on with their hard work as long as they possibly could. The quarters for the sick were most inadequate, there were practically no medicines or attendants. Some of the symptoms of the disease were extremely disagreeable: an irrepressible aversion to even a scrap of food (which was an additional danger to life) and terrible attacks of delirium. The worst case of delirium was suffered by a friend of mine who thought that he was dying and wanted to pray. In his delirium he could not find the words to do so. *To avoid these attacks of delirium, I tried, as did many of the others, to keep awake for most of the night. For hours I composed speeches in my mind. Eventually I began to reconstruct the manuscript which I had lost in the disinfection chamber of Auschwitz, and scribbled the key words in shorthand on tiny scraps of paper.* (p. 55)

These quotes show how Frankl shifted attention from the immediate horror of the here and now to other issues. Particularly, he thought of his wife and his relationship with her. His was a sane response in an insane situation. At a more basic level, Frankl found meaning outside the horror of the immediate situation, which gave him strength to cope with life's difficult reality.

There are times when problems cannot be solved—the rape has occurred, the HIV infection proven by a medical test, an automobile accident prevents the client from returning to previous employment. In such cases, how we think about what happened and the meaning of our lives—our cognitions—are as important as or more important than any concrete behavioral change we can make.

Central Theoretical Constructs and Techniques of Logotherapy

The task for the logotherapist is to help the client find meaning and purpose in life—*and then to act on those meanings.* Logotherapy could be described as a therapy balanced between the listening skills of Rogers and the influencing skills of Perls, with a greater stress on the importance of generalizing change to the real world.

Logotherapists are interested in carefully learning how the client constructs a worldview. Once they have this understanding, they are willing and ready to move actively to promote client change. Logotherapy, like much of the cognitive-behavioral tradition, is also a metatheoretical orientation in that its practitioners will not hesitate to use techniques from other orientations to help clients find meaning and real-life goals.

Cognitive Change and Finding Positive Meanings

Many Vietnam and Persian Gulf veterans will raise issues of the meaning of life in therapy, as will a Latina/o youth who has experienced discrimination and feels beaten. Almost all clients of any cultural background will bring problems relating to meaning. Since the definition of meaning sometimes depends on the religious, ethnic, and cultural background of your client, you need to be prepared to deal with a variety of meaning and belief systems ranging from Christian and Jewish to Mormon to Islamic. Being a gay male or lesbian, physically challenged, economically disadvantaged, or from a particular ethnic/racial group will also challenge and change the structure of the meaning system.

Helping Clients Find Meaning in Difficult Life Situations.   The route toward intentionality and meaning is through carefully listening to the client's construction of meaning of the world. Then, if necessary, the logotherapist will intervene directly and actively to facilitate change in the client's construct or meaning system, but in accord with the cultural tradition of the client. Frankl is keenly aware that meaning is constructed not only in the individual, but also from the cultural tradition of the client.

Cultural Issues Are Important in Meaning Making.   Cultural and family traditions are often keys to meaning change in clients. This change in meaning may be represented in thought or played out in direct action. It is important that you be aware of many differing types of constructed meaning systems among individuals of varying cultural backgrounds. The listening aspect of Frankl's logotherapy seems close to that of Rogers, and the influencing aspect is almost as powerful and direct as that of Perls. Yet logotherapy extends existential-humanistic thinking and practice in its awareness of cultural traditions as part of meaning making.

Searching for Positive Meanings.   To help clients find personal meaning and to make more sense of their lives, Frankl offers a positive philosophy, as exemplified by his life and by his influential writings. Talking with or listening to Frankl personally is an exercise in life itself — a sermon in motion — and in this sense, Frankl is very similar to Rogers. The person you are in the interview is as important as or more important than your therapeutic skills. *In addition, you must find the person in your client and what is meaningful to that child, adolescent, man, or woman before you.*

Many clients suffer from day-to-day problems of meaning. How does one make sense of a meaningless job, learn to cope with a less-than-satisfactory personal relationship, or relate to difficult parents or in-laws?

Helping clients find positive meanings obviously is not a technical skill of helping. There is no formula that can be easily applied to any one client or group. The kind and hopeful approach of Rogers to humanity is helpful, that of Perls is demanding, and that of Frankl provides a basic philosophy that helps us to focus on meaning and may enable us to search with our clients as they find their unique meanings — perhaps differently constructed meanings than ours, but nonetheless workable for them.

Taking Meaning into Behavioral Action

Frankl (1946/1959, 1969) has framed a theory and a method of helping that are gaining increasing prominence (see also Mahoney & Freeman, 1985). The techniques he developed — dereflection, paradoxical intention, and change of attitudes — are current popular methodological and research areas (Frankl, 1985b; Lukas, 1984; Fabry, 1984). Frankl's conceptions around change of attitudes and dereflection may be found in varying forms in cognitive-behavior modification, rational-emotive therapy, and the structural/systemic family theories. Paradoxical intention is one of the key "new" methods that can be used to produce rapid change, yet it was used by Frankl as early as 1929.

Lukas (1984) is a major logotherapy theorist and practitioner. She has outlined four main logotherapy techniques that therapists can use to facilitate client growth and movement toward meaningful living: modification of attitudes, paradoxical intention, dereflection, and the appealing technique.

Modification of Attitudes

Clients can hold negative attitudes toward themselves despite overtly positive life situations. For example, an extremely attractive and personable client may see him- or herself quite negatively. Alternatively, clients may have really serious problems and be unable to do anything about them. In each case, the logotherapeutic task is to change the way the person thinks about the situation — a goal similar to that of the cognitive approach. Modification of attitudes is most often conducted directly through sharing opinions, arguing (as in Ellis's rational-emotive therapy), or offering positive suggestions with the client. At issue is assisting the client to take a new view of the situation.

Reframing Attitudes.   The positive asset search or positive reframe (chapter 3) is one technique in logotherapy for modification of attitudes. However, it is of crucial importance to first listen carefully to clients' negative meanings and constructions. Clients need first to tell their stories fully and completely and to feel heard. If you use the techniques of positive reframing or the positive asset search too early, the client may likely turn away from you. An important guideline is: *Do not try to modify attitudes or cognitions until the client feels thoroughly and respectfully heard.*

The following brief example from a videotaped interview illustrates the specifics of finding positive meanings in negative situations:

Counselor: (after listening to the client's deepest fears and hearing how he thought himself close to death in quicksand — the client had talked about feelings of guilt about survival — "Why me?") Is there anything positive? I know it sounds like a totally negative experience. Was there anything you could see that was positive about what happened?

[*This short counselor comment catches the essence of the search for positive meanings. It is a simple point, so direct that its importance is sometimes lost in professional jargon and theorizing.*]

Client: Well, it sure felt good when they saved me. I was scared, I felt guilty, but at least they came and got me.

Counselor: So you felt that help was there even though you were afraid.

Client: And you know what, one of the guys who helped get me out I thought didn't like me before. But he asked me to work for him the following week. I never thought of that before. (Ivey, 1984)

The ultimate existential issue is *survival* and finding something positive in the simple act of being-in-the-world. Those who have experienced the Vietnam war, child abuse, rape, AIDS or other terminal illness, or other trauma have all survived. Mere survival for some will be sufficient to satisfy existential needs, but the issue will be more complex for others. Resources for understanding the worldview and specific needs of trauma victims can be found in the work of Wilson (1989) on veterans, Katz (1984) on survivors of rape, Miller (1990) on child abuse, and Sue and Sue (1990) on racial discrimination.

Deciding for the Future. Although what is past is past, one can modify and change the way one thinks about it. Thinking of the past negatively is making a "decision for the past." By questioning the client's past interpretations, the therapist can help the client make a decision for the future. Those who suffer trauma often make decisions for the past—and for very good reason, since it is difficult not to focus on the negatives of trauma. The modification of attitudes, as demonstrated in the foregoing interview, undergirds much more complex survivor issues. Combining an understanding of the specific needs of trauma survivors with the basic approaches of Frankl or Lukas will give you a good foundation for helping your clients live and cope with the effects of trauma.

Frankl (1985b) reminds us that some people must live with impossible situations and impossible memories:

> This was the lesson I had to learn in three years spent in Auschwitz and Dachau: those most apt to survive the camps were those oriented toward the future, toward a meaning to be fulfilled by them in the future. . . . But meaning and purpose were only a necessary condition of survival, not a sufficient condition. Millions had to die in spite of their vision of meaning and purpose. Their belief could not save their lives, but it did enable them to meet death with heads held high. (p. 37)

Modification of attitudes cannot change the past, but it can help people live with the past and the present more intentionally. The point is to find something positive, something to live for out of and beyond the trauma experience. As a therapist or counselor, you will need a good deal of patience, strength, belief, knowledge, and power to help your clients modify their attitudes toward these impossible traumatic situations.

Paradoxical Intention

Frankl was the first therapist to use the concept of paradox. In 1929 Frankl had a phobic client who was suffering from severe agoraphobia. Analysis and other methods were not working. Improvising, Frankl suggested that instead of being afraid of fainting on the street, the patient should deliberately try to collapse. Frankl (1985a) unequivocally defines his paradoxical intention technique as "encouraging the patient to do, or wish to happen, the very things [she or] he fears—albeit with tongue in cheek." The next week the patient was cured. Frankl did not recall what he had advised, so the patient told him, "I just followed your advice, Doctor. I tried hard to faint but the more I tried, the less I could, and consequently—the fear of fainting disappeared!" Thus the technique was born.

Paradoxical intention has become an important therapeutic skill. Ascher and Turner (1979) were the first to experimentally validate the clinical effectiveness of paradoxical intention in comparison with other behavioral strategies. Prior to this work, Solyom et al. (1972) proved experimentally that paradoxical intention worked.

However, Frankl (1985a) warns of confusing paradoxical intention with so-called symptom prescription. In symptom prescription, the patient is told to exaggerate the symptom, say, a fear. In paradoxical intention, however, the patient is encouraged to wish to happen what he or she fears to happen. In other words, the fear itself is not dealt with, but rather the object of fear.

Clarifying Paradox through an Example.   Frankl's hospital had a patient suffering from a severe washing compulsion who had been washing her hands several hundred times a day. One of the doctors suggested that, instead of being afraid of bacteria, the patient should instead desire to contract an infection. She was advised to tell herself: "I can't get enough bacteria. I want to become as dirty as possible. There is nothing nicer than bacteria." The patient diligently followed this advice. She asked other patients to let her borrow from them as many bacteria as possible and came up with the resolution no longer to wash "the poor creatures" away but instead to keep them alive. None of Frankl's staff would have dreamed of recommending that this patient no longer wash her hands several hundred times a day. However, it would be in accord with "symptom prescription" to advise her to do so several thousand times a day.

Humor and Paradox.   As one can see from the above case history, "an integral element in paradoxical intention is the deliberate evocation of humor" (Lazarus, 1971). After all, a sense of humor is an aspect that logotherapy regards as a specifically human capacity, namely to be self-distancing.

Some authorities (for example, Lankton, 1980; Bandler & Grinder, 1982) argue that the client should not know that a paradoxical intervention is being used. Clinical experience and new research data suggest that clients can profit from knowing that a paradoxical technique is being used. It may even be helpful to explain to the client your theory as to why the technique works.

Dereflection

Dereflection, according to Lukas (1984), uses our ability to "forget ourselves" and brings about a therapeutic reordering of attention—turning it from the problem toward other and positive contents of our thinking. Many of us "hyper-reflect" on our problems and our negative feelings and experiences. The objective of dereflection is systematically to change the focus of our attention. Put in its most simple and direct terms, the task of the therapist is to encourage the client to think about something else other than the problem.

Refocusing Attention.   Techniques of dereflection may be as simple as encouraging a person who has lost a limb to start thinking about a new career, helping a cancer patient focus on helping others rather than on self, or encouraging a retired person to find an interesting hobby. It is true that the facts of the situation cannot be changed and that it is difficult to reframe problems of illness, age, and loneliness as having positive components. However, it is possible to find something else on which to focus one's attention.

Changing the "Meaning Core" of One's Life.   Instead of being depressed about the loss of a limb, the handicapped person, through refocusing of attention, can work toward a new goal, the cancer patient can think about others, and the aging individual may make new friends in the process of enjoying a new hobby. The concept of refocusing has many important variations that are clearly described by Frankl (1946/ 1952) in a chapter on dereflexion, in which he also devotes special attention to issues of sexual functioning. Lukas (1984) is another useful source for ideas about this concept.

Dereflection and Sexual Dysfunction.   Dereflection may be especially useful in therapy with those with sexual dysfunction. For example, impotence can be caused when the man focuses excessive attention on whether or not he will have an erection. He is hyper-reflecting on himself and his fear, which in turn causes more impotence. The logotherapist would help this client dereflect and possibly focus attention on the wife or on sexual stimuli. When one focuses attention on another, it is difficult to think about oneself; at such a time, natural autonomic functions start working effectively.

A similar approach may be used with a person suffering from insomnia. Instead of trying to fall asleep, the individual may decide to use this time to study or for an enjoyable activity. After a relatively short period of time, many clients will naturally get tired and fall asleep.

This simple technique is partly born of logic and of common-sense. However, it takes considerable creativity and expertise to find what each individual client needs to avoid hyper-reflecting on the negative. Furthermore, changing patterns of attention may require you to use modification of attitudes as well as some form of paradoxical intention.

The Appealing Technique

The appealing technique, Lukas (1989) suggests, may be effective for clients experiencing drug or alcohol detoxification or for those clients you cannot reach via other methods. The appealing technique is reminiscent of the concepts used by Alcoholics Anonymous (AA) and some drug therapy groups. In this approach, one simply appeals to the client to do better and to change. The counselor takes the position that the client's situation is not hopeless and directly attempts to bring the client to a similar awareness. For example, the drug abusing client may be asked to state out loud, "I am not helpless. I can control and direct my fate."

In some situations, with an understanding and supportive counselor or therapist, the appealing technique can work. It is clearly different from the "sophisticated" techniques of psychoanalysis or behavior therapy. Some helpers find themselves embarrassed by this approach. Some feel it does not have sufficient theoretical implications. However, if you as a helper *believe,* you will find that some clients will respond to this exhortative approach, which appeals to the human spirit. Witness the effectiveness of AA and some drug treatment programs that use similar techniques to the appealing process.

Maintaining Flexibility of Approach. Logotherapy in the application of technique is an intentional approach to change. There are theoretical and practical reasons for trying to help a client change in a certain direction, but if the first technique does not work, logotherapy does not hesitate to "mix and match" and change the approach to meet the unique human needs of the client.

Exhibit 12.1 offers a practice exercise in some dimensions of logotherapy that you may find beneficial in your own work in counseling and psychotherapy.

Exhibit 12.1

An Exercise in Logotherapy

Viktor Frankl and his colleague, Elisabeth Lukas, give almost as much attention to hearing and understanding the worldview of the client as does Carl Rogers and person-centered therapy. Thus, you can easily adapt exhibit 11.2 of the preceding chapter, "An Exercise in Person-Centered Counseling," to logotherapy.

Particularly good topics for this exercise include procrastination, a difficulty with a colleague or housemate, boredom, or concern over illness or the loss of someone important. Indicate to your real or role-played client that you are going to be talking about what the problem means to her or him and that problem solving will be secondary.

Stages 1, 2, and 3.
Rapport/Structuring, Data Gathering, Determining Outcomes

It is suggested that you use the same structure of the interview in exhibit 11.2

for the first three stages of the interview. Basically, use listening skills and the basic listening sequence to draw out the problem.

However, add one central dimension: Ask yourself and your client, "What does this mean to you?" "What does this say about your deeper values?" "Why is this important?" Ask these meaning-oriented questions after you have heard the problem defined clearly. And, as you reach the third stage of the interview and the goal is established, ask what the goal *means* to the client and why the client *values* that goal. In the process of asking questions about meaning, you will find that a new depth is added to the interview and that clients frequently start talking about their lives when before they were talking about problems. In this process you will want to add the skill of reflection of meaning. A reflection of meaning is similar to the paraphrase, but focuses more on deeper issues underlying the surface structure sentence.

Stage 4. Generating Alternative Solutions

Once having heard the client and the client's meaning, you have two central alternatives:

1. You may summarize the problem and its meaning to the client and contrast it with a summary of the ideal goal and its meaning. Through the summary you will have pointed out possible discrepancies and mixed messages in the client's meaning system. Then, through listening skills and reflection of meaning, you can encourage further self-exploration. The goal here is to discover the underlying, more deeply felt meanings guiding the client's action.
2. If the client wishes to act on meaning, select one of the four major techniques of logotherapeutic action (change of attitudes, paradoxical intention, dereflection, or the appealing technique). If the first technique does not work, try another. Logotherapy does not hesitate to try several approaches in an attempt to meet the unique needs of your client.

Out of this portion of the interview, your goal is to facilitate client examination of meaning and through the influencing approach to help your client change and act on her or his meaning system.

Stage 5. Generalization

As with other existential-humanistic orientations, logotherapy does not give extensive attention to generalization and maintenance of behavioral change. It is suggested that you may ask your client to "think about" the interview over the next few days and talk with you personally or by phone. If it seems relevant, ask your client to try one thing differently during the time period before you have a follow-up talk.

Multicultural Implications of Logotherapy

Logotherapy grew out of cultural oppression—the German treatment of Jews during the Holocaust. Frankl's powerful existential-humanistic approach appeals to the human spirit and thus is particularly adaptable to multicultural counseling and therapy. Many culturally diverse groups may find Frankl's philosophy and specific methods particularly applicable because they represent a response to personal and cultural oppression.

The listening style of Rogers is particularly compatible with Frankl's ideas, and it is easy to integrate the views of humankind put forth by Rogers and Frankl. Each was an admirer of the other's work. Such mutual respect is rare in the sometimes highly competitive world of psychological theory and practice.

Adapting Logotherapy to Multicultural Practice.   Logotherapy leaves considerable room for you to generate your own culturally relevant integration of theory and practice. Frankl would endorse drawing from traditional and meaningful helping techniques from each culture. Perhaps more than any other single theory of helping, logotherapy is represented throughout the world with commitment and passion from its adherents. Logotherapy appears to be highly adaptable to multicultural and to gender differences. It is interesting that Frankl, a male theoretician, now is represented internationally by a woman, Elisabeth Lukas.

Spirituality and Psychotherapy as Reconciliation.   The title of a recent paper by Lukas (1989) is "From Self-Actualization to Global Responsibility." In this paper she talks about "education toward responsibility" and maintains that individual self-examination is a most limited way to view therapy and counseling:

> We must be concerned about a *future worthy of human beings*. . . . This concern deserves the trouble to look up from our navels and focus our feelings on something beyond our Ego — feelings which in turn could release energies for the spiritual renaissance of our generation. (p. 5)

Lukas argues for three sensitivities: the feeling for the sacred, the feeling for the necessary, and the feeling for Otherliness. The sacred is spiritual being — our relationship with transcendence and Nature. The necessary represents our ability to deal with challenging situations — for example, trauma, oppressive situations, physical disfigurement. Life, as Frankl discovered in the Nazi concentration camp, is not all positive. We must do all we can to cope with the impossible.

The feeling for Otherliness speaks to our relations with friends, family, and strangers. "The Otherliness of the other person is not something just to be tolerated; it is, instead, something to behold, something that in fact enriches the beholder" (p. 15). Lukas stresses that we must learn to accept and appreciate the Other — "The I and the very different You can be integrated in a common We." Lukas describes logotherapy as an *agent of reconciliation*. Logotherapy seeks to reconcile us to God and Nature, to the most difficult of challenges we face, and to each other.

Fritz Perls and Gestalt Therapy

Frederick (Fritz) Perls devised Gestalt theory to fill the theoretical gaps of psychoanalysis, and he came to be regarded as a "guru" of existentialism in the 1960s. So popular was Perls that his "Gestalt Prayer"[1] was widely available in poster form:

> You do your thing, and
> I'll do my thing, and
> If by chance we meet, it's beautiful.

A relatively large group of admirers waited outside the hospital in Indianapolis when he passed away in 1970. It seemed the end of an era.

"Doing your own thing" in many ways captures the essence of Perls and his approach to therapy and explains the relationship of his movement to existentialism. Perls deeply believed that individuals who became aware of themselves and their experience in the immediacy of the here and now could become more authentic and purposeful human beings. Many of his techniques were directed to helping individual clients and groups become aware of who they were and what they really wanted.

Perls saw human nature as holistic, consisting of many varied parts that make a unique individual. We start life more or less "together," but as we grow and develop, we encounter experiences, feelings, and fears in life that cause us to lose parts of ourselves. These "splits" from the whole, or the gestalt, must be reintegrated if we are to live intentional, self-actualized lives. Thus, Gestalt therapy is centrally concerned with integrating or reintegrating our split-off parts into a whole person.

The Gestalt worldview is that people can be responsible for their actions in the world and, further, that the world is so complex that very little can be understood at any given moment. Thus, Gestalt therapy tends to focus extensively on the present-tense, immediate, here-and-now experience of the client. These two key constructs are reflections of the basic existential view.

Case Example: Gestalt Dreamwork

The following excerpt is typical of the work of Perls (1969a). In this case, he was working with a client's dream. In Gestalt dreamwork, each part of the dream is believed to represent a part of the dreamer. The task of the Gestalt therapist is to find how the parts relate together as a unity. Note particularly the consistent present-tense immediacy in the session and the willingness to direct client action. It is astonishing that these techniques, now thirty to forty years old, still catch our interest and astonish us with their power.

1. *Meg:* In my dream, I'm sitting on a platform, and there's somebody else with me, a man, and maybe another person, and — ah — a couple of rattlesnakes. And one's up on the platform, now, all coiled up, and I'm frightened. And his head's up, but he doesn't seem like he's gonna strike me. He's just sitting there and I'm frightened, and this other person says to me — uh — just, just don't disturb the snake and he won't bother you. And the other snake, the other snake's down below, and there's a dog down there.

2. *Fritz:* What is there? [*Open question*]

3. *Meg:* A dog, and the other snake.

4. *Fritz:* So, up here is one rattlesnake and down below is another rattlesnake and the dog. [*Paraphrase; note how Perls works in the present tense. The emphasis is on immediate sensorimotor and concrete experience rather than formal operational analysis.*]

5. *Meg:* And the dog is sort of sniffing at the rattlesnake. He's — ah — getting very close to the rattlesnake, sort of playing with it, and I wanna stop — stop him from doing that.

6. *Fritz:* Tell him. [*Directive*]

7. *Meg:* Dog, stop! /*Fritz:* Louder. /*Meg:* Stop! /*Fritz:* Louder. /*Meg:* (shouts) STOP! /*Fritz:* Louder. /*Meg:* (screams) STOP! [*This example is particularly representative of Gestalt repetition exercises. Repeating words again and again often leads to deeper, more emotional experience.*]

8. *Fritz:* Does the dog stop? [*Closed question*]

9. *Meg:*   He's looking at me. Now he's gone back to the snake. Now—now, the snake's sort of coiling up around the dog, and the dog's lying down, and—and the snake's coiling around the dog, and the dog looks very happy.

10. *Fritz:*   Ah! Now have an encounter between the dog and the rattlesnake. [*Directive*]

11. *Meg:*   You want me to play them?

12. *Fritz:*   Both. Sure. This is your dream. Every part is a part of yourself. [*Directive, interpretation*]

13. *Meg:*   I'm the dog. (hesitantly) Huh. Hello, rattlesnake. It sort of feels good with you wrapped around me.

14. *Fritz:*   Look at the audience. Say this to somebody in the audience. [*Directive*]

15. *Meg:*   (laughs gently) Hello, snake. It feels good to have you wrapped around me.

16. *Fritz:*   Close your eyes. Enter your body. What do you experience physically? [*Directing. This type of sensorimotor body technique is particularly emblematic of Perls and Gestalt therapy. Emotions are to be experienced immediately rather than reflected on abstractly. As such, Gestalt exercises should be used with care with children and many less verbal clients.*]

17. *Meg:*   I'm trembling. Tensing.

18. *Fritz:*   Let this develop. Allow yourself to tremble and get your feelings . . . (her whole body begins to move a little) Yah. Let it happen. Can you dance it? Get up and dance it. Let your eyes open, just so that you stay in touch with your body, with what you want to express physically . . . Yah . . . (she walks, trembling and jerkily, almost staggering) Now dance rattlesnake . . . (she moves slowly and sinuously graceful) . . . How does it feel to be a rattlesnake now? . . . [*Directive, open question. The building and magnification of sensorimotor experience are considered basic to Gestalt work.*]

19. *Meg:*   It's—sort of—slowly—quite—quite aware, of anything getting too close.

20. *Fritz:*   Hm? [*Encourager*]

21. *Meg:*   Quite aware of not letting anything get too close, ready to strike.

22. *Fritz:*   Say this to us. "If you come too close, I—" [*Directive*]

23. *Meg:*   If you come too close, I'll strike back!

24. *Fritz:*   I don't hear you. I don't believe you, yet. [*Feedback*]

25. *Meg:*   If you come too close, I will strike back!

26. *Fritz:*   Say this to each one, here. [*Directive*]

27. *Meg:*   If you come too close, I will strike back!

28. *Fritz:*   Say this with your whole body. [*Directive*]

29. *Meg:*   If you come too close, I will strike back!

30. *Fritz:*   How are your legs? I experience you as being somewhat wobbly. [*Open question, feedback. Perls was often concerned about clients' bodies being physically grounded on the earth.*]

31. *Meg:*   Yeah.

32. *Fritz:*   That you don't really take a stand. [*Interpretation*]

33. *Meg:*   Yes, I feel I'm . . . kind of, in between being very strong and—if I let go, they're going to turn to rubber.

34. *Fritz:*   Okeh, let them turn to rubber. (her knees bend and wobble) Again . . . Now try out how strong they are. Try out—hit the floor. Do anything. (she stamps

several times with one foot) Yah, now the other. (stamps other foot) Now let them
turn to rubber again. (she lets knees bend again) More difficult now, isn't it?
[*Directive, closed question*]

35. *Meg:*   Yeah.

36. *Fritz:*   Now say again the sentence, "If you come too close —" . . . (she makes an
effort) . . . (laughter) . . . [*Directive*]

37. *Meg:*   If — if you . . .

38. *Fritz:*   Okeh, change. Say "Come close." (laughter) [*Directive*]

39. *Meg:*   Come close.

40. *Fritz:*   How do you feel now? [*Open question*]

41. *Meg:*   Warm.

42. *Fritz:*   You feel somewhat more real? [*Interpretation*]

43. *Meg:*   Yeah.

44. *Fritz:*   Okeh . . . So what we did is we took away some of the fear of being in
touch. So, from now on, she'll be a bit more in touch. (pp. 162–64) [*Interpretation and the beginning of formal reflection on the experience*]

It is useful to compare Perls and Rogers on their use of microskills. In Rogerian
counseling, attending and listening skills are primary, whereas Perls predominantly
used the influencing skills of directives, feedback, and interpretation. Whereas Rogers emphasized empathy and warmth and positive regard, Perls was somewhat personally distant and remote during the session. His respect for others showed only
when they became truly themselves. Although both Rogers and Perls sought genuine
encounters with others, Rogers tended to wait patiently for them, whereas Perls de-
manded that authentic relationships develop quickly and strongly.

Central Theoretical Constructs and Techniques

Gestalt can be described as centrally concerned with the totality of the individual's
being-in-the-world. The complexity and possibility of the world can be dealt with,
according to existential thought, in a wide variety of ways. Perls chose to emphasize
here-and-now present-tense experiencing as a way to integrate people in relation to
themselves, others, and the world. There is thus a corresponding decrease in emphasis on past or future.

Perls (1969a) writes: "Whenever you leave the sure basis of the now and become
preoccupied with the future, you experience anxiety" (p. 30). Perls suggested that the
mode of being-in-the-world is to center on oneself and get in touch with one's own
existential experience; this makes for a very "I-centered" individualistic view of therapy.

The Role of Relationship

The focus of Perls on individuals making decisions alone — "doing their own thing" —
is similar to the emphasis of Rogers on self-actualization, but Perls carries the idea

considerably further. In terms of actual practice, Perls did not give much attention to the individual-in-relationship. Yet when his clients truly were able to find themselves, to identify themselves as authentically in real relationship to others, Perls would often embrace them with joy.

Thus, although Perls's system does not focus on relationships, it should be stressed that *real and authentic relationships* were important to him. In the final stages of his life, he established a Gestalt community on Vancouver Island, British Columbia. The idea of the community was to extend Gestalt ideas of the "whole" to group and community interaction. Unfortunately, Perls died before his ideas could be tested. Clearly, in his last works he was moving toward environmental and interpersonal interaction and action.

Lerman's (1991) critique of Perls is more gentle than her commentary on Rogers. She recognizes that Gestalt therapy is more concerned with environmental reality than with person-centered theory. However, she feels that Perls gave insufficient attention to the role of trauma in therapy and that he uncritically accepted a Maslow (1971) type of need hierarchy. In her view, the emphasis on self-actualization misses the importance of self-in-relation.

Gender and Multicultural Issues.   Enns (1987) gives special attention to Gestalt therapy's implications for women. She suggests that Gestalt exercises can be helpful for women in three ways: (1) helping women become aware of themselves as distinct individuals having their own power (particularly in that "I" statements are used); (2) facilitating the expression of anger through any of a variety of Gestalt exercises; and (3) enabling more choice. Gestalt therapy is highly concerned that individuals make their own choices and, as such, can be very helpful to women who have been culturally discouraged from making their own choices.

These same three choices above, however, may be less beneficial for individuals of various cultural groups. The direct personal affirmations of individual choice suggested by Perls can come into serious conflict with the cultural values of Asian-Americans and Native Americans, who may tend to believe that decision making is made in context rather than as a purely individual matter. Rigney (1981) spoke to the condition of the Australian Aboriginal, making specific comments on how unsuitable much of traditional counseling and therapy is for many cultural groups, particularly the Aboriginal.

The word *gestalt* implies that the individual is a whole in a context of family and community. It seems clear that clients of many cultures can and will respond to Gestalt interventions, if used with cultural sensitivity and an egalitarian, nonhierarchical approach. The culturally sensitive use of Gestalt therapy requires that you be sure that your client is ready and understands why you are using these particular interventions.

Gestalt Techniques

Perls was a charismatic, dynamic therapist who was trained in classical psychoanalysis but profoundly aware of its limitations. He brought his formal knowledge and a formidable clinical talent to the counseling interview. He and his coworkers have been able to document both Gestalt therapy theory and technique in a rather complete form (see Perls, Hefferline, & Goodman, 1951; Fagan & Shepherd, 1970; Perls, 1969a, 1969b). However, the most effective way to understand Gestalt therapy is to experience it.

Although Gestalt theory can be discussed in considerable detail, the primary purpose of this section is to examine some techniques for enhancing awareness of interpersonal experiencing developed by Perls and his coworkers. It can be argued that Perls's major contribution is methodological rather than theoretical. Over the years, he developed a wide range of techniques that vitalize existential experiencing.

The following techniques should always be used in a working relationship and with a full sense of ethics. *Reading about them will be of no value unless you practice them experientially.* These methods are easily integrated into interviews, regardless of theoretical orientation.

1. *Here-and-now experiencing.* Most techniques of Gestalt therapy are centered on helping the client experience the world *now* rather than in the past or future. What is done is done, and what will be will be. Although past experiences, dreams, or future thoughts may be discussed, the constant emphasis is on relating them to immediate present-tense experience. In the transcript, Perls again and again directed the client to awareness of the here and now.

2. *Directives.* Gestalt therapists constantly tell their clients what to do in the interview, although decisions for their own later action are clients' own. For example, Meg (number 5) talks in the past tense about her dream. Perls, through the simple directive "Tell him," brings the past to the present. Throughout this session, Perls constantly directs the movement of the client. Feedback (number 24), questions relating to feelings (number 30), and interpretations (number 32) give additional strength to the directives.

3. *Language changes.* Gestalt clients are encouraged to change questions to statements in the belief that most questions are simply hidden statements about oneself. For example, "Do you like me?" may actually be the statement "I am not sure that you like me." The therapist suggests that the client change questions to "I" statements. Clients are also often asked or told to change vague statements about some subject to "I" statements, thus increasing the personal identification and concreteness in the interview.

The client is frequently directed to talk in the present tense ("Be in the here and now"), as this also adds power and focus to the problem. Gestalt therapists point out that the counselor can see and understand only what is before him or her. Talking about problems is considered less effective than experiencing them directly. Although questions are generally discouraged, "how" and "what" questions are considered more acceptable than "why" questions, which often lead to intellectualization.

4. *The empty chair technique.* Perhaps the best-known and most powerful of the many Gestalt techniques, the empty chair technique is also one of the easiest to use in counseling practice. When a client expresses a conflict with another per-

son, the client is directed to imagine that the other person is sitting in an empty chair and then to talk to that person. After the client has said a few words, the counselor directs the client to change chairs and answer as if he or she were the other person. The counselor directs a dialogue between the client and the imaginary other person by constantly suggesting chair changes at critical points. Through this exercise, the client learns to experience and understand feelings more fully. The client also often learns that he or she was projecting many thoughts onto the other person.

5. *Talking to parts of oneself.* A variation of the empty chair technique is to point out client splits, immobility, or impasses to the client. The two sides of an issue, or conflicting parts within the person, are drawn out. Sometimes the therapist seeks details for clarity; at other times, the counselor moves immediately to the exercise. The two sides of the person then engage in a dialogue, using the empty chair technique. By discussing the conflicted issues reflected by the split, the person often spontaneously generates a new solution or answer.

A variation on the foregoing often occurs when the counselor notes incongruities or mixed messages in client body language or between client body language and words. In such cases, the Gestalt therapist may have the tense right hand talk to the loose left hand or the jiggling right leg talk to the upset stomach. Through such imaginative games of body dialogue, quick and important breakthroughs in understanding often occur.

6. *Top dog and underdog.* Gestalt therapists constantly search for the authoritarian and demanding "top dog," which is full of "shoulds" and "oughts." In contrast, the "underdog" is more passive, apologetic, and guilt ridden. When these two dimensions are observed, the empty chair technique or a dialogue often helps the client to understand and experience them more fully.

7. *Staying with the feeling.* When a key emotion is noted in the interview, particularly through a nonverbal movement, the Gestalt therapist will often immediately give attention to the feeling and its meaning. Perls's suggestion (number 18) to Meg to let her trembling develop exemplifies the use of this technique. *This is a simple technique, but it can be invaluable whether you are a Rogerian, a psychodynamic helper, or a feminist therapist.*

8. *Dreamwork.* In dreamwork, the Gestalt approach most closely resembles its psychoanalytic foundation. Yet, unlike psychoanalysis, Gestalt does not use dreams to understand past conflicts, but rather as metaphors to understand present-day, here-and-now living. The parts of a dream are considered as aspects of the client. Any piece (person, object, scene, or thing) of a dream is a projection of the client's experiential work. Through acting out the dream, the client can integrate the split pieces into a whole person.

Each of these techniques can be used in multicultural settings, *providing there is a base of sufficient understanding and trust between client and therapist.* For example, Gestalt dreamwork can be expanded to include the multicultural family and dream concepts mentioned in the psychodynamic chapter. When combined with Gestalt interventions, such dreamwork can be very powerful and emotional. For other examples, the empty chair technique can be used to increase a woman's or gay male's understanding of how another person may have maltreated them. The top dog/underdog technique is made to order for discussion of oppression.

Through these and other powerful techniques, Perls made an impressive impact on the practice of counseling and psychotherapy. More than any other therapist, he has been able to show that clients can rapidly be moved to deep understanding of themselves and their conditions. Although his theoretical foundations have been criticized and there is little empirical evidence validating his approach, there is no question that his work and life are an important expression of the existential-humanistic tradition.

Perls and Rogers

Like many other orientations to helping, Gestalt therapy has been influenced by the Rogerian tradition. For example, in a recent discussion of the present state of Gestalt theory, Yontef and Simkin (1989) place a greater emphasis on the relationship of client and therapist and argue for more softness, as compared with the "hard-ball" approach of Perls.

Unfortunately, research studies comparing Rogerian and Gestalt methods are virtually nonexistent. In fact, there is very little research on Gestalt therapy itself. However, opinion is that Gestalt therapy facilitates change faster than do Rogerian methods, but that it also has the potential for more destructive impact on the client if the therapist moves too fast. The Gestalt therapist is often seen by the client as a "guru," which means that the therapist has even more power. Strupp and Hadley (1976) have documented thoroughly the dangers of the charismatic therapist for fragile clients.

It seems wise, particularly for beginning counselors and therapists, to use these powerful techniques with a real sensitivity to the worldview and experience of the client. Be advised to seek specific training and supervision before implementing these techniques.

Limitations and Practical Implications of the Existential-Humanistic Tradition

As an existential-humanistic theorist, Frankl's work sometimes tends to be verbal, reflective, and formal operational in nature. Perls's direct sensorimotor approach may be inappropriate for clients who are not ready, and if Gestalt exercises are used too soon, they may even be personally and culturally offensive.

As stressed throughout this book, manipulative and insensitive therapists are the greatest danger in the field. Theories may not always be personally and culturally sensitive, but if you are aware and growing, you can almost always adapt theory to meet the needs of the client.

The powerful Gestalt activation exercises described in this chapter have become an important part of the techniques of many effective therapists of varying orientations, from cognitive-behavioral to psychodynamic and even those with a specific multi-cultural orientation. There are now relatively few individuals who practice Gestalt as a theory by itself. Transactional analysis (Berne, 1964; James & Jongeward, 1971) has incorporated many Gestalt techniques into its framework.

Current theory and practice may lead one to conclude that the balanced listening and influencing approach of Frankl may gradually come to center stage as the most prominent existential-humanistic theory. This approach deals openly and honestly with issues of pain and how to surmount these difficulties through personal action with the support of the therapist or counselor.

NOTE

1. Perls was also criticized for his individualistic approach. For example, the journal *Rough Times* (1972, *3*, p. 7) published "The Getsmart Prayer." The first three lines are the same as above, but *Rough Times* added the following as their conclusion:

> You are you and I am I,
> And if by chance we find
> Our brothers and sisters enslaved
> And the world under fascist rule
> Because we're doing our thing—
> It can't be helped.

REFERENCES

ASCHER, L. M., & TURNER, R. M. (1979). Controlled comparison of progressive relaxation, stimulus control, and paradoxical intention therapies for insomnia. *Journal of Consulting and Clinical Psychology, 47* (3), 500–508.

BANDLER, R., & GRINDER, J. (1982). *Reframing: Neurolinguistic programming and the transformation of meaning.* Moab, UT: Real People Press.

BERNE, E. (1964). *Games people play.* New York: Grove Press.

ENNS, C. (1987). Gestalt therapy and feminist therapy: A proposed integration. *Journal of Counseling and Development, 66,* 93–95.

FABRY, J. (1984). Personal communication. *International Forum for Logotherapy.*

FAGAN, J., & SHEPHERD, I. (1970). *Gestalt therapy now.* Palo Alto, CA: Science and Behavior Books.

FRANKL, V. E. (1952). *The doctor and the soul.* New York: Bantam. (Original work published 1946)

FRANKL, V. E. (1959). *Man's search for meaning.* New York: Pocket Books. (Original work published 1946)

FRANKL, V. E. (1967). *Psychotherapy and existentialism.* New York: Simon & Schuster.

FRANKL, V. E. (1969). *The will to meaning.* New York: New American Library.

FRANKL, V. E. (1985a). Logos, paradox, and the search for meaning. In M. J. Mahoney & A. Freeman (Eds.), *Cognition and psychotherapy* (pp. 259–75). New York: Plenum.

FRANKL, V. E. (1985b). *The unheard cry for meaning: Psychotherapy and humanism.* New York: Simon & Schuster.

IVEY, M. (1984). Reflection of feeling [Videotape]. In A. Ivey, N. Gluckstern, & M. Ivey, *Basic attending skills.* North Amherst, MA: Microtraining.

JAMES, M., & JONGEWARD, D. (1971). *Born to win: Transactional analysis with gestalt experiments.* Reading, MA: Addison-Wesley.

KATZ, J. (1984). *No fairy godmothers, no magic wands: The healing process after rape.* Saratoga, CA: R & E Publishers.

LANKTON, S. (1980). *Practical magic.* Cupertino, CA: Meta.

LAZARUS, A. A. (1971). Behavior therapy and beyond. New York: McGraw-Hill.

LERMAN, H. (1991). The limits of phenomenology: A feminist critique of the humanistic personality theories. In L. Brown & M. Ballou (Eds.), *Personality and psychopathology* (pp. 8–19). New York: Guilford.

LUKAS, E. (1984). *Meaningful living.* Cambridge, MA: Schenkman.

LUKAS, E. (1989, June). *From self-actualization to global responsibility.* Paper presented at the seventh World Congress of Logotherapy, Kansas City.

MAHONEY, M., & FREEMAN, A. (Eds.). (1985). *Cognition and psychotherapy.* New York: Plenum.

MASLOW, A. (1971). *The farther reaches of human nature.* New York: Viking.

MILLER, A. (1990). *The untouched key: Tracing childhood trauma in creativity and destructiveness.* New York: Doubleday.

PERLS, F. (1969a). *Gestalt therapy verbatim.* Moab, UT: Real People Press.

PERLS, F. (1969b). *In and out of the garbage pail.* Moab, UT: Real People Press.

PERLS, F., HEFFERLINE, R., & GOODMAN, P. (1951). *Gestalt therapy: Excitement and growth in human personality.* New York: Dell.

RIGNEY, M. (1981, April). *A critique of Maslow's self-actualization theory: The "highest good" for the aboriginal is relationship* [Videotape]. Aboriginal Open College, Adelaide, Australia.

SOLYOM, L., GARZA-PEREZ, J., LEDWIDGE, B. L., & SOLYOM, C. (1972). Paradoxical intention in the treatment of obsessive thoughts: A pilot study. *Comprehensive Psychiatry, 13* (3), 291–97.

STRUPP, H., & HADLEY, S. (1976). Contemporary view on negative effects in psychotherapy. *Archives of General Psychiatry, 33,* 1291–1302.

SUE, D., & SUE, D. (1990). *Counseling the culturally different* (2nd ed.). New York: Wiley.

TAUB-BYNUM, E. B. (1984). *The family unconscious.* Wheaton, IL: Quest.

TAUB-BYNUM, E. B. (1992). *Family dreams: The intimate web.* Ithaca, NY: Haworth Press.

WILSON, J. (1989). *Trauma, transformation, and healing.* New York: Brunner/Mazel.

YALOM, I., & LIEBERMAN, M. (1971). A study of encounter group casualties. *Archives of General Psychiatry, 25,* 16–30.

YONTEF, G., & SIMKIN, J. (1989). Gestalt therapy. In R. Corsini & D. Wedding (Eds.), *Current psychotherapies* (4th ed.) (pp. 323–61). Itasca, IL: Peacock.

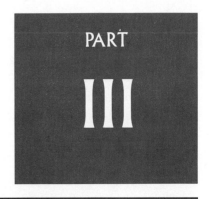

PART

III

FAMILY COUNSELING AND THERAPY
AND THEORETICAL INTEGRATION

The individual develops in a family within a cultural context. Although the primary emphasis in this book is on individual counseling and therapy, there also has been a consistent emphasis on family and multicultural considerations. An attempt has been made to demonstrate that it is possible to use both family and multicultural theories and methods in the individual interview.

The Importance of Family Theory

It is now time to consider family counseling and therapy theory as part of the mainstream in individual work. Practicing individual counseling without awareness of the main constructs of family therapy will leave you with a constricted and somewhat limited awareness of the human condition. Chapter 13 presents three basic family theories and a way to integrate these ideas with other constructions of this book.

Bowen's intergenerational family theory has much in common with psychodynamic

orientations, whereas Whitaker's symbolic/experiential approach relates to the existential-humanistic tradition. Minuchin's structural approach is unique, and his techniques are often helpful in cognitively reframing client problems. Each of the family therapy techniques described can be adapted for individual counseling and therapy. As such, they have special multicultural relevance, as the family of origin is where the client's culture manifests most clearly.

Multicultural issues are important in family therapy, and family theorists may have discovered the importance of this area before individually oriented theorists. Examples of multicultural contributions to family therapy theory, as generated by Cheatham and Attneave, are featured in the chapter.

Integrating Theory and Practice

As chapter 13 was being written, one of the authors happened to talk to a graduate student now practicing counseling and therapy. The student was asked, "Which theoretical orientation in your courses do you find more helpful now that you are really working with clients?" The graduate responded (the comments are paraphrased and summarized):

> Well at the time I finished the counseling program, I could discuss and write about the various theories fairly easily and directly. I knew how they were similar and how they differed. Now that I work with *real clients,* I find that I've integrated theory in such a way that I seldom think of it anymore. I'd be hard pressed to know which theory is my favorite, but I do know "what works" with various people I see.
>
> Psychodynamic theory helps me conceptualize clients and their developmental history. I never think of Rogers anymore, but somehow I know he is

with me. I find that cognitive-behavioral techniques work, and I wish I had learned more of them when I had the chance. But my clients are increasingly culturally different now, and I feel less able to work with people whose background is different from my own. Some workshops I've completed on family therapy concepts have been especially helpful.

You will be asked in chapter 14 to summarize key theoretical constructs in a brief fashion and generate your own ideas about counseling and psychotherapy. While you do this, be aware that the field is changing and growing. You will be a part of that growth. This book, now in its third edition, is very different from what it was ten years ago. With your help and participation, the field will continue to evolve and adapt to the needs of its clients for years to come.

Family Counseling and Therapy: Theoretical Foundations and Issues of Practice

Sandra A. Rigazio-DiGilio

CHAPTER GOALS

The goals of this chapter are to:

1. Describe the systemic worldview that undergirds family therapy approaches to treatment.

2. Present the central constructs of family theory, along with a description of healthy family functioning and normative life-span events.

3. Stress the importance of a multicultural perspective when providing counseling and psychotherapy to families.

4. Discuss the basics of four family therapy models.

5. Demonstrate the underlying conceptual connection between individual counseling, family therapy, and the network therapy model emphasized at several points in this text.

Why Family Therapy?

When asked how to treat common mental or behavioral dysfunctions such as anxiety, depression, and eating disorders, the traditional approach has been individual psychotherapy and counseling. First-force psychodynamic theory, second-force cognitive-behavioral theory, and third-force humanistic theory all have their origins in the focus on the individual.

However, it is clear that the individual lives in a family and multicultural context. Fourth-force multicultural counseling and therapy is founded on this fact. Furthermore, the supporting foundational theories, such as empathy dimensions, microskills, and decisional counseling, all give prominence to the development of the individual in a family context. You have also seen that psychodynamic, cognitive-behavioral, and existential-humanistic theory is coming to an increasing awareness of these issues as well.

In the 1950s, the work of pioneering family therapists was virtually unknown among individual counselors and therapists. The early work in family therapy was based on a systemic conceptualization called *cybernetics* and the anthropologist Gregory Bateson emerged as a leading theoretician. Cybernetics points out that each action, whether individual or family, reverberates throughout an entire system of relationships.

A significant breakthrough occurred when Bateson and his colleagues documented that some severe psychiatric disorders could be accounted for by an analysis of family communication patterns. The group labeled this concept the *double bind hypothesis* and clearly demonstrated the significant role of family dynamics (Bateson et al., 1956). Bateson documented that clients treated within a family context suffered fewer relapses and improved more quickly than clients treated individually.

This work, and the efforts of other theoreticians and practitioners who recognized the need to enlist the family's support for change, laid the groundwork for an alternative form of treatment that included families. This alternative is now being enlarged to encompass networks of individuals who may have an impact on the client's functioning and recovery. Now, when asked how to treat issues such as anxiety, eating disorders, drug abuse, and many other mental health issues, the answer often includes family therapy.

The Systemic Worldview

What was the essence of the shift from an individualistic perspective to a family context perspective? How does this alternative worldview affect the conceptualization of illness and treatment? Isn't a systemic worldview equivalent to an individual worldview, only multiplied by the number of members in a family? These and other questions will be examined in this section.

The traditional, *psychological* worldview focuses on the individual as the primary actor, with all others relegated to supporting roles. The *systemic* worldview considers the family as the primary unit and holds that all members of the family are important contributors to its functioning. Families and larger systems, such as networks, are observable through the structure of relationships, rules, and roles.

1. *Relationships.* Some practitioners have considered the family to include not only family members, but also relatives and friends (see Speck & Attneave, 1973). As such, a systemic worldview is concerned with relationships both inside and outside the family. Systemic theory holds that each unit is a subsystem of an even larger system. For example, a person is a subsystem of a family, which is a subsystem of a network, which is a subsystem of a community, which is a subsystem of a nation, which is a subsystem of a culture, and so on.

2. *Rules.* Families are viewed as systems, and intrafamilial patterns of communication are the focal point for understanding family functioning. The family's use of routinized and regulated communication assists each member to make meaning of life within the family. Examples of routinized communication are the simple exchanges you have with your family when you come to breakfast, or how you know to end a conversation when the TV is turned on. Through observation of repeating patterns of communication, family therapists learn the unconscious and conscious rules under which a family operates.

3. *Roles.* The roles members are permitted to fulfill within a system are also communicated to each person. Bateson found that the most vulnerable member of certain families was often given the role of the *identified patient.* The roles of family mascot, peacemaker, and gatekeeper are just a few of the expected ways of behaving that individual members might perform in a family or network.

Cultural Impact and Extensions of Family Systems

This definition of the family as a system with specified relationships, roles, and rules applies to a wide variety of family types (gay and lesbian, single-parent, blended, and nuclear). Furthermore, in African-American, Latina/o, and Native American cultures, the extended family and even the broader network of relationships may represent the family. You will also find family dynamics in living arrangements such as college dormitories and group homes. A promising new area of consultation and treatment is in the business community, where many work groups operate much like dysfunctional families.

Cultural expectations infuse every family and group experience. Children in Western society are encouraged to excel on an individual basis, be it in sports, school, charm, or physical looks. Children in China are encouraged to excel in cooperative activities that benefit first the community, then the family, and then the self. Culture, because it is manifest in all that we are exposed to, becomes a significant ingredient in our construction process.

The systemic worldview has been the touchstone of the family therapy movement. Cottone (1991) reports that this worldview is also infiltrating other disciplines of mental health such as group, school, and rehabilitation counseling. Further, Cottone notes that all therapists/counselors should be aware of this worldview and cognizant of the treatment implications of a systemic perspective, even for individual counseling.

Central Constructs of Family Theory

The primary construct of family theory is the *system*. For family counseling and therapy, the family is the system of focus. The term *family* means different things to different people. Some corporations consider themselves "families," whereas two elderly siblings living together might conceive of "their family" as only their offspring. The family worldview is multicultural and open in nature: a family is simply a group that lives together in some significant way.

Family Developmental Life Cycle

A sequence of stages of family development over the life span has been utilized by family theorists to provide an explanatory context for the specific tasks family groups must master over time. This is an important contribution in that issues and concerns faced by families vary over the developmental cycle. Family assessment and treatment stress the value of knowing key developmental tasks and life stages of the family group.

When counseling any individual or family, it is important to know what is going on developmentally. For example, you may be working with a European-American teenage client just starting to engage in drug abuse. Developmentally, this teen may be working with issues of identity and intimacy, but what is going on in the family? You may find that the parents have just filed for divorce, thus disrupting the life cycle. Family theory would argue that it is naive to treat the teen without awareness of what is occurring in the family.

Key points in the family life cycle often bring a client into treatment. For example, the developmental stage of adolescents leaving home, or of retirement, often can create conflict in the family, which can express itself in various family members as individuals. Table 13.1 presents a life-cycle model that has been adapted from the work of Haley (1979) and Carter and McGoldrick (1988).

Each of the six transition points listed in table 13.1 must also be considered within a cultural context to give a full appreciation of the stress families experience at critical life junctures. The launching of children for lives on their own, for example, is handled very differently in different cultural contexts. For example, a midwestern Swedish-Canadian may be expected to move out on his or her own very directly and quickly, whereas an Italian-Canadian or Chinese-Canadian may be expected to live in the home until marriage. Each culture's way of handling this important family transition can result in varying types of issues.

It is particularly important that you be aware of your own cultural expectations regarding these developmental stages. For example, imagine the issues of a counselor of Swedish background imposing her or his values on the Italian or Chinese, or vice versa. Healthy family functioning in one culture may be viewed as potentially pathological by another.

Table 13.1   The Stages of the Family Life Cycle

Developmental Stage	Emotional Process of Transition	Separation and Attachment Issues
Young adulthood	Accepting emotional and financial responsibility for self.	Increasing attachment with peers. Separation from family of origin. Selection of mate.
New couple	Commitment to new system formation.	Attachment to mate and new friends. Separation from parents. Attachment to in-laws. Reattachment to parents.
Childbirth and childrearing	Accepting new members into the system.	Separation from mate and attachment to infant. Renegotiation of relations with parents, in-laws, and peers. Beginning detachment from child as school begins.
Middle marriage	Increasing flexibility of system boundaries to include children's independence and grandparents' frailties.	Progressive separation from children. Increased reattachment with mate or further separation. Refocus on midlife issues.
Leaving home	Accepting a variety of ways to exit and enter the family system.	Children separate from parents. Increased reattachment with mate. Beginning attachment to child's mate. Renegotiation of relationship with family of origin, in-laws, and peers.
Families in later life	Accepting the shifting of generational roles.	More attachment to mate. Adult children reattach as caregivers. Dealing with loss of spouse, siblings, or peers. Preparing for own death.

SOURCE: B. Carter and M. McGoldrick, The Changing Family Life-Cycle: A Framework for Family Therapy, © 1988. Needham Heights, MA: Allyn & Bacon. Used with permission.

Healthy Family Functioning

The primary function of the healthy family is to provide stability for its members while at the same time changing to adapt to new situations. The characteristics of functional families that facilitate this ability to support family members and respond to needs for change are defined by Bochner and Eisenberg (1987) as:

1. A strong sense of trust. Family members do not engage in strong oppositional attitudes and avoid blaming each other.
2. Enjoyment. Healthy families enjoy humor, wit, and spontaneity.
3. Lack of preoccupation with themselves. Family members do not overanalyze their issues, looking for hidden motives. Life is not taken too seriously.
4. Maintenance of firm, yet flexible boundaries. Optimal families have strong parental coalitions and clear relationships with other subsystems inside and outside the family.

Healthy families recognize the *interdependence* of family members and strive to provide support for individual as well as family growth. Relationships are important to healthy families, and these family bonds are considered simultaneously fragile, yet capable of withstanding extreme pressure. Adaptive families are capable of making adjustments in their rules, communications, and behavioral patterns to accommodate change, while at the same time not disrupting supportive intrafamilial roles and relationships.

The definition of a healthy family must be general, because no one type, organizational structure, or relational configuration typifies optimal family functioning. The family unit is the culture bearer and we need to remember that the nature of the family and its concepts of health vary widely among cultures.

Multicultural Issues in Family Therapy

As emphasized in chapter 2, a significant component of our self-concept is derived from our ethnic heritage. Often, when asked to describe ourselves, we use our family's nationality as a primary descriptor: "I am Irish, Jewish, Puerto Rican, Japanese, African-American." McGoldrick, Pearce, and Giordano (1982) note that until recently, ethnicity has been largely ignored by family therapists.

Attitudes toward Mental Health and Treatment

Research indicates that ethnicity is a filter through which families and individuals understand and interpret their symptoms, their beliefs about the cause of their illness, their attitudes toward helpers, and their preferred treatment methods (Giordano & Giordano, 1977; Tseng & McDermott, 1981). For example, Italian and Jewish family members may use their tendency toward emotional expressiveness in sharing suffering, whereas those from Irish and British backgrounds may tend to pull into themselves and not discuss their feelings with others.

Attitudes toward mental health professionals also vary. Italians, in general, rely primarily on the family and seek professional assistance only as a last resort. The church is the only extrafamilial institution that many African-Americans trust and feel safe with when they are in need of help (Cheatham & Stewart, 1990; Hines & Boyd-Franklin, 1982). Exhibit 13.1 explores family therapy in the African-American context. Many Puerto Ricans, Chinese, Norwegians, and Iranians experiencing psychological stress often report physical symptoms and seek medical rather than mental health services. Research indicates that Irish, African-Americans, and Norwegians tend to place blame for their issues on themselves, whereas Greeks, Iranians, and Puerto Ricans tend to blame others for their issues (McGoldrick, Pearce, & Giordano, 1982).

Exhibit 13.1

Family Therapy with African-American Families

Cheatham and Stewart (1990) contend that therapies with the most promise for serving African-Americans are those that set aside abstract theoretical notions of how therapy is done. Models that adopt active, intervention-oriented strategies emphasizing social functioning over inner feelings are more appropriate. The mental health professional needs to attend to the specifics of the African-American's historic and cultural experiences, particularly an awareness of the history and presence of racism in North America.

Additionally, the culturally sensitive family therapist should be aware of the important roles that extended family members and social institutions (particularly the church) play in the lives of African-American families. These external agents and agencies can be causes of stress or support, and their influence needs to be considered in the solution-determination process. The following five elements of Cheatham's intervention model address the modifications to

family work he feels are prerequisites to success.

1. *Discussion of Role and Expectancy.* What the family and the therapist expect to happen in and as a result of therapy needs to be discussed and clarified. The issue of power must also be recognized and negotiated. The therapist can facilitate this process by refraining from familiarity with the family until given permission. This means that the formal salutations of Mr., Mrs., or Ms. should be used until the family invites you to use first names. In general, use the given name and avoid nicknames. Changes in the times and location of therapy communicate a willingness on the part of the therapist to modify the power quotient. Difference in therapist ethnic background from that of the family should be discussed, particularly if the therapist is not African-American.

2. *Identification and Interpretation of the Situation.* The therapist should be mindful that the family cultural norms and values are important and that a good deal of pride attends to them. As the family begins to define and explore the presenting issue, the sensitive therapist should facilitate this exploration in a manner that does not violate the family's sense of cultural propriety. Cheatham advocates empowering African-American families to evaluate the situation *within their cultural context.*

3. *Resource Inventory.* Cheatham has families conduct a resource inventory. This is similar to the positive asset search of microskills or Rogers's positive regard. It is critical to consider those persons (and networks) who will assist in the resolution process who may not be present during the family sessions.

4. *Trying Out for Legibility.* The next stage is to assist the family to enact and own the plan. Is the family able to *read* and *understand* the plan? The therapist can facilitate skill transfer and affirm the family's positive self-expectations through the use of guided practice and corrective feedback. The therapist must be skilled and conscientious in efforts to provide the family with culture-relevant and culture-specific reinforcers and suggestions that are important to the unique family.

5. *Evaluation.* The final stage is evaluation, with family members, of the adequacy of the solution. Are the new behaviors working as well as was originally expected? Are there other issues that the family would now like to work on? How will the family handle a relapse? As necessary, the process returns to the identification and interpretation stage and then proceeds sensitively through each of the subsequent stages.

The Definition of Family

Who comprises the family also differs across ethnic groups. The intact nuclear family is associated with the Northern European culture. Italians extend the membership of the family to include three to four generations and may consider godparents and close friends as part of the family. The Chinese take this extended view one step further to include all living or deceased ancestors and descendents as members of the family. African-Americans also view the family from a multigenerational perspective. Some Native Americans consider the entire membership of their community as their family (Attneave, 1969).

Although these generalizations have been documented by sociologists, psychologists, and family researchers, we must remember that many families today are, in fact, a union of individuals from different cultures. Many marriages result from the attractive differences a person of another ethnic group offers (for example, Spanish expressiveness may combine with Norwegian stability). The role of the family counselor/therapist today is often to help the family explore the influence of ethnic heritage and belief systems, and to differentiate those thoughts and behaviors from personal attacks on the spouse (Falicov, 1983). Consider the following example.

Edward and Maria, a Greek/Italian couple married for one year, entered counseling because of the "constant conflict and tension" they were experiencing. In the first session, Edward provided a reserved critique of Maria's dramatic nature, labeling her as "hysterical and impulsive." Maria immediately countered with a louder complaint about Ed's "self-controlled, judgmental, and distant" way of talking with her. By the time treatment was initiated, both were convinced that their partners were being intentionally hurtful and wondered if they were still loved by the other. An essential component of treatment involved helping both Edward and Maria understand their behaviors within an ethnic context.

Although the list of examples of cultural differences could go on for chapters, it is important to note fundamental assumptions that ground the work of a culturally sensitive family counselor/therapist:

- Be aware of his or her own ethnic heritage.
- Avoid stereotyping members of any ethnic background.
- Demonstrate empathy for members of other cultures.
- Realize that ethnicity may be an essential ingredient in a treatment plan.

Network Therapy

Attneave has also developed an action-oriented form of extended family therapy. As described by Speck and Attneave (1973), network therapy (NT) stresses the importance of *interdependency* within the social ties of natural support systems found in families, tribes, clans, and other community groups, such as schools, church congregations, and service organizations. At first, Attneave's work was primarily with Native Americans, but it was later adapted to treat inner-city families when she worked with Minuchin, Haley, and Speck at the Philadelphia Child Guidance Clinic. Currently, basic concepts of network therapy have been used to frame social policy in Great Britain and Scandinavia.

The primary goal of network therapy is to empower people to cope with life crises with the support of their natural social relationships. This treatment involves convening groups of relatives, friends, neighbors, coworkers, and oftentimes personnel from other human service agencies to work on the issue. Network interventions have been proven to offer a better understanding of the issue, more open and creative issue solving, more efficient coordination of community resources, and an increased likelihood that the benefits will be experienced by more than just the identified client (LaFromboise & Fleming, 1990).

The primary focus of this therapy is to enable the group to renew itself over and over again, as new needs and issues emerge. This concept of *group renewal* is viewed as a cycle having six phases: retribalization (group consensus), polarization (activating conflicting positions within the system), mobilization (channeling energy constructively), depression (working through resistance), breakthrough, and finally exhaustion/elation. Network therapy's emphasis on the larger social context has profound implications for family counseling and therapy, feminist therapy, and mental health services.

Major Theories of Family Therapy

The field of family therapy has experienced an explosion of treatment models since the early 1970s, and it would be impossible to cover each in depth. This section summarizes some key theoretical frameworks. Family therapy is moving toward an integration of the various techniques. Just as it is recommended that you become conversant with the major theories of individual therapy, family theorists are now advocating that you gradually become skilled in multiple orientations.

However, let us first examine an overview of the multiple approaches available. Table 13.2 presents a worldview classification system that divides the systemic therapies into three categories: historical, existential, and interactional.

Table 13.2 Classification of Systemic Therapies

Perspective/Orientation	Representative Theorists/Models
Historical	
Historical theories view the family as shaped by past forces and events.	M. Bowen—intergenerational family therapy N. Ackerman—psychoanalytic J. Framo—psychoanalytic D. & J. Scharff—object relations
Existential	
Existential theories focus on understanding and expanding each individual's subjective experience, including family members and the treating therapist.	C. Whitaker—symbolic/experiential A. Napier—symbolic/experiential V. Satir—process/communication R. Levant—client-centered W. Kempler—Gestalt
Interactional	
Interactional theories principally focus on identifying and expanding cognitive understanding, behavioral sequences, and family rules and structures.	S. Minuchin—structural P. Watzlawick—strategic M. Selvini-Palazzoli—Milan J. Haley—structural and strategic G. Patterson—behavioral R. Stuart—behavioral R. Liberman—marital J. Alexander—functional B. & L. Guerney—relationship enhancement C. Anderson—psychoeducational

SOURCE: Adapted from Grunebaum and Chasin (1982).

For illustrative purposes, one model from each of the three categories will be explained. Information about the major contributors to the approach, a brief description of the theoretical constructs and treatment goals, and an outline of the therapeutic techniques associated with each model will be described. Following this review, an integrative framework based on systemic cognitive-developmental therapy (SCDT) (Rigazio-DiGilio & Ivey, 1991) will be presented.

Historical Perspective: Intergenerational Family Therapy

Bowen (1960) was a leading proponent of the intergenerational approach. He and his colleagues at Georgetown University articulated a concise theory that explicates the process of individual *differentiation* within the family context. More than anyone else, this group has shown us how family behaviors, thoughts, and feelings are passed from one generation to the next.

Central Theoretical Constructs

The central concept of Bowenian theory is the *emotional system*. This concept refers to the governing dynamics that control the functioning of a system, such as reactions to the environment, relationships, biological needs, and feeling states. All individuals have their own emotional system, and all families have a collective emotional system. This emotional system is similar to the concept of family unconscious as described by Taub-Bynum in chapters 7 and 8.

Bowen states that within this system there are two primary opposing forces that shape and direct the behavior of the members of that system. The force within a system that pulls members toward each other is labeled a togetherness force or *fusion*. The pull to be together can be so extreme in some families that the members cannot function without each other.

The second force in the system propels individuals to seek their own individuality. Bowen uses the term *differentiation* to describe the ability of an individual to separate emotions from cognitions, thereby retaining some choice between behavior governed by thinking and behavior governed by emotional reactivity. Mature individuals, according to Bowen, are able to avoid being overwhelmed by whatever emotions are predominant in the family. Although Bowen did not emphasize cultural context, the level and method of differentiation vary from culture to culture.

Bowenian theory conceives that symptoms currently being manifested by an identified patient have their origins in failed differentiation attempts that occurred in previous generations. This *multigenerational transmission process* influences interactional patterns of the current family. Parents tend to transmit their level of undifferentiation to their children, and these children, as adults, continue the transmission process. For example, Sorenson and Rutter (1991) suggest that family factors such as family history of suicide attempts and mental disorders are significantly related to individual suicidal ideation and attempts.

The intensity of family disruption due to the multigenerational transmission process is related to two factors: the degree of immaturity or undifferentiation of the parents and the level of stress or anxiety the family experiences. Research efforts by Sabatelli and Anderson (1991) indicate that the emotional patterns of parental and marital functioning do influence an adolescent's ability to appropriately separate from the family. Adolescents who reported the highest level of depression were those who perceived their parents' marital relationship to be most dysfunctional.

Bowen also noted that unstable, two-person systems under stress seek to regain balance by bringing in another person. This new *triangle* is the basic building block in a family's emotional system. Triangles are not limited to three separate individuals. They can be made up of entities such as work, substance abuse, friends, or children as the third side of the triangle. Triangles are used to project the couple's anxiety onto another, thus relieving the twosome of the unwelcome stress. The role of scapegoat is often the third member of a family triangle, and it is not uncommon to see a parent triangulated by two siblings.

Central Treatment Goals

According to Bowen, the goal of therapy is to assist family members to achieve higher levels of differentiation of self. Specifically, individuals should be able to separate themselves from their families and become more inner directed and autonomous. The family should be able to support both the cognitive and emotional development of each member in a fashion that does not trap that member into only one way of thinking or behaving. Needless to say, this orientation is obviously European-American in orientation and would not be culturally appropriate for all clients. Bowen's theories need to be adapted, but nonetheless the general constructs are useful in multicultural situations.

The therapist's role is to help the family evaluate intergenerational issues. It is here that Bowenian theory becomes particularly relevant to multicultural counseling. You can expect clients, regardless of cultural background, to enact their cultural history with you in the individual and family session.

To facilitate multigenerational understanding, the therapist helps clarify relational boundaries around the spouses and enables the family to identify triangles and family projection processes. The therapist assumes a position outside the family in order to avoid being triangulated. The use of *"I" statements* helps the therapist stay grounded in her or his own experience and models differentiation for the family.

Primary Therapeutic Techniques

Genogram. The genogram is one of the most useful diagnostic tools in the field and is utilized extensively by Bowenian family therapists and increasingly by individual counselors as well. The genogram is a graphic representation of the multigenerational family tree. When used effectively, it can render covert family patterns overt. Genograms can help families see the intergenerational transmission process at work and identify existing triangles. By using *focusing skills,* the therapist can make recurring themes and behaviors that flow from one generation to the next become visible. Genograms can be effectively integrated with individual or family counseling to help clients concentrate on family and cultural influences.

Exhibit 13.2 presents the basic symbols and rules needed to complete a genogram and provides a family genogram exercise. Demographic, psychological, medical, and behavioral information about each member is added to the chart along with any pertinent qualities of the family relationships. Figure 13.1 shows a completed genogram.

Exhibit 13.2

Tools and Information for Completion of a Genogram

Demographic Data

1. Write out the names of all family members for at least two or three generations.
2. Fill in the dates of birth, marriage, separation, divorce, death, and other significant life events.
3. Make notations regarding occupations, places of residence, illness, and changes in life course.

Basic Relationship Symbols

Close	≡≡≡
Enmeshed	≣≣≣
Estranged	—//—
Enmeshed and conflictual	AAAAAA
Distant	- - - - - -
Conflictual	MWWW
Separated	—/—

Family Genogram Exercise

As a counselor, it is important to be aware of your own intergenerational issues, because these issues can affect your life, and can be stimulated by your clients. To increase your conscious understanding of your family's legacy, take some time to complete a family genogram.

Begin by talking to your immediate and extended family. Go through family memorabilia. Then using the above symbols, begin mapping your family genogram. Be sure to include your own perceptions of the relationships with and between family members as well as those of other family members. It's always interesting to see how different family members view each other. Share the genogram with your family and look for patterns and themes. Then share it with a friend or someone who is not a member of your family.

Compare the insights gleaned from the family exploration and the nonfamily description. Which was easier? Which generated more emotions? What themes are important in your family? What personal and professional issues were raised by this exercise?

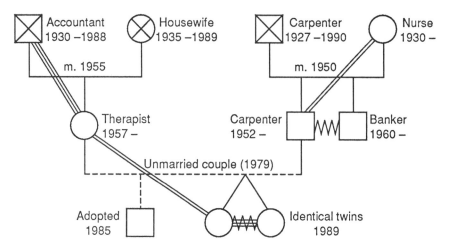

Figure 13.1   A Completed Genogram

In addition to the genogram, other questions, assignments, and activities are presented to the family in order to discover the nature of the family emotional system. Interventions are aimed at assisting family members to work through the differentiation process through cognitive analysis as opposed to emotional reactions. Bowen encourages clients to "go home again," not for confrontational purposes, but to use the knowledge learned in therapy to truly see their family-of-origin members as they themselves do.

Existential Perspective: Symbolic/Experiential Family Therapy

Basically a clinical approach, experiential/symbolic family therapy emphasizes the here-and-now phenomena of the encounter of family and therapist. Whitaker (1967) and Napier (1978) are the most notable proponents of this approach. Experiential therapists mainly focus on the present experience of the family, as opposed to exploring the family's past.

Central Theoretical Constructs and Goals

Whitaker believes that the *symbolic meaning* family members attach to their intrapersonal and intrafamilial life are the essential structures that influence behavior and emotions. How one feels and thinks about the family is of utmost importance. If a mother believes her daughter is devious, no matter what that daughter does, the mother will always suspect her daughter's motives. Symbolic/experiential therapists consistently attempt to identify and explore these explicit and often implicit images.

Theory does not have a significant role in symbolic/experiential therapy. Unlike Bowen, Whitaker adheres to the belief that therapy should be creative, spontaneous, and authentic. He asserts that rigid theories of how therapists should behave and how families should interact are oversimplifications of reality and do more harm than good.

The primary task of the experiential therapist is to help the family become aware of the underlying symbolism that is influencing family functioning. The ultimate purpose of this work is to assist families to support the creative efforts of their members to balance the need for belongingness and the freedom to individuate. Providing opportunities for family members to examine their symbolic interpretations of family life, to play, and to feel more powerful as a team are all objectives of this approach.

Primary Therapeutic Techniques

Whitaker advocates a *cotherapy* or *multitherapist team* approach to family therapy. He believes this allows for greater creativity, buffers the possibility of becoming enmeshed in the family's pathology, and provides peer support for thinking about the therapeutic situation. Some additional specific intervention techniques that experiential family therapists have used to help the family become aware of their symbolic structures are described below. Each of these techniques is aimed at helping the family redefine symptoms as efforts on the part of the identified patient to grow and to bring out the family's creative abilities in the service of finding new alternatives for healthy development.

Family Sculpture.   A family member is asked to position and direct the other members in a typical scene that might be evident when the issue is observable. This technique can help answer such questions as Where are people in relation to one another? What are they doing? and How do they act? The technique also affords the other family members insight into the perception of the sculptor.

Family Art Therapy.   Utilizing art therapy techniques, experiential therapists ask family members to draw images of their family. Individual or joint drawings can be generated and then explored to gain insight into the family's functioning. One technique, "joint family scribble," requires each member to make a quick scribble. The whole family then incorporates the scribble into a unified picture. The relational implications of this activity are considerable. How does each person feel as represented by the scribble, and who do they feel connected to as represented by the finished picture?

Symbolic Drawing of Family Life Space.   Using the psychodrama technique of a sociogram, the therapist draws a large circle. The space inside the circle represents the family, whereas all other persons and institutions not considered part of the family are placed outside the circle. Family members are directed to draw a small circle that represents where they are in relation to others.

The Family Floor Plan.   As with the other experiential techniques mentioned here, the family floor plan is used for two purposes: first, to get the family comfortable with expression, and second, as a diagnostic tool. Members are asked to draw the floor plan for their current family. Sometimes parents are also asked to draw the floor plan of their family of origin.

The Use of the Self.   The essential element of a successful intervention, as defined by Whitaker, is the *use of the self* by the therapist. Whitaker believes that no theory can truly capture the evolution of the therapeutic process. Therapists must move beyond rigid interventions or theories and rely on their own feelings, impulses, and ideas, which are generated in the interactional relationships with the family.

Interactional Perspective: Structural Family Therapy

Minuchin is noted for having popularized and legitimized the use of family therapy. His book, *Families and Family Therapy* (1974), became a handbook for most practicing family therapists. The book articulated a clear way of diagramming family structure using easily understood maps and symbols.

Central Theoretical Constructs

Structural family theory provides the practitioner with a clear map of what constitutes functional family life. This map can be used to determine the degree of variance presented by any family. With this, a direction for treatment can be developed. There are obvious cultural and gender limitations inherent in this map that need to be recognized by those who use the model.

Structural therapy's basic family map reflects the *traditional hierarchical* structure that Minuchin sees as universal. In the hierarchical organization, parents exercise more power than children, and older children have more responsibilities as well as privileges than younger ones. Most often families seeking therapy are not aligned in such a hierarchical structure and have developed their own idiosyncratic family structure, which is generating symptomatic behavior. In effect, the children sometimes run the family, or a parent may be aligned with a child against another parent.

Three significant concepts bring meaning to the interpretation of family organization: structure, subsystems, and boundaries.

Structure.   All families have many rules that determine the family structure. These rules translate into an invisible set of functional demands that organizes the way family members relate to one another. The behavior patterns established by the rules form structures that position various family members and subsystems into an organized unit.

Subsystems.   Minuchin has outlined three types of subsystems: the *spouse subsystem,* the *parental subsystem,* and the *sibling subsystem.* Subsystems can also be organized around other issues, such as gender, generation, common interests, and functions. Any member of the family is her or his own subsystem and is also a member of many other subsystems, such as dyads, triads, or larger groups.

Theoretical groupings of parental, spousal, and sibling subsystems are often less powerful than the real subsystems that have been established over time in the family. Subsystems may cross generational lines and include various combinations of parents and children. Many times families seeking treatment will present with an organization that reinforces a child in the parental subsystem.

Boundaries.   Boundaries delineate individuals and subsystems and define the amount and kind of contact allowed between members of the family. Boundaries can vary in the degree of firmness and flexibility. Some subsystem boundaries are very permeable or diffuse. In this case, the boundaries between individuals are so open that the relationship is described as *enmeshed.* Children may rule the family. Excessive cohesiveness could lead to a lack of individuation of family members.

Another type of dysfunctional boundary is the impermeable or *rigid* type. Here communication and affect are blocked at the boundary. Parents with rigid boundaries may foster autonomy in their children but not supply or receive affection. In this type of family structure, family members must search elsewhere for support and nurturance.

The final type is the healthy or *clear* boundary, which is firm yet flexible. Clearly defined boundaries between subsystems help maintain separateness, while also emphasizing a sense of belongingness. In this situation, the autonomy of members is not sacrificed, and at the same time, care, support, and involvement are available as needed.

Central Treatment Goals

The primary goal of the interactional approach is to restructure the family's system of rules and interactional patterns in order to improve its flexible adaptation to the environment. Therapeutic change is viewed as the process of releasing family members from rigidly defined positions within the system. The restructuring process frees family members to utilize new resources and to enhance their ability to cope with stress and conflict. The aim of the therapist is to help the family realign the structural composition of its interactions and to work with family members until they are able to maintain this new configuration on their own.

Primary Therapeutic Interventions

Three major structural interventions include relabeling or reframing, straightforward directives, and unbalancing techniques.

Relabeling, or Reframing.   Relabeling, or reframing, is a form of positive connotation that translates the symptomatic behavior as adaptive behavior. In this fashion, the family's understanding of the behavior is shifted, thus freeing the members to think and behave differently. This new interpretation releases the potential for a more appropriate solution to the issue. Relabeling can be used to connote specific individual behavior, for example, "Johnny's excessive drinking is a cry for help" or "Your father's anger when you violate the curfew is a sign of his love for you." Reframes can also be used to relabel family behavior.

Straightforward Directives and Homework Assignments.   Directives and homework assignments are clear requests for the family to take specific action. Some directives include asking family members to directly discuss the issue or to identify the negative aspects of change. Homework assignments may engage the parents to not make any decisions about the children until all have discussed the issue.

Unbalancing Techniques.   These are used to create a disequilibrium within the family so that the family's symptomatic patterns are disrupted. For example, the therapist may side with one family member or subsystem to move the family to a new interpretation of the issue. Specifically, the myth that boys do not show emotion may be unbalanced when a male therapist sides with the mother and tells the son "It's alright to cry." In this type of unbalancing, the weight of the therapist's authority is used to break a stalemate by supporting one of the sides in a conflict. Unbalancing can explode dysfunctional myths that render the family ineffective.

Exhibits 13.3 and 13.4 provide an exercise in structural assessment and research findings on structural family therapy, respectively.

Systemic Cognitive-Developmental Therapy: An Integrative Framework

Systemic cognitive-developmental therapy (SCDT) emphasizes the importance of providing a suitable therapeutic environment for facilitating family growth (Rigazio-DiGilio & Ivey, 1991). SCDT is oriented toward providing:

Exhibit 13.3

Exercise on Structural Assessment

1. Think of a rule that you know exists in your family. For instance, who must do a certain task or play a certain role, or who isn't permitted to do a particular task or play a certain role?

2. What evidence do you have that this rule exists? What behavior, feelings, and thoughts are controlled by this rule?

3. How and where did this rule originate?

4. How does the family react when attempts are made to change the rule?

5. What structural changes would your family have to make in order to revise this rule?

6. If you were a therapist treating this family, what structural interventions would you initiate?

=== **Exhibit 13.4** ===

Research in Family Therapy

In the mid-1970s Minuchin and his colleagues (1978; 1975) presented two well-designed studies that demonstrated family therapy's success in the treatment of anorexia nervosa. Their work, perhaps more than any other, initiated research on the efficacy of this new approach.

Some example studies in which family therapy has been found more effective than individual approaches include:

- Substance abuse (Stanton, Todd, & Associates, 1982).
- Conduct disorders (Patterson, Chamberlain, & Reid, 1982; Fleishmann, 1981).
- Psychosomatic disorders (Minuchin & Fishman, 1981; Schwartz, Barrett, & Saba, 1985).
- Marital therapy (Beach & O'Leary, 1985; Baucom & Hoffman, 1985; Jacobson, Follette, & Elwood, 1984).
- Schizophrenia (Falloon, Boyd, & McGill, 1985; Anderson, Reiss, & Hogarty, 1986).
- Juvenile delinquency (Tolan, Cromwell, & Brasswell, 1986).

Based on comprehensive reviews by Gurman et al. (1981; 1986), Becvar & Becvar (1988) have selected the following findings to illustrate the effects of family therapy treatment:

1. The preferred treatment for alcohol-involved marriages is conjoint couples treatment in groups. Such treatment may be superior to individual therapy with the alcoholic spouse.
2. Cognitive conjoint marital therapy may be more effective than individual therapy for marital issues.
3. Improvement can be expected with about 71 percent of childhood or adolescent behavioral issues when any one of a variety of family therapy methods are used.
4. When compared to no treatment, cognitive marital and family therapies are effective in about two-thirds of cases.
5. Successful outcomes occur in relatively few (one to twenty) sessions.
6. Cotherapy has not been demonstrated to be superior to marital or family therapy by one therapist.
7. Higher-level "therapist relationship skills" appear to be necessary for positive outcomes in therapy. Basic technical skills may prevent worsening of the issue, which merely maintains the pretherapy status of the family.

- A theoretical integration of the diverse theoretical alternatives in the family therapy field
- A system for assessing family cognitive, behavioral, and emotional style
- A framework for action in the interview that is oriented toward family style

SCDT is concerned with focusing on the uniqueness of the family; providing an array of alternative interventions; and facilitating cognitive, behavioral, and emotional growth. In order to accomplish these aims, therapists should be able to select methods from a variety of family therapy models. SCDT encourages this type of therapeutic flexibility as a means of ensuring that the family's needs are being addressed in the most appropriate fashion.

SCDT proposes that collectively, families also move through cognitive-emotional developmental orientations, much as proposed by developmental counseling and therapy (DCT) in chapter 6. The systemic translation of cognitive-developmental constructs results in a family therapy model that permits the therapist to identify at any point in the interview the predominant orientation being used by the family through the natural language of the family.

The four cognitive-developmental orientations framed from a systemic perspective and tied to specific treatment environments are as follows:

1. *Sensorimotor Families: Focusing on the elements of immediate experience.* The interactions and relationships of families functioning primarily at this orientation are often guided by emotions. The emotional life of families seeking treatment may be overwhelming, and there may be a loss of family stability and continuity. SCDT suggests that a *firm, yet flexible structure* be a prominent aspect of the therapeutic relationship.

2. *Concrete-Operational Families: Seeking situational descriptions.* These families present in a straightforward, unidimensional fashion characterized by simple cause-and-effect reasoning. They may continue to use "tried-and-true" solutions even though the situation has changed. Although they are "in control" of their emotions, they have great difficulty recognizing patterns of nonadaptive behavior and thoughts. SCDT recommends a *behaviorally oriented coaching style* of therapy for these families.

3. *Formal-Operational Families: Exploring the family-in-context.* Identifying and analyzing patterns that are embedded within their cognitive, affective, and interactional experiences are easy for families predominantly at this orientation. Overreliance may promote logic-tight assumptions about functioning, which may impede the family's ability to alter behavior when necessary. SCDT believes that a *client-directed or consultative style* of intervention is useful with these families.

4. *Dialectic/Systemic Families: Integrating the family-in-context.* These families realize the powerful influence of the environmental context on their functioning. Intergenerational, intrafamilial, and societal forces can be analyzed and evaluated by the family. Exclusive functioning at this level can lead to a diffuse, abstract sense of family identity that inhibits a collective ability to deal with concrete and sensorimotor reality. SCDT considers a *collaborative or mutual therapeutic environment* appropriate for these families.

Families repeatedly progress through these cognitive-developmental orientations over the life span or, at times, become stuck and immobilized in one orientation. The meanings, emotions, and actions a family shares about specific issues tend to be framed by one orientation. For example, a family faced with a child leaving home may become very concrete and controlling with a subsequent rebellion. The task is to help the family "move on" by exploring the feelings (sensorimotor) and generating new meanings (formal and dialectic) associated with separation.

Central Theoretical Constructs

SCDT holds that families develop a collective worldview that organizes predictable ways of thinking, feeling, and acting. This worldview may be a blending of each member's cognitive-developmental orientation, or a combination of some subsystem in the family—for example, a dominant member or the parental subsystem. The family's worldview is anchored in one of the four orientations and serves as the primary filter that the family uses to understand its world.

By using listening skills along with a sequential set of questioning strategies, an SCDT therapist can identify which orientation the family is operating primarily from, as well as its ability to use the other cognitive-developmental orientations. In other words, the therapist can identify whether the family can experience (sensorimotor), act on (concrete operational), and understand the patterns (formal operational) and origins (dialectic) of the issues promoting treatment. The degree of organization at a particular orientation and the range of movement between other orientations is labeled as the family's *cognitive-developmental structure*.

The concept of *equilibration*, or how a family maintains a balance between its worldview and its changing environment, is also an important element of this theory. When faced with new situations or emotions, the family must work to either integrate these new data into its existing worldview or to modify its own perspective, thereby altering its worldview. Functional families have demonstrated the capacity to do both as needed. These families have the ability to use multiple orientations to integrate new data. For example, when a healthy, concrete operational family is faced with the death of a grandparent, the family can feel the sorrow of that loss (sensorimotor) and can assist each member to make sense of this experience (formal operational), while taking care of the necessary legal arrangements (concrete operational).

Conversely, dysfunctional families choose extreme methods of integrating new data. On the one hand, families with *rigid* cognitive-developmental structures hold very strongly to one orientation. Even in the face of contradictory experience, they do not alter their worldview or consider alternative perspectives from which to understand their experience. Given the same scenario as the previous example, the rigid, concrete operational family would take care of the appropriate funeral and legal details but the emotions that might be triggered by this loss would not be acknowledged. Some family members might feel they must repress their feelings. Over time these feelings could turn to resentments and serve to separate family members.

On the other hand, families with *diffuse or underdeveloped* cognitive-developmental structures are highly reactive to changes in their environment and haphazardly move within and between several orientations without concern for family stability or continuity. They often lack a strong foundation at any particular orientation and cannot fully utilize the perspective of the orientation they are working within. Using the same example, the diffuse family is not grounded in any orientation, so one might see severe mood swings from deep sorrow to intense denial about the grandparent's death. Specific details would be completed in a haphazard fashion, and the family members would not be able to assist each other to integrate this experience.

Central Treatment Goals

The goals of SCDT are to assist families to function effectively within and between the different cognitive-developmental orientations, to empower them to view their issues from multiple perspectives, and to generate solutions that are appropriate to their developmental needs. Ideally, families would leave therapy with the ability to use all four orientations, but in reality, the true outcome of therapy is sometimes to help families be aware of all four perspectives and be comfortable using a limited subset. As noted in our first example, the healthy family used only three orientations to help the family adapt to the loss of the grandparent.

Primary Therapeutic Techniques

SCDT begins with a structured interview process that identifies the family's cognitive-developmental structure in general and specifically, in relation to the presenting issue. Based on the results of this assessment strategy, the therapist creates an environment that helps the family use multiple orientations to explore different perspectives of the issue. In this regard, SCDT does not offer new techniques beyond specific questioning strategies, but rather integrates methods from other family approaches within a cognitive-developmental framework. To illustrate this point, table 13.3 correlates the four cognitive-developmental orientations with the primary therapeutic interventions of the three major family therapy models addressed in this chapter.

SCDT believes that change is brought about in one of two directions. The first is helping the family elaborate and explore the further reaches of its current prevailing cognitive-developmental orientation. This type of movement is labeled *horizontal* change. The second type of movement is *vertical* and involves assisting the family to move to other cognitive-developmental orientations.

To illustrate these two concepts, consider a concrete family that has been asked to complete a genogram. At first, as the family is directed to gather more and more specific information about the intergenerational family network, the therapist utilizes the family's natural descriptive skills. In this fashion, the therapist makes a horizontal intervention aimed at helping the family use and extend its descriptive abilities. The completed genogram then becomes the focus of therapy as the family is encouraged to search for patterns of interactions. This move to a more formal operational skill is an example of vertical movement.

It is important to note that many strategies lend themselves to multiple orienta-

Table 13.3   Classification of Orientations and Therapeutic Strategies

Model	Sensorimotor	Concrete	Formal	Dialectic
Intergenerational	Genogram: attaching photos	Genogram: organizing family information "Going home" technique	Genogram: analysis of patterns	Genogram: interpretation of cultural and intergenerational influences
Symbolic/experiential	Art techniques Family sculpture	Floor plan	Use of self Analysis of art, sculpting	
Structural	Unbalancing	Directives	Reframing	

tions and that it is the *intentionality* of their use that will determine the impact on the family. For example, the family sculpture activity can be used to help a family identify interpersonal closeness (sensorimotor), describe a typical family scene (concrete operational), analyze a recurrent pattern (formal operational), or consider the impact of contextual forces (dialectic/systemic). By using this SCDT conceptualization system, a therapist is empowered to use a variety of therapeutic interventions in a horizontal or vertical direction, depending on the specific developmental needs of the family.

SCDT is an emerging theory of family therapy that presents practical methods to unite concepts of family development with the strategies of clinical practice. Additionally, SCDT provides a framework for family counselors and therapists to integrate the approaches of various models using a developmental perspective. In this way, SCDT offers an alternative paradigm for the assessment, treatment, and conception of family issues.

Limitations and Practical Implications of Family Counseling and Therapy

Over the past forty years, family therapy has made its mark on the counseling field. With a cadre of charismatic leaders, new forms of family treatment have emerged and have found a wide audience of practitioners and researchers. One reason why these methods caught on so quickly is because they appear to work, and research is mounting as to family therapy's importance and usefulness. Any individual therapist who does not consider family issues is simply missing an important dimension of treatment. The systematic focus on the family as a context of individual behavior is one method of integrating family counseling strategies within an individual treatment setting.

Some limitations of the family therapy models include issues of philosophical orientation and larger sociocultural concerns. It is difficult for some therapists to consider the family as a system when they are so concerned with the intrapsychic world of the individual. Further, many therapists feel overwhelmed when confronted with the depth and intensity of a family in trouble. Training and supervision in family systems theory is an important element of being able to develop a systemic worldview.

The contextual concerns about existing major approaches to family therapy (structural, intergenerational, and experiential/symbolic) have been criticized from two perspectives. First, cultural sensitivity is not an important element of the foundations of these models. McGoldrick, Pearce, and Giordano (1982) have clearly articulated the need for family therapists to acknowledge and work within a multicultural perspective.

The second contextual criticism comes from feminist family therapists, who contend that the major models only replicate the male-oriented status quo of our culture. Luepnitz (1988) and others (Goldner, 1988; Hare-Mustin, 1978; Lerner, 1986) stress that if family therapy is to be viewed as ultimately bringing about real change for families, then larger social and cultural forces as well as power distribution within the family must be addressed. Furthermore, all members of the family must be empowered to deal with these issues.

Both concerns, feminism and ethnicity, are forcing family therapists to stop and reevaluate their worldview in order to reduce cultural and gender bias. It will be a long struggle, but in the future, the quality of effective therapy will be measured not merely by the removal of family symptomatic behavior, but also by the demonstration of consideration for cultural diversity and gender equity.

REFERENCES

ANDERSON, C., REISS, D., & HOGARTY, B. (1986). *Schizophrenia and the family.* New York: Guilford.

ATTNEAVE, C. (1969). Therapy in tribal settings and urban network interventions. *Family Process, 8,* 192–210.

BATESON, G., JACKSON, D., HALEY, J., & WEAKLAND, J. (1956). Towards a theory of schizophrenia. *Behavioral Science, 1,* 251–64.

BAUCOM, D., & HOFFMAN, J. (1985). The effectiveness of marital therapy: Current status and application to the clinical setting. In N. Jacobson & A. Gurman (Eds.), *Clinical handbook of marital therapy.* New York: Guilford.

BEACH, S., & O'LEARY, K. (1985). The current status of outcome research in marital therapy. In L. L'Abate (Ed.), *Handbook of family and psychotherapy.* Belmont, CA: Wadsworth.

BECVAR, D., & BECVAR, R. (1988). *Family therapy: A systemic integration.* Needham Heights, MA: Allyn & Bacon.

BOCHNER, A., & EISENBERG, E. (1987). Family process: System perspectives. In C. Berger & S. Chaffee (Eds.), *Handbook of communication science* (pp. 540–63). Newberry Park, CA: Sage.

BOWEN, M. (1960). A family concept of schizophrenia. In D. D. Jackson (Ed.), *The etiology of schizophrenia.* New York: Basic Books.

CARTER, B., & McGOLDRICK, M. (1988). *The changing family life-cycle: A framework for family therapy.* Needham Heights, MA: Allyn & Bacon.

CHEATHAM, H., & STEWART, J. (1990). *Black families: Interdisciplinary perspectives.* New Brunswick, NJ: Transactional Publishers.

COTTONE, R. (1991). Counselor roles according to two counseling worldviews. *Journal of Counseling and Development, 69,* 398–401.

FALICOV, C. (1983). *Cultural perspectives in family therapy.* Rockville, MD: Aspen Systems.

FALLOON, I., BOYD, J., & McGILL, C. (1985). *Family care of schizophrenia.* New York: Guilford.

FLEISHMANN, M. (1981). A replication of Patterson's "Intervention for boys with conduct problems." *Journal of Consulting and Clinical Psychology, 49,* 343–51.

GIORDANO, J., & GIORDANO, G. (1977). *The ethno-cultural factor in mental health: A literary review and bibliography.* New York: Committee on Pluralism and Group Identity, American Jewish Committee.

GOLDENBERG, I., & GOLDENBERG, H. (1991). *Family therapy: An overview* (3rd ed.). Pacific Grove, CA: Brooks/Cole.

GOLDNER, V. (1988). Generation and gender: Normative and covert hierarchies. *Family Process, 27,* 17–33.

GRUNEBAUM, H., & CHASIN, R. (1982). Thinking like a family therapist: A model for integrating the theories and methods of family therapy. *Journal of Marital and Family Therapy, 8,* 403–16.

GURMAN, A. S., & KNISKERN, D. P. (1981). Family therapy outcome research: Knowns and unknowns. In A. S. Gurman & D. P. Kniskern (Eds.), *Handbook of family therapy.* New York: Brunner/Mazel.

GURMAN, A. S., KNISKERN, D. P., & PINSOF, W. M. (1986). Research on the process and outcome of marital and family therapy. In S. Garfield & A. Bergin (Eds.), *Handbook of psychotherapy and behavior change (3rd ed.).* New York: Wiley.

HALEY, J. (1979). *Leaving home: Therapy with disturbed young people.* New York: McGraw-Hill.

HARE-MUSTIN, R. (1978). A feminist approach to family therapy. *Family Process, 17,* 181–94.

HINES, P., & BOYD-FRANKLIN, N. (1982). Black families. In M. McGoldrick, J. Pearce, & J. Giordano (Eds.), *Ethnicity and family therapy.* New York: Guilford.

JACOBSON, N., FOLLETTE, W., & ELWOOD, R. (1984). Outcome research on behavioral marital therapy: A methodological and conceptual reappraisal. In K. Hahlweg & N. Jacobson (Eds.), *Marital interaction: Analysis and modification.* New York: Guilford.

LAFROMBOISE, T., & FLEMING, C. (1990). Keeper of the fire: A profile of Carolyn Attneave. *Journal of Counseling and Development, 68,* 537–47.

LERNER, G. (1986). *The creation of patriarchy.* New York: Oxford University Press.

LUEPNITZ, D. (1988). *The family interpreted: Feminist theory in clinical practice.* New York: Basic Books.

McGOLDRICK, M., PEARCE, J., & GIORDANO, J. (1982). *Ethnicity and family therapy.* New York: Guilford Press.

MINUCHIN, S. (1974). *Families and family therapy.* Cambridge, MA: Harvard University Press.

MINUCHIN, S., BAKER, L., ROSMAN, B., LIEBMAN, R., MILMAN, L., & TODD, T. (1975). A conceptual model of psychosomatic illness in children. *Archives of General Psychiatry, 32,* 1031–38.

MINUCHIN, S., & FISHMAN, H. (1981). *Family therapy techniques.* Cambridge, MA: Harvard University Press.

MINUCHIN, S., ROSMAN, B., & BAKER, L. (1978). *Psychosomatic families: Anorexia nervosa in context.* Cambridge, MA: Harvard University Press.

NAPIER, A. (1978, January). The rejection-intrusion pattern: A central family dynamic. *Journal of Marriage and Family Counseling, 5*–12.

NICHOLS, M., & SCHWARTZ, R. (1991). *Family therapy: Concepts and methods.* Needham Heights, MA: Allyn & Bacon.

PATTERSON, G., CHAMBERLAIN, P., & REID, J. (1982). A comparative evaluation of a parent-training program. *Behavior Therapy, 13,* 638–50.

RIGAZIO-DiGILIO, S., & IVEY, A. (1991). Developmental counseling and therapy: A framework for individual and family treatment. *Counseling and Human Development, 24,* 1–19.

SABATELLI, R., & ANDERSON, S. (1991). Family system dynamics, peer relationships, and adolescents' psychological adjustment. *Family Relations, 40,* 1–7.

SCHWARTZ, R., BARRETT, M., & SABA, G. (1985). Family therapy for bulimia. In D. Garner & P. Garfinkel (Eds.), *Handbook for the psychotherapy of anorexia nervosa and bulimia.* New York: Guilford.

SPECK, R., & ATTNEAVE, C. (1973). *Family networks.* New York: Random House.

SORENSON, S., & RUTTER, C. (1991). Transgenerational patterns of suicide attempt. *Journal of Consulting and Clinical Psychology, 59,* 861–66.

STANTON, M., TODD, T., & ASSOCIATES. (1982). *The family therapy of drug abuse and addiction.* New York: Guilford.

TOLAN, P., CROMWELL, R., & BRASSWELL, M. (1986). Family therapy with delinquents: A critical review of the literature. *Family Process, 25,* 619–49.

TSENG, W., & McDERMOTT, J. (1981). *Culture, mind and therapy: An introduction to cultural psychiatry.* New York: Brunner/Mazel.

WHITAKER, C. (1967). The growing edge in techniques of family therapy. In J. Haley & L. Hoffman (Eds.), *Techniques of family therapy.* New York: Basic Books.

Toward an Integrated Counseling and Psychotherapy Approach

CHAPTER GOALS

This chapter seeks to:

1. Review the major concepts of this book.
2. Help you start generating your own personal view of the helping process in a more concrete fashion.

Becoming a Samurai

Japanese champions of the sword learn their skills through a complex training program. The special movements and philosophy of sword work are broken down into specific components that are studied carefully, one at a time.

In learning the precise handling of the sword, the naturally gifted person often finds that there is a temporary decrease in dexterity and performance. Awareness of many components can interfere with coordination. Nonetheless, the skills and concepts are learned thoroughly and practiced again and again.

Once the skills reach close to virtuoso level, the samurai retire to a mountaintop to meditate. They deliberately forget what they have been learning. When they return to the valley, they find their discrete skills have been naturally integrated into their style or way of being. They seldom have to think about skills at all: they have become samurai.

Consider the samurai and your own experience. You may be naturally talented as a musician, dancer, writer, or athlete. And you may have found that practicing scales helped you become an even more proficient musician, that repeating new steps to perfection helped make you a better dancer, that learning to write on a computer enabled you to shape your ideas more easily, or that practicing the fundamentals of a sport made a large difference in your performance.

Just so, you may be a naturally gifted helper. This book contains many skills, concepts, and theories—all of which can help you become even more accomplished as a counselor or therapist. The rehearsal and practice of these basics can build a new understanding, which later becomes integrated into your own natural style.

The Search for the "Best" Theory

> If Sigmund Freud was alive today, he'd be turning over in his grave.
>
> Yogi Berra (cited in Cummings, 1988)

In many ways it was more simple during much of Freud's lifetime. There was really only one major theory, and all one had to do was to learn it. Second-force cognitive-behavioral theory and third-force existential-humanistic concepts complicated the matter, but still one only had to decide which was the "best" theory. The task for new counselors and therapists as recently as twenty years ago remained simply to decide on a single theoretical commitment.

The Growth of Eclecticism

Currently, theory and practice options are as varied and plentiful as the therapists who originate them. "What treatment, by whom, is most effective for this individual, with that specific problem, and under which set of circumstances?" is a classic statement made by Gordon Paul in 1967. At this point, eclecticism—drawing from the best of all theories—became respectable. However, eclecticism has nonetheless been criticized for lacking a central theoretical rationale for therapeutic action.

Over time, research and clinical practice have revealed that first-, second-, and third-force theories have considerable value. At issue is how they can be integrated in a meaningful fashion. Eclecticism as a systematic frame lacks a rationale for changing theories or methods with clients other than the intuitive preference and clinical experience of the practitioner.

Lazarus's multimodal therapy (1981, 1986) was a major attempt to organize therapy theory, primarily from a behavioral frame of reference. He divides treatment into seven parts, the "BASIC-ID" (*B*ehavior, *A*ffective response, *S*ensations, *I*mages, *C*ognitions, *I*nterpersonal relationships, and *D*rugs). He draws from each dimension to create a holistic treatment plan. Lazarus was one of the first to move eclecticism to a more coherent and organized way of thinking.

Integrative theorizing is currently becoming more common and influential. Meichenbaum's discussion of cognitive-behavioral theory brings diverse theories together in a coherent fashion and thus is broader in scope than traditional behavioral frames of reference. Developmental counseling and therapy (DCT) reframes Piagetian theory and provides an overall rationale for moving from sensory methods to behavioral to cognitive to systemic approaches. DCT, perhaps more than other theories, emphasizes sensorimotor and systemic/cultural foundations of experience, arguing that network treatment is essential if change is to be maintained over time.

You will be asked in this chapter to generate your own integrated view of counseling and psychotherapy. You have been exposed to many alternatives that have stood the test of time or, if new, show some promise of influencing future change. As a professional, you will be part of the process moving the field toward a new view. How can you continually add new dimensions while retaining the best of the past?

The Multicultural Fourth Force

Multicultural counseling and therapy (MCT) and developmental counseling and therapy (DCT) do not dismiss traditional methods of helping but instead recognize their value, *as long as they are employed in a culturally meaningful and culturally sensitive fashion*. MCT and DCT start from a different place than traditional theory, beginning with client assessment of individual, family, and cultural experience. Rather than impose a theory on the client, these approaches seek to find how the client constructs and makes meaning in the world and stress an egalitarian, nonhierarchical therapist/client relationship. They suggest that counselor and client together draw from other theories in an integrated fashion to meet individual, family, and cultural needs.

In effect, the multicultural orientation works to turn the history of counseling and therapy "on its head" and seeks a major new direction. The issue is not to impose a theory on a client, but rather to *work with the client in a culturally sensitive fashion* to find a technique, strategy, theory, or set of theories that meets the client's needs. *Self-in-relation* becomes the focus rather than individually oriented self-actualization.

MCT might expand Gordon Paul's earlier statement with the following additional specifics:

What set of treatments, by whom, is most effective for this individual or family with that specific problem (issue, or concern), with what specific culturally and individually appropriate goal, under which set of circumstances? How can relapse of treatment be prevented? Moreover, how can we involve this client (and family) in network treatment planning in a culturally sensitive fashion? (p. 111)

How might you rephrase the above ideas? How would you personally organize this exciting, but extremely complex, field? A final exercise in this book asks you to start the process of generating your own integrated approach and consider such questions as: How would you utilize first-, second-, and third-force theories? What sense do you make of the integrative approaches such as those of Meichenbaum and DCT? Would you place multicultural issues at the core of your theory or would they be more peripheral? These are important questions that will define you as a professional. Not only will you be making these decisions, you also will be asked to define the rationale for what you decide. Your work will be with some very important people—interviewees, clients, and patients.

The following summary of major theories is designed to help you work toward your own integration of helping theories.

A Summary of the Four Major Theoretical Forces of Counseling and Psychotherapy

There are many ways to consider the field of counseling and psychotherapy, and no one perspective has all the answers. This book is about multiple perspectives on reality. Clients often can get "stuck" in a single perspective. The theories and practice presented in this book and summarized in this section offer a range of ways of thinking that may be helpful with clients.

The four broad orientations to counseling and therapy stressed in this book are summarized in table 14.1. As you review these theories, think about how you personally would integrate them. There are many ways to describe the field. What are your own preferences at this moment? What concepts appeal to you personally? And what can you find in your own developmental history, family history, and multicultural background that might help explain your answers?

Integrating Multiple Approaches with a Client or Family

Attneave's network therapy, drawn from her work with Native Americans, reminds us that multiple interventions are often necessary to produce and maintain change (Attneave, 1969, 1982; Speck & Attneave, 1973). Furthermore, action needs to be conducted in the larger community to change systems that continue to adversely affect individuals and families.

Throughout this book, there has been frequent emphasis on the importance of multiple, multilevel interventions to support client change. Developmental counseling and therapy focuses on multiple approaches to clients and families. DCT argues that interventions planned at the sensorimotor, concrete, formal, and dialectic/systemic levels are needed if change is to be initiated and secured. DCT endorses the multicultural counseling and therapy approach as essential in any choice of treatment.

Case Management: Integrating Network Treatment and DCT

It is critical to arrange many interventions for complex client cases and for lasting change. Also, you will find that many clients need only one or two interventions to provide a lever for permanent change. Figure 14.1 visually indicates that any intervention can be conducted at one or more cognitive-developmental levels. Moreover, it is possible to integrate concepts of DCT and relapse prevention as part of the overall treatment plan. The following list summarizes individual, family, group, and community interventions that can be used in a case management/network treatment approach. Developing a network of interventions to provide change is the best way to prevent relapse.

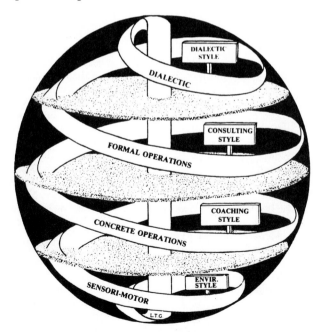

Figure 14.1   The Multilevel Nature of Therapeutic Intervention

SOURCE: This figure was originally conceived and drawn by Lois T. Grady and is used here with her permission.

Table 14.1   Overview of Four Major Forces in Counseling and Psychotherapy Theory

Theoretical System and Relationship to Foundational Theories and Family Theory	Worldview	Major Concepts and Techniques
Multicultural Counseling and Therapy (The Fourth Force)		
Foundational theories (empathic dimensions, microskills, decisional counseling, developmental counseling and therapy) explicitly and implicitly utilized as part of overall theoretical conception, but modified with cultural frames of reference. Family therapy concepts considered essential. Attneave's network therapy often an essential ingredient.	Counseling and therapy have been culturally encapsulated. The individual and family are based in the culture. The counselor or therapist needs to approach counseling with multicultural awareness. Many authors stress issues of development in the family and society. Seeks to integrate first-, second-, and third-force theories as part of worldview and counseling and therapy theory and case conceptualization.	As a newly evolving major theoretical group, the main point of agreement is that issues of culture, gender, and other multicultural issues need to take a central place in the helping process. Collaboration and network treatment planning are essential. Consciousness raising about ethnicity/race and gender issues often critical in the helping process.
Psychodynamic (The First Force)		
Foundational theories not explicitly considered, but post hoc examination shows that these concepts help explain the value of these orientations and makes their implementation more explicit. Family concepts not prominent, although attachment theory and the family unconscious are adding this emphasis. Bowen's intergenerational theory especially compatible. Historically, minimal attention to gender and multicultural issues.	The past is prelude to the present, and much of the past is held in the unconscious. Individuals are deeply influenced by the past, and we must understand this past if we are to facilitate individual growth. Sigmund Freud is major philosopher. The pragmatic and optimistic Bowlby stressed that we can facilitate growth through understanding and action. Taub-Bynum focused on family and cultural history playing themselves out in the individual.	These are the most complex set of theories available. The development of the person rests on early life experience. The interaction of person and environment is largely played out in the unconscious. Traditional Freudian theory emphasizes the Oedipal complex as central to development, whereas object relations and attachment theories focus on early infant and child experience as more important. Free association, dream analysis, and awareness of transference, countertransference, and projective identification are important.
Cognitive-Behavioral: Behavioral Foundations (The Second Force)		
Foundational theories often integrated into understanding and planning treatment. Decisional counseling and social skills portion of mi-	Deeply rooted in the idea of progress and faith in science to solve human problems. B. F. Skinner often seen as major philosopher.	Through functional analysis, it is possible to understand the antecedents, resultant behavior, and consequences of the behavior. Many highly

Table 14.1   (continued)

Theoretical System and Relationship to Foundational Theories and Family Theory	*Worldview*	*Major Concepts and Techniques*
croskills a standard part of counseling and therapy. Family concepts historically have not been important, but behavioral family approach illustrates how theory can be integrated.	Meichenbaum's more recent construction is more humanistic in orientation and provides a new integration of behaviorism with other theories. **Cheek** supplies a culturally-relevant view.	specific and proven techniques of behavioral change available. Has had profound influence on popular cognitive-behavioral movement, particularly the work of Meichenbaum in social skills training.

Cognitive-Behavioral: Cognitive Foundations (The Second Force)

Foundational theories tend to be implicit rather than explicit. Cognitive aspects of developmental counseling and therapy may help integrate this framework more closely with MCT, particularly action at the sensorimotor and systemic level, which is often missing in CBT. Family concepts historically have not been important, but are compatible.	Roots lie in stoic philosopher Epictetus—"We are disturbed not by events, but by the views we take of them." Attempt to integrate ideas about the world with action in the world. Ellis's rational-emotive therapy. Beck's cognitive therapy. Glasser's reality therapy.	Currently a popular theoretical orientation, as the system allows integration of many ideas from seemingly competing theories. Major focus is on thinking patterns and their modification, but maintains a constant emphasis on homework and taking new ideas out into the world and acting on them. Glasser's work is similar, but focuses very effectively on schools and youth in institutions.

Existential/Humanistic (The Third Force)

The foundational concepts of empathy and the listening portion of microskills have been derived from this orientation. Family concepts historically have not been important, but are compatible. Whitaker's experiential family orientation is especially compatible. Has not consciously embraced MCT but is compatible.	The human task is to find meaning in a sometimes meaningless world. Rogers stresses the ability of the person to direct one's own life; Frankl, the importance of positive meanings; and Perls, that people are wholes, not parts, and can take direction of their own lives. Heidegger, Husserl, Binswanger, and Boss have been most influential at a basic philosophical level. Rogers's person-centered theory. Frankl's logotherapy. Perls's Gestalt therapy.	Each individual constructs the world uniquely. Rogers stresses the importance of self-actualization and careful listening to the client. Frankl emphasizes spirituality and a variety of specific techniques to facilitate the growth of meaning. Perls, with his many powerful techniques, may be described as the action therapist.

1. *Individual Interventions*

   Counseling and therapy (drawing from first, second, third, fourth, or other major theoretical orientations)

   Helping clients fill basic needs for money, shelter, clothing

   Advocating and crisis intervention

   Medication

2. *Family Interventions*

   Family therapy and counseling

   Family education in parenting skills

   Marital counseling

   Divorce, legal issues

   Mediation

   Family support groups

3. *Group Interventions*

   Group counseling and encounter groups

   Multicultural consciousness-raising groups (women, African-Americans, Vietnam vets)

   Self-esteem groups

   AA, ACOA, and other self-help groups

   Psychoeducational and skills training groups

   Peer counseling

4. *Community Interventions*

   Network therapy

   Racism/oppression training

   Community action (organizing local government, church, and school groups)

   State and federal action and advocacy

Relapse Prevention

Change gained through therapy often disappears in the complexities of life after therapy unless change is planned. Although we may help clients feel less anxious via Rogerian therapy or by implementing assertiveness training, both techniques may fail if there is no plan for follow-up and treatment generalization. At this time, it may be useful to return to chapter 4 on decisional counseling and review the steps of relapse prevention.

Relapse prevention can be greatly facilitated by the case management/network approach suggested in the foregoing list. Relapse prevention is a multidimensional, multimodal approach to maintaining human change. If we want to avoid relapse and therapeutic failure, we may have to work with families, schools, and other systems as well.

A Suggested Exercise

Review figure 14.1 as you might apply it with a client with whom you have worked. If you have not yet seen clients, imagine a client. Given certain types of concerns, particularly those that result from conflict or oppression in the family or community, working to change institutions may be as important as or more important than helping the client. If we return clients to the same system that helped create their difficulties, we can expect them to return for more counseling and therapy in the not-too-distant future.

Although individual counseling and therapy is the topic of this book, it should be clear that if human change processes are to be lasting, we also need to consider issues beyond the unique individuals we see. Chapter 2 related the analogy of people drowning in the river. It is indeed important to pull out those about to sink, but it is perhaps even more important to move upstream and find out who is throwing them in the river. The case management approach helps us remember that as an individual counselor or therapist, we are but a portion of a network of helpers. Unless other important parts are in place, our efforts are bound to fail.

Constructing Your Own View or Theory of Counseling and Psychotherapy

In preparation for therapeutic practice, it is important that you think through your own view of the helping process. This book has suggested that you be familiar with multiple theoretical approaches and the skills and techniques of many orientations. Despite this recommendation, it is recognized that no one individual can "do it all." However, a network of cooperating helping professionals indeed *can* do it all. Thus, it is also crucial that you define your own place in a network of counselors and therapists and assess how you can collaborate with these other professionals for the benefit of clients. In the following pages, you are asked to think about yourself and your own personal reactions to the many ideas presented in this book.

Importance of Worldview

The construction you make of the helping process is derived from your worldview. Chapter 1 defined worldview as how you think the world works. A worldview is a *theory about the nature of things.* In turn, a theory may be described as a framework in which you organize facts and their relationship one to another. Identifying your own worldview is critical to your role as a professional and your own integration of the helping field.

Ahia (1991) challenges the traditional "objective" approach implicit in much of our traditional theory, maintaining that "who you are determines your use of theory—counseling and therapy are issues of *being.* We counsel from our *being.*" The objective approach means that we "objectively" select a theory, much as Paul (1967) suggests, and then apply it correctly to the client. Ahia (1991) and DeEsch (1991) argue for *intersubjectivity,* which may be defined as the awareness that we make our choices from often unconscious family and multicultural experience. Intersubjectivity also implies that the therapist is sensitive to both his or her own and the client's family and multicultural self.

Figure 14.2, repeated from chapter 2, visually represents the intersubjectivity in the counseling and therapy process.

Exhibit 14.1 provides questions that will help you evaluate yourself, your worldview, and your intersubjective thoughts and feelings about clients and yourself.

Qualitative Research — You as Scientist-Practitioner

Most authorities would argue that an ethical practice of counseling and therapy is a practice that, among other things, constantly examines and evaluates effectiveness. Furthermore, the importance of reading and conducting one's own research is often stressed. Research and reading keep us all alive and aware of new developments.

But too often counselors and therapists think about research as something that is "elsewhere" — something found in professional journals and not part of "real life." The busy practitioner sometimes finds journals boring and irrelevant and often cannot find the time to read. However, reading, research, and writing can be important and even vital to avoiding burnout and staying alive in the profession. It is unfortunate that some therapists choose not to read or conduct research and thus often continue to provide therapy that research data and new theory clearly show to be irrelevant, time consuming, expensive, and perhaps even damaging to the client.

How can you surmount this challenge? Lia Kapelis (personal communication, 1981) organized a model therapeutic research program at Flinders University Clinic in Adelaide, Australia. Kapelis is a professor who teaches counseling and therapy skills, but she also conducts therapy herself and supervises the clinic. Kapelis decided that *every* case she and her staff worked with would involve some form of research. Exhibit

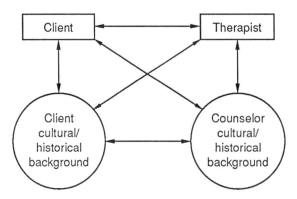

Figure 14.2 Cultural/Historical Background and the Counseling/Therapy Process

Exhibit 14.1

What Is Your Counseling and Therapy Worldview?

The purpose of this concluding exercise is to ask you to consider your own construction of counseling and therapy. What is important to you? Where do you stand? Where are you heading? How does your family and cultural history relate to these issues?

1. How do you view the goals of counseling and therapy?

Client-centered theory focuses on self-actualization; behavioral theory, on behavioral change; psychodynamic theory, on awareness of unconscious forces; family theory, on an adequate family organization; feminist theory, on awareness of one's gender; multicultural theory, on becoming aware of how individual and family have been shaped and affected by the environment and history. These are only a few of the types of goals offered by different theoretical orientations.

Consider these and other personal goals and values of your own. What do you want to have happen for your clients in your work as a counselor and therapist? Write a statement of your values and convictions regarding the key goals and values you have for the helping process.

2. Where do your values and convic-

tions come from? How were they derived? Do they come from reading this book? Or are they influenced by your own life-span developmental process? How does your family, gender, and multicultural background affect your values?

The key constructs in your worldview are generated in a gender, family, and multicultural context. Write a statement in which you discuss how your own life-span development relates to your selection of worldview and goals.

3. Where might your worldview be limited with some of your clients? Given the vast array of multicultural experience you will encounter, what types of groups do you need to learn more about? What types of values and behaviors might give you difficulty?

None of us can relate equally well with all clients. Write a statement describing areas in which you need to learn more, and indicate some specific steps you plan to take to reach an expanded awareness.

4. What additional questions would you ask of yourself and others? The questions here are only the beginning of serious questioning on the nature of counseling and psychotherapy practice.

14.2 shows how individual qualitative research could be used in the active practice of counseling and psychotherapy.

Research can be an integral part of one's practice, or it can be ignored. You will have to make your own decision about the place of data and research in your own clinical and counseling work. Some survive in the field without any up-to-date aware-

Exhibit 14.2

Using Qualitative Research in Counseling and Clinical Practice

Ponterotto and Casas (1991) define four key characteristics of qualitative research methodology.

1. *Use an inductive approach based on observation of client needs and wishes.* Imagine you are working with a client who presents you with issues of anxiety and tension. Rather than deciding beforehand what to evaluate or measure, focus on your observations of this particular client and generate hypotheses about what issues might be important in therapy. In addition, think about ways in which you might evaluate whether or not therapy is helpful to this client.

2. *Take a holistic stance and set joint client-counselor objectives for evaluation of therapy.* Much of quantitative research focuses on single dimensions of human experience. You are working with a whole client who comes from a family and cultural background. As part of a holistic stance, you will want to consider the whole life of the client, not just single dimensions. Obviously, you cannot measure everything in your client's life, but with your client you can set goals for therapy that can be validated by both you and the client.

At Flinders University in Australia, Kapelis (personal communication, 1981) builds on the concept of joint goals and, with the client, selects concrete thought, feeling, and behavioral changes based on jointly agreed-on criteria for success. In some cases, standardized tests are used, but in these cases, the client is al-

ways a participant in the selection. With a client struggling with anxiety, you might jointly decide that feeling relaxed and easy in interpersonal contacts is one objective of therapy. Another objective might be sleeping through the night. These objectives lead to certain specific types of treatment plans (for example, assertiveness training, relaxation training).

3. *Be flexible and change objectives and evaluation design as therapy progresses.* Establishing joint goals for counseling is important, because therapy does not always proceed as you and the client predict. You and your client may find new objectives as therapy progresses. For example, the client may discover in the process of stress management training that he or she had an abusive family history. If your qualitative research contract is open ended, with a joint commitment for exploration, you will be better positioned to evolve a new evaluation design as therapy enters new areas. For example, a short-term evaluative research agreement may be client satisfaction with the process. At the same time, you must work to concretize such a goal more precisely at the next stage of counseling or therapy.

4. *Emphasize clinical significance.* This point is vital to the qualitative researcher. The change and evaluation design must be important to the client and to the therapist.

Ponterotto and Casas list a variety of possibilities for qualitative research, including journal entries, case studies, structured interviews, reports by the client's family members or friends, asking the client to audio- or videotape certain types of interactions, and so on. Again, when conducting qualitative research with your client, it is essential that he or she be involved in the process throughout.

ness of new research findings. Most psychologists, counselors, and social workers, however, make a constant attempt to update themselves through reading and workshops on the latest new ideas and research findings.

You as an Integrative Theorist in a Multicultural World

Some might argue that it is impossible not to have a theory. But many of us need to look at ourselves, our values, and our competencies so we can make our implicit theories more explicit and understandable both to ourselves and others. This book argues that the task of the professional counselor and therapist is to know as many theories and techniques as possible—their similarities and differences—and to select from each theory concepts that are most helpful to the client.

Theories from your frame of reference, however, may not be enough. It is also important to enter and understand the client's world in a nonhierarchical, egalitarian fashion. We have suggested that rather than imposing a theory of your choice on clients, you may engage your clients as coparticipants in this process, as more and more authorities suggest. Furthermore, it is your task to learn how your client constructs and makes sense of the world—to consider the nature of their meaning-making systems.

The theories in this book are only views—constructions of the world. Chapter 1 began with the Escher print "Relativity," which shows that there is no "right side up." By turning the print, you can gain a new view, a new way of thinking. There are many ways to view the print and to view "reality."

Similarly, we must recall that *theory is simply description, a way to examine reality, a set of constructs.* If we become enmeshed in the belief that our theory of counseling and therapy *is* reality, then we enter an illusion. An illusory view of the world may be functional for you, but not for everyone.

You will likely encounter some people engaged in the practice of counseling and therapy who believe they have found the "truth," the "final answer," "the way" to conduct counseling and therapy. We suggest that these people are very likely false prophets. However, as the authors of this book have learned over time, even false prophets sometimes present important, albeit partial, truths. Thus, it is important to listen and learn and be willing to consider alternative perspectives of the world and of new theories.

For example, there was a time in the field when meditation was considered irrelevant and outside the range of counseling and psychotherapy practice. Meditation is now a standard technique in many stress management programs. Similarly, issues of women's development and multicultural understanding were once considered to be peripheral and unimportant "fringe areas" of study. However, these areas have become increasingly central. The lesson to be learned is: *Beware of prophets proclaiming a new truth—they just may be right!*

Exhibit 14.3 provides a final exercise in which you are asked to review your own thinking about this book and organize its meaning in your own way.

Exhibit 14.3

Ten Questions to Ask Yourself about Your Own Construction of the Counseling and Psychotherapy Process

1. What is your overall worldview, and how does it relate to multicultural issues? Have you carefully elaborated your worldview and its implications for your future practice?

2. What are the central dimensions of your definition of ethical practice? (These dimensions were introduced in chapter 1. The effective professional is constantly examining ethical and moral issues.)

3. As you think about each of the empathic concepts, what is your personal construction of their meaning? What sense do you make of them?

4. With which microskills and concepts do you feel particularly comfortable? Which have you already mastered, and which need further work so that they can actually be used in the clinical session?

5. How do you make sense of the focusing concept? How might you choose to focus your interventions? Can you focus on individuals, family context, and the multicultural surround?

6. What is to be your position on research and keeping up with new ideas?

7. What is your understanding and integration of the challenge of multicultural counseling and therapy? What place will this fourth force of helping have in your mind and in your practice?

8. What theories of counseling and therapy appeal to you? What type of integration of these diverse theories are you moving toward? (This book has attempted to stress that all theories are potentially valuable to some clients, but you are not expected to be immediately skilled in all. Learning theories in more depth is a lifelong practice.) From what approach do you personally plan to start practice, and what type of professional curriculum for further learning do you see for yourself in the future?

9. How many of the practical counseling and clinical exercises presented in this book have you completed and with what level of mastery? (If you have engaged in practice exer-

cises to examine yourself, have tried the specific clinical skill exercises, and have practiced varying interviewing styles, you may have established a beginning "clinical portfolio" on which you can build for the future. If you have approached this book from an experiential practice frame of reference, you will have gained a more solid understanding than those who have chosen merely to read. Taking theory into practice and seeing if it "works" is where one truly integrates theory and skills and makes them part of one's being.)

10. Have you examined how your personal developmental history in family and culture affects your answers to the above questions? (It is critical that you constantly be able to reflect on yourself and how your personal history and present life issues affect your performance as a counselor or therapist.)

The general or metatheoretical position requires that each counselor or therapist develop her or his own conception of the counseling process and remain constantly open to change and examination. A student working through the draft of this book commented, "I think I've got the point. I find myself rewriting the book in my own way. I use some of it, but ultimately the book I am rewriting in my head is mine, my own general theory that is similar in some ways to the book, but in other ways very different."

We hope that you will rewrite this book and use it authentically in your own way. At the same time, we hope that you will extend that same privilege to your clients. How might they seek to help you rewrite and reconstrue your constructions of counseling and therapy? Counseling and therapy are very much about listening and learning—for all of us as therapists and for our clients as well.

REFERENCES

AHIA, E. (1991, October). *Enhanced therapeutic skills: Family and ethnic dynamics, part I.* Paper presented at the North Atlantic Association for Counselor Education and Supervision, Albany, NY.

ATTNEAVE, C. (1969). Therapy in tribal settings and urban network interventions. *Family Process, 8,* 192–210.

ATTNEAVE, C. (1982). American Indian and Alaska native families: Emigrants in their own homeland. In M. McGoldrick, J. Pearce, & J. Giordano (Eds.), *Ethnicity and family therapy* (pp. 55–83). New York: Guilford.

CUMMINGS, N. (1988). Emergence of the mental health complex: Adaptive and maladaptive responses. *Professional Psychology, 19,* 308–15.

DEESCH, J. (1991, October). Enhanced therapeutic skills: Family and ethnic dynamics, part II. Paper presented at the North Atlantic Association for Counselor Education and Supervision, Albany, NY.

LAZARUS, A. (1981). *The practice of multimodal psychotherapy.* New York: McGraw-Hill.

LAZARUS, A. (1986). Multimodal therapy. In J. Norcross (Ed.), *Handbook of eclectic psychotherapy.* New York: Brunner/Mazel.

PAUL, G. (1967). Strategy of outcome research in psychotherapy. *Journal of Consulting Psychology, 31,* 109–18.

PONTEROTTO, J., & CASAS, M. (1991). *Handbook of racial ethnic minority counseling research.* Springfield, IL: Thomas.

SPECK, R., & ATTNEAVE, C. (1973). *Family process.* New York: Pantheon.

Name Index

Subject Index

Positive regard (*see* Facilitative conditions of empathy)
Positive reinforcement (*see* Reinforcement)
Practice exercises (*see* Exercises for interviewing practice)
Problem-solving training (*see* Decisional counseling)
Projective identification, 208–211, 364
Psychodynamic counseling and therapy, 161ff, 183ff
    multicultural issues, 163–164, 171–180, 199, 202–206
    worldview, 162–163
Psychodynamic theory, 4, 63, 81, 85, 127, 128, 135, 137, 252, 273, 281, 288, 291, 293, 321, 334, 364 (*see also* Dreamwork)
Psychoeducation, 82–83
Psychosomatic disorders, 351

Q

Qualitative research, 368–371
Questions (*see under* Microskills)

R

Race (*see* Ethnicity)
Rape, 204–206, 247–248, 316
Rational-emotive therapy, 254–264, 365
    multicultural issues, 253–254, 262
    self-help form, 260–261
    worldview, 252
Rationalism, 230
Rational Recovery (AA), 263–264
Reality therapy, 134, 137, 275–281, 365
    multicultural issues, 253–254
    worldview, 252
Real self, 304
Reflection of feeling (*see under* Microskills)
Reframing, 349–350 (*see also* Interpretation)
Regression, 204–206, 274
Reinforcement, 216, 224–225, 233–234
Relapse prevention, 85–89, 228, 230, 244, 247, 255, 266, 334, 366
Relational orientation, 13–15, 76, 99–100, 116–119, 146, 155, 221, 290, 324, 335 (*see also* Interdependence; Network therapy; Self-in-relation)
"Relativity" (Escher print), 2, 371
Relaxation, 232, 235–240, 246–247, 255
Religion (*see* Spirituality)

Repetition compulsion, 205
Research issues (*see also* Scientist-practitioner):
    Ainsworth-Bowlby research on attachment theory, 174
    attending behavior and microskills research, 50–51
    cognitive-behavioral assessment and treatment of agoraphobia, 231–232
    defining cognitive-developmental level, 141
    effectiveness of counseling and psychotherapy, 12
    empathy research, 24
    family therapy with African-Americans, 339–340
    meta-analysis of Ellis's RET and Beck's cognitive therapy, 265
    person-centered theory research, 291–292
    psychotherapeutic services for ethnic minorities, 110–111
    qualitative research in counseling and clinical practice, 370
    single-case evaluation research, 89–90
    structural family therapy, 351
    transference in Rogerian therapy, the Gloria film, 305–306
Resistance, 197, 206–207
Respect (*see* Facilitative conditions)
Rigid boundaries, 349 (*see also* Separation)
Rigid structures, 353

S

Samurai, 360
Schema theory, 130–131, 155
Schizophrenia, 351
Scientist-practitioner, 1, 11 (*see also* Research issues)
Selective attention (*see under* Microskills)
Self-actualization, 288–289, 365
Self-disclosure (*see under* Microskills)
Self-in-relation, 111–112, 187, 195, 285–288, 297–298, 335ff, 361 (*see also* Coconstruction; Egalitarian approach; Interdependence; Relational approach)
Senoi dreamwork, 203–204
Sensate focusing, 255
Sensorimotor cognitions/emotions, 132ff, 144, 185–186, 199, 204, 352, 355, 363, 366

Separation, 173–175, 285–287, 337
Sex role development, 171–172
Sex therapy, 255, 318
Single-case evaluation research, 89–90
Snake phobia, 240–241
Social class (*see* Socioeconomic issues)
Social skills training, 232, 241–242, 247
Socioeconomic issues, 106–108, 148, 253, 289
Spirituality, 199, 321
Stereotyping, 37–38
Stoic philosophy, 252
Strange situation procedure, 174
Stress inoculation (*see* Stress management)
Stress management, 238, 246–248
Structural assessment, 350
Structural family therapy, 348–350, 355, 356
Style-shift counseling, 133
Substance abuse, 274–275, 351 (*see also* Alcoholism)
Subsystems, 348
Suicide, 343
Superego, 165–166
Survivor (as contrasted with victim), 205–206
Symbolic/experiential family therapy, 346–348, 355, 356
System (*see* Family issues and theory)
Systematic desensitization, 232
Systemic cognitive-developmental therapy, 350–356

T

Training as treatment, 64–65
Trait and factor theory, 73ff

Transference, 197, 206–208, 213, 363
Translation issues, 105–107 (*see also* Language)
Trauma, 106, 108, 179, 188, 190, 191, 203, 204, 205–206, 274 (*see also* Abuse; Logotherapy; Vietnam veterans' identity theory)
  normalizing, 205–206
Treatment plan, 113–117, 143–146, 363, 366 (*see also* Network therapy)

U

Umwelt, 286, 288, 289, 299, 304
Unconscious, 195, 211
Universal approach, to MCT, 95–98, 105, 108–109
Upstream approach, 22–23

V

Vertical development, 137–138, 354
Vietnam veterans' identity theory, 102–103

W

War issues, counseling, 293–294
Warmth (*see* Facilitative conditions of empathy)
White culture, 37
White identity theory, 102–104, 120
Wild analysis, 212
Wolf Man, 206
Women's identity development theory, 102–103
Women's issues (*see* Gender; Self-in-relation)
Worldview, 1–8, 194, 369, 372